DIGITAL MEETS HANDMADE

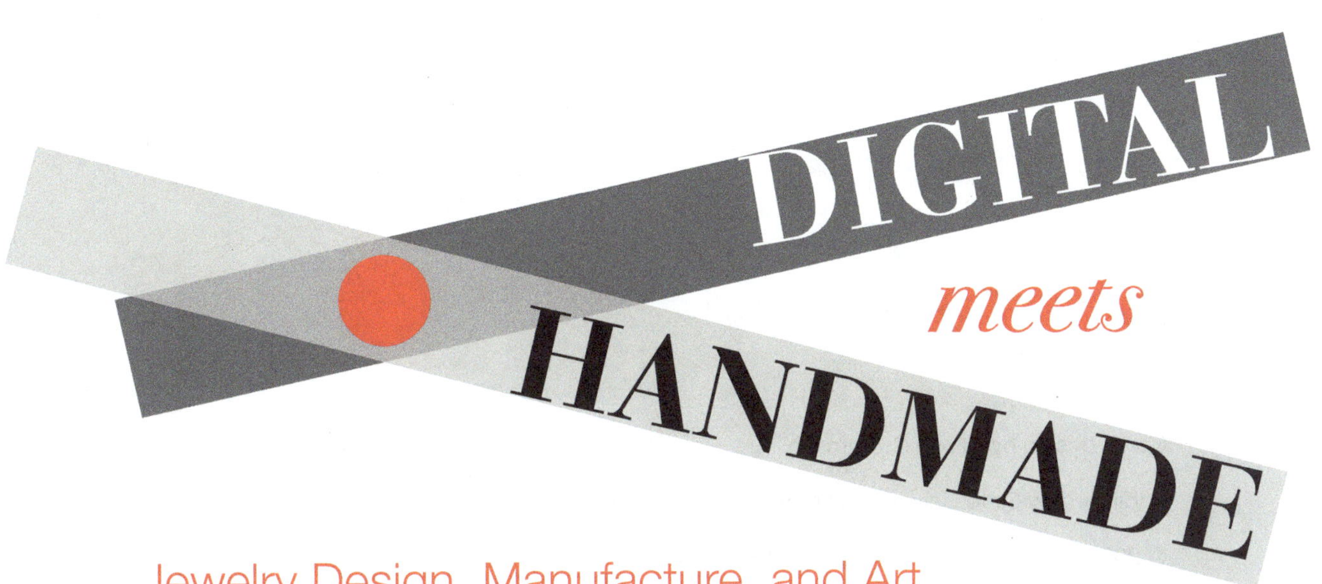

DIGITAL *meets* HANDMADE

Jewelry Design, Manufacture, and Art in the Twenty-First Century

Curated by
Wendy Yothers and Alba Cappellieri
with Susanna Testa

Foreword by
Troy Richards, Dean, School of Art & Design,
Fashion Institute of Technology

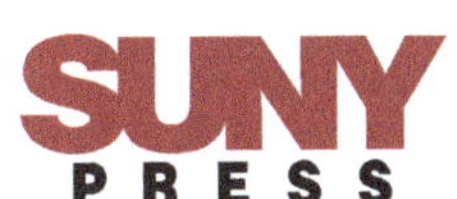

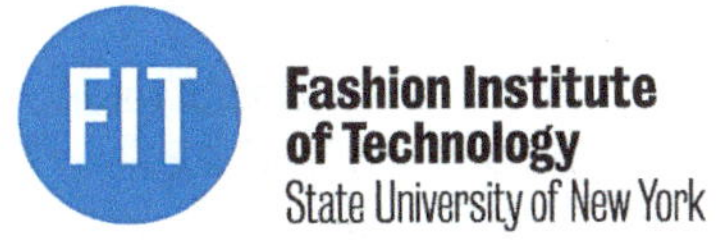

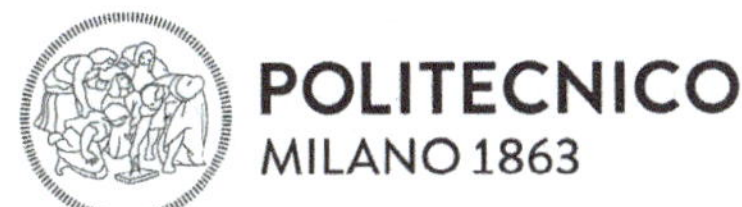

Cover design by Aimee C. Harrison

Published by State University of New York Press, Albany

Printed in the United States of America

For information, contact State University of New York Press, Albany, NY
www.sunypress.edu

Library of Congress Cataloging-in-Publication Data

Names: Digital Meets Handmade: Jewelry in the 21st Century (Symposium) (2018 : Fashion Institute of Technology, New York, N.Y.), author. | Yothers, Wendy, editor. | Cappellieri, Alba, editor. | Fashion Institute of Technology (New York, N.Y.), sponsoring body. | Politecnico di Milano, sponsoring body.
Title: Digital meets handmade : jewelry design, manufacture, and art in the twenty-first century : proceedings of the International Symposium, May 15th-16th-17th 2018, Fashion Institute of Technology, NY / curated by Wendy Yothers and Alba Cappellieri with Susanna Testa.
Description: Albany : State University of New York Press, [2021] | "Fashion Institute of Technology; State University of New York; Politecnico Milano 1863." | Includes bibliographical references.
Identifiers: LCCN 2021025084 | ISBN 9781438487663 (paperback) | ISBN 9781438487656 (ebook)
Subjects: LCSH: Jewelry—Congresses. | Technology—Social aspects—Congresses.
Classification: LCC NK7300.5 .D54 2018 | DDC 739.37—dc23
LC record available at https://lccn.loc.gov/2021025084

Thanks to the Fashion Institute of Technology, in the persons of President Dr. Joyce F. Brown, Dean Troy Richards, Vice President for Academic Affairs Dr. Giacomo Oliva, and Deputy to the President for Industry Partnerships and Collaborative Programs Joanne Arbuckle.

Thanks to the Jewelry Program at Politecnico di Milano for their partnership in the symposium, and in particular to Professor Alba Cappellieri and Dr. Susanna Testa, who coordinated the Organization Committee.

CONTENTS

Preface

Wendy Yothers, Fashion Institute of Technology, NY, USA
Conference Chairwoman

In May of 2018, the Jewelry Design department of the Fashion Institute of Technology (FIT) and the Jewelry and Accessories master's program of the Politecnico di Milano collaborated to present the international symposium *Digital Meets Handmade: Jewelry Design, Manufacture, and Art in the Twenty-First Century*. The three-day event was held at FIT in New York City. Its purpose: to provoke a lively debate on how digital technology and traditional making by hand duel for influence in the aesthetics, the use, and the cultural contexts of jewelry—as a manufactured product and as an applied art form.

Disruptive Innovation: "Digital vs Handmade"

There has been a seismic shift in jewelry design and manufacturing. Digital design, digital model making, and prototyping have elbowed their way into common practice and proven themselves both invaluable and disruptive to the jewelry profession. As planners of the symposium, we wanted to create a venue for discussion of the friction caused by the disruptive impact of "digital" on the notion of value embedded in "handmade" jewelry.

Our call for papers attracted artisans, educators, students, mavens from the realm of fine jewelry, artists, renegades from the wild west of the maker movement, and innovators from the digital engineering sector.

Thirty-seven speakers were selected from this diverse group. They came from across the US, as well as thirteen countries in Europe, Latin America, and Asia. As structure for the discourse, four primary questions connected the broad conversation around how digital technologies and virtuoso handcraft can coalesce in the education and practice of artists and jewelers:

How can digital software and new forms of output support hand-making techniques?

How does direct manufacturing by 3D printing with precious metals change jewelry manufacturing, with regard to the aesthetics, profitability, and traditional perceptions of quality in fine jewelry?

How must we respond to the ways computer-aided design (CAD) and rapid prototyping are redefining perceived value, driving aesthetics, and creating new contexts in wearable art?

What are best practices for bringing technology into the jewelry classroom, in regard to integrating CAD as an aid in ideation and tool making; introducing it into curriculum as a core aesthetic; or re-imagining the way we might teach art and craft to a generation of digital natives?

We were surprised...

We expected a collision of cultures. We were prepared to break up fistfights between "fine jewelry" craftsmen, who believe the sterility of CAD compromises their art, and engineers, who reckon the expediency of the technology is too elegant and too obvious to question. We expected that artists who use CAD and rapid prototyping exclusively, as well as those who blend it with handcraft, would lock horns with jewelers who use the "made-by-hand" quality of their work to create their distinctive brand and their artistic voice.

What happened was a total surprise. Instead of conflict, the main theme running thorough the presentations was how both sectors embrace CAD and adapt the technology to their own purpose.

The papers presented, and the conversations that sprang up between sessions, have engendered further research. In fact, the discussion has grown legs. The discourse that began in New York at *Digital Meets Handmade* has carried forward in international symposiums, articles, and papers from Santa Fe, New Mexico to Birmingham, UK and beyond. To our surprise and delight, getting all the stakeholders in our industry together in the same room had one lasting, unexpected consequence: everybody got to look over the fence to see what everyone else is doing. The consensus (if there can be said to be one) is summed up in this quote from the historian Richard Sennett:

The experimental rhythm of problem solving and problem finding makes the ancient potter and the modern programmer members of the same tribe. (The Craftsman, Yale University Press, 2008.)

The three days of intense discussion introduced us to what we have in common, and is still inspiring collaborations that blur the boundaries between digital and handmade.

Thoughts expressed in this preface have been abstracted from "The Next Generation: Digital Meets Handmade: Conversations about Jewelry, Technology, and Education." written by Troy Richards and Wendy Yothers, that appeared in *Metalsmith Tech* (1), no. 2, 2018, published by the Society of North American Goldsmiths.

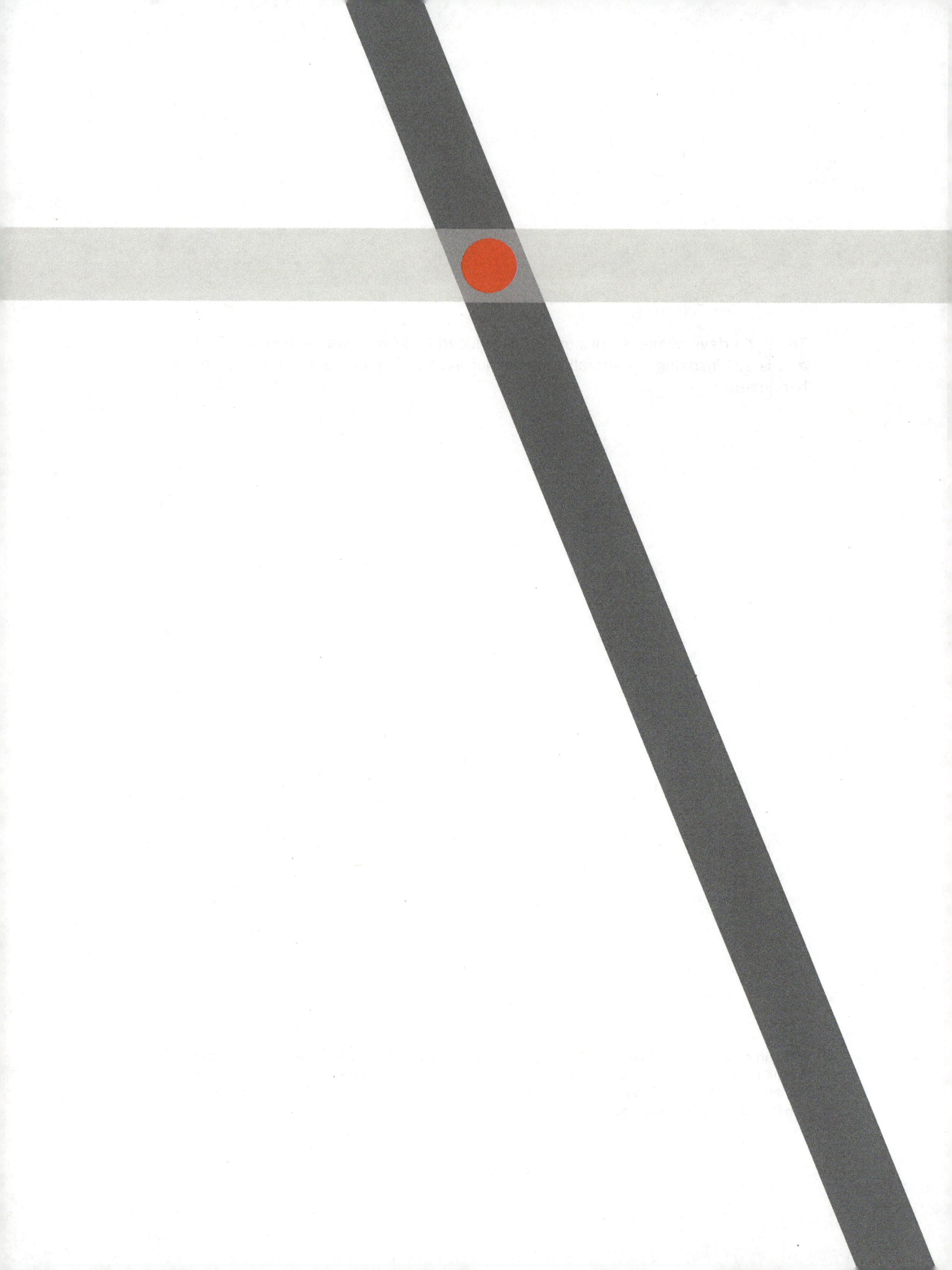

Preface

Alba Cappellieri, Full Professor at Politecnico di Milano, Italy
Susanna Testa, Research Fellow at Politecnico di Milano, Italy

The shift from a handcraftsmanship-based methodology to new models of productive processes was marked by the first industrial revolution: the handcraft know-how had been gradually flanked and, for some sectors, entirely replaced by the use of machine tools, with significant benefits in terms of quantity, speed, and efficiency. It is during the industrial revolution, the transition from artisanal manufacture to mass production, that for the first time the contrast between *manus* (hand) and *machina* (machine) comes to light, two opposing elements that have characterized every productive and artistic sphere for the centuries ahead.

The jewelry sector, thus, has also been affected by the dichotomy generated from the manufacturing revolution. Hand manufacturing and mechanized production, respectively hand and machine, has marked and settled over time two opposite ways of creating and therefore conceiving jewelry: on one side the manufactured object, one of a kind, often custom-made, targeted towards an elite; on the other side the piece of jewelry industrially produced, standardized, affordable and addressed to the mass market. The jewelry sector, like many other productive and artistic areas, had for a long time been somewhat skeptical towards technology: on the one hand, the manual work was nostalgically ensuring the production quality and it was associated with positive values, such as exclusivity, spontaneity, and authenticity; on the other hand, the machine was seen as synonymous with progress and accessibility, but it was also linked to the idea of inferiority and homologation.

The current revolution has marked the transition from an analog era to a digital one (and maybe post-digital?) and it has globally fluidified the system: in the age of digital technology, the distinction among the different spheres is increasingly less defined, and the productive paradigms tend to blend and to contaminate each other, progressively reducing the antithetical distance between hand and machine. Even though the dichotomy still represents a significant characterizing element for the jewelry field, the boundaries between the two different production processes are becoming more and more blurred, and the cases of a hybrid approach are more frequent. The changing nature of the relationship between manual labor and mechanical work not only represents a challenge to established assumptions, handed down by the goldsmith tradition, but also constitutes an important stimulus in fostering technological innovation for the sector, making it possible to achieve results that would have never been carried out without this synthesis and to encourage the spread of a new aesthetics.

HANDMADE

The term "handmade" refers to a manual process, to the creation of a non-industrial product, therefore forged through the use of hands. In particular the inquiry concerns the entirely handcrafted jewelry, traditionally resulting from the abilities of the artisan-demiurge to shape the matter starting from an idea. Regardless of whether it is a product made by traditional or post-digital craftsmen, the handworked-piece of jewelry is the result of a long process of trials and errors, which requires study, precision, and continuous experimental application in order to reach remarkable results. The handmade quality in fact is achieved not only through precision and attention to details, but also through the uniqueness of the manufactured object, the time spent by the artisan in crafting it. The craftsmanship is therefore the outcome of a constant striving between handwork and creativity, traditional repertoire and innovative techniques, use of precious materials and material experimentations.

DIGITAL

The deployment of digital technologies had such a great impact on the society that it has been defined as an authentic revolution. Indeed, today it is possible to design, to produce, to distribute, and to communicate through the web: this has drastically changed the relationship among designer, product, production, and final consumer.

In this context, the word "digitalcraft" refers to varying production processes that combine hand and mind to digital media. The integration among new technologies and craftsmanship has also involved the jewelry sector: productive methods and tools have been adapted from industrial reality to the collective practices of the designer-makers. These new digital artisans share productive technologies and creative processes thorough the Internet, in an integrated system of mutual connections. Open source technology, algorithmic models, laser cutting machines, and additive manufacturing allow the production of products with a high level of complexity and definition, custom-made pieces starting from a digital file.

Digital Meets Handmade: Jewelry in the Twenty-First Century International Symposium, organized by the Fashion Institute of Technology with the collaboration of the Politecnico di Milano, explored the relationship between jewelry and production processes, fostering the investigation of the cultural and symbolic meaning of the binomial hand/machine for the jewelry sector in its historical evolution. The different contributions here presented delve into the increasingly slippery borders between handcraft and new productive technologies in the field of contemporary jewelry and identify new scenarios through case studies of best practice. The discussion is not only oriented to the outcome of the different crafting procedures, but it proposes a reflection on the production and distribution processes themselves, their implications with the social context in terms of sustainability, and their impact on research and on education.

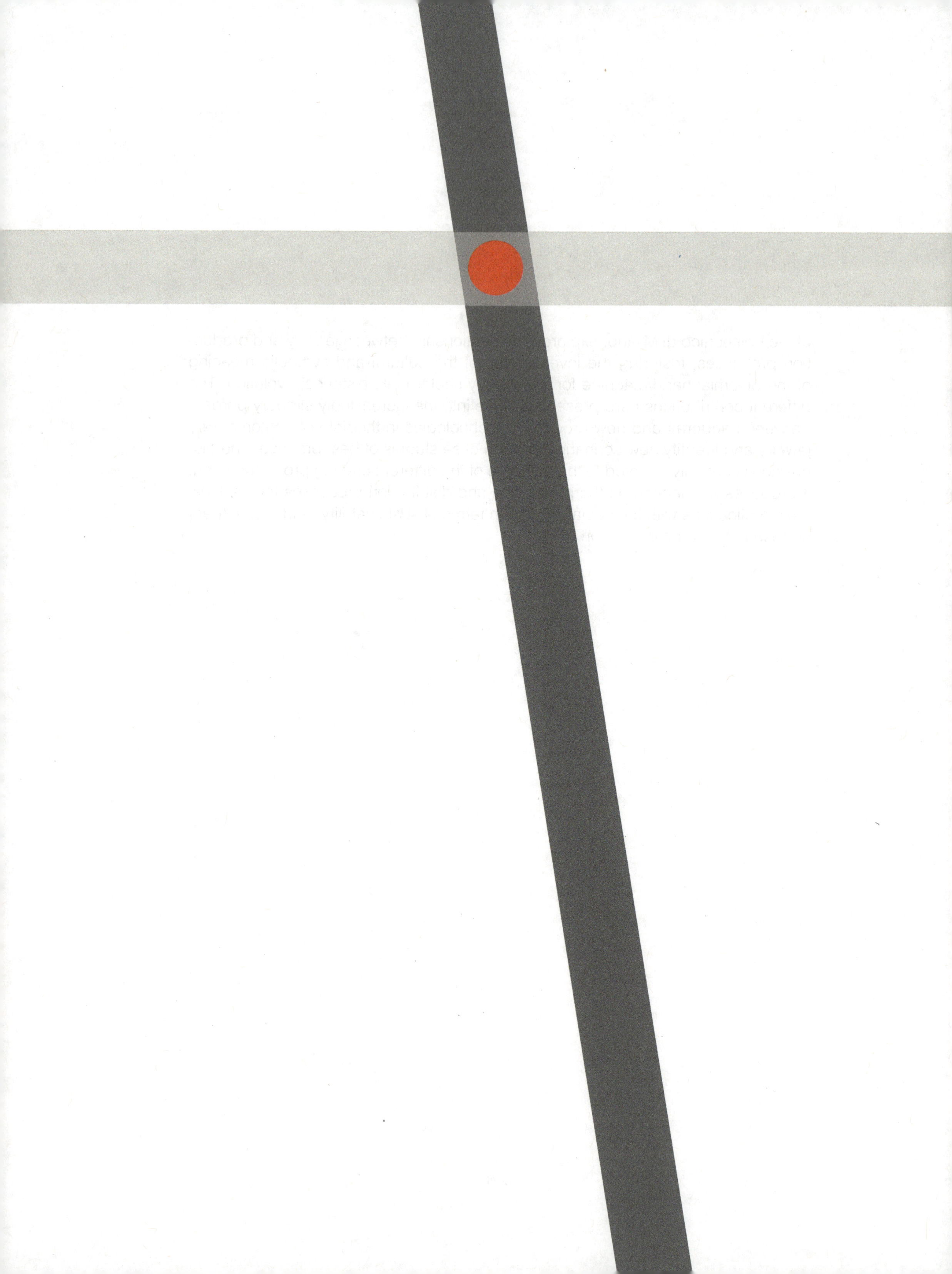

Introduction

Troy Richards, Dean, School of Art & Design,
Fashion Institute of Technology, NY, USA

In 1946, weighing 28 tons, occupying a large room and requiring 170,000 watts of power to run, the first computer was developed. The first personal computers, sold in kits, were introduced in 1975 and the first Apple desktop was released in 1977. Depending on which date you choose, we are somewhere in the fifth to eighth decade of the digital era. What has been referred to as a digital revolution has been, in reality, an evolution. While a discovery or invention may be heralded as groundbreaking or disruptive, in reality it takes time for new ideas and ways of making to take hold and gain acceptance. It takes even longer for individual designers and industry to accept, master, and fully integrate these tools and ideas in practice and manufacturing. This is true across many industries, including jewelry design. Humans have been making jewelry for thousands of years. As they've mastered new technologies the designs and aesthetics have changed as materials and tools have changed. This evolution has continued with digital techniques where new fabrication processes are impacting how we make, but also what we are capable of producing.

But just as photography emphatically did not replace painting as painters once feared, digital design will not replace handcraftsmanship. But is digital design just another tool—a fabrication technique? A new material or method, a product differentiator to be exploited in advertising? Or is it such a departure that it can reset the entire industry?

Our thirty-seven speakers from around the world gathered at FIT in May 2018. Each is an expert in the field and brings, with that expertise, a unique point of view. However, each has had to grapple with the changing reality of the field of jewelry design. In this book you will find these designers and academics applying their creative and critical minds to a number of issues, among them:

Annika Pettersson, a Swedish jewelry designer, investigates how the digital "noise/tool mark" to copying and printing digital models can effect design—and can be deliberately exploited in creating new aesthetic statements.

Lynne Heller and Dorie Millerson, both assistant professors at the Ontario College of Art and Design, in their research "Craft, Pedagogy and the Digital Challenge: A Jewelry Perspective" point out a "generational shift" in the learning orientation of their students, the first generation of "digital natives," as they grapple with learning and applying more traditional skills.

In her paper, Alba Cappellieri, Full Professor at the Fashion Design program at the Politecnico di Milano, suggests a classification of the different types of interaction systems enabled by jewelry as a medium: the static linear system (analog jewelry), the dynamic linear system (relational jewelry), the close circuit dynamic system (jewelry made with smart and reactive materials), and the open circuit dynamic system (wearable technologies).

Jeff Deegan, along with Jane, his wife and partner, founded Jeff Deegan Designs, takes a more critical approach in his paper referring to the democratization of design that has occurred as a result of digital revolution. For the first time in memory anyone, whether or not they possess bench skills, can, by sending a file, generate a 3D jewelry model. Deegan asks, "What is the soul at the core of the piece?" He argues that most successful and passionate designs will continue to require attention to technical detail and be in accord with real world methods necessary to manufacture.

The issue of making or wearing designs that digital techniques make possible, or the issues of economy and the speed at which the designs can be developed and marketed, was argued at the event. But for me and many participants as educators, bigger questions emerged:

— How do we teach digital techniques?
— How can we continue to afford to buy the ever-more-sophisticated machines our students and faculty need to learn it?
— How can we compensate teachers for the time necessary to become enthusiastically proficient in these new technologies?
— Should we continue to teach digital design in its own silo? Or should digital design be part of everything an institution such as FIT teaches?
— And what of industry? An industry that is shared by organizations and artisans making pieces of jewelry by the millions and pieces as unique one-off creations?

Different students and different faculty members will bring different talents and different priorities to institutions such as ours and to eventual employers.

I do not wish to guide readers one way or another, but rather to stimulate readers into considering the full range of ideas presented here. To an overwhelming degree the participants in this symposium warmly embrace new digital software, prototyping equipment, and production equipment. For many, adapting to and integrating technology in their practices has been a decades-long process. The fact that for each designer that adaptation has taken on a different and idiosyncratic form demonstrates that a personal vision, and the artist's hand, is still at the heart of jewelry design. Creative individuals willfully select from all of the tools available to them to make and solve problems.

This brings me back to my role as Dean of FIT's School of Art & Design and as a lifelong educator. I, my colleagues, and my peers have to figure out how to teach this stuff and to find and fairly allocate the resources—human, institutional, technical, and monetary—to continue moving into and expanding this exciting field. We cannot ignore it. We cannot even remain neutral.

I think you will agree after reading these thoughtful and stimulating papers that we most wholeheartedly embrace these new creative gifts and meld them into the canon of established design norms already in our curriculum, continuing to expand humanity's range as we continue to evolve.

Just as we learned to melt and shape materials and to bend wire, we will learn and embrace digital techniques.

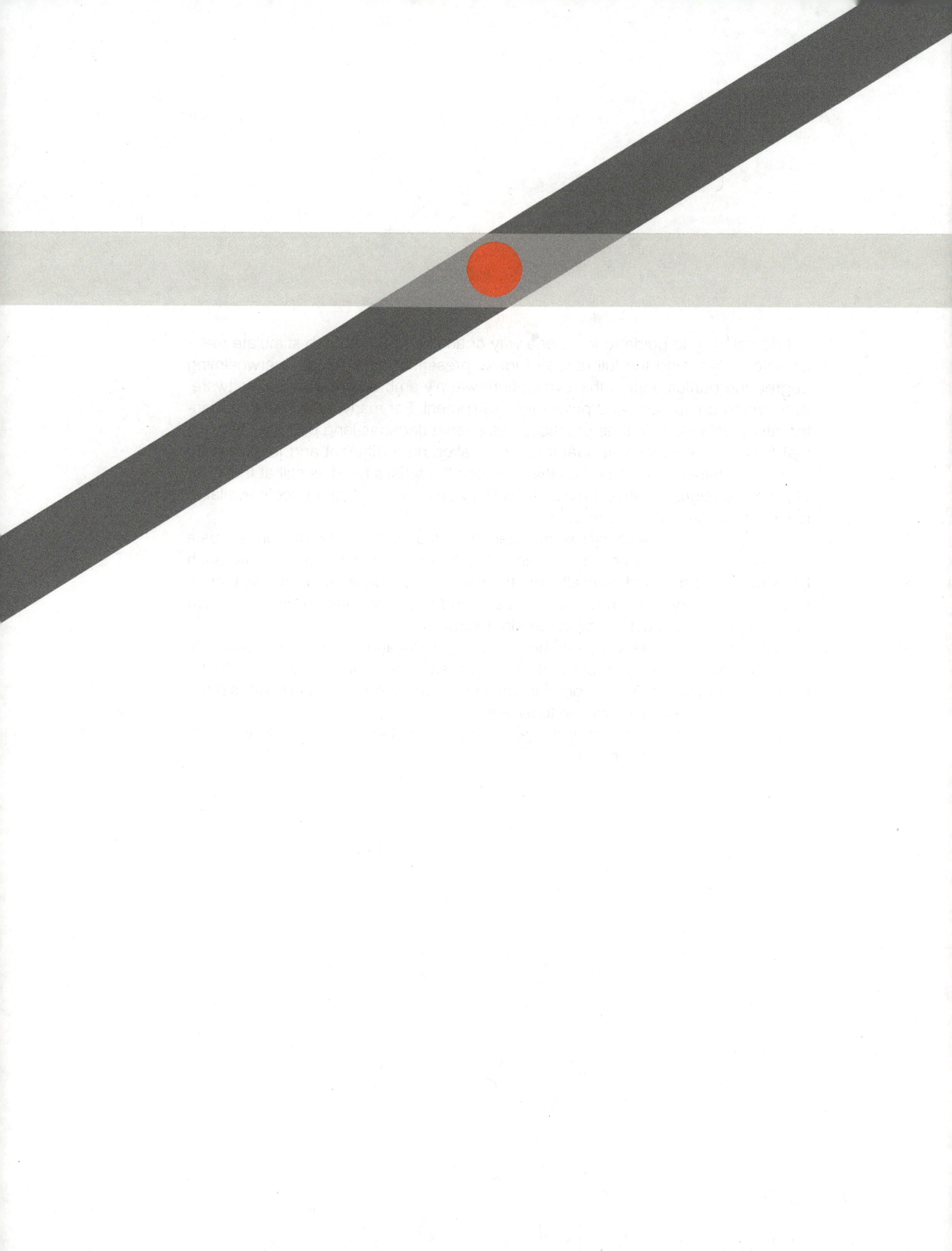

Jewelry Interactions: From Analog to Digital

Alba Cappellieri, Politecnico di Milano, Italy
Livia Tenuta, Politecnico di Milano, Italy
Susanna Testa, Politecnico di Milano, Italy

Abstract

Digital technologies and scientific advancements, besides having revolutionized the entire jewelry supply chain, overturning the phases and the roles of the actors involved, have permeated the products themselves, affecting their physical and aesthetic features and the systems of interaction they enable.

This paper aims to investigate the different systems of interactions within the field of jewelry, focusing on the transition from an analog to a digital context.

First, the effects of digital technologies on the supply chains in terms of interaction are briefly described. In particular, the paper finds a possibility to generate an important value for the consumers in open structures, engaging them in co-creating the products along the different phases.

Furthermore, the analysis focuses on the product, describing the evolution of interaction mediated by jewelry conceived as an interface, from analog to digital.

To this end, the paper suggests a classification of the different types of interaction systems enabled by jewelry as a medium: the static linear system (analog jewelry), the dynamic linear system (relational jewelry), the close circuit dynamic system (jewelry made with smart and reactive materials), and the open circuit dynamic system (wearable technologies). The different systems are described in terms of relationships, features and elements of interaction.

The analysis demonstrates how circular open systems represent a turning point for the evolution of body ornaments. This system resulting from new technological and scientific advancements enhances some features that were already intrinsic in the more traditional jewelry systems, such as the relational component it also offers and, other powerful tools to create a one-of-a-kind and made-to-measure experience for the wearer.

1. Jewelry from Emotion to Experience

The inclusion of digital technologies has revolutionized the jewelry system, shattering and fluidifying it. The distinction among the different areas is increasingly blurred, the production paradigms tend to blend and contaminate each other. During the last century jewelry was univocally conceived in terms of precious materials, and characterized for passing to future generations. The contemporary jewelry landscape instead is extremely heterogeneous, animated by such a plurality of languages, concepts, and meanings, sometimes in contrast among themselves, that makes it difficult to formulate a univocal definition (Cappellieri, 2016, p.18).

Investment or fashion accessory, ornament or sculpture, industrial or handmade, mass produced or one-of-a-kind, the multiplicity of interpretations suggest a common element: the emotional component intrinsically linked to jewelry (Carcano at al., 2005).

The value of the ornament can be connected to the attributed meaning, to the emotion that it is able to raise. Whether it is associated with its uniqueness, the preciousness of materials and the manufacturing expertise, the symbolic value of representing a memory or a gift, the ornamental spectacularity, the idea, or the project value, jewelry may convey emotions for the wearer. The widespread distribution of digital technologies, despite having affected the process in terms of optimization and improvement of performances for jewelry companies, has also created the possibility of impacting the final consumer experience. The new powerful technological tools in fact describe an open system, allowing the consumer to take part in the different phases of the process. This systemic interaction generates an added value in terms of experience, amplifying the product's emotional component.

New technologies in fact enable the designer to engage the final consumer in a dynamic way from the design phase to the production. This leads to products' ability to respond to the needs of the clients, in terms of wearability and aesthetics.

Additive technologies and parametric modeling software have not only revolutionized the aesthetics of the final product, allowing the implementation of shapes and finishing otherwise unobtainable because of timing and cost with traditional tools, but have also put into effect the possibility for the user to intervene in the production of physical objects, starting from digital tools.

Digital co-creation platforms set up a new virtual space for collaboration, where the role of the designer is no longer related to the definition of the final structure of the object, but consists in regulating and programming the very procedure; therefore, design lies increasingly in defining parametric algorithms able to generate structures with infinite variations, thus maintaining a common coherent matrix. A pioneering example of virtual interactions within the jewelry sector is represented by Nervous System. This tech-oriented design studio, recurring to generative systems, additive manufacturing and digital platforms, enables consumers to easily create their own customized products. Through the use of these tools users can directly interact with the graphic interface, creating unlimited formal variations, generating organic-like structures, such as the perfect geometry of fractals, extremely complex and always new figures, which become one-of-a-kind pieces, produced on demand.

Virtual platforms valorize the role of consumers, shortening the supply chain while making the process interactive. Shapeways, Sculpteo, and Igniverse are examples of companies whose use of technology enables users to upload digital sketches, choose materials, prototype pieces, and potentially sell them online.

New technologies not only allow the user to create highly customized and one-of-a-kind products, but also "made-to-measure" pieces, adjustable to the size of each and every body. 3D scanners offer the possibility of measuring and accurately tracing the three-dimensional shape of the human figure. The end product will fit the precise contours of the intended client.

The advantages of digital technologies are not only addressed to optimize processes and to create highly adaptive products, scattering the concept of "size," but also to create sparks for creative experimentation within the sector. *Portrait Me*, the project by Vivian Meller and Laura Alvarado, for example, reinterprets the traditional cameo in a modern and ironic way. The characters have been dressed up with historical costumes and then accurately reproduced through the use of a 3D scanner. The shapes were then printed with a laser sintering technique in a brooch collection.

Digital technologies have also revolutionized the retail experience, offline and online. This has not only overturned the dynamics of product distribution and sale through e-commerce, but also promoted the development of online spaces enabling interactive experiences where the user can virtually try on the product via augmented reality before buying it. Boucheron is one of the first luxury brands that understood the potential of this digital marketing strategy. Since 2010, through the use of augmented reality, the company has been offering customers the opportunity to try on its precious creations and digitally visit the boutique on the website.
New technologies, besides having highly influenced the entire productive system, overturning the phases and the roles of the actors involved, have permeated the products themselves, affecting their aesthetic features, increasing their performances, and conferring new meanings.

2. Jewelry as Interface

Traditionally, jewelry has always acted as a cultural vehicle, transmitting information about the identity of the wearer. However, ornaments have also played the role of a practical tool, with shapes, functions and meanings that have changed over time.

The practical functionality was highly emphasized in the first pieces of jewelry produced by ancient civilizations: Kenyans utilized finger-knives to cut shrubs and gather berries, Indians recurred to the use of heavy bracelets whose weight and sharp profiles made it a great tool for personal defense (Cappellieri et al, 2014). The instrumental utility of the ornament has fallen by the wayside, until it almost completely got lost during the modern history. The introduction of digital technology has partially restored the binomial of function and aesthetic: this has marked the transition from aesthetic-ornament to prosthetic-ornament, reactive objects, highly autonomous, designed with the ambition of overtaking the limits imposed by the human body, which is amplified, empowered, and monitored.

The introduction of the technological element changes the nature of the product that, from a mostly static piece, becomes an open, dynamic, and functional structure.

To this purpose, Baudrillard's (2005) considerations about the concept of functionality are particularly interesting. The term "functional" moves away from its common sense of responding to a precise scope, but adapts to a specific order or system: functionality is the property of organically integrating in a context. Therefore, the functional object, according to Baudrillard, is not an object whose primary aim is to satisfy a need, but an element of gaming, of combination and calculation in a universal system of signs. The objects are conceived as open structures, characterized by a configuration that makes them assimilated to concepts: despite their apparent formal finitude, they are not defined in use and content. This margin of indetermination makes them highly interpretable. This has influenced the consumers' experience of use: users not only wear the piece of jewelry, but they contribute to complete its sense, defining it, conferring a meaning. These objects "liven up," thanks to the voluntary or involuntary interaction they have with the wearer and/or the surroundings. They are highly customizable because they can perfectly adapt to the wearer's behavior. The most essential difference compared to traditional jewelry is this degree of indetermination: incomplete objects, interface-jewelry items, that are defined in the moment of use, enabling dynamic interactions at different levels.

The transition from the analog context to the digital system has modified the features of the interaction, not only between the users and the piece of jewelry, but also of the relationship, mediated by the ornament, among users, users and environment, users and their own bodies, and users and other objects, enabling other forms of interactions, such as the one with the system.

This research aims to outline and classify the different types of systems enabled by jewelry items. To this end, the following macro categories have been identified:

- the static linear system: analog jewelry;
- the dynamic linear system: relational jewelry;
- the close circuit dynamic system: jewelry made with smart and reactive materials; and
- the open circuit dynamic system: wearable technologies.

The areas are described in terms of systemic and relational features that result from the different interaction enabled by jewelry.

Even though the technological and scientific experimentations have facilitated complex dynamic systemic interactions to a significant degree, the seed of the relational component can be seen also in some typologies of jewelry within the traditional analog system.

3. Analog System Interaction

3.1. The Static Linear System

The traditional jewelry system describes a mainly static system, where the consumer interacts with the piece of jewelry wearing it, conferring different meanings to it. This procedure doesn't contemplate either a practical instrumental functionality, nor the possibility of actively taking part to the design phase and modifying the aesthetic features.

The traditional system provides an experience between the user and the product mainly based on analog inert components, such as the physical features of the material, the surface treatments, and the overall shape.

The interaction within this context is mostly based on voluntary inputs by the wearer and passive feedbacks from the objects, usually visual or tactile. Besides the first degree of relationship between the user and the piece of jewelry, the enabled system also provides a second degree of the relationship, mediated by the physical and aesthetic features of the ornament, between different users and users with their own bodies. These interactions describe a static linear system, where the jewelry interface passively behaves without engaging with the context.

The convergence of jewelry with design culture led to concepts that tend to overlook the preciousness of materials, to celebrate the intangible preciousness of ideas, giving value to the role of people's experiences and behaviors.

3.2. The Dynamic Linear System: Jewelry as Relational Analog Interface

Within the analog system, a particular category of jewelry is designed to enable the dynamic interactions it figures in. These pieces of jewelry can be referred to as "relational," since they are specifically designed to enable relationships of different degrees among various actors. The jewelry item becomes a relational prosthesis for the body.

The fertile unitary system that takes shape not only links the users to the ornament in a dynamic way, inasmuch configurable and reconfigurable, but also allows them to interact with their own body, with other people, with other objects, and with the context. All these different elements are asked to take part in the sense and the aesthetics of the project.

Between users and jewelry items

Jewelry can become the interface itself if designed to enable the interaction between the wearers and its own aesthetic features.

These are reconfigurable and customizable objects, designed to leave the final consumer free to establish a relationship with the product, ensuring a wide margin of intervention.

Historically the goldsmith field did not structurally contemplate the active intervention of the consumer, both in terms of interaction in the process stages and in the aesthetic definition of the product. There are, however, in the traditional repertoire, some interesting examples, such as sentimental jewelry.

Extremely rooted in human culture thanks to their ability to convey feelings and emotions, sentimental jewelry can be traced back to ancient times and reaches its maximum expression during the Victorian age (Cappellieri, 2014). The nineteenth-century sentimental jewelry was designed to celebrate a wide range of feelings: not just love, passion, and joy for new births, but also mourning and condolence, preferring primarily poor materials to emphasize the symbolic and immaterial value. These ornaments were often designed to be customized: the traditional type of chest-jewel meant to guard the memory of the loved ones in the form of rings, medallions, pendants, and bracelets, equipped with small cavities to contain hair locks of the missing person. The pieces of jewelry were conceived as empty frames that reached aesthetic and design fullness in the moment they are animated by the wearer.

The preciousness of materials leaves room for the preciousness of feelings, for the value of the gestures of donating and receiving, thus strengthening the physical and emotional bond between people. It is the case of modular jewelry given to newborn babies during the rite of baptism. The modular elements were then gradually added to celebrate the important moments of life: the piece changed and grew over time along with the person who wore them.

This trend has been reinterpreted over time: it is the case at Pandora, the multinational giant that started a jewelry business from the concept of customization. The bracelets, made in precious metals, can be gradually enriched with the addition of new charms or pendants with different shapes and meanings.

These typologies are based on the concept of open structure and combinational invention, in which the consumer has the possibility to personally affect the aesthetics or the mode of operation of the product by modifying the arrangement of preexisting parts.

Sentimental jewelry is therefore an interesting example of interface-ornament that enables an interaction between the user and the object itself (through aesthetic reconfiguration) and between different users.

In contemporary times, designers carry out customization at various levels.

Modular jewels allow the users to intervene in the arrangement of predefined parts, to combine them and wear them in various ways. It is the case of *Molecole Preziose* by Massimiliano Adami, a collection made up of sub-multiples, assemblable parts, each constituting the core of structural elements of jewelry. Units are assembled as parts of a kit, as in the project of Drilling Lab that creates a precious alphabet by reinterpreting the structures of industrial clamps. Manuganda's *Compo* describes a modular chain that can be disassembled and reassembled in different ways, stimulating the creativity of the wearer. Maria Jennifer Carew with *LessIs* reinterprets the brooch to promote combinatorial innovation: the project not only offers the possibility to compose a variety of elements, but also to arrange them on garments in different ways, wearing them without any rule.

Between users and their own bodies

The most immediate relational system is the relationship between the ornament and the body of the wearer. Jewelry has always been conceived and designed for the human body, not only to enhance it, but also to modify it, to emphasize its features,

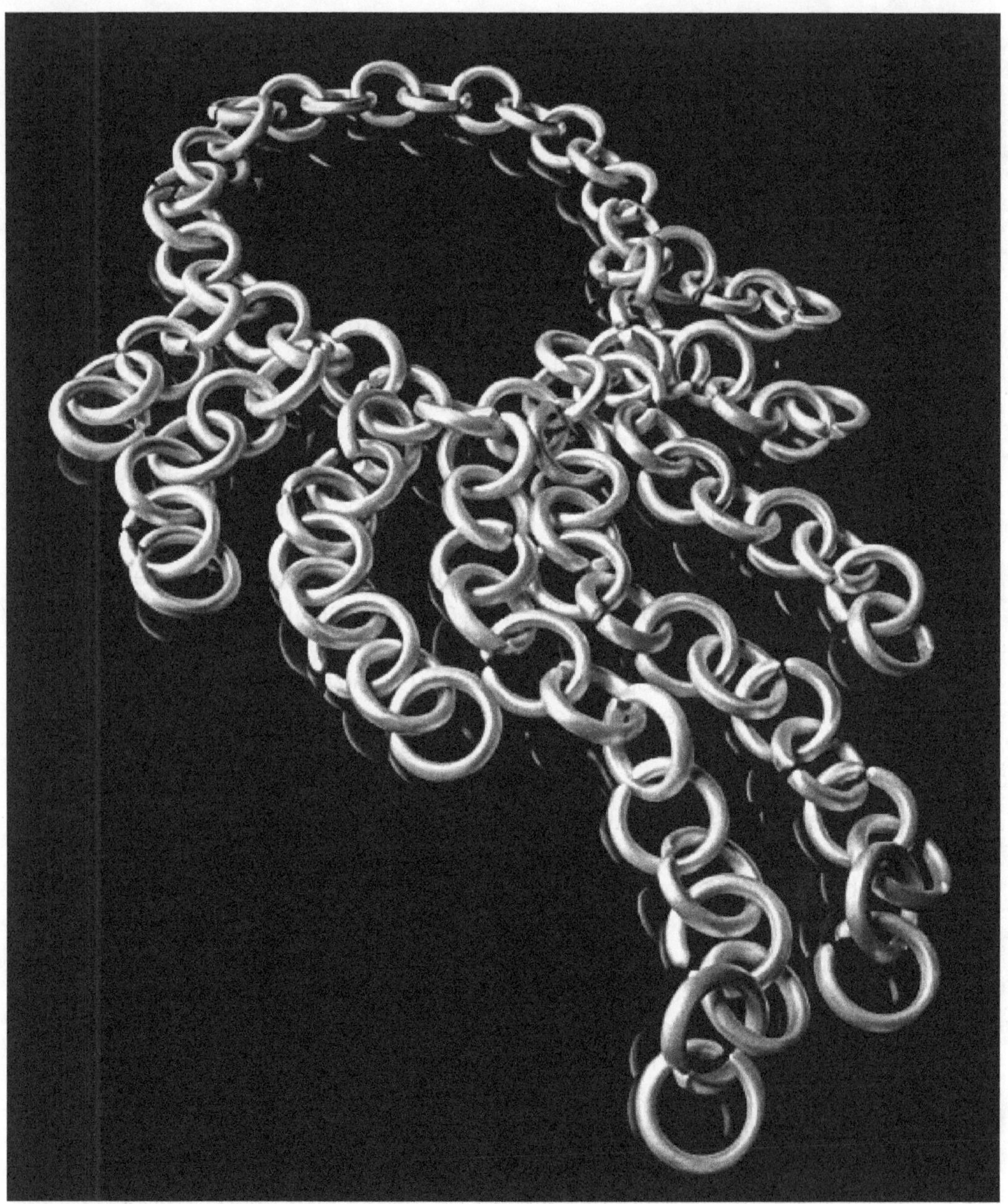

Figure 1. Manuganda, Compo Necklace, 2007, anodized aluminum.

making it theatrical, imprisoning it, forcing its transformation, temporarily or permanently. The ornament is not only able to change the aesthetics of the wearer's body, but also alter the senses.

Body modification using ornaments is a practice already popular in the different cultures of the world in ancient times. This habit is still common among some specific ethnic groups, such as the Mursi's labial plate or the Kayan women's neck rings in Thailand. These body altering practices, besides having a specific symbolic value, allow the user to join certain aesthetic criteria and thus to stress their own identity of belonging to a specific ethnicity.

The jewelry-mediated relationship between users and their own bodies has been extensively investigated in contemporaneity, raising the interest of designers and artists who have explored the jewel-body interaction through experimentations in different ways.

These are mostly conceptual and paradoxical projects, whose aim is to astonish and to offer cause for reflection to the observer, the beneficiary of the work. The wearability of these pieces is secondary to the message that the designer-artist wants to communicate.

Jewelry can embody temporary traces on the body, exhibited and declared as in the case of Gijs Bakker's *Shadow Jewelry* series, or hidden and intimate, as it is for Ineke Hans's jewel for Chi Ha Paura? (*Forever Yours*). They may be designed to hide part of the face, taking on the behavior of masks that change the real perception of the wearer's body, as in Akiko Shinzato's *Another Skin Jewelry Collection*, or as in Mint Design's protection masks.

Jewelry can also be disruptive in the body modification process. The following projects describe situations where the skin is forced to temporarily adapt itself to "unwearable" ornaments. Real body cages made by Ren Kurosawa, who reinterprets the prohibition of the fundamentalist Catholic religion in a metaphorical way. Sascha Nordmeyer focuses on the mouth, creating ironic and eccentric objects with the aim to force the smile in unusual grim faces, while Naomi Filmer designs jewelry to lock the hands in precise positions. Jennifer Crupi also refers to gestures and is particularly interested in the communication between people through body language. She created a collection of sculptural jewelry that encourages precise actions and specific plastic poses.

The reflection and the more-or-less veiled critique about the role of aesthetic surgery in defining a common aesthetic in contemporary society is an inspiration for several designers. They can be eye-catching objects such as Zhilu Cheng's *Self Image* collection, made with stainless steel elements that make the gums visible and stretch the mouth in different and unpleasant ways; or they may be in the form of a series of discrete prostheses designed to distort facial and body expressions like Imme van der Haak's and Burcu Büyükünal's projects. *Urban Dolls* by Valma Vaiciule, a series of micro prostheses that partially alter the face, challenges the canon of common beauty, while Studio X creates an object halfway between an ornament and an aesthetic surgery device that corrects somatic features, modifying the shape of the eyes. Lucy McRae and Bart Hess (Lucyandbart) deal with ornaments and low-tech cosmetic surgery. At the MU gallery in 2008 they set up a performance during which they applied hooks on the face of visitors to redefine their aesthetic features.

Some designers, on the other hand, explore the relationship between functionality and beauty, placing themselves in a hybrid area between orthopedics and accessories: Francesca Lanzavecchia, for example, reinterprets temporary disability prosthesis by designing embroidered collars, while Una Burke was inspired by the world of orthopedic braces to create her *Re.Treat* collection, where sculptural shapes that, like casts, force the movements of the human figure.

The *Medically Prescribed Jewelry* collection by the Portuguese designer Olga Noronha is fully involved in the medical field. Hers is an alternative approach to jewelry, exploring the mix of science, medicine, and ornament. The project involves the combined use of real surgical instruments mixed with precious materials with the aim of creating functional jewelry that not only is closely in contact with the body but also substantiates it: some pieces are in fact implanted, they disappear into the skin, becoming visible only through X-rays.

This category not only includes jewelry designed to modify the body, but also prosthesis-ornaments that can alter the perception of reality. In fact, jewelry can be designed with the aim of mediating the sensory experience of the wearer. They can enhance, alter, or cancel the senses involved. After the famous Getulio Alviani's *Monorecchino*, a work of art that, amplifying the ear-piece size, increases the hearing ability of the wearer, Gina Hsu also focuses on hearing, designing *Hear Ring* for Chi Ha Paura? It is a small acoustic-instrument-shaped ring that amplifies sounds when brought to the ear. Emilie Voirin, on the opposite side, addresses her *Earbling*—a silver necklace with small colored ear-plugs—to those who want to indulge in moments of isolation.

Natha Khunprasert's *Finger Tips* challenges the sense of touch, altering the sensitive perception of fingers, trapping them in glass spheres, while Zoé Bezençon designed a phalanxes ring whose tuft allows brushing against objects without directly touching them.

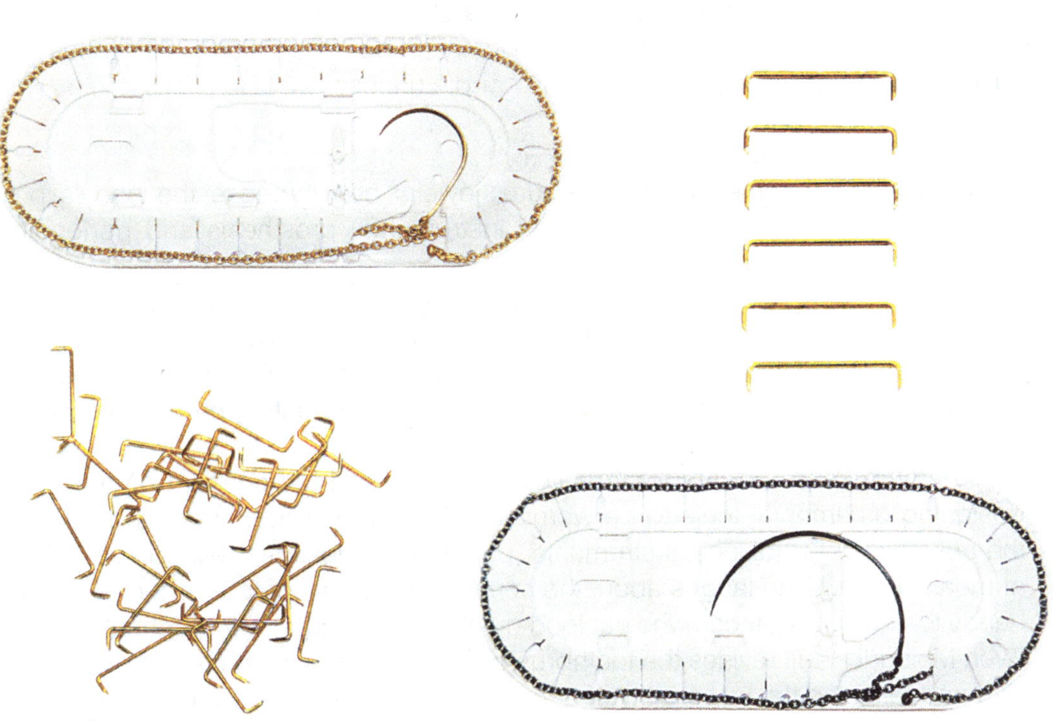

Figure 2. Olga Noronha, Sub-Dermal and Exo-Dermal, Medically Prescribed Jewelry, 2013, suture staples and suture wires, precious metals. Source: olganoronha.com.

Studio Eric Klarenbeek has designed contact lens jewelry to improve the sense of sight, and Ana Blagojevic created *Senza Sensi*, a set of elements to be worn together, each of which cancels a specific sense: the destruction of all senses amplifies the perceptual experience for the couple (Finessi, 2012).

Between users and other objects
As an extension of the human structure, jewelry can increase the body's performances by wearing it, becoming an instrumental prosthesis and performing practical functions.

Jewelry belonging to this category is no longer merely an aesthetic ornamentation, but becomes useful, enabling the relationship between the wearer, the environment, and other objects. The aesthetic of these ornaments expresses their functionality: these items are designed to be used, suggesting precise modalities of intervention by the consumer.

Already in 1987, Alessandra Cusatelli revolutionized the concept of cutlery by designing ornamental tools to be worn directly on the fingers, revisiting not only the aesthetics of traditional instruments, but also the gestures related to the ritual of meals. Paolo Ulian laughs about the contemporary way of feasting, designing a handy toothbrush for those who eat food quickly and frequently throughout the day. Even Moloudi Hadji revises the toothbrush: the personal hygiene tool is reduced in size and takes on the wearability of a tongue piercing. For literature lovers, Matteo Ragni has designed a small object with wings that serves as a precious and functional ring: it keeps a book open, allowing a "handy" reading.

Some jewels may be transformable, in a reversible or irreversible way, turning from purely ornamental into functional objects fulfilling a certain purpose. *Nap Collection* by Camille Cortet, for example, consists of objects that can be converted as needed: the spherical necklace pendant, if opened, becomes a small portable pillow for emergencies.

Drawing Tools by Laimé Lukosiunaite are used to stimulate creativity: chalk-ending claws that transform the limbs into drawing tools; Hilary Sanders's graphite ring instead is more wearable and subtle, enabling the user to new gestures, to a new dimension of artistic performance. Kyeok Kim designed a collection of soap-shaped rings—in contrast with the value of eternity conferred to jewelry, the ring dissolves with few gestures, leaving behind only a sweet aroma.

In all these examples, shapes are closely related to functions, suggesting the users' behaviors and partially predefined intervention procedures.

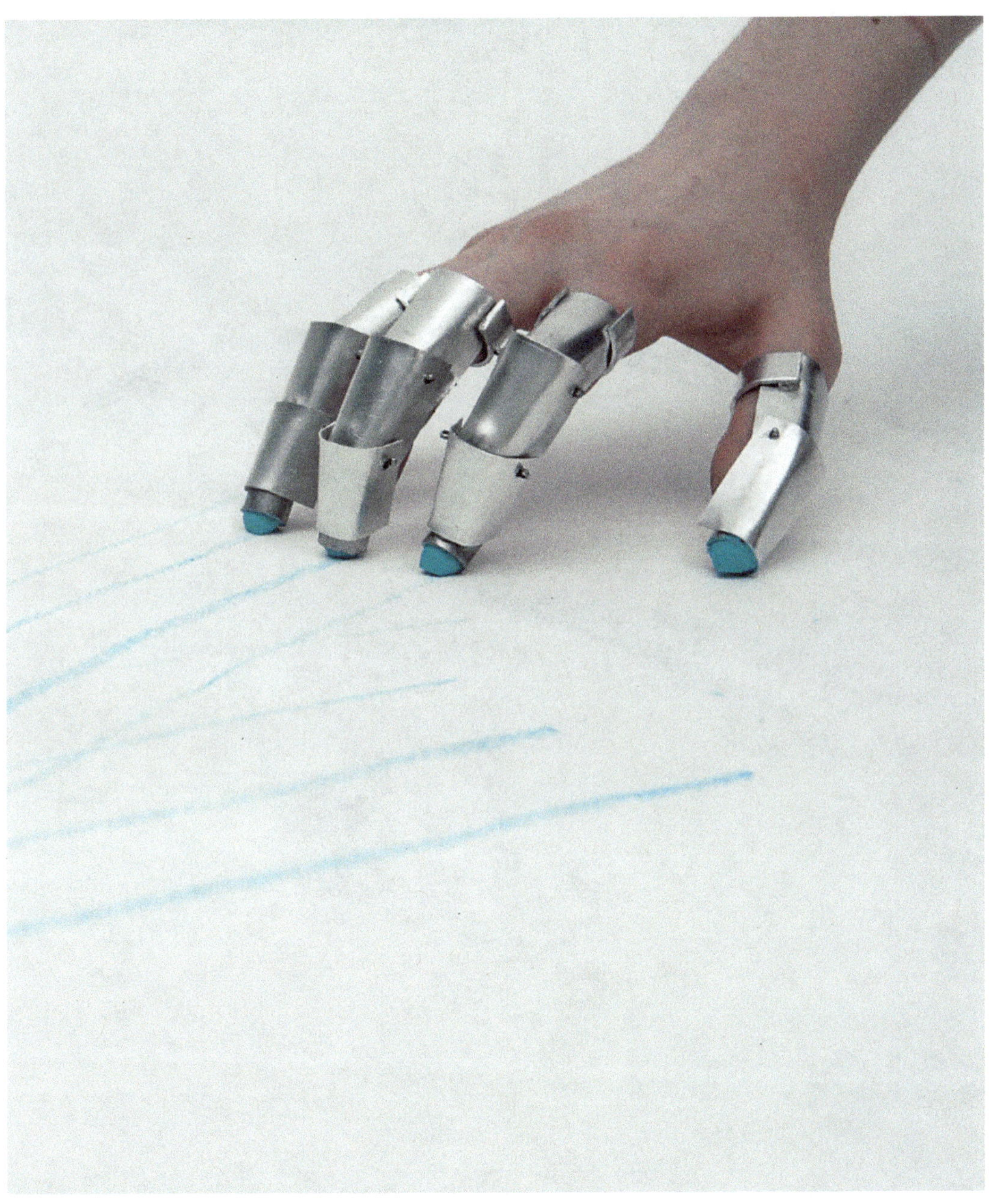

Figure 3. Laimė Lukošiūnaitė, Drawing Tools.
Source: laimeluko.com.

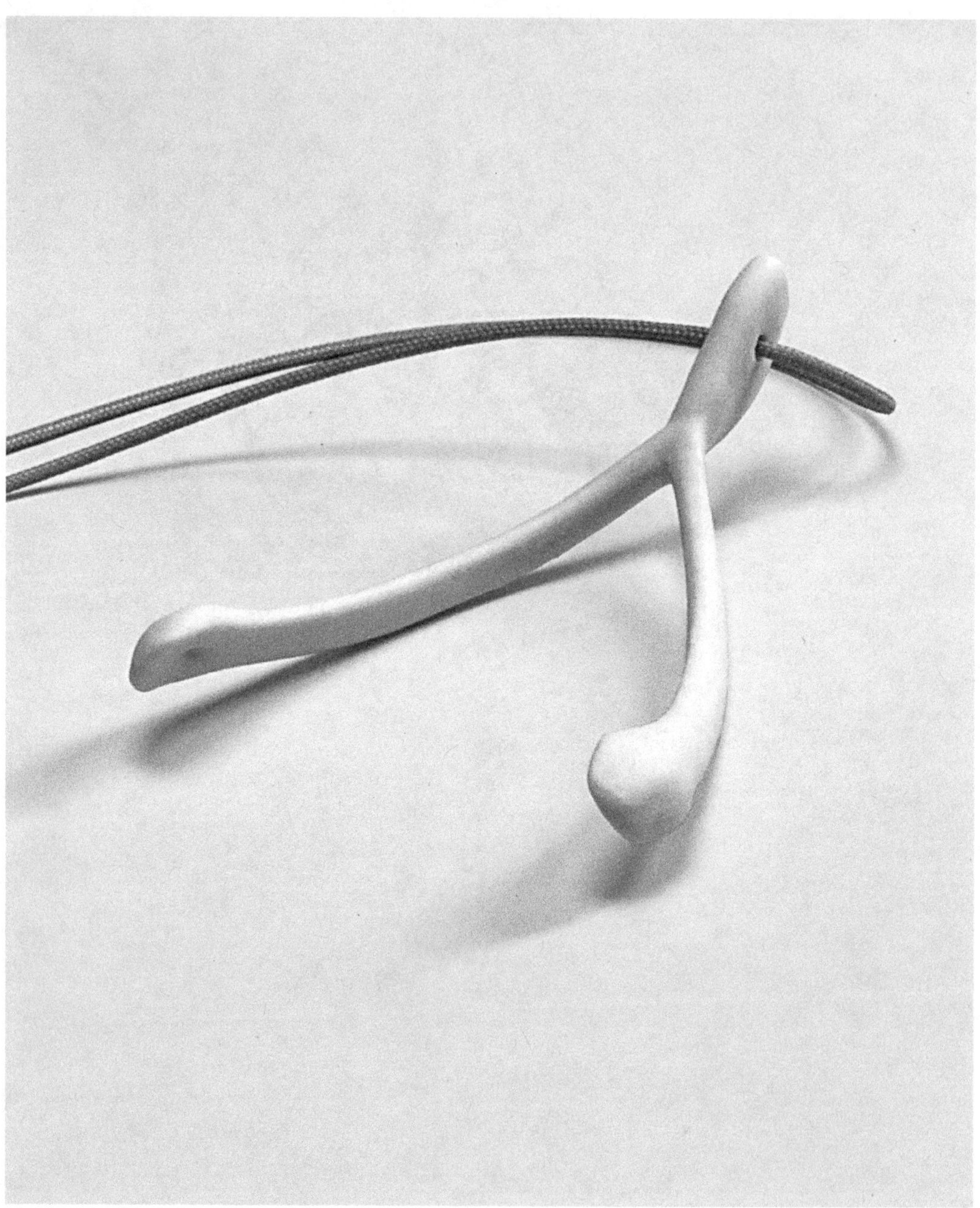

Figure 4. Michael Leung, Wishbone, 2007, pendant, porcelain. Source: chpjewelry.com.

Between users

From ordinary complementary heart-shaped pendants, which in their entirety create an overall readable figure, to *Vera Laica* by Angelo Mangiarotti, the wedding ring that works thanks to the two parts that compose it, the history of sentimental jewelry conveys several examples of ornaments that can bind people in an experience, both metaphorically and physically.

These relational products not only exploit the value of the ornament as a communicative interface between individuals, but also suggest interactive actions thanks to their aesthetics, telling what people can do, together. They are not entirely defined dynamic products, whose essence suggests a sharing experience among several actors, creating new rituals. *Wishbone* by Michael Leung for Chi Ha Paura?, for example, is a fragile porcelain pendant that can be broken together with a friend while making a wish. The very fracture confers a customized aesthetics to the piece.

Jewelry can measure relationships, as *Friend or Foe* by Lin Cheung proves. It is a ribbon necklace that ironically attributes a label to the rapport depending on the distance between people. But jewelry can also facilitate and moderate relationships, such as in Didier Faustino's prosthesis accessory: a mask for two, which induces and facilitates a kiss action.

Jewelry may even physically bind people. *Ring for Two* by Otto Künzli and *Pair* by Sun Kyoung Kim are tandem rings designed for a couple.

All these jewels require a joint participation of people to create the experience, creating contextual, extemporized, and unique performances, involving individuals in their sociality. These objects generate a physical and emotional bond between people, evoking relational meanings.

4. Close Circuit Dynamic Interaction

Technical-scientific experiments brought by the Third Industrial Revolution have significantly influenced the evolution of both natural and artificial materials by introducing the concept of designed material.

The matter is molded at micron resolution, and its features are designed considering specific functions to solve technical problems. These interventions alter and improve the characteristics of the materials, making them appropriate for targeted purposes: not only high performances, and innovative functionality but also responsiveness and behavioral autonomy. Smart materials are in fact special materials designed to describe and incorporate complex behaviors, to produce specific action-reaction depending on the stimuli produced by the human body or the surrounding environment (Ferrara and Lucibello, 2009).

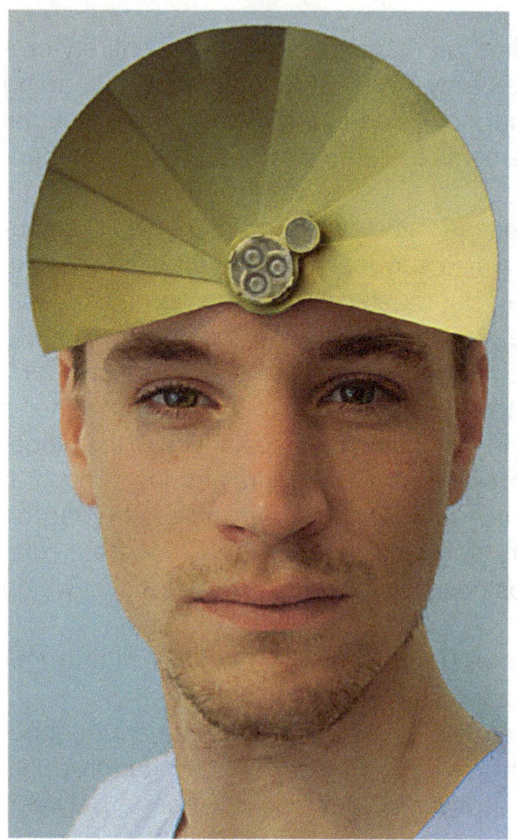
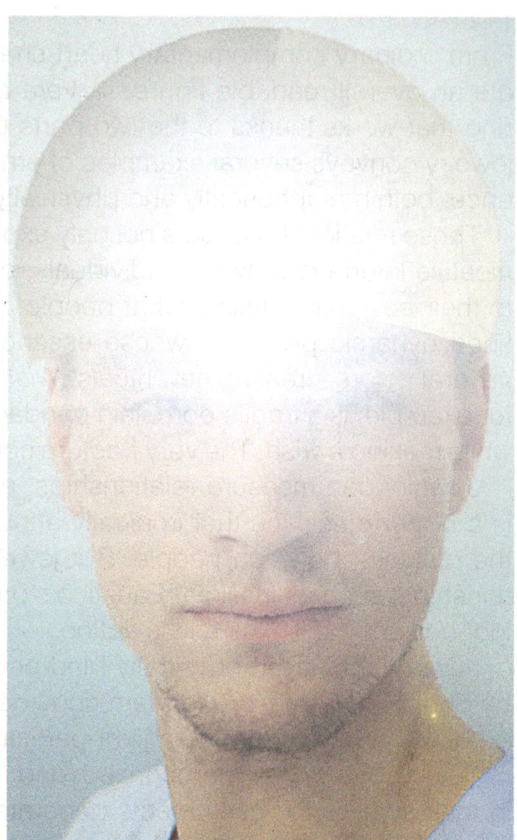

Figure 5. Formafantasma for Chi Ha Paura?, My Own Show, 2013, head piece, titanium.

With the concept of material design, the idea of the static nature of matter fails: the material changes, assuming different features.

Widespread in the field of active wear, these smart and programmable materials have opened the jewelry field to unprecedented opportunities, for practical and aesthetic applications.

From the simplest and most common thermochromic jewelry to those that exploit the reactive properties of some particular stones, Elena Corchero creates pendants with Albedonite, which, if stimulated by the sun rays, passes from light pink to intense magenta, to warn of the danger of UV exposure.

Federica Francisco for *Lumina Biomorphic* collection takes advantage of the phenomenon of photoluminescence: tapered glass stones collect daylight and release it into the dim light, illuminating who wears them. *My Own Show* project by Formafantasma moves around the theme of light. The shining head ornament makes it impossible to take pictures of the wearer: it reacts to the flash of the camera with an intense light that covers the user's face, blinding the photographer.

The dynamics of natural mechanisms are often a source of inspiration for innovative design solutions. For example, Neri Oxman and the MIT Media Lab team designed a series of 3D "wearable skins" that can facilitate synthetic biological processes allowing humans to survive on other planets. *Wanderers: An Astrobiological Exploration* is a four-piece collection made with a living substance. They interact with the environment and create a micro-habitat suitable for humans by chemically modifying the atmosphere.

Smart materials confer to jewelry a partial behavioral autonomy, creating a dynamic interaction between the wearer and the surrounding environment.

This close circuit system binds the involved actors in a circumscribed dialogue. The interaction inputs of the wearer are often unintentional, material reactions only partially controllable and hardly quantifiable from a numerical point of view.

5. Open Circuit Dynamic Interaction

The 1980s are the period in which, alongside the Internet explosion, consumers witnessed the entry of the first wearable technologies, *Walkmans*, mobile technologies, mobile phones, and laptops into the everyday life. With the birth of computers, industrial machines leave room for intangible assets, moving from hardware to software (Dery, 1996).

A dense and pervasive network system spreads out, progressively encasing what finds on its way: The Internet of Things. Materiality of products is here combined with immateriality of connections, whose crossroads are made up of everyday objects.

The technology-enabled system describes an open, conversational circuit that transforms the product into a highly responsive and time-sensitive interface-subject, a "spime" (Sterling, 2005), able to communicate with other interfaces by transforming the user from recipient to mediator.

The main feature of these products relies in their ability to enable users to new interactions, connecting them with their own body, with other users, and with the surrounding environment. In order to improve and guarantee new performances for the user, these connections generate a multitude of discrete data that can be used in real time but also exchanged and archived through a constant dialogue with the pervasive system.

A greater part of wearables is smart bands. These bracelets with embedded technology are mainly used in the sports field, as measuring tools for performances that then can be compared. Fitbit, for example, aims to monitor physical activity and is presented in different versions, from a smaller free screen to a bulkier one approaching aesthetics similar to a watch. The Sony Smart Band, Samsung Gear, or Garmin vivosmart additionally receive notifications of phone calls or messages; Razer Nabu creates a social network among all those who wear the smart band to exchange information and compare similar interests. All these products have a poorly designed aesthetic in common: wrist bands, with or without screens, interacting with the wearer through sounds or vibrations signals. The Lumo Lift brooch, thanks to a reduced number of functions, aspires to almost imperceptible dimensions. The smart brooch monitors the posture and alerts the user with a slight vibration to remind to keep shoulders back and head raised. Some products are linked to the medical sector: Embrace by Empatica prevents seizures besides measuring stress, anxiety, and sleep. The Moodmetric Smart Ring measures emotions and monitors nervous system signals in order to control and improve the quality of life. From the connection to the body and with other people to the one with other objects, jewelry can become the interface for the smartphone. Thanks to access via smartphones, some jewels take advantage of the power of images: Purple Locket, harking back to the traditional aesthetics of a medallion, is a tool to share pictures, or the Tago Arc, a wrist Kindle that can be customized by the user with different textures. The "projectables" are based on the role of images as interfaces: in most cases they exploit holograms to reproduce the screen of the smartphone, as in the Cicret bracelet, and in other cases they simply have an aesthetic function, as the Neclumi.

The smartphone is not the only object that can be controlled by these technological ornaments. A range of jewels have been designed to enable gestures to control the music volume, to take photos, or to answer phone calls, as in the case of Logbar. Hiris allows the user to control all smart devices at home, and Neyya transforms each phalanx in a controller to adjust the sound, make phone calls, or send messages.

Some pieces of jewelry aim to create a connection between the user and the environment. Juno by Netatmo records the amount of UV rays hitting the body and alerting the user.

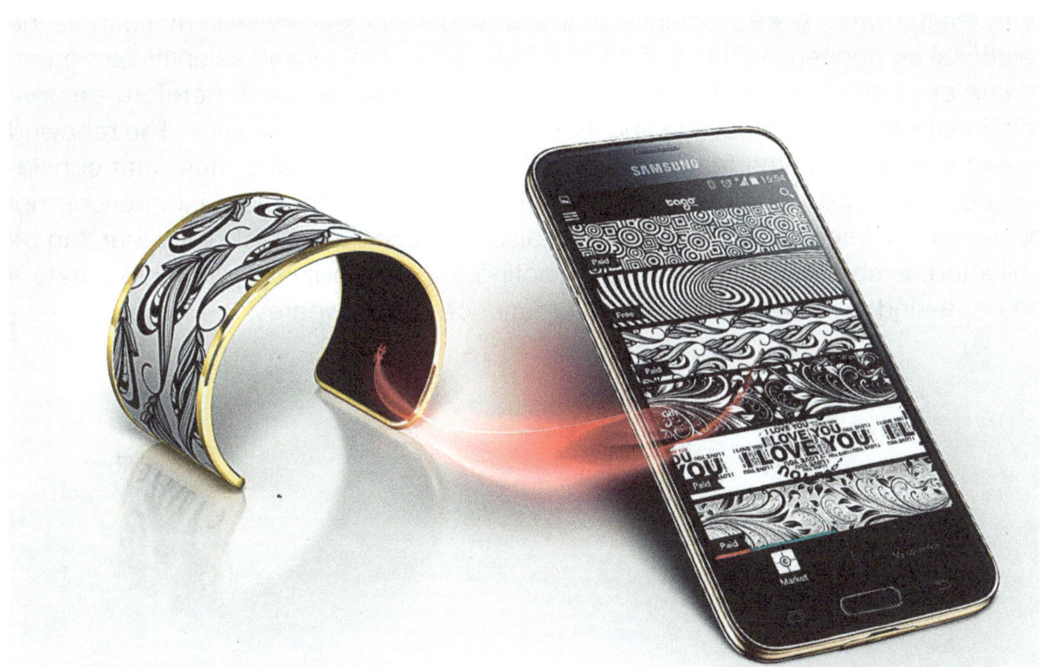

Figure 6. LIBER8 Technology, Targo Arc, 2015, Bracelet, golden metal, E Ink display.

Instead, the Shanghai government has adhered to the use of *Shuashua*, a bracelet enabling payments with Near Field Communication (NFC) not only for public transportation, but also for restaurants, supermarkets, gas stations, movie theaters and hospitals.

Widespread multifunctionality, constant connectivity, intuition, and immediacy. The trend of interaction has shifted from being screen-centric (systems where users interacted with devices through keyboards, or screens, generating a series of new gestures) to interaction everywhere. The most avant-garde projects developed by the biggest multinational companies are trying to enable interactions with every kind of surface, eliminating the physical element, transforming the gesture into the interface.

6. Conclusions

This analysis demonstrates how circular open systems represent a turning point for the evolution of body ornaments. These advanced products tend to stress some features that were already intrinsic in the analog linear jewelry system, such as the relational component. Within this context new technological and scientific advancements are transforming objects from open, customizable, and therefore passive relational interfaces to reactive and increasingly autonomous entities. The renewed interaction takes on the feature of a dialog, a conversational system that considers objects to be able to behave independently. Technological interactions not only enable all-senses experiences, but also produce quantifiable data that can be collected, exchanged, and stored, impacting the possibility for jewelry to create a one-of-a-kind and made-to-measure experience for the wearer.

References

Baudrillard, J. 2005. *The System of Objects*. London, UK: Verso.

Cappellieri, A. 2016. *Brilliant: The Futures of Italian Jewellery*. Mantua: Corraini.

Cappellieri, A., B. Del Curto, and L. Tenuta. 2014. *Around the Future: New Materials and New Technologies for Jewellery*. Venice: Marsilio.

Cappellieri, A. 2014. *Sentimental Jewellery*. Venice: Marsilio Editore.

Carcano, L., A. Catalani, and P. Varacca Capello, in collaboration with Club degli Orafi, 2005. *Il gioiello italiano ad una svolta. Dalla crisi alla costruzione di nuove opportunità*. Milan: Franco Angeli Editore.

Dery, M. 1996. *Escape Velocity*. New York: Grove Press New York.

Ferrara, M., and S. Lucibello. 2009. *Design Follows Materials*. Florence: Alinea.

Finessi, B. 2012. *Ultrabody. 208 opere tra arte e design*. Mantua: Corraini.

Sterling, B. 2005. *Shaping Things*. Boston: MIT Press.

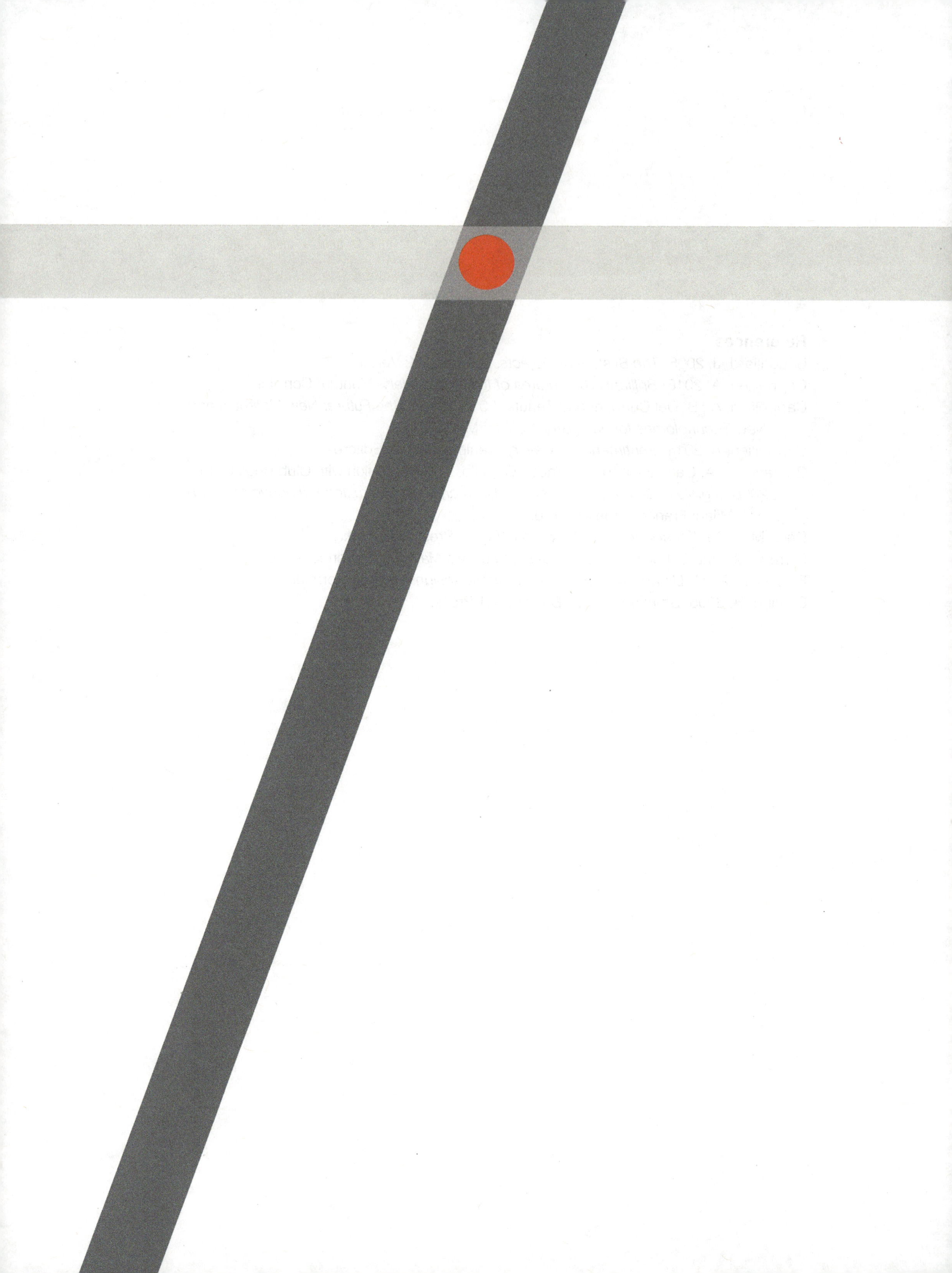

The Future of Jewelry Programs in Higher Education: The Intersection of Technology and Handcraft

Sunyoung Cheong, University of Kansas, KS, USA

Abstract

In recent years, jewelry programs in colleges and universities in the US have transformed to place more extensive emphasis on computer-aided design (CAD) and computer-aided manufacturing (CAM) in education. New technologies such as digital design software, 3D printing, Computer Numerically Controlled (CNC) milling as well as laser cutting have been adapted to classrooms. This innovation could provide students with new ways to create jewelry more efficiently and productively and at the same time technology could expand the possibilities of creativity and open new artistic boundaries.

This paper discusses on how to integrate technology into traditional jewelry programs; the potential challenges in CAD/CAM education, such as the reliability and misconception of technology; and better ways to educate students by using both CAD/CAM and handcraft with less confusion and frustration.

Introduction

Technology, like art, is a soaring exercise of the human imagination . . . art and technology are not separate realms walled off from each other. Art employs techne, but for its own ends. Techne, too, is a form of art that bridges culture and social structure, and in the process reshapes both. (Bell 1991, p.20)

Bell highlights that the impact of technology has changed our lives and our culture throughout history. Technology influences every aspect of our society including how we think, how we connect, and how we make. It provides us with more efficiency and productivity while it encourages us to be more innovative and creative. The recent rise of digital culture has taken technology into traditional art and craft.

About 60 years ago Dr. Patrick Hanratty, the father of CAD, created the first numerical control system, which would later become Computer Aided Design or CAD.

With this new technology, the precision, versatility, and edit-ability of CAD designs revolutionized the engineering, architecture and manufacturing landscape. (Beck n.d)

Since then, CAD has widely been used in industrial fields, designing aerospace, and product designs as well as drafting. (CADAZZ 2010) Despite this widespread use of CAD, jewelry craft was the last discipline among all design fields to use this technology. Compared to industrial fields, arts and crafts have slowly adapted technology into their realm. In the beginning, artists and craftsmen were hesitant to accept technology because of its contrary nature of handcraft. It seems that they still have doubts and concerns that technology will undermine traditional handcraft.

Historically, jewelry is one of the oldest artifacts in thousands of years. However, the same fabrication techniques such as forging, chasing and repousse, lost-wax casting, granulation, and enameling have been used in the jewelry making process. Even though there have been a lot of new automated tools and technological developments available, some hand tools and techniques have been unchanged from ancient history to create jewelry. Since technology has been added to these ancient tools, jewelry craftsmen have been able to create more sophisticated and precise works.

From the late 1980s, a few jewelry programs in higher education in the US integrated this new technology into their traditional jewelry programs (Dalrymple, 2010). The intersection of technology and craft began to be explored by these pioneers. But at that time, bringing technology into the formal jewelry education was not an important matter to the most of jewelry programs because they simply did not foresee the potential contribution of new technology for traditional crafts.

In a 1990s article by Lewton-Brain, however, he seemed to anticipate the future of CAD/CAM education in industry and art schools. According to him, "As art schools computerize in response to market pressures on graphic design, textiles and animation departments a unique opportunity arises for jewelry and metals departments to educate their students in CAD as well" (Lewton-Brain, 1990).

As the importance of CAD/CAM in art and craft rises, jewelry programs in universities and colleges have begun to embrace CAD/CAM education into their curriculum. However, digital education in jewelry programs, especially in public universities, are still at the nascent stage due to the high cost of initial investment and high maintenance expense. More importantly, incorporating the new curriculum into well-established traditional jewelry courses is not a simple task.

The rapid transformation of technology in the jewelry industry is deeply associated with embracing digital technology in jewelry programs. Technologies such as CAD softwares, 3D printing, and laser cutting are becoming an essential tool in jewelry education due to industry requirement and social needs. Universities and colleges may offer digital jewelry classes as a part of their coursework or as a special topic in response to these shifts. However, it would be ideal to have CAD/CAM as the major requirement for jewelry students at a jewelry program. It is necessary to teach the fundamental knowledge of CAD/CAM the same way we teach the fundamentals of jewelry class: piercing, soldering, riveting, raising, etc. Taking one or more CAD/CAM classes with the traditional jewelry education will augment their design skills and it will also help them understand more about the jewelry industry's manufacturing process.

Digital Tools in the Artist's Hand

A worn-out bench, timeless anvil, rows of different hammers and uncountable small tools are typically found in a jewelry studio. Some studios might be equipped with comprehensive tools and machines, but the basic making process remains the same as "hand" has been the most important tool for the whole process physically and conceptually.

The terms digital and handmade/craft are contradictory. Recently, however, we have used these seemingly opposing terms in the same context as "digital handmade" or "digital craft." This combined term has slowly inspired traditional artists and craftsmen to utilize technology in various craft mediums.

McCullough (1998, p.10) explained a traditional craft,

Virtual craft still seems like an oxymoron; any fool can tell you that a craftsperson needs to touch his or her work. This touch can be indirect—indeed no glassblower lays a hand on molten material—but it must be physical and continual, and it must provide control of the whole process.

He also pointed out that "as a part of developing more engaging technology, as well as developing a more receptive attitude toward new opportunities raised by technology, we must understand what matters in the traditional notion of practical, form-giving work" (1998, p.19). In art and craft, it is common knowledge that we use our hands to transfer ideas and concepts to materials. We draw, hammer, carve, and sew physically with a hand by holding different tools. According to Merriam-Webster, the definition of "handmade" is made by "hand" or "hand process." In this sense, artists and craftsmen who try to integrate technology into their works seem absurd and it can be controversial issues. Yet, digital technology is already affecting art and craft increasingly. Many traditional artists and craftsmen have integrated technology into their works and played an important role in a new creative movement.

In the beginning of the late twentieth and the early twenty-first century, there has been extensive research and articles regarding technology's influence on art and craft fields. These studies show how technology, especially CAD/CAM (computer-aided design and computer-aided manufacturing), has made an enormous impact on the process of making in art and craft as well as the industry itself. Most importantly, for jewelry education, some researchers predicted that traditional jewelry programs in art schools would embrace technology in the near future.

Although CAD/CAM was introduced to the jewelry education a few decades ago, CAD/CAM has not yet been broadly used in jewelry programs. However, some schools are beginning to utilize CAM technology in classrooms gradually: laser cutter, CNC router, or 3D printer. Sooner or later, CAD/CAM might be included in most jewelry programs in higher education.

Challenges in Digital Education

The role of the educator is highly significant in digital education in jewelry programs at universities and colleges because there is no perfect pedagogical model available so far. Numerous challenges and obstacles are inevitable to set up the learning environment for the CAD/CAM education.

In digital education, teaching technology in jewelry programs could be a daunting task due to lack of resources, many misconceptions, and a slow communication system at the university. CAD/CAM educators often have a role as an IT or technician or both. Just like any other art education, creating the best environment for teaching technology requires great support from universities and colleges. Furthermore, communicating with administrative and IT departments is critical to improving teaching and the learning environment.

Technology rapidly changes. A lot of new tools and abundant information comes into the world every moment. CAD/CAM educators must decide what needs to be added or changed in their curriculum from these continuous changes and updates. It is important to have a flexible curriculum to adapt to these variations.

One of the most important things is that educators should clarify to students that CAD/CAM is not the easy way or shortcut to create jewelry. In many cases, students believe that technology can replace hands. Educators must let students realize that good work comes from understanding both traditional jewelry techniques and

CAD/CAM skills. Keeping our traditional skills is indispensable. If we decline the hand skills and basic training of jewelry making, it will affect the quality of works and it may even affect our traditional principles negatively. Lewton-Blain (1990) stressed that "it should be noted that an art school would not be churning out computer operators but rather placing computers as a tool for expression in the art school environment."

It is important to understand the opportunity and limitation of digital design; It may only exist in the digital world, and it may not make into real objects. Designing a real object in a virtual sketchbook (CAD interface) requires the use and understanding of technology and materials and manufacturing process. The basic knowledge of jewelry fabrication augments the design possibility of CAD/CAM.

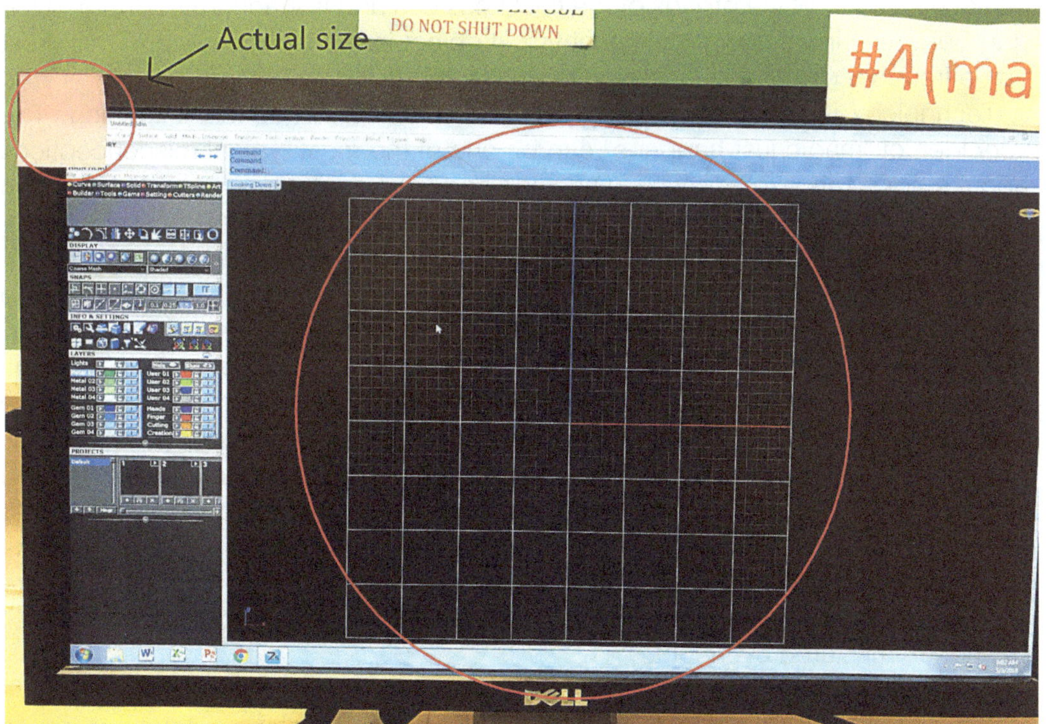

Figure 1. A paper on the left corner is the actual size of a grid that is 40mm by 40mm.

Most students (American students) in my beginning Jewelry CAD class are frustrated with the metric system and scale when they are first introduced to CAD programs such as Rhino or Matrix. Students often have a hard time envisioning their creation into an actual size. One student said, "The most difficult thing for me was learning how to navigate and learn all of the tools and their functions so that I could execute a particular design. Also, the scale was difficult for me to grasp. I made things too thin or too small or too big."

When students are working on a large computer monitor, the scale and proportion can be very confusing. Because of this confusion, the first main training in a CAD class is to make students aware of metrics and the size of the grid (usually 40mm by 40mm on Rhino or Matrix). Students need to learn the metrics of a scale, proportion, and element relationships to make a good design. It requires a lot of practice designing, printing, cutting waxes, and learning production standards to improve this challenge. The latest CAD program does not offer tools that correct the design if the size of the prongs or the thickness of a ring is inaccurate. Bridging the gap between virtual design and a physical object is a critical issue and this must come from both traditional and digital jewelry experience.

Technology is like magic. Mastering magic demands constant training. The very idea of "magic just happens" can be one of the most typical misconceptions about magic. This explains why 3D design and 3D manufactured jewelry are often neglected by the public or peer artists because they think technology is easily manipulated with no effort. It can create sophisticated and complex designs that were difficult and challenging by hand. This is only made possible after learning how to use this magic correctly, efficiently, and creatively.

The CAD program is like a virtual sketchbook and a virtual drawing pencil. Students must learn how to use this tool and put a lot of hours into practice, just like traditional studio hours. Even if 3D software is becoming more user-friendly, it still requires extensive learning time to be a professional. As McCullough (1998, p.61) states, "tools take practice." He continues to emphasize "You must learn how to bring skills and intentions together. You must learn how each tool works, how one tool works with another, and how all are maintained. You must know what tools are for." We must understand that learning technology is a lifelong commitment and it cannot be mastered overnight.

Maintaining technology is the most important part of running the classroom since CAD/CAM classes rely entirely on technology. If you have any glitches or issues with computers, CAD programs, or 3D printers in the classroom, it is difficult to carry out the lesson. Having a good IT support from a school is a must to run CAD/

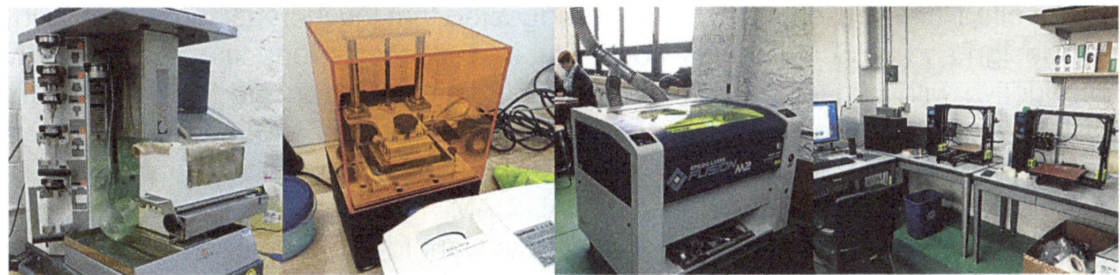

Figure 2. Various technologies are available to students. Maintaining these machines is crucial to teach CAD/CAM.

CAM classes smoothly, and constant communications between the CAD/CAM instructor and an IT department is strongly recommended.

Learning CAD programs can be challenging and frustrating when students are introduced due to their complexity and variety. Although CAD programs are becoming more user-friendly and more accessible, this does not mean that they are easy to learn. The complex interface of CAD programs easily intimidates most students who come to CAD/CAM classes. It is very important for students to get familiarized with the CAD interface first and, at the same time, they should have a realistic expectation during their limited time in school.

Even though CAD/CAM technology has been around for some time, using technology in jewelry programs in higher education is still in the early stage. One of the main reasons could be the initial investment. Although the price of technology is getting lower, it is still expensive for the public university. Some companies offer a educational discount for CAD program and upgrades. But it is still a big investment for jewelry program in public universities. Furthermore, annual technical support contracts and constant upgrades may be added to CAD/CAM expenses. Even so, it is very clear that jewelry programs in higher education can no longer afford to ignore this digital revolution.

Complementary Relationship with the Jewelry Industry

New materials and technologies, including CAD/CAM, have been introduced to the jewelry industry with many advantages: productivity, high detailing in design, easy editing, and innovative design. Technology has been showing what could be possible, and it gives the jeweler a new tool they did not know existed. CAD/CAM is increasingly becoming the most important tool for the jewelry industry. McCullough

(1998 cited in Adamson, 2010, p. 310) suggested that the increasing power of digital design and fabrication tools would make small shop production economically productive with large-scale manufacturers. Some people in the jewelry industry still have apprehension about these digital transformations and they want to keep making jewelry the same way. But this perception has been shifting to accept new technology because of the benefits of CAD/CAM. The same thing is happening in jewelry programs in higher education. People want to keep the tradition of jewelry making, and they feel left behind by the latest changes at the same time.

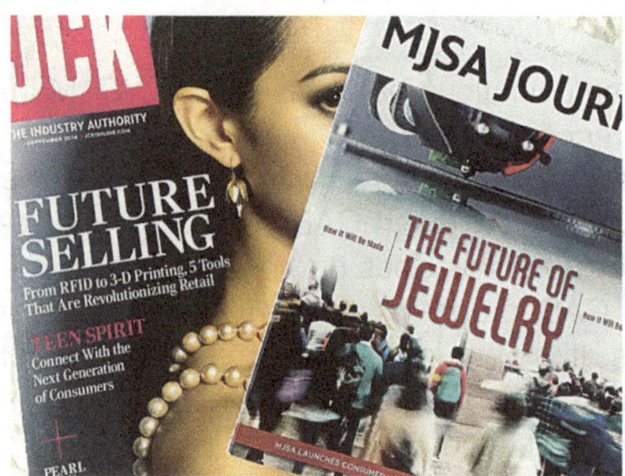

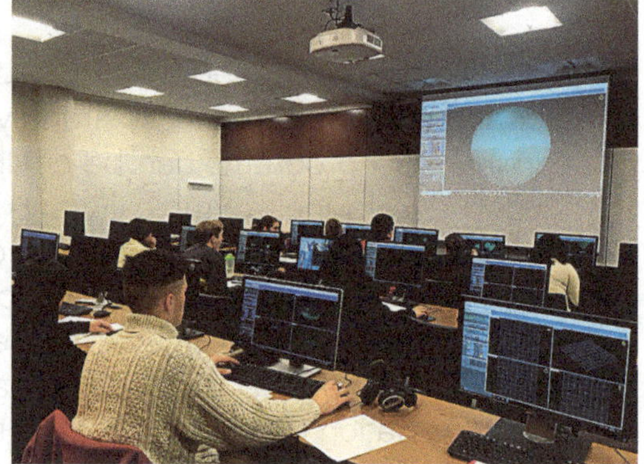

Figure 3. Magazines from Manufacturing Jewelers and Suppliers Association (MJSA) and the Jeweler's Circle Key (JCK) in the US and digital jewelry class at the University of Kansas.

Some students go to graduate school after they receive a BA or BFA degree, but most students go into the job market and would like to start their career in a jewelry-related field. We, as teachers, expect them to be working in the jewelry industry or other creative areas as a designer, bench jeweler, gemologist, etc. Jewelry programs should incorporate technology as a part of their education to meet the industry's needs since the jewelry industry have been deeply using cutting-edge technologies. The importance of CAD/CAM education in jewelry programs cannot be overemphasized due to the jewelry industry's dramatic change. If the jewelry industry changes, jewelry programs in higher education need to learn these changes. We should profoundly consider what students need for their future after college and provide appropriate tools that can support them in various opportunities in their future.

Gen Z[1]—The New Generation

According to the leaders of the World Economic Forum, we are now in the beginning of the fourth industrial revolution, a digital transformation where changes are happening at breakneck speed (Kulpa, p. 22). These new technologies will impact all disciplines, economies, and industries, and even challenge our ideas about what it means to be human (Marr, 2018).

This digital revolution has tremendously affected us, especially the new generation called *Gen Z,* or *digital natives* who were born after 1997, according to a Pew Research Report (Demock, 2018). This generation is the first generation to have widespread access to the Internet at an early age and they are more global and open-minded than other previous generations.

This means that this generation officially entered colleges and universities since around 2016 and will be the majority of the population in a classroom (Konzinsky, 2016). Konzinsky stated that "as a digital generation, Generation Z expects digital learning tools such as these to be deeply integrated into their education." This means that Gen Z is are ready to accept new technology into their learning experience and, without the fear of technology, this generation may fully adapt to CAD/CAM education.

Conclusion

From production jewelry to art jewelry, the possibilities of technology are beyond our imagination. A lot of jewelry programs in art schools consider developing curriculum for CAD/CAM after acknowledging the necessity of technology education. Jewelry programs are structured with the skill-building, conceptual developments, and knowledge about the history of the discipline and they also offer a creative environment for students. Students are not only learning skills and techniques but also cultivating creative and innovative minds while they are in art school.

We need to aware that it is possible to have a drawback from educating CAD/CAM in traditional practice. Students may work with CAD/CAM as a tool to take a shortcut without even trying traditional techniques. For that reason, balancing and bridging the gap between technology and traditional principles should be the fundamental strategy to teach students. It is crucial that our main goal is to protect our unique creative environment.

1 Born: 1995 - 2012
Digital Natives: One of the first generation to have widespread access to the Internet at an early age.
Fingertip Generation (Thumbies). They are more global and open in mindset than any previous generations.
Current Population: 23 million and growing rapidly. They are driving force in the innovation of new learning tools. - Source: Forbes & NY Times

There are a lot of tools and machines available to students in our metals studio. When we add CAD/CAM to our classroom, we must look at technology not as a substitute for traditional handcraft, but as one of many tools we use in our studio every day. Students should choose tools that are right for their needs. Mongeon (2016, p. 9) mentions that "you do not know what you can do until you know what you can do, and once you learn what you can do with this technology, possibilities will blow your mind."

Technology, in conjunction with the jewelry and creativity training of art school, may be at an advantage in the jewelry field. Some people in jewelry education are concerned that if technology intervenes into traditional jewelry making, there will be a negative impact on traditional craft. However, digital technology built on traditional discipline will make jewelry education more successful in the future. It will help to produce many talented jewelry artisans and keep our jewelry program in higher education for a long time. Digital technology should be considered not an alternative or replacement but a tool in the artist's hand. It gives us more freedom and possibilities in creativity, but it may come with great responsibility to implement this technology for artistic creation. Students with both traditional jewelry education and digital literacy will shape the future of the jewelry programs of the next generation.

References

Adamson, G. 2010. *The Craft Reader*. New York: Berg.

Bell, D. 1991. *The Winding Passage: Sociological Essays and Journeys*. New Brunswick, NJ and London, UK: Transaction Publishers.

Beck, A. n.d. "60 Years of CAD Infographic: The History of CAD since 1957."https://partsolutions.com/60–years-of-cad-infographic-the-history-of-cad-since-1957.

CADAZZ. 2010. "CAD software—history of CAD CAM." http://www.cadazz.com/cad-software-history.htm.

Dalrymple, J. 2010. "CAD/CAM Impact on Jewellery Fabrication." https://www.ganoksin.com/article/cadcam-impact-jewellery-fabrication.

Dimock, M. 2019. "Defining Generations: Where Millennials End and Post-Millennials Begin." *Pew Research Center*, January 17, 2019. http://www.pewresearch.org/fact-tank/2018/03/01/defining-generations-where-millennials-end-and-post-millennials-begin.

Kozinsky, S. 2017. "How Generation Z is Shaping the Change in Education." *Forbes*, July 24, 2017. https://www.forbes.com/sites/sievakozinsky/2017/07/24/how-generation-z-is-shaping-the-change-in-education/#2b1149bf6520.

Kulpa, S. 2018. "In the Making: Technologies Transforming How Jewelry Will Be Made." *MJSA Journal* 13, no. 1.

Lewton-Brain, C. 1996. "CAD/CAM Systems for Metals and Jewelry." https://www.ganoksin.com/article/cadcam-systems-metals-jewelry.

Marr, B. 2018. "The 4th Industrial Revolution Is Here—Are You Ready" *Forbes*, August 13, 2018. https://www.forbes.com/sites/bernardmarr/2018/08/13/the-4th-industrial-revolution-is-here-are-you-ready/#6b7ab76b628b.

McCullough, M. 1998. *Abstracting Craft: The Practiced Digital Hand*. Cambridge, MA: The MIT Press.

Mongeon, B. 2016. *3D Technology in Fine Art and Craft: Exploring 3D Printing, Scanning, Sculpting, and Milling*. Burlington, MA: Focal Press.

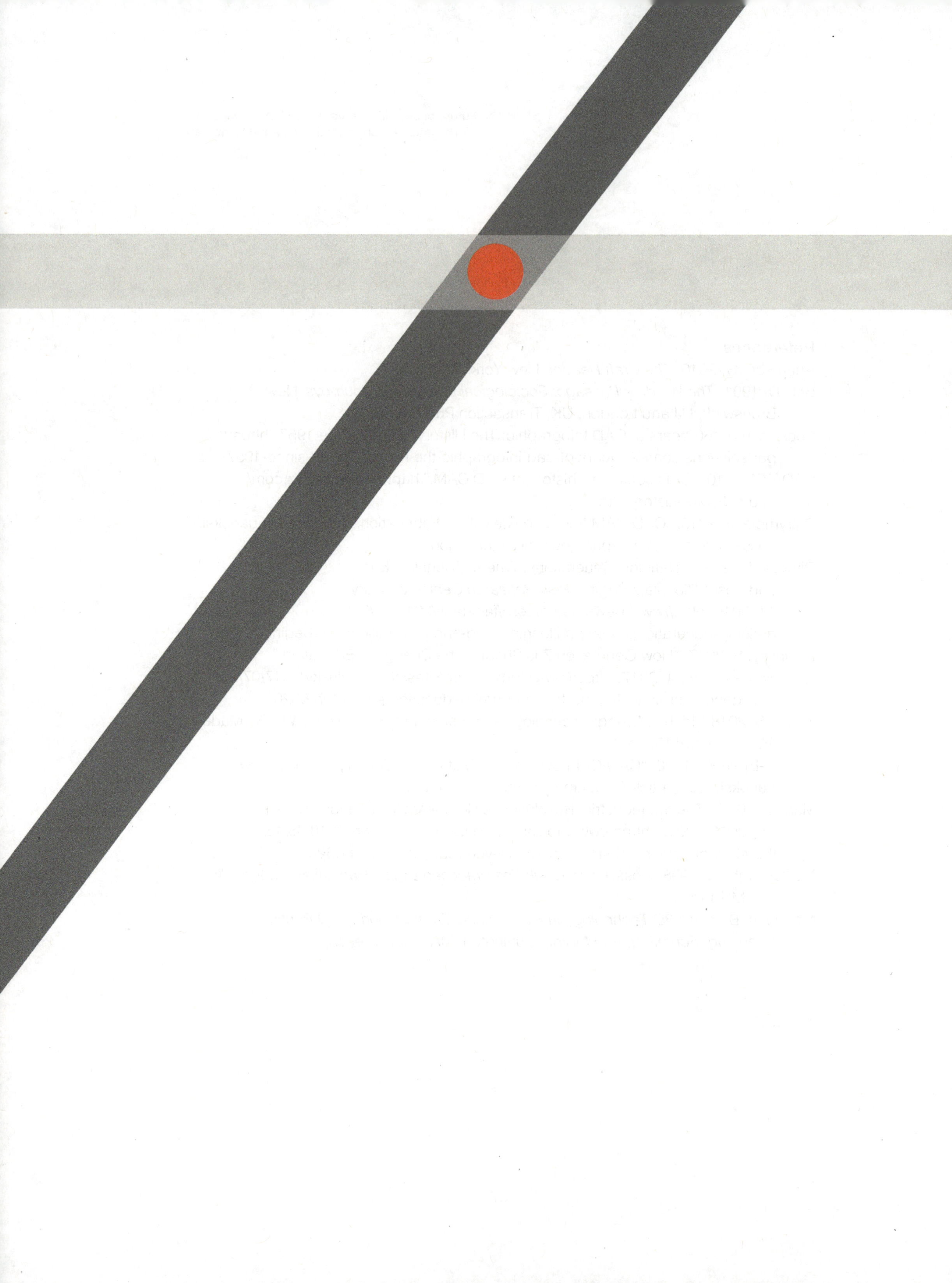

Finding the Sensuous in Digital: Can "the Hand of the Maker" Survive the Digital Age?

Jeff Deegan, Jeff Deegan Designs, USA

Abstract

I intend to address important considerations in the evolving prominence of digital platforms for the design and production of jewelry. My own work has, for 45 years, has been predominately handcraft. For me jewelry work is quite sensual. The design concept from sketch to finish is informed by countless tactile informed decisions. To paraphrase the author James Joyce, my relationship to digital is akin to pornography. That is it (digital) is often exciting to behold but then leaves me cold and empty.

The first reason I've identified is the digital revolution has created what I refer to as the democratization of design. It is a tool with a transformative power quite unlike tool and tech advances of the past. For the first time in memory anyone whether or not possessing bench skills can, by sending a file, generate a 3D jewelry model. An experienced technician/model maker prior to the jewelry being created often no longer interprets a designer's sketches and concepts.

The second reason is the uncanny perfectionism of digital down to the minutest detail visible. These perfect models whose early novelty led to existential feelings of inadequacy over my skills now seem so soulless as there has been a proliferation. Soullessness is defined as lacking any humanizing qualities or influences. Jewelry is, at its best, a poetic craft communicating memories, status, and passion.

The question is how to keep the passion alive. What is the soul at the core of the piece? I will argue that most successful and passionate designs will continue to require attention to technical detail and be in accord with real world methods necessary to manufacture.

The cleverest designers will integrate handcraft skills with digital's efficiency to not just express today's ideas, but to achieve the freedom to make a leap to ever more elevated expression of their visions. This integration will require a holistic and informed approach to aesthetics and methods of traditional jewelry making.

Yes, there can be democratization of design and it will be so much better with an informed electorate.

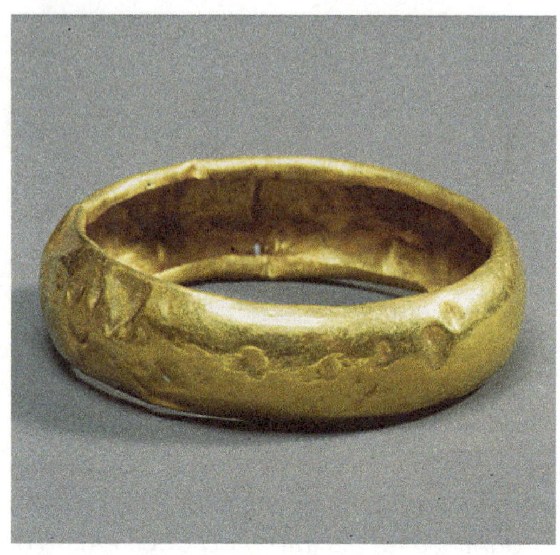
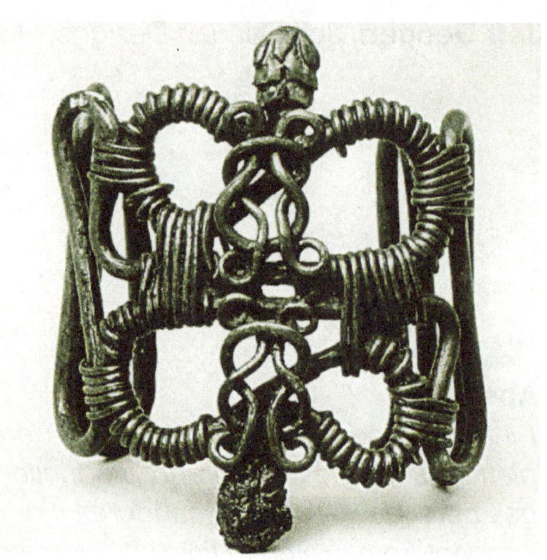

Figure 1. Gold earring, Sumerian, ca. 2600–2500 BC, and silver bracelet, Egypt, 304–364 BC, Source: Metropolitan Museum of Art.

Introduction

Our relationship to jewelry and adornment is surely one of humankind's earliest fascinations. Decoration, beginning at the dawn of human existence, indicated a wearer's tribal affiliation and chronicled his or her status (Borel, 2001). The wearing of, and our response to, jewelry has been rarely about non-contextual decoration. Wearing it, we signal our wealth, we attempt to enhance our attractiveness to potential partners, and we flout our devotion to a single mate with bands of gold. It is sentimental as well as a bit profane; both materialistic and sacred. The magic of the jewelry arts is their connection to our humanity. The architect Louis Kahn might have been describing jewelry when he declared succinctly, "art strives to communicate in a way which reveals the human" (Schutte, 1975, p. 18).

This article will address how digital work platforms have affected perception of the term, "the hand of the maker." Computer aided design and manufacturing (CAD/CAM) has revolutionized design and jewelry making. What happens when digital work platforms meet this most personal of craft forms, and 3D printers are replacing the hand of the maker?

I will make some specific remarks on some of the challenges of integrating digital with jewelry making and I will confine my remarks to designer or high jewelry.

Jewelry defined as the product of sophisticated design married to precious materials and, more often than not, limited production.

I will also discuss a future I believe will happen: where jewelry continues to be "the poetic craft" (as I once heard it described), through a renewed awareness and appreciation of the maker's hands to the process.

Part I: Digital Disruption

In his encyclopedic 1982 book, *Jewelry Concepts and Technology*, the master metalsmith, educator, and author Oppi Untracht posits that: "a survey of the work of today's artist-jeweler might bring the conclusion that change is the single constant and that the underlying thrust is design through conceptual and technological eclecticism" (Untracht, 1982, p. 205). Though we're a generation beyond the era when Untracht wrote that, clearly adoption and the leveraging of change continues to be a constant for the jewelry craftsman or craftswoman. Whether it is economic conditions, fashion dictates, or novel technology—the influence on design and making is self-evident (Sranton, 1997).

The ubiquity of digital would have been the stuff of science fiction when the author published his book. Digital design and manufacturing have disrupted the industry in profound ways, bringing both tremendous advantages and a jarring impact on the handmade tradition.

My own work over the past 45 years has been primarily analog. The feel of my tools in my hands and the familiar challenge of forming material are central to my metalsmithing experience. As for digital, to paraphrase the great Irish author James Joyce, my relationship to digital has been more akin pornography. I find them both to posses a certain excitement that ultimately leaves me unfulfilled.

In Joyce's novel *A Portrait of the Artist as a Young Man*, the protagonist, Stephen Dedalus, delivers a lecture on how he defines the nature and appreciation of beauty, especially in art. Stephen contrasts "proper," or static art, with "improper," or kinetic art. Static art (from the Greek word stasis) causes the viewer's mind to be "arrested," entering a state of contemplation and reflection that produces a higher level of aesthetic appreciation, believes Stephen. Kinetic art, by contrast, brings upheavals to the senses instead. Joyce writes: "the arts which excite (the senses are) pornographic or didactic (and) are therefore improper arts" (Joyce, 1964, p. 205).

All too often digital design has been like Joyce's "improper" art for me: exciting—and technically a marvel. The early creations I saw simultaneously elicited in me wonderment, envy of the flawless execution, and dread for the future of handmade.

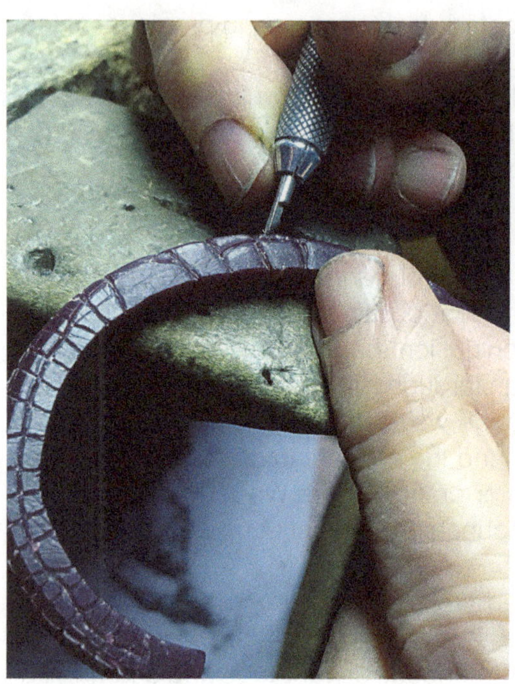

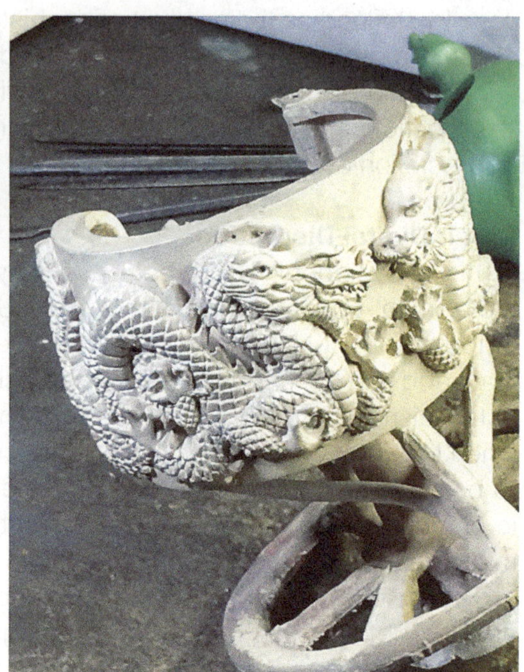

Figure 2. Wax carving and cast bracelet.
Source:
Jeff Deegan.

Yet, to this day, rarely does the digitally produced design arrest me in my tracks, and appeal to my aesthetic mind. I find the monotony of form and busy detail to be most often devoid of a life spark. When the digital design's perfection of line is accompanied by a profusion of symmetric detail, it reads to me as self-contained and distancing, isolating me, the viewer. The evidence of "the hand of the maker" is absent. Gone is any glimmer of the human soul, and with it the ability to feel connection with the humanity of the artist.

The digital revolution has been sweepingly transformative, creating what I refer to as the "democratization of design." Design is now a field anyone can participate in. Design has become "easy" and accessible with the multitude of art and CAD programs. Keyboard skill is the new foundational basis for creation, eclipsing accomplished craftsmanship. While this democratization is bringing fresh talent to the pool of creativity, it is also disrupting the craft of jewelry making and the relationship of it to the maker in profound and lasting ways.

Jewelry has a long history of conceptual designers, imaginative people who through sketches or other form of communication bring to the jeweler/model maker their ideas to be translated into reality. Digital technology turns this process on its head. No bench skills, no problem. In CAD, a file is created and can be sent directly to a CAM servicer for printing or milling. For the first time in history, anyone with a computer can produce from the conceptual stage a fully sculpted model executed with a fit and finish to match or exceed the efforts of a master model maker's hands.

A conceptual designer is now liberated from the need to own tools or develop through training the manual skills to manipulate them to create, define, and decorate a form or, alternatively, engage with a skilled craftsman. The machine can do all that. Lost is the crucial conversation between the designer and the skilled specialist who, prior to digital, would have collaborated in bringing the sketch to life as a successful and wearable piece of jewelry.

This jeweler specialist, drawing on skills and experience acquired over years or decades, would construct the new design with allowances and modifications necessary

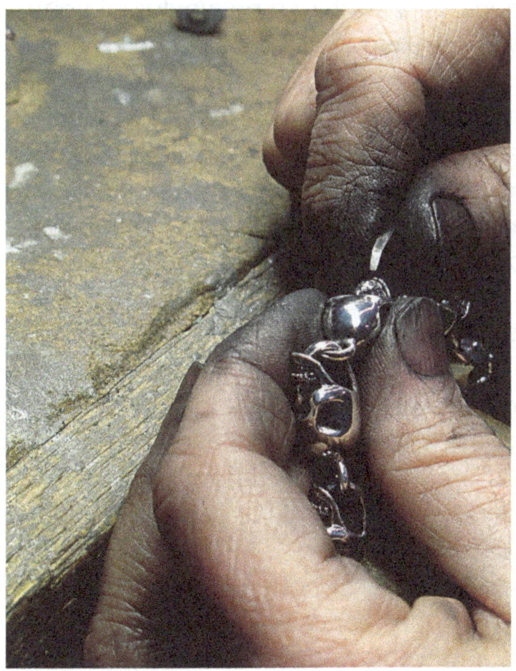

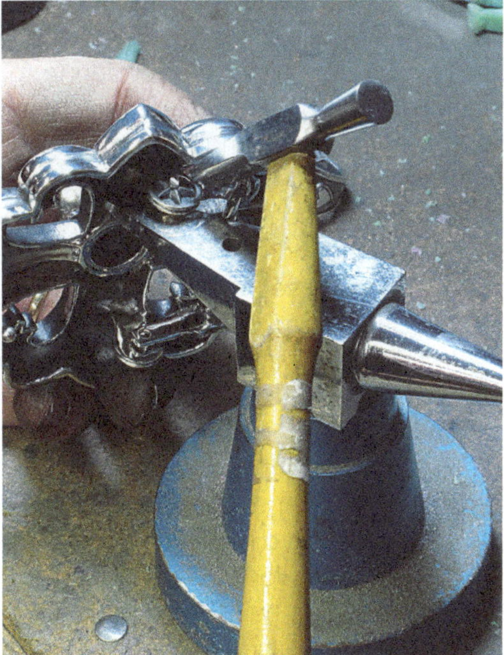

Figure 3. Stonesetting and riveting at the bench.
Source: Jeff Deegan.

to production. The model maker's influence would occur in at least several instances. There might be voiced suggestions. During construction, shifting conditions of material, tools, and form require reconsiderations and adjustments (Trilling, 2001). The push/pull collaboration between concept and construction of designer and jeweler has over the years produced some breathtaking leaps of artistry (Trilling, 2001).

In the creation of a piece, "we assume that only aesthetic choices determine the aesthetic character of an object" (Trilling, 2001, p. 16). More likely, however, the finished piece is the product of a maker's accumulated skill in tool handling, as well as, a response to the mutable conditions of the material and, truth be told, slips and mistakes. The responses or choices are informed by an accumulation of experience that is a fundamental component of a master maker's skill.

Now that non-bench skilled designers can proceed directly to machine production of their concepts, I've witnessed countless real world consequences that were not at all evident while working on a large color computer screen. Tolerances that looked reproducible and disregard for the actual process of finishing or polishing the item are some commonly encountered problems. In CAM operation, the digital file makes no adjustments or reconsiderations as a craftsperson would. Of course there are now experts in both CAD and jewelry making who work with the CAD-only designer to alter his or her rendering to make it manufacturable. But the changes that take place on screen feel to me like engineering problems to be solved technically, rather than a hands-on process creating a work of art.

This disruption of the traditional design and developmental process exists in a larger world, an environment where digital fluency increasingly erodes the knowledge of manual craft. The sensual skill of a human-guided tool connecting with material gets closer to extinction.

Nick Benson, a 2010 MacArthur Fellowship recipient and stone carver, recently made this point with an observation about our digitally obsessed culture. He believes that humans are increasingly viewing the world through a "digital filter" which removes humanity from direct connection to the physical world. He feels this is true in so many cases, but is abundantly obvious in contemporary design. Young architects, designers and artists increasingly define and confine their capabilities to the parameters of the digital realm (Benson, 2018).

To step into the John Steven's Shop, Benson's Newport, Rhode Island workspace, is to quite literally go back in time, specifically 1705, the year of its founding. Benson relates that some visiting design students, upon viewing his work, automatically assume a computer-driven router machines the meticulous letter carving. It just does not occur to them, in the frictionless universe of digital, to relate the work to an actual maker's hands.

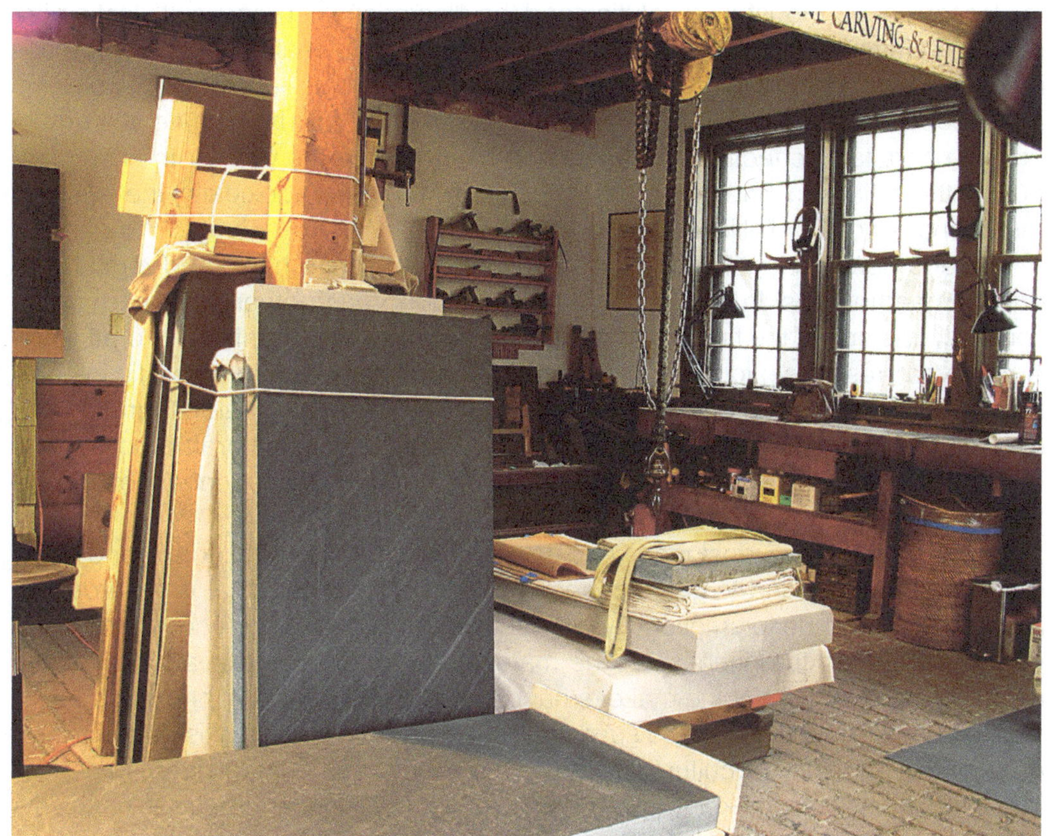

Figure 4. View of the John Steven's Shop, Newport, RI. Source: Jeff Deegan.

Part 2: The Best of Both Worlds

Van Day Truex, the Tiffany & Co. design director who hired legendary jewelry artist Jean Schlumberger in 1956, observed that "the only really different ideas in our contemporary world are appearing because of a new material discovery or a new means of evolving a shape" (Truex, 1975, p. 1). The new digital means of evolving shape, together with the speed and accuracy it brings, offers tremendous leverage to artisans who discriminately integrate it with the more traditional approaches to fabrication, engineering, and aesthetics.

We remain too close to the beginning of the Digital Age to have an accurate perspective as to how it will eventually play out as pertains to craft. We might look to the lessons of the industrial revolution and the disruptions of process. Its lasting impacts on craftsmanship are felt to this day. That the industrial revolution and mass mechanization seemed to drain creativity from many objects—including jewelry—is an antecedent worthy of our remembrance (Becker, 2014). The nineteenth century pursuit of crafted perfection can be said to have "paved the way for the rise of industry, the extinction of the craft-based economy, and (paradoxically) the eventual resurgence of craft" (Trilling, 2001, p. 16).

Perhaps now, during the digital revolution, the maker's hand and digital production need not reside in dialectical relationship to each other. Informed by the soulless missteps of the first age of mechanization and the fetishizing of craft in the Art Nouveau response, for example, might we not formulate a more holistic integration of this newest mode of mass production? Can we strive for an integration that exploits the tension between digital advantages and traditional craft process, in a way that does not dictate the aesthetic, while affording the maker enhanced opportunities to expand his or her virtuosity?

Clever, imaginative designers and jewelers will continue to adapt and innovate for expression and to gain economic advantage. Jewelry that is regarded as inspired will continue to emotionally connect with the consumer. A connection produced not just by the richness of the materials but the visceral realization of the masterful achievement of the maker's hands in concert with appropriate tools.

The question of the continued survival of the "hand of the maker" is part of a larger story of the vitality of culture itself. Craftsmanship has always been somewhat imperiled. For jewelry makers, raw material, skill acquisition, and patrons have never been so easily obtainable as to be taken for granted.

I identify three factors as contributing to the continued prestige and appreciation for objects produced by a skilled maker.

First, design institutions, both schools and museums, can play a leadership role in maintaining and fostering an appreciation of craft as integral to the design process. Knowledge of process is eroding; newer generations possess a blind spot when it comes to the experience of craftsmanship. In their embrace of the new to teach the latest technology, it is paramount that curricula remain inclusive and broad, reinforcing the relationship of craft to successful design. The discernment of good design derives from exposure to and fluency in the historical context of design and process.

Second, jewelry designers and makers bear a responsibility for their own viability. Besides cultivating a broad perspective on design and technique to execute their work to full aesthetic and efficiency levels, they must step up to advance their narratives. Relating your personal design journey is one of the best ways to

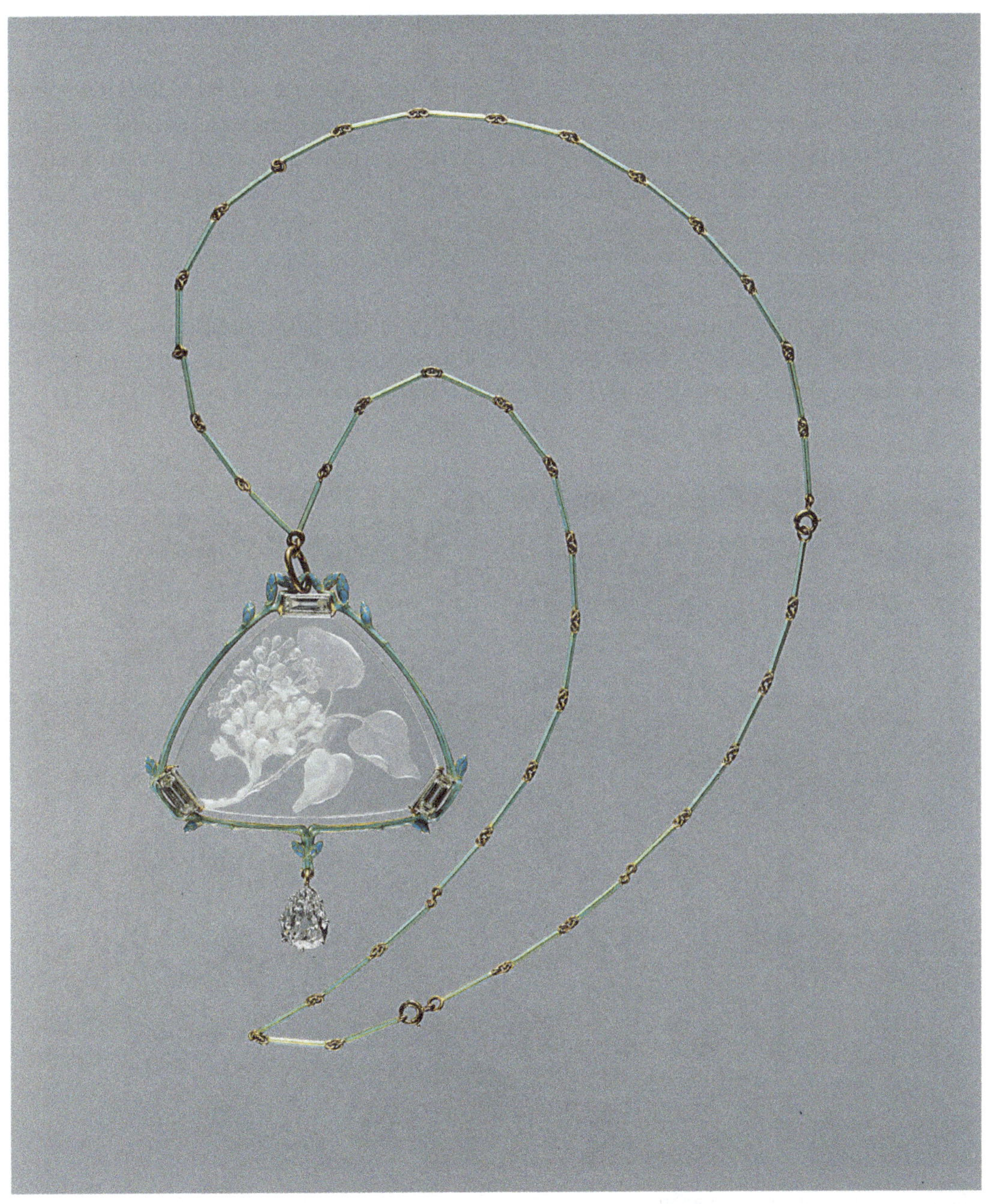

Figure 5. Pendant and Chain, René Jules Lalique, ca. 1905. Source: Metropolitan Museum.

help educate and promote appreciation for well-made design with your audience. Bottom line, consumers relate to a story.

Third, as pertains to the consumer, a continued appetite for fine designs made with human and technical mastery persists. The three elements listed by Tiffany & Co. President Walter Hoving in the 1970s as key to arousing consumer interest were: authenticity of material represented, quality of workmanship, and quality of design (Hoving, 1975). In a mass production world of anodyne products, jewelry design that is made with passion will continue to have a status in inverse proportion to its relative rarity.

In conclusion, the designers and artisans who uphold the tradition of jewelry designed and made with aesthetic zeal will be those who "... took the triumph of industrial design for granted, and worked to humanize it" (Hoving, 1975, p. 2).

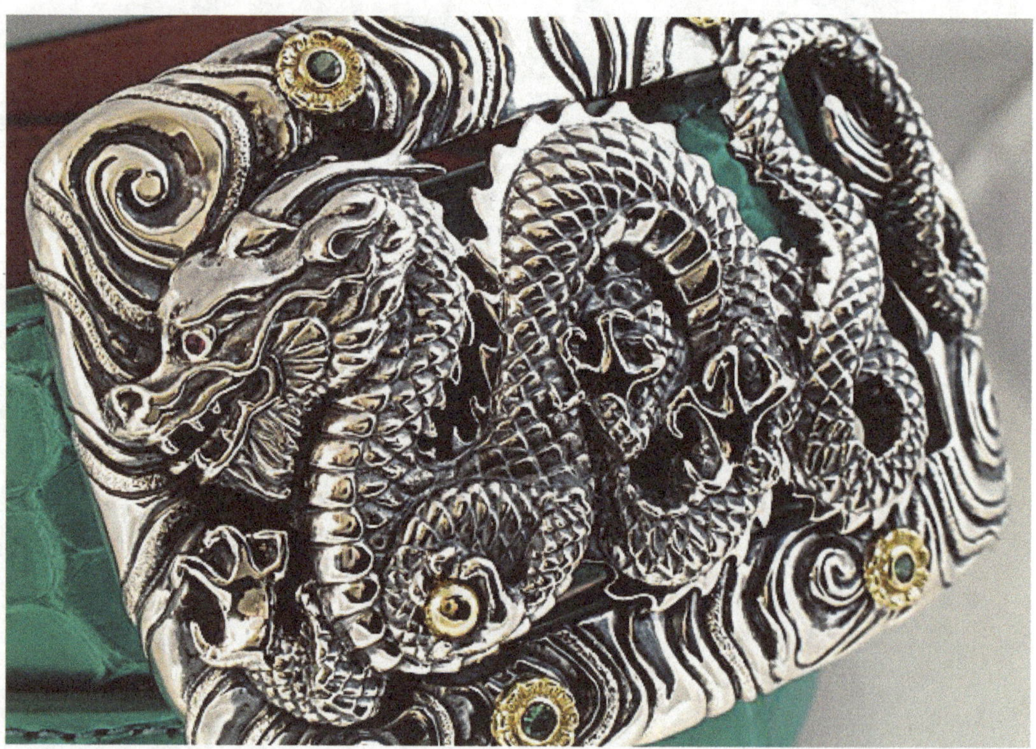

Figure 6. Sterling and gold "dragon in the clouds" buckle. Source: Jeff Deegan.

References

Becker, V. 2014. *Art Nouveau Jewelry.* London: Thames & Hudson.

Benson, N. April 2018. Interview with the author.

Borel, F. 2001. *The Splendor of Ethnic Jewelry.* New York: H.N. Abrams.

Hoving, Walter. 1975. "The Crisis of Design Management." *Design in American Business*, edited by Thomas F. Schutte, 2. New York: Tiffany.

Joyce, J. 1964. *A Portrait of the Artist as a Young Man.* Viking Press.

Schutte, Thomas F., editor. 1975. *Design in American Business.* New York: Tiffany.
Schutte, T. 1975. *The Art of Design Management.* New York: Tiffany.

Sranton, P. 1997. The Horrors of Competition: Innovation and Paradox in Rhode Island's Jewelry Industry, 1860–1914. *Rhode Island History* 5 (2): 47–67.

Trilling, J. 2001. *The Language of Ornament.* London: Thames & Hudson.

Trurex, Van Day. 1975. "The Environment for Creating Good Design, the Art of Design Management." *Design in American Business,* edited by Thomas F. Schutte, 81. New York: Tiffany.

Untracht, O. 1982. *Jewelry Concepts and Technology.* Garden City, NY: Doubleday.

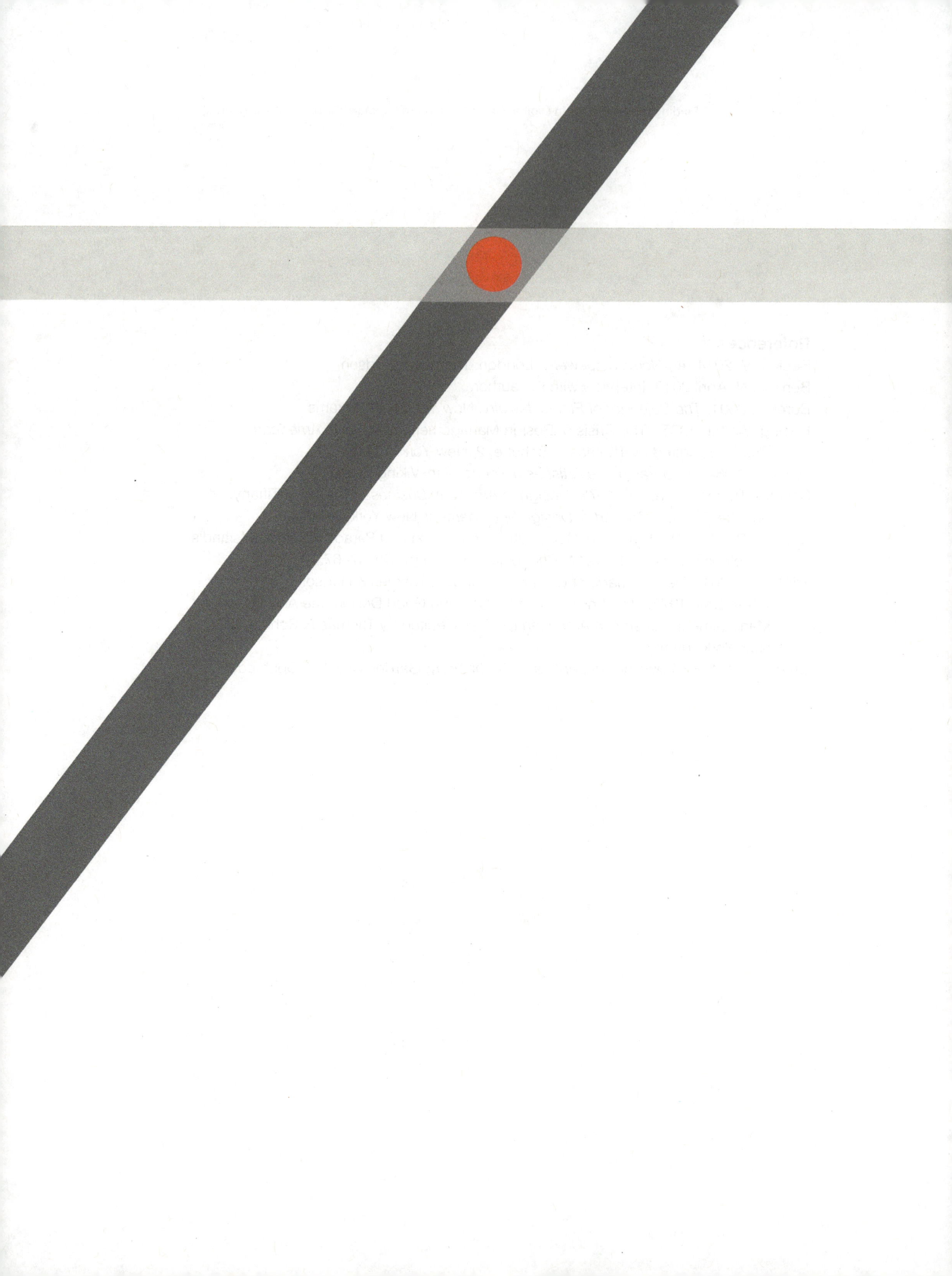

Digital Tooling and Handcrafting

Karen-Ann Dicken, Duncan of Jordanstone College of Art & Design, University of Dundee, Scotland
Sandra Wilson, Duncan of Jordanstone College of Art & Design, University of Dundee, Scotland

Abstract

Craft practitioners have been reluctant to embrace new 3D digital approaches. Tool making, however, is a fundamental aspect of being human and this paper presents examples of digital toolmaking whilst the work itself is still handcrafted.

This paper presents a variety of examples from the authors dating from 2005, including 3D printed resin jigs for laser welding steel wires to make jewellery and bowls; a multi-purpose stone setting tool; a laser sintered planishing hammer and laser cut and pressed bowls and computer numerical control (CNC) milled press forms for creating differently shaped bases in silversmithing.

We conclude that making your own tools is an important way of generating your own visual aesthetic. We also hope that this approach to digital tooling enables craft practitioners to retain the uniqueness and handcrafted expression as well as the handcrafted finish in their work. This approach also enables a more diverse range of forms to be achieved, perhaps not possible via conventional handcrafted approaches.

Finally, however, those embarking on digital toolmaking still need to have a sound knowledge of different materials, for example different types of wood and their grain structure, if their objects are to have structural integrity.

It is hoped therefore that this approach will encourage many craft practitioners to embrace digital tooling.

Introduction

Toolmaking is recognised as an essential aspect of being human. It has played a key role in our evolution and abilities and has allowed us to build and craft ever more innovative items, with less effort or impact on the human body.

But only with the aid of the tools that these more primitive species learnt to use was it possible for the human man of today to evolve, losing much in bodily strength and speed, but more than compensating for this loss by developing a brain and hands and eyes that enable him to call to his aid his many tools and machines that made him master of the world" (Lilley 1948, p. 1).

Recent developments in modern technologies such as 3D printing and CNC milling machines have seen a change or advancement in production methods that moves us into the next industrial revolution. Although toolmaking, craft and historic design movements are well recognised, the implications of using these digital technologies as tooling, in the craft making process, and the impact on the wider society, is currently under researched.

Our ancestors began with simple stone tools and progressed to developing handles to create an extension to our arms. In the first to third industrial revolutions, with the use of steel and machinery, we were able to eliminate very labour intensive jobs and replace them with machines.

We have now entered a new revolution, recognised by Flusser (1999) as the robot revolution and by Marsh (2012) as the fifth industrial revolution, recognising the fourth revolution as being the computer revolution, starting circa 1950.

The dangers and fears of the robot revolution are that they can entirely remove the human input for creating artifacts. An object that has been designed using computer-aided design (CAD) which is then 3D printed to become a finished item, has very little human input. They can be mass produced, and we may question whether these objects will have the same value as a handcrafted object using traditional techniques. It is human nature to craft and make art and it is integrally linked to human evolution and behaviour. Dissanayake's research explains the links between the human brain, tooling, and the development of society as well as the roots of the arts.

The fact that people everywhere value the arts and take the trouble to express themselves aesthetically suggests to an evolutionary biologist that there is a reason: doing this (rather that not doing this) contributes to human evolutionary fitness.' (Dissanayake 1988, p. 62)

It is this human behaviour, evolution, and tradition of making objects to show status or specialness that gives handcraft its value and worth, as opposed to more mass produced items of today's disposable culture.

At the same time this new industrial revolution varies from the previous four. The previous revolutions required a large part of the population to have knowledge of working machinery, tooling, and making processes. Our new robot revolution requires less knowledge from the masses about past making and construction methods. Robots build more robots, which make our objects for us, and the danger in this is that more people require less knowledge about construction and craft. This is also part of the increasing dematerialisation of culture. A good example of this is the rapid evolution in music from vinyl to the virtual storing of your record collection in the cloud.

This study therefore seeks to integrate modern technologies with traditional handcraft. In particular, this practice-based investigation, studies the ways in which contemporary craftspeople are integrating 3D printing with traditional hand fabrication through digital toolmaking.

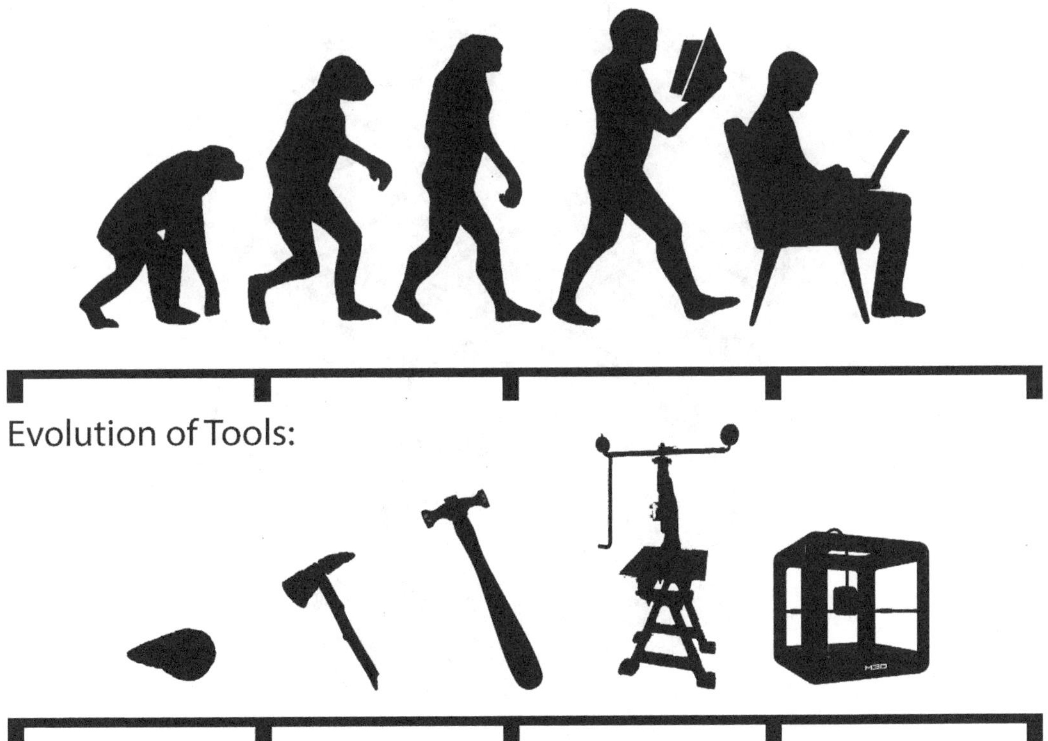

Figure 1. Evolution of tools. Source: Author (Dicken), 2017.

Karen-Ann Dicken

My first experimentation with digital tooling came in 2005–2007 whilst studying an MA in goldsmithing, silversmithing, metalwork and jewellery design at the Royal College of Art in London (RCA).

I introduced CAD into my work, but not in a way I had done in the past. During my degree I used this as a visualisation tool to present and visualise 3D designs I had in my head but couldn't draw on paper. At the RCA I merged the use of CAD and handcraft in my practice by using CAD to create tooling that allowed me to make designs more accurately and intricately than what would otherwise have been possible by hand.

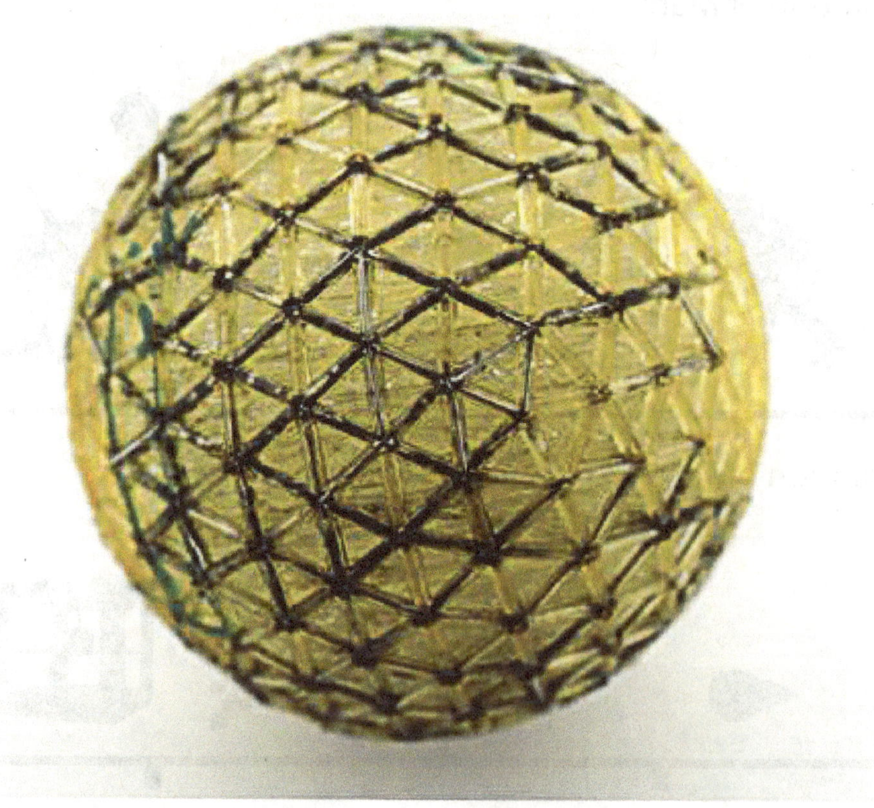

Figure 2. Karen-Ann Dicken, resin jig for holding wires in position, 2007.

Figure 2 shows a stereolithography resin SLA resin jig I designed and made at the RCA. I designed these in Rhino 3D, printed them in resin, and used them to hold wires together while I laser welded my constructions together. In this example the partially constructed frame can be seen. The wires are welded through the tiny resin tubes.

The use of CAD and 3D printing as a tool enabled me to create jewellery with the soul, sweat, and value that handcrafted items hold as opposed to jewellery entirely CAD made.

Figure 3 is the bowl I produced from the resin jig. This piece took over a month to make and contained over 1,200,000 welds. After laser welding the initial frame into

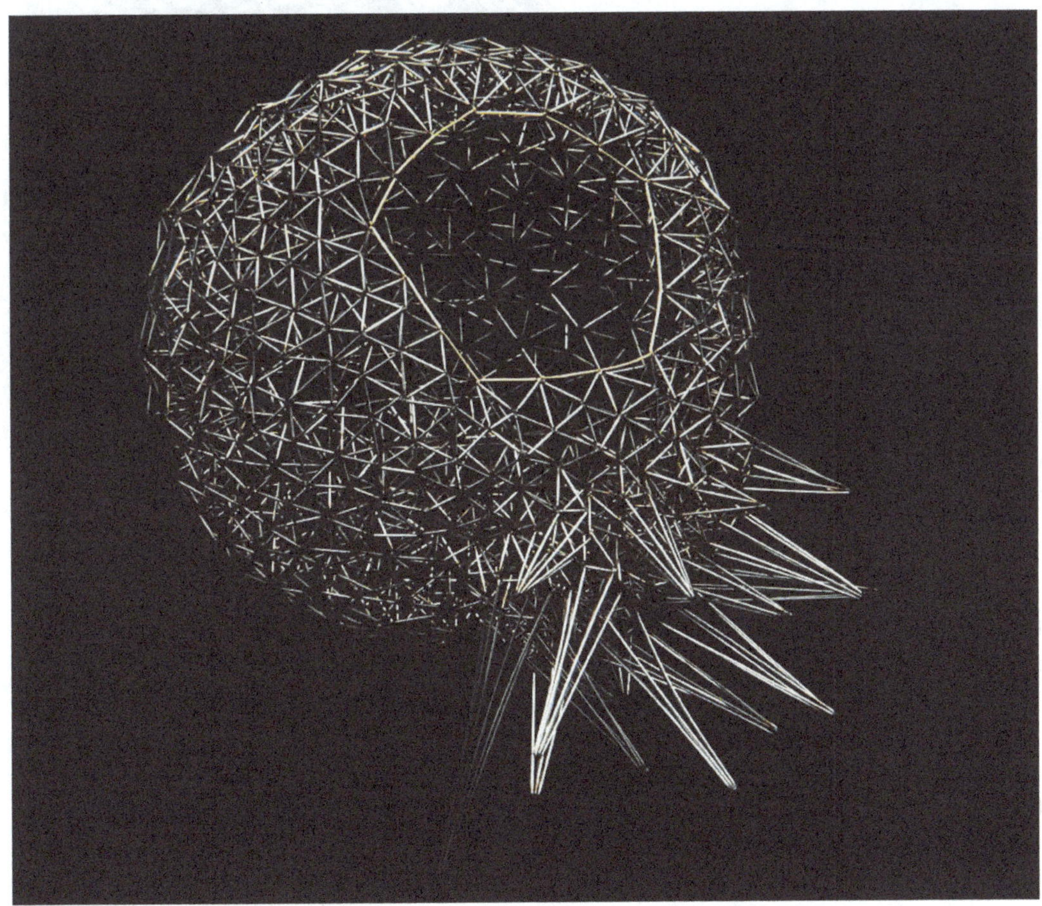

Figure 3. Karen-Ann Dicken, 18ct gold and steel bowl, 2007.

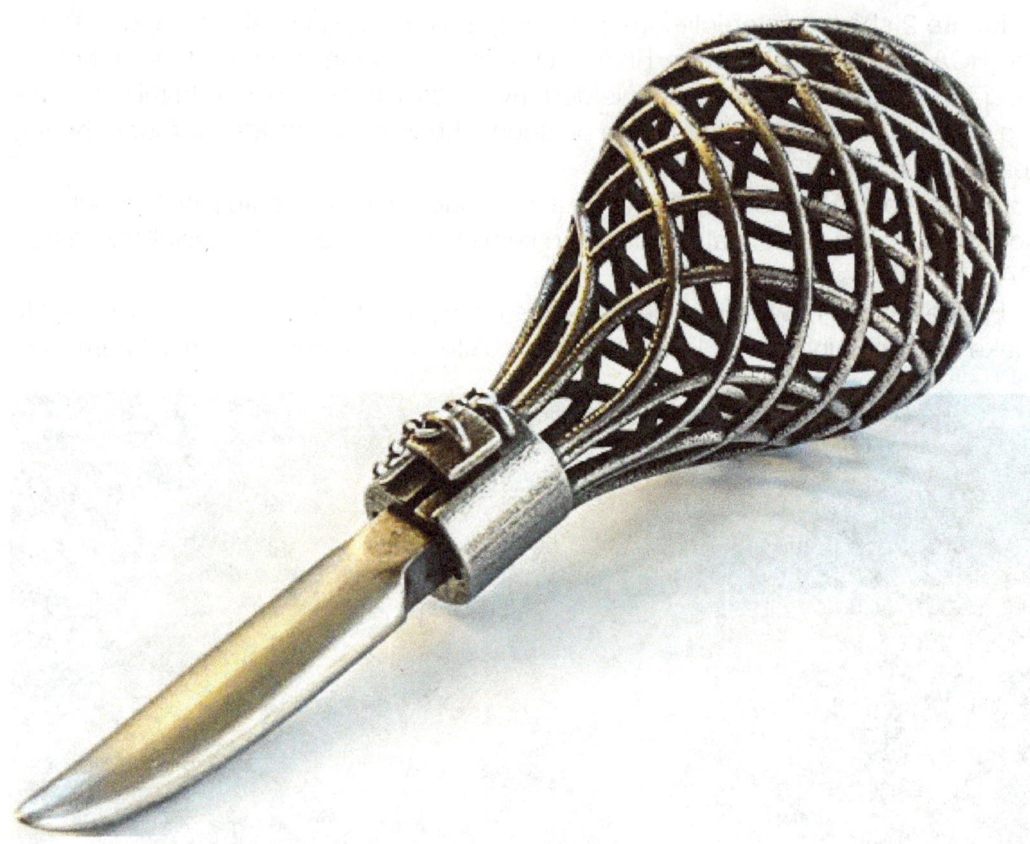

Figure 4. Karen-Ann Dicken, steel laser sintered multipurpose stone setting tool and burnisher, 2017.

the jig I burned off the 3D print to leave an accurate structure that would otherwise not be possible to make by hand.

More recently I have been looking at making 3D printing tooling more usable and accessible to jewellers, such as figure 4, designed in CAD, a multi-purpose stone setting tool. It has detachable ends that can be exchanged on the handle to become a burnisher, bezel pusher, rocker, or bezel setting stake tools. These pieces were direct laser sintered at Shapeways.com (a 3D printing bureau service) into bronze infused steel. This tool is personalised and with multi purpose tool ends would cut down the amount of individual tooling a jeweller requires.

I have experimented with making a range of hammers for various purposes. Figure 5 shows a planishing hammer that was laser sintered. The head of this soon broke off after I had used it because the inside of the hammer was made of a less hardened steel powder; however, Shapeways use a green part process and there are now printers that will print solid parts, so I believe this is still possible to achieve.

During my most recent project I wanted to test more intensely the properties and materials available through 3D printing and use modern technologies as tooling for craft. So I set one simple form that I would adapt to each technology and production method. The outside of the designs would be direct from machines and the inside would be handcrafted, but made using modern technologies to make the tooling.

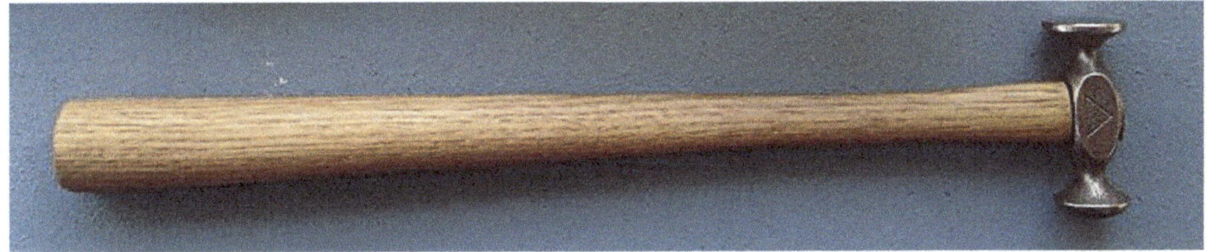

Figure 5. Karen-Ann Dicken, steel laser sintered planishing hammer, 2017.

The first technology I used was laser cutting. I cut the outside of these pieces in acrylic. They slotted together easily to create the outer structure. The inside bowl was created by laser cutting a press form. I then used this to press a sheet of copper to fit the outer bowl exactly. The final bowl was then sanded and oxidised—see figure 6.

I tested a range of 3D printing and used different 3D filaments to create tools. For the first bowl I 3D printed the outside section in .brass polylactic acid (PLA) filament—see figure 7. The inside section I created a press mould through 3D printing. I found that the durability of this using PLA was not great as the edges soon folded under the pressure and after multiple uses made a less and less accurate edge. Other experimentation of using 3D printing for press forming has worked well using metal plates to counteract this. My most recent piece is a sterling silver vase where I 3D printed the form in PLA plastic and cast into silver. I found problems with ash residue inside the moulds which left a hole in the casting. So I rectified this by using pressurized air on the mould before casting, which worked very well and gave a good casting without holes—see figure 8. Using 3D printing to directly cast can allow the maker much more intricate designs than might otherwise be makeable by hand and leads to a wider palate of forms and shapes available. The time spent designing and 3D printing the form is far reduced from hand carving process, more accurate, and allows for fresh aesthetics to emerge.

Sandra Wilson—Setting a Base on a Vessel

My practice has recently shifted from making jewellery into silversmithing using a method known as dutch raising that starts by raising at the outside edge (Wilson, 2018) rather than the centre associated with angle raising. Traditionally with small bowls it is quite common in silversmithing to create a round indented base through using a wooden block and punch in a fly or hydraulic press. A round base is most commonly used partly because the round tool can be easily created on a wood

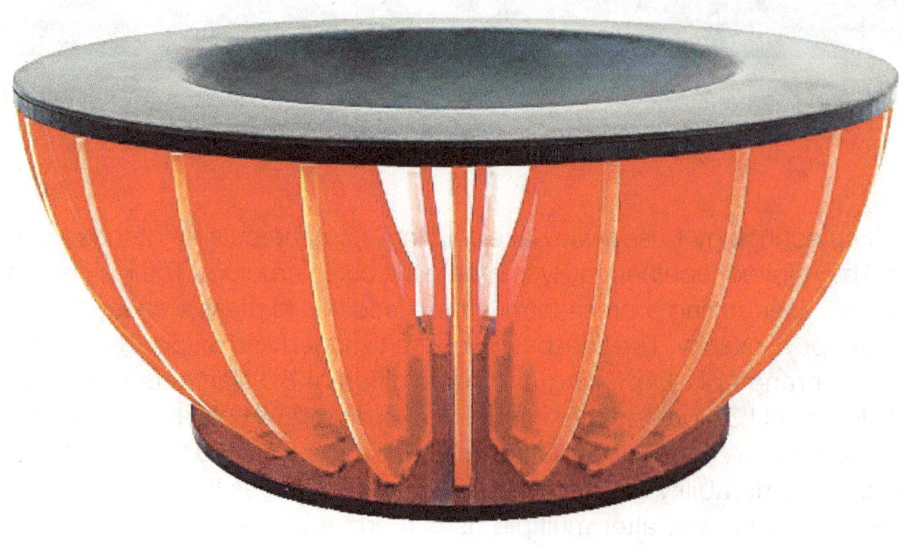

Figure 6. Karen-Ann Dicken, laser cut acrylic and copper press formed bowl, 2017.

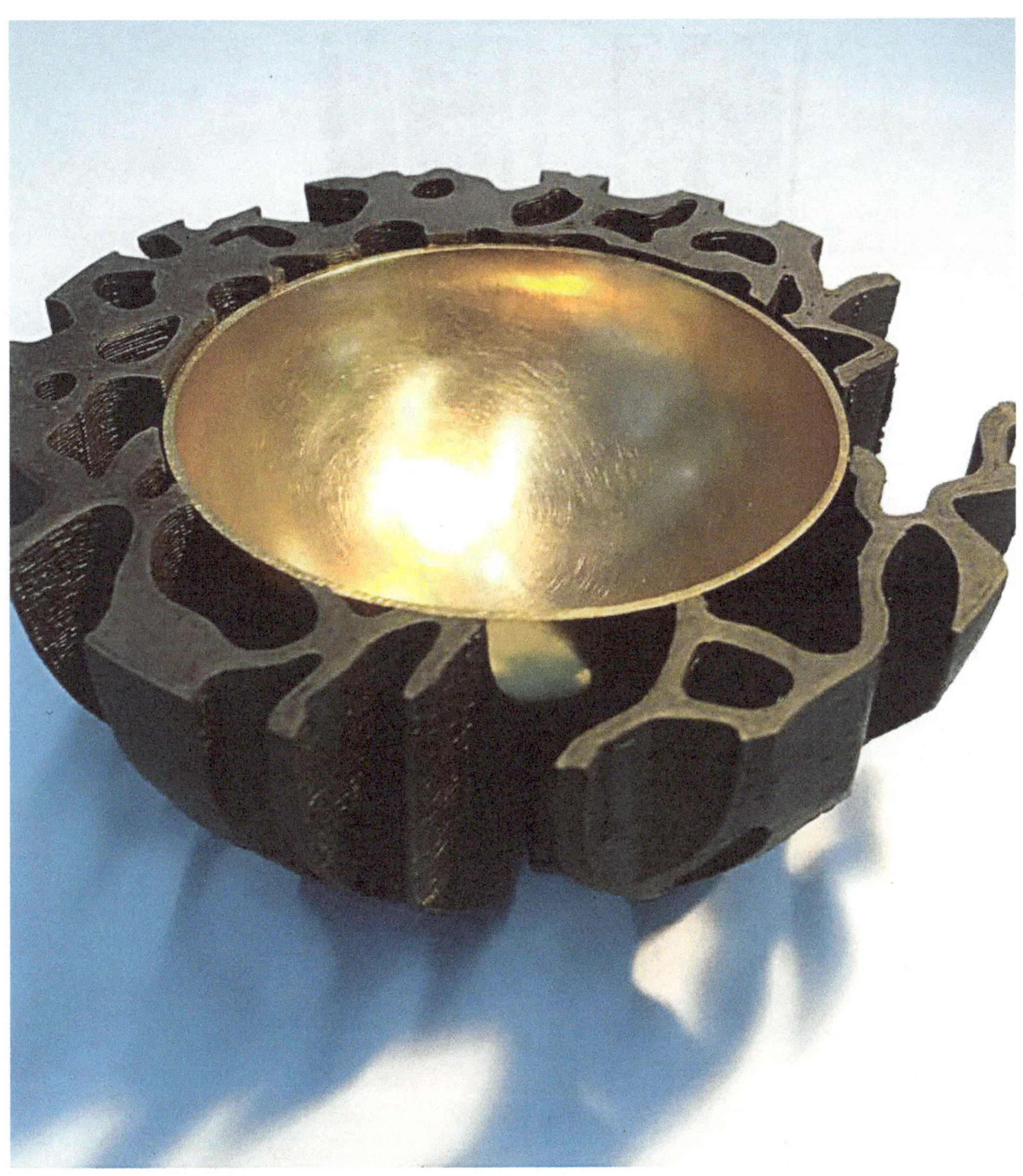

Figure 7. Karen-Ann Dicken, brass PLA and gold plated copper bowl, 2019.

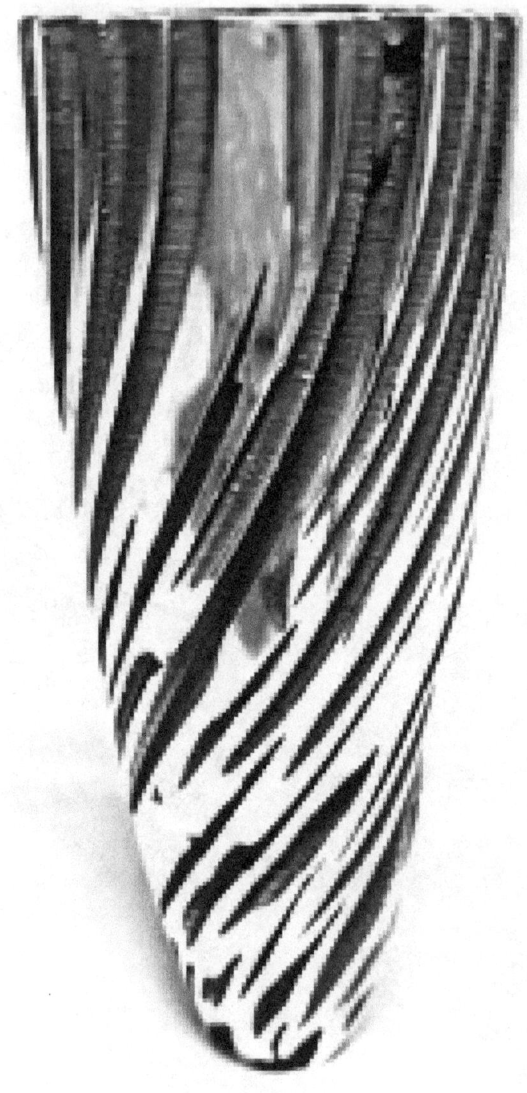

Figure 8. Karen-Ann Dicken, cast sterling silver vase, 2018.

lathe and a corresponding hole of the same size created in a wooden block with a drill bit.

It occurred to me that with the introduction of CNC (computer numerically controlled) milling, blocks and punches of different shapes could be produced, for example three-sided shapes, squares, and ovals. I am currently working on a series of bowls to demonstrate this, the first of which is completed. I have started with a fairly simple shape to begin with although the forms can become more adventurous once it is clear how far the metal can be pushed.

To make a block and punch for my three-sided base see figure 10—I created a file in Rhino 3D, using only a few basic commands—firstly creating a square block using one of the primitive tools, extruding the curve of the shape for the punch, and using the patch command to make the base of the punch slightly concave. Using the patch command was probably the hardest part of the process to figure out. I then made a copy of the punch shape and made it around 1mm larger and then used Boolean difference to subtract the punch shape from the block. It is important to leave this gap between the block and the punch so that there is room for the metal. Overall it took around fifteen minutes to make both parts in Rhino 3D. The file was then exported as .stl file for CNC milling. See figure 9 to see the Rhino file for the distorted oval base, the next in the series.

The tool was made on a Denford Router 6600 Pro using a 6.35mm ball nose cutter. The ball nose cutter is effectively a round drill bit that forms the shape of the punch and cuts out the base through repeated removing of unwanted material. This subtractive process took around one hour to perform. Using a round drill bit also means that the shape of the base will inevitably have slightly rounded corners. The Janka scale rates the relative hardness of different types of wood. For this three-sided base I used Beech, which rates as 1686 ibf. I have also used Ash (1320 ibf) and Walnut (1010 ibf) to good effect. A hardwood is important if you want to repeat the operation on several vessels and so extend the life of the tool. So it is clear that some knowledge of wood as a material is important, including which direction the wood grain should be set on the CNC milling machine. This would be particularly important when CNC milling, for example, a hammer handle, as if the grain was facing the wrong direction then the handle would snap quite easily. See figure 10 for an image of the wooden block and punch after CNC milling.

Once the basic shape of the silver vessel is raised, it is important to use a process called back raising—where metal is moved with raising hammers towards the centre of the bowl. Through back raising a "pimple" of spare metal is created that can be stretched by the block and punch to form the base. The rest of the vessel

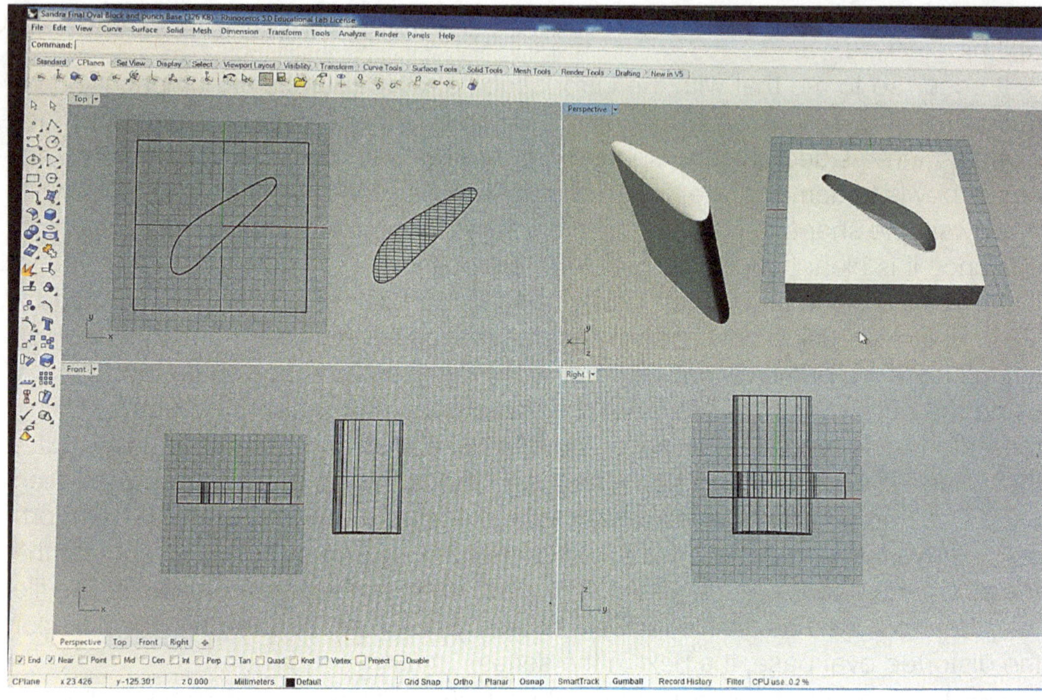

Figure 9. Sandra Wilson, Rhino 3D file for a distorted oval base block and punch, 2019.

can then be planished smooth. The setting of the base should be one of the last actions performed on the piece. So skill is required to judge how much metal is needed to be stretched for the base and in setting the bowl inside the block and positioning the punch under either the hammer or the fly press. I personally prefer using the press as it can give you more control over how much pressure to add and pressure can be added slowly, unlike with a large heavy hammer.

Another significant part of my current research is exploring recovering precious metals from electronic waste and so I have added some gold chloride solution to the work—this is one of the chemicals I have encountered in my research. The finished bowl is figure 11.

The hardwood for the tool cost around £20 and the time taken on the CNC machine around one hour for both block and punch at an average cost of around £45 per hour. So this is very good value to create a custom designed and unique tool that, if used with care, could create a base for several vessels.

Through this process we can see how new technologies lead to new advances and innovations in the form and shape of artifacts. These forms could have been achieved through other methods, for example chasing with steel punches in pitch, however we have not seen much evidence of this, perhaps because it would be very time consuming. The use of the CNC milled wooden block and punch also requires the skill of the maker to ensure the metal is placed in the right position, and that enough back raising has been carried out to ensure there is enough metal to spread for the base and the right amount of force is applied. Consequently, even

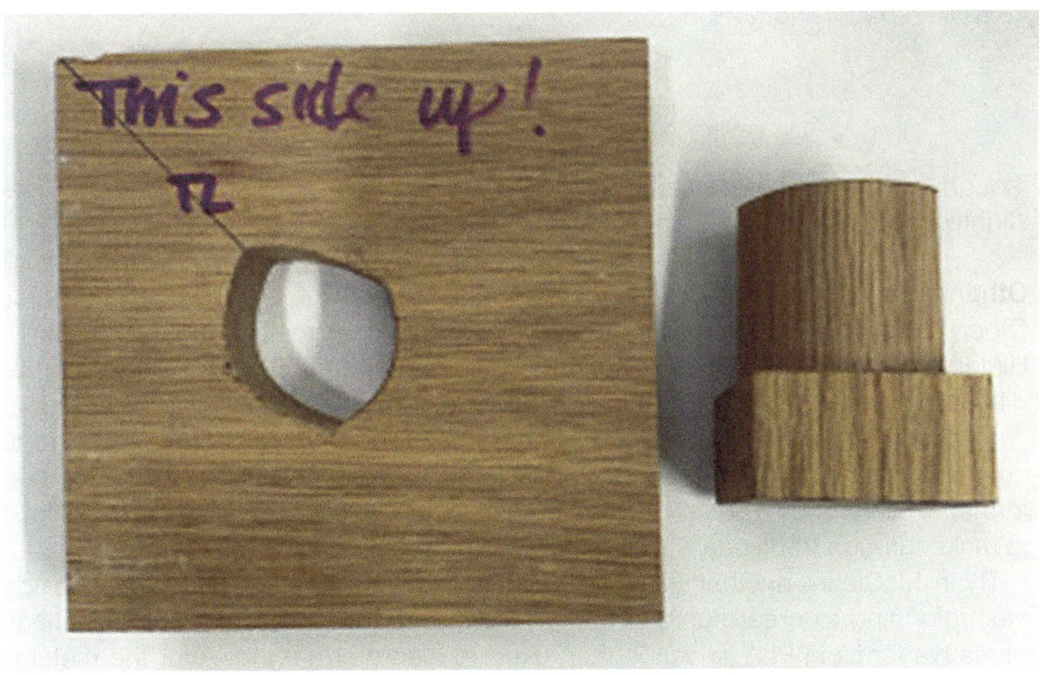

Figure 10. Sandra Wilson, CNC milled block and punch in beech hardwood, approx. 20 cm square with 4cm x 5 cm punch shape.

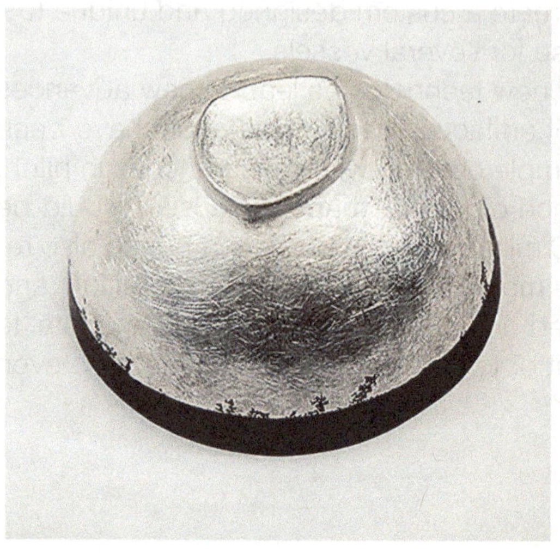
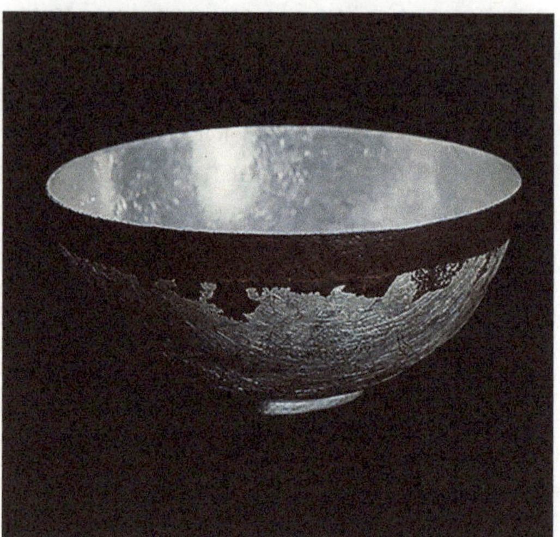

Figure 11. Sandra Wilson, gold chloride bowl with 3 sided base, Britannia silver, 2018.

though you are using the same block and punch each vessel will look and feel slightly different to each other.

Other Artists

Other artists in the field using digital tooling within their making includes Kathryn Hinton, a Scottish silversmith who uses 3D printing and CNC milling alongside traditional techniques such as casting.

Her more recent work has been using CNC milling in hard resins and wood to create press forming tools. The CNC milling allows her to create accurate faceted forms, which can be transfered into the metals that would otherwise prove difficult to make through traditional silversmithing methods.

Ryan McClean, another British based silversmith, uses 3D printing alongside electroforming to create unique flowing vase forms based on fractals. McClean prints his forms in PLA, which is then used to elecroform on to. After the metal is thick enough the vase is removed and the PLA is burned out to leave the final metal form.

Conclusion

In conclusion, we feel that as makers we should be taking the approach of embracing new technologies available to us and using them in innovative ways to integrate into the wide range of skills that we have acquired through thousands of years of handcraft. We should embrace the qualities that these new tools have to offer and at the same time retain the quality and love that goes into handcrafted object in order to create fresh and innovative designs that have a sense of vitality.

Making your own tooling is an important way of creating your own unique aesthetic. It can be something that can differentiate your work from everything else out there in the market place. By using new 3D printing and CNC milling digital tools to create our own unique tools for handcrafted work we can create new forms, textures, and ways of creating shape and pattern. These examples demonstrate how existing tools can be made through digital tooling that enables us to expand on their current capabilities as in the case of creating different shaped bases for vessels. We can also potentially create new tools not yet encountered before and this is the next phase in Dicken's PhD research.

Craft makers have traditionally been reluctant to embrace new digital processes fearing the loss of the hand made and the uniqueness associated with personal expression and handmade work. We hope that these examples demonstrate that these qualities can still be maintained by using digital tooling.

The integration of digital tooling is allowing makers to create tools that are personal to them and offers opportunities to create fresh and exciting new forms within their work from embracing digital tools, whilst still maintaining the quality and vitality that emanates from a handcrafted item. 3D printing technologies has enabled makers to create otherwise un-makeable items by using handcraft alone, for example 3D printing complicated jigging for laser welding. The speed and low cost of 3D printing tooling enables makers to have more control over what they can produce, in the example of Wilson's CNC wooden press forms. Through embracing the toolmaking approach using digital technologies, makers are able to open up their tool box to a much wider range of form and expression. Makers are able to have more control over the aesthetic of their finished designs through embracing and integrating both new technologies alongside traditional handcraft.

It is still vitally important, however, that makers have a basic knowledge of different materials such as wood and their main characteristics and how they need to be worked. For without this knowledge the tools created through digital means may simply fall apart quite quickly. A maker needs to have a good understanding of material qualities in order to apply this towards a digital making process in order for the designs to work well and to be able to apply their own personal expression of an object through digital toolmaking.

Digital toolmaking is a continuation of the long history of people's desire to shape their world. This development in tool making as with previous developments opens up new forms, textures, and patterns, particularly lattice style forms as in the work of Dicken and pixelated forms as in the work of Hinton. The wider jewellery industry can learn much from jewellery artists and silversmiths working with digital tooling. For example, if the industry partnered with jewellery and metal design artists, this would also create opportunities for growth within the wider marketplace based on the new aesthetics possible.

References

Dissanayake, E. 1988. *What is Art for?* Seattle: University of Washington Press.

Flusser, V. 1999. *The Shape of Things: A Philosophy of Design.* London: Reaktion Books.

Lilley, S. 1948. *Men Machines and History.* London: Corbett Press.

Marsh, P. 2012. *The New Industrial Revolution: Consumers, Globalisation and the End of Mass Production.* New Haven, CT: Yale University Press.

Wilson, S. 2018. "The Mystery of Dutch Raising." *Silver Studies* 33.

For more information on digital tooling and access to open source files see Karen-Ann Dicken's PhD blog http://www.3dprinttooling.com/home.html.

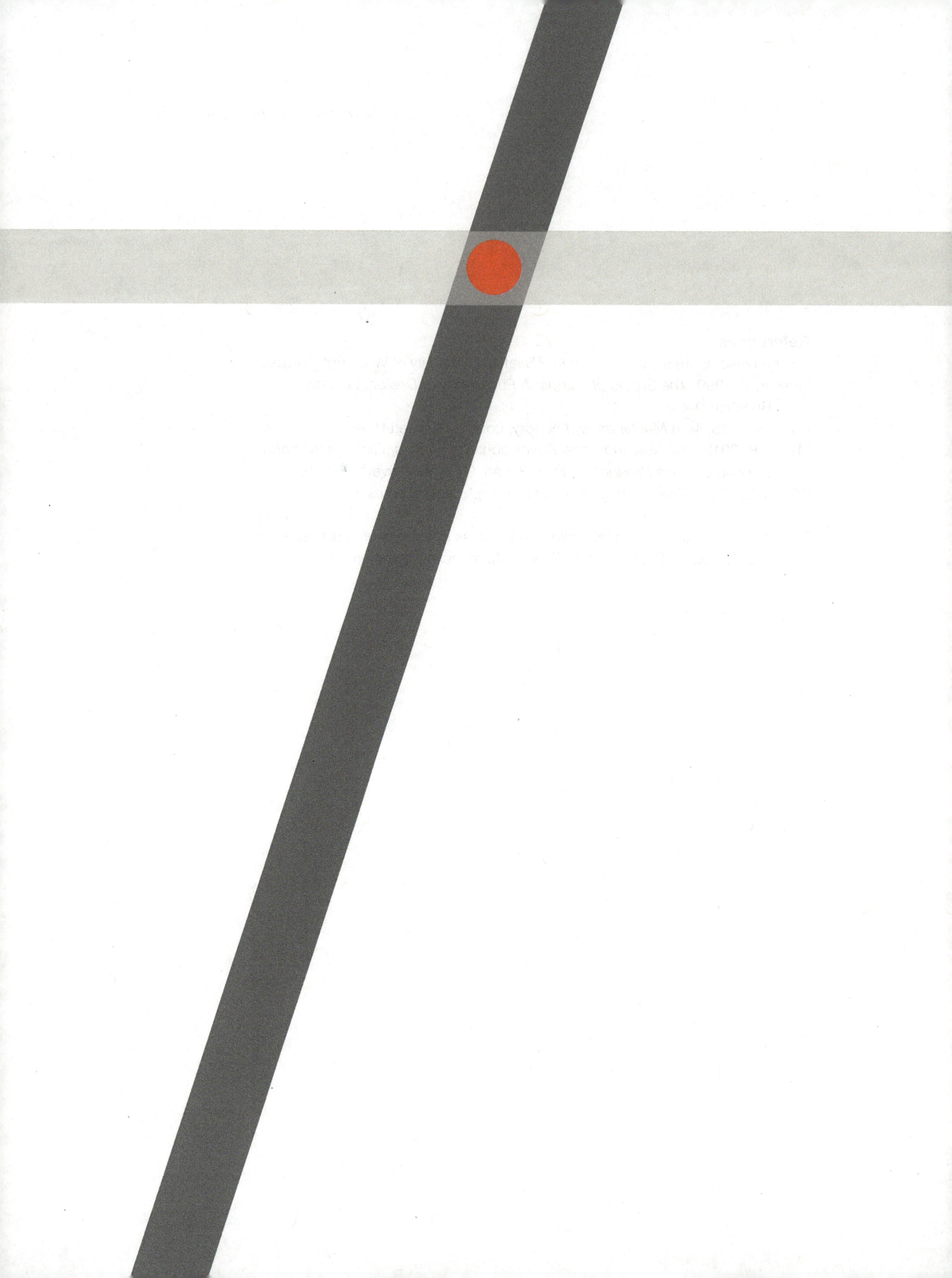

The Grid, from Colonial to Digital: The Role of Digital Technology in Craft Making

Bin Dixon-Ward, RMIT University, Melbourne, Australia

Abstract

In this paper, I present a practice-based research project in which I explore the constructed environments of grid-based cities and produced jewellery using 3D printing technology. The research draws on experiential jewellery practice focusing on the cities of Melbourne, Shanghai, and New York. I explore the interconnectedness of the process of making the artworks and the objects themselves, and argue that it is only through letting go of any sense of separateness from technology that the complexity of my relationship to digital tools and materials can be revealed.

Drawing on three key theorists, Martin Heidegger (1889–1976), Donna Haraway (1944–), and Peter Dormer (1949–1996), I describe my relationship with digital making tools. In the first instance, Heidegger's concept of ready-to-hand is used to explore the way in which my 3D technology becomes "assumed'" by me; its presence is not the primary focus of the use, rather, the work being done. Donna Haraway's argument of the hybrid machine/organism where the tool becomes a pairing of our bodies and machines (prosthesis), adds to the understanding of my relationship to the technology. Finally, Peter Dormer's concept of tacit knowledge, whereby through frequent use, the maker develops an unconscious knowledge relationship with the tool, might be seen to encompass the entire project.

These relationships with digital tools are evident in the finished works—jewellery and small objects, which reveal four states of the city grid and interpreted these as jewellery and small objects. These states of the grid are: rigid and incising, protecting and containing, mutable and changeable, and dissolving and disintegrating. The jewellery follows these forms as they were found in the city grid: from rigid orthogonal forms that control landscapes to fluid forms that conform to the human body, while all the time maintaining the underlying structure of the grid.

A parallel interrogation of the controlled logic of the urban grid and the organic nature of human interaction was threaded through the research. Commencing with an examination of the city grid as an organising and framing device, shaping human activity, I reveal ways in which human activity shapes the grid. In isolating and downsizing the forms of the city grid, I produced work of a human and wearable scale. Through duplicating, layering, and distorting forms of the grid, the objects are abstracted from their origin, allowing an organic interaction with the wearer, while a trace of the source, that is, the rigid grid, remains as a gesture to its origins.

My research reveals the relationship between artist, tool, wearer, material, and object as not only adaptable and mutable but integral to their making and meaning. The jewellery contributes to contemporary debates relating to the role of digital technologies in making, and the relationship between the maker and the machine.

The Grid, from Colonial to Digital: The Role of Digital Technology in Craft Making

In this paper, I present a practice-based project in which I researched the constructed environments of grid-based cities and produced jewellery using Rhino 3D (Robert McNeel and Associates) and SLS (selective laser sintering) 3D printing technology. Through the project I explored the process of making the jewellery and its manifestation in the objects themselves. I argue that it is only through letting go of any sense of separateness from technology that my relationship to digital tools and materials can be revealed. The meta-narrative is one of a parallel between the role of the grid in city making and the digital grid's role in my jewellery making.

Through the course of the research, I explored stages of urban development from colonisation to digital city, with each stage providing new insights into the grid. This process revealed four states of the city grid. I identified the first of these grid states as a rigid orthogonal form that served to control the landscape and its inhabitants; the second form of the city grid is a device that protects and contains its occupants, while also excluding outsiders; a third state of the city grid is mutable and fluid, demonstrating that where people interact with the city grid they transform it; and the final state of the grid sees it disassembled and reconstituted through other vectors of movement and intersections in the contemporary city grid, most particularly that of digital interactions.

The rigid orthogonal grid emerged from my examination of the historical use of a grid-based street plan, employed by surveyors and city planners as a process of colonising the landscape. I explore the impacts of the grid street plan on the

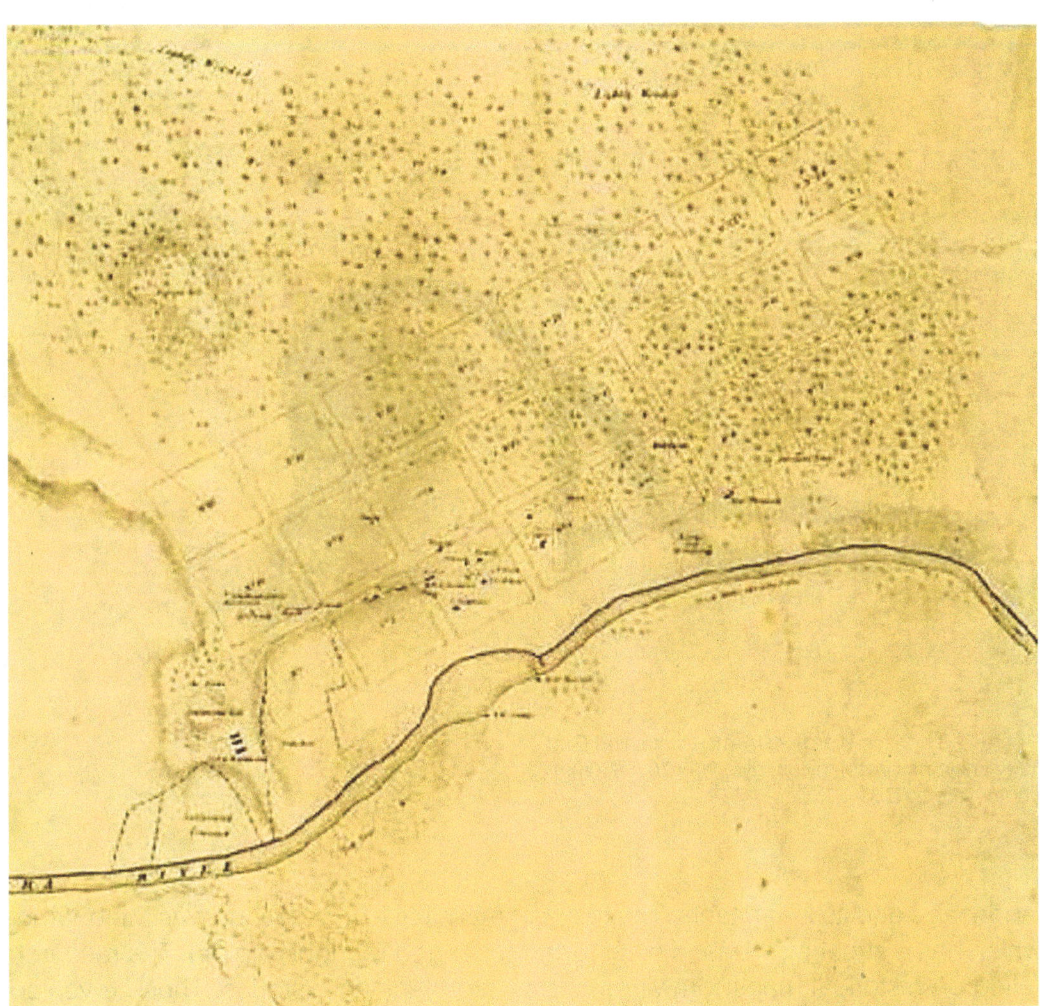

Figure 1. Map showing the site of Melbourne and the position of the huts and buildings previous to the foundation of the township by Sir Richard Bourke in 1837. Source: cartographic material surveyed and drawn by Robert Russell (detail).

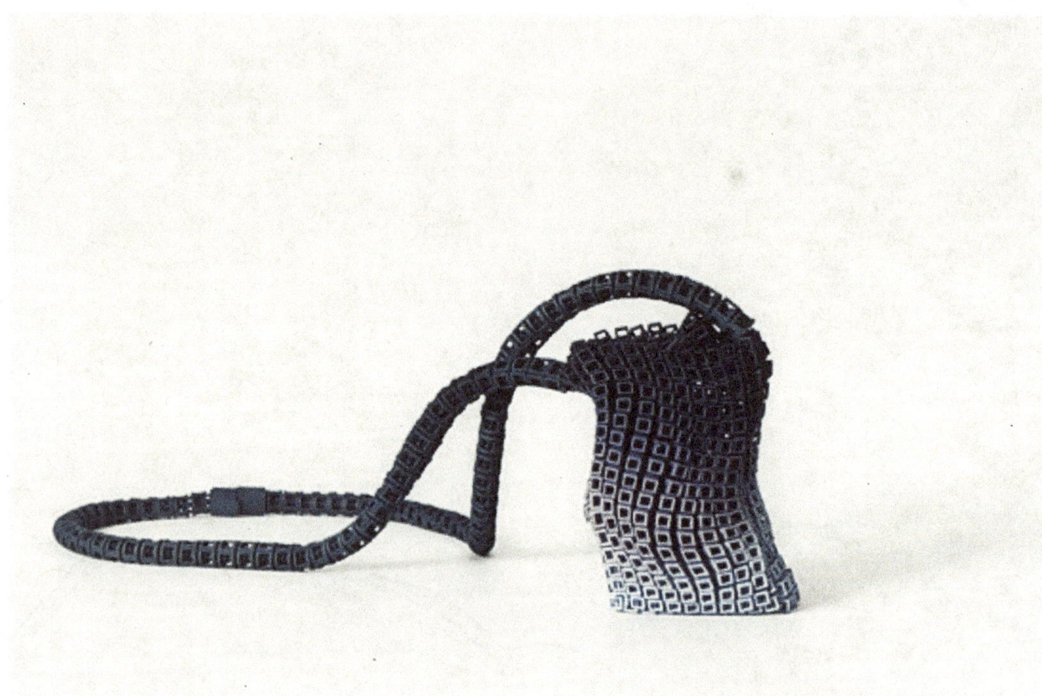

Figure 2. Bin Dixon-Ward, 2014–16, Containing Grid #2 (work in progress), nylon, dye, 90 x 70 x 600mm. Photo: Jeremy Dillon.

landscape and its inhabitants. The focus of my initial investigations was Melbourne, which has a street plan based on an orthogonal grid (at right angles). The research relied on historical maps, drawings and urban planning histories. These revealed the narratives of history, mapping, and colonisation through interpreting the shapes of the sites where the grid was laid.

The grid in the context of Melbourne's history was identified as being a rigid, incising instrument, a technology of control; the jewellery objects created during the course of this enquiry relate in a similar way to the body of the wearer. Russell's grid (see figure 1) shows the topographical features of the site where Melbourne is located (known to the local indigenous Kulin nation as Narrm). This part of my research produced rigid forms that, while wearable as a brooch, sit on the body rather than responding to its contours and movements.

The second form of the city grid that I identified is the *containing and protecting technology* for its inhabitants; a barrier, an exclusionary device for outsiders. The works created in this series of investigations see the grid become more flexible, yet still maintain its structural foundations. They share common features: all are tightly grouped, interlinked, container-like objects, which offer a sense of protection and safety while also being exclusionary. This phase of the research examined the material and tools that create the conditions under which a grid can emerge through digital fabrication technologies, from a rigid state to one that conforms to the human body. Further, through exploring Heidegger's concept of *enframing* (Waddington, 2005, p. 572), I came to see the colonial grid as enframing the landscape and, by defining its boundaries, conferring control to the grid's creators and inhabitants and therefore determining who is included and who is excluded.

In relating the colonial city street grid to the landscape, Heidegger's concept of enframing stems from his notion of "challenging-forth," a useful paradigm in that

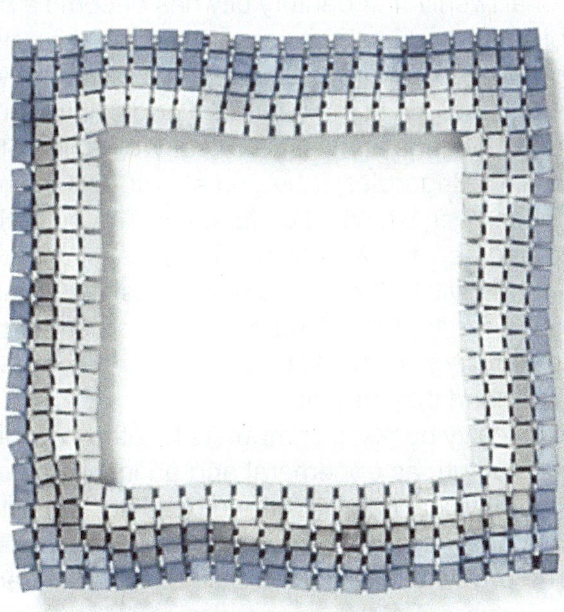

Figure 3. Bin Dixon-Ward, 2016, Enframing Grid 1, nylon, ink, 310 x 320 x 15mm. Photo: Jeremy Dillon.

it accounts for the transformation of the materials of the natural environment from their essential nature to that of a resource for our use and to be available when we want them. This, as Heidegger explains, is a state of "standing reserve" (available for our use) and being "set-upon" (or ordered and systematised) (Heidegger, 1977, p. 10). Standing reserve, Heidegger argues, places material and objects subordinate to human agency, so that we have control over them. So too, it is in this way that the landscape is subjugated to the technology of the colonial grid. As such the landscape is challenged-forth and set-upon. Heidegger proffered that when we view nature this way we are "enframing;" that is, we are ordering, managing, controlling, and training nature.

The third series of works embraced the mutability and fluidity of the grid in the context of human interaction. The resulting celebratory group of artworks, capture the ways in which people interact with the grid, and in so doing, the grid is transformed. The grid's agency as controller is disrupted, opening up a space where the city inhabitants create their own environments. The objects produced in this phase embody the grid, and demonstrate the capacity for people to transform the shapes of the grids they occupy.

The multidimensional twenty-first-century city has become a permeable arrangement of physical objects and digital entities. In this fourth iteration of the grid, it is broken down, disaggregated, and reconstituted in a myriad of ways, as are digital files as they flow through the grid of the Internet. People, infrastructure, utilities, and services move through city grids at massive rates, yet, while potentially chaotic, an underlying order remains. Regardless, the grid structure is maintained as the base framework or foundation upon which cities function. The potential for disorder and order were explored and new forms emerge. The disassembly and reassembly of formal shapes and forms within the grid emerges as the primary vehicle whereby new ways are found for the grid to respond to the human body. The city grid is unrecognisable in *Intersections* (2017); instead, the piece gestures towards the digital grid, the "cloud," and the Internet.

While the cloud is in reality banks of computers located in large secure buildings, we envision this infrastructure as ephemeral and an infinite net or cloud floating in space. In a sense, the physical nature of the digital city is of little consequence; it is the online social connections, the interactions that connect people, which make up the digital city. The physical forms of the built environment are almost irrelevant to this city, it is the capacity for infinite connection and communication that is at the fore. The open lace-like network of *Intersections* with both positive and negative

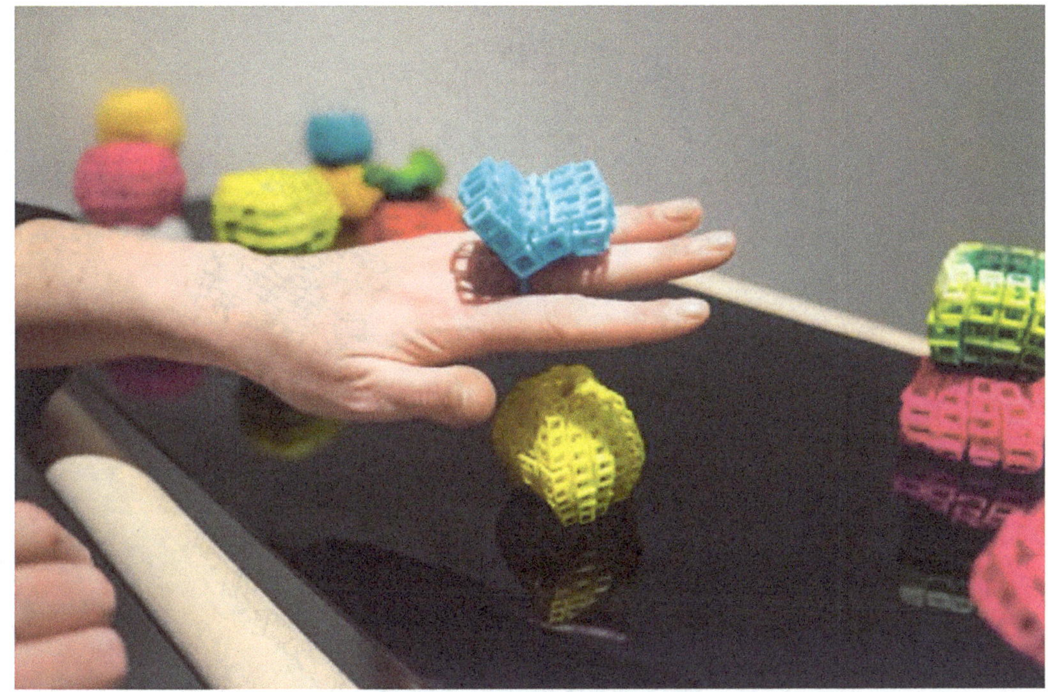

Figure 4. Bin Dixon-Ward, 2014, Small City Rings, SLS, nylon, ink, installation in Grids, Craft Victoria, August 2014. Photo: Heather Lighton.

space reflects the openness and porosity of the digital city. It is possible to engage at any time, from any place.

Any discussion of technology and material cannot ignore Heidegger's (1977) analysis of the tool. And it is to this that I now turn. Heidegger's concepts of "present-at-hand" describes situations where the tool is at the fore of the users thinking. In contrast his concept of ready-at-hand describes how the tool recedes from the users consciousness.

UK academic Alan Dix offers an interpretation of Heidegger's text from a carpenter's perspective. Dix (2010) argues that the carpenter's knowledge of the hammer, developed over ten years of use of the tool, positions the hammer to be in a state of readiness-to-hand. He argues that ready-to-hand is a state in which the tool or technology is assumed by its user and its presence is not the primary focus of the

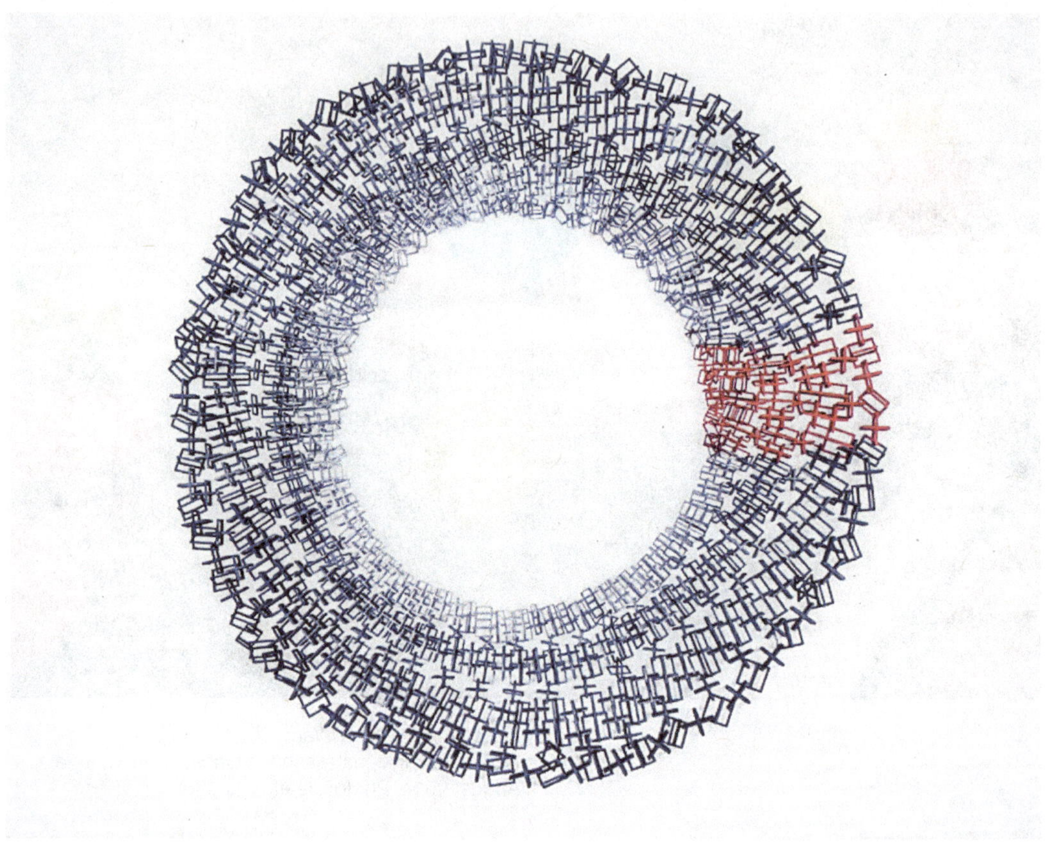

Figure 5. Bin Dixon-Ward, 2017, Intersections, nylon, ink, 500 x 500 x 15 mm. Photo: Giulia McGauran.

use, rather, the work being done with the tool central is to the task. This is contrasted with Heidegger's "present-at-hand" (Dix, 2010, p. 3), where the tool is present in the mind of the user, occupies the thoughts, or is in the view of the user.

Dix argues that the present-at-hand state, in fact, comes from a breakdown between the user and the tool. In other words, when it draws attention to itself. That is, that the hammer becomes present-at-hand when one bends a nail or bangs a thumb or is not the right-shaped hammer for the job at hand and creates an unwanted impression in a sheet of metal. In practice these states of using a tool are not either-or: they coexist. A user may at one moment be using a tool in a state of readiness-to-hand and the next in present-at-hand.

In the context of my use of computer-aided design (CAD) in making a jewellery objects, there were numerous situations in which I used this tool in a state of ready-at-hand or, as Dormer (1997) describes, with tacit knowledge or embodied knowledge, coming to the fore. In other situations in which I was trying to achieve an outcome not previously realised, this thinking and testing and problem solving tool use/outcome is perhaps a manifestation of Heidegger's present-at-hand. As I seek ways to find solutions, the tool (i.e., CAD) is at the fore of my thinking. In approaching a new work using new forms and types of connections, my concerns are with the work sequences, methods, and tools that will achieve my desired outcome. While undertaking the task I also engaged my embodied, tacit skill or ready-at-hand tools, that is, the fundamentals of the software, cut, copy, paste, move, rotate, etc. At the same time I needed to learn and experiment with new methods, new workflows and new (to me) Rhino tools. It was in this process of experimenting and learning that I employed the two modes of ready-at-hand and present-at-hand in the making of a new object.

Just as skills in the use of tools are a vocabulary to be drawn upon and used to realise a particular idea, so was my familiarity with 3D printing and CAD. In time, and with constant use, skills became innate and unconscious. Left mouse button, or right, press "enter" or scroll the mouse wheel. Hand-eye coordination is no longer a conscious activity as tools become a part of the maker's physicality. This is the tacit knowledge that Peter Dormer describes, but it is also the tool as prosthesis, as Donna Haraway envisages.

The machine is not an it to be animated, worshipped and dominated. The machine is us, our processes, an aspect of our embodiment. We can be responsible for machines; they do not dominate or threaten us. We are responsible for boundaries, we are they (Haraway, 2016, p. 60)

The mouse in my hand becomes a part of me as I move the object in the screen as easily as if it is in my hand in the same way with a hammer or a pencil.

I find it useful to think of the digital technologies employed in my jewellery making as co-contributors to an art making process. By understanding their potential to enframe our thinking or to see them as standing reserve, their role can become clear and their contribution acknowledged. The complex interlinked forms developed in my last series of experiments, in which I interconnected cubic frameworks to form a flexible fabric-like structure, could not be made in any way other than 3D printing, and more specifically, using the selective laser sintering process. It is the unique combination of the material, tooling, and making process, and CAD, that allowed these forms to come into being. With this way of thinking about the role of the tool in my making, I felt liberated to acknowledge I was not the sole author, that the forms came into being through a collaboration between me, the digital tools, and materials. This made sense to me, as it mirrored my thinking about the ways in which human/grid interaction shapes the city. I began to see my making process as part of a wider engagement between humans and technology.

To conclude, on one level, the jewellery created during the research demonstrates the connections between the city and digital grids. My jewellery and objects also play a part in theoretical debates regarding the role of artist and digital technologies; the role of the grid as an elemental structure of urban development; and the potential for art making to be enabled by digital technology

I have argued that my use of technology can be understood as an extension of the Heideggerian approach to the tool. The digital design process has been shown to be both ready-at-hand and present-at-hand. I have demonstrated how the technology in my practice has shifted between these two states, at times problem solving with the technology as ready-to-hand, but also working alongside the technology in a form of co-creation.

Bibliography

Dix, A. 2010. "Struggling with Heidegger." Blog. August 12, 2010. http://alandix.com/blog/2010/08/12/struggling-with-heidegger/.

Dormer, P. (ed.) 1997. *The Culture of Craft.* Manchester University Press, Manchester.

Haraway, D. 1991. "A Cyborg Manifesto: Science, Technology, and Socialist-Feminism in the Late Twentieth Century." In D. Haraway, *Simians, Cyborgs and Women: The Reinvention of Nature*, 149–81. New York: Routledge.

Heidegger, M. 1977. *The Question Concerning Technology and Other Essays.* New York: Harper & Row.

Waddington, D. 2005. "A Field Guide to Heidegger: Understanding 'The Question Concerning Technology.'" *Educational Philosophy and Theory* 37, no. 4: 567–83. https://www.academia.edu/540032/A_Field_Guide_to_Heidegger_Understanding_The_Question_concerning_Technology.

Maps and Images

Russell R. 1837(?). *Map Shewing the Site of Melbourne and the Position of the Huts & Buildings Previous to the Foundation of the Township by Sir Richard Bourke in 1837.* Cartographic material, surveyed and drawn by Robert Russell. http://search.slv.vic.gov.au/MAIN:Everything:SLV_VOYAGER1872264.

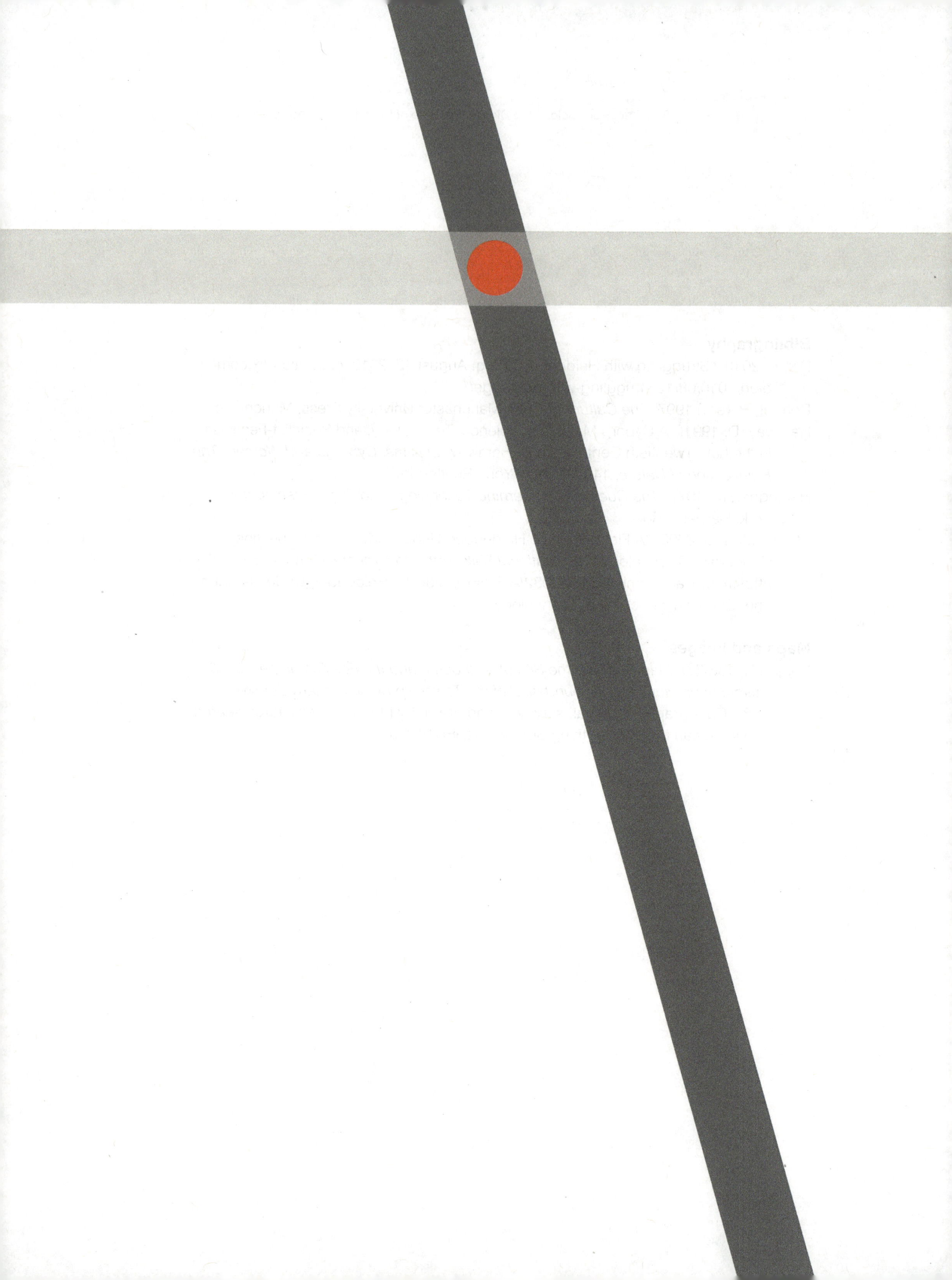

Craft, Pedagogy, and the Digital Challenge: A Jewelry Perspective

Lynne Heller, OCAD University, Toronto, Canada
Dorie Millerson, OCAD University, Toronto, Canada

Abstract

In the Material Art & Design undergraduate program at OCAD University (OCAD U) in Toronto, students are taught traditional fabrication techniques in ceramics, jewelry/metalsmithing, and textiles alongside digital design and production methods such as 3D printing, laser cutting, and computerized textile machinery. The jewelry faculty have led the way in integrating 3D digital technology into the curriculum but there remains a divide between the ways in which traditional and digital approaches are taught in the studio. This divide is seen in the use of separate classes and spaces for teaching traditional or digital fabrication along with the limited accessibility of tools such as 3D printers that tend to be operated by technicians rather than students. Teaching with digital technology also requires the learning or updating of skills on a constant basis and an ability to impart how traditional and digital fabrication methods can work together. The need to consider the place of digital craft in relation to traditional craft in potentially de- and re-skilling practitioners is of paramount importance as we prepare students for professional practice in jewelry. In this paper we present perspectives on the teaching and learning of digital craft tools at OCAD U based on an ongoing research project that began in 2017. In the first part of our project, we conducted a series of interviews with faculty, technicians, and administrators who teach or facilitate digital technology in the digital futures, jewelry/metalsmithing, textiles, wood, and rapid prototyping areas. In a subsequent study, conducted with the Faculty & Curriculum Development Centre (FCDC), we surveyed the experiences of first- to third-year jewelry and textiles students who were beginners or intermediate learners in digital technology.

The discoveries from this investigation have been extensive, but we have identified six themes that helped us analyze our data. The first, "Thinking in and Resisting Binaries," speaks to perceptions of difference between the analog and the digital. With "Impact of Time" we seek to compare the realities of time with expectations. In "Nostalgia for the Hand" we reflect on the connection participants made between traditional craft learning and embodiment. With "Generational Difference/Bias," perspectives around digital competency and age are presented. "New Models of Learning" addresses ways that the use of digital resources has expanded options for learning. "Communication and Agency" highlights the interactions between stakeholders and the role of autonomy when controlling or outsourcing production.

Digital processes have been an exciting development at our institutions, but they have also led to the need for re-training, concerns of sustainability, and deeper insight. In a climate where crafts-based programs are often challenged to explain their relevance in contemporary post-secondary education, questions around the use of digital technology are compelling and time sensitive. This is a prescient moment for investigating a new paradigm for the pedagogy, theorizing, and activity of making jewelry.

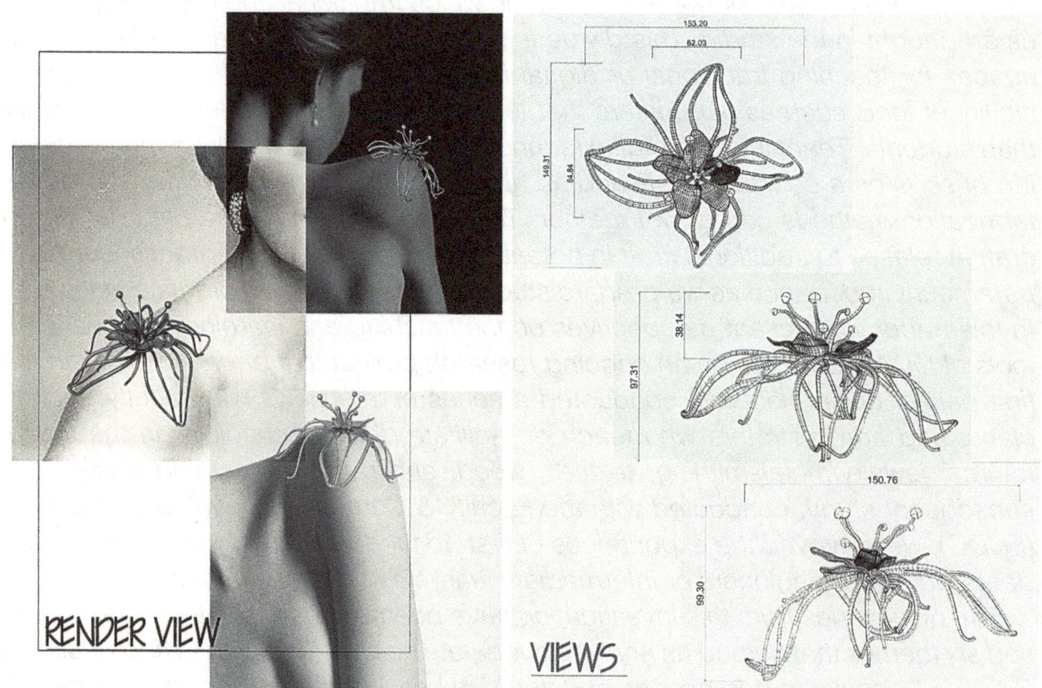

Figure 1. Anonymous, Study ID 180037, With a Lily, 2018, Instructor Greg Sims, OCAD University.

1. Introduction

In 2007, craft historian Sandra Alfoldy published the anthology *Neocraft: Modernity and the Crafts* (2007), including contributions that analyzed craft and the digital field (Harrod, 2007; Jönsson, 2007; Press, 2007). Twelve years later, it is timely to revisit and update issues around the evolution of craft and digital technology. Simultaneously, there is a renewed interest in maker culture (Labb and Neely, 2014), evidenced by the strong enrolment in craft-oriented classes from students from across art and design disciplines at institutions such as OCAD University (OCAD U) in Toronto.

This paper is based on an ongoing research project that seeks to consider the place of teaching and learning digital craft in Material Art & Design (MAAD) at OCAD U, a four-year undergraduate program with studies in Ceramics, Jewelry/Metalsmithing, and Textiles, from the perspectives of faculty, students, staff, and technicians. This was a two-part study supported by OCAD U, in which we first focused on faculty, technicians, and administrators who teach or facilitate digital technology and then we surveyed textile and jewelry students about their perceptions and experiences of learning and using digital technology. All aspects of the project have been conducted in accordance with the ethical review guidelines of OCAD U. All faculty, technicians, and staff gave consent to be named in the study while the students had the option to choose to have examples of their work credited or remain anonymous. By studying the data from interviews with eight members of faculty, technicians, and administrators and examining the surveys of about 50 students taking either a digital design class or conducting a digital project, we started to define some of the challenges and strategies for negotiating the space between traditional craft teaching and the use of digital tools.

As co-investigators of the initial stage of the project, we looked across craft disciplines and interviewed five faculty members (who taught digital design, jewelry, textiles, and wood fabrication), two technicians (of textiles and rapid prototyping), and one head of studio management. We asked each participant a series of questions about how they acquired their knowledge of and learned to teach digital craft processes. We were interested in how their experiences teaching/facilitating have changed over time and how their teaching may develop in the future. We also asked what kind of goals and outcomes they set when teaching digital designing and making processes and how they evaluate the results.

In the second phase of the study, conducted in collaboration with an expanded research team, including Dr. Cary DiPietro and Travis Freeman from OCAD U's Faculty & Curriculum Development Centre (FCDC) and faculty member Greg Sims as co-investigators, we analyzed students' opinions of time, money, efficacy, level of confidence, and agency in relation to digital technology. We worked with students and faculty in six classes: three first-year classes that introduced 3D digital design and modeling to jewelry and textiles students; two second-year classes that consisted of a digital jewelry class and a stitching class that incorporated digital embroidery; and one third-year digital technology elective class taken by students across the design disciplines. Research methods consisted of an initial survey followed by a final survey along with the collection of samples of students' work (see figures 1 and 2). We looked at the visual work in relation to the surveys to discover how the students talked about the digital experience in relation to what they made.

Potential de- and re-skilling of practitioners is of paramount importance for educators, as one of our goals is to prepare students for professional practice in jewelry. The term deskilling and its corollary, reskilling, are grounded in Marxist theory (Braverman, 1974) and refer to the phenomenon of the division and mechanization of labor, historically tied to capitalism and its drive to devalue labor by reducing the expertise needed to complete a process and thereby eliminating the need for skilled workers. Craftspeople have often resisted the tendency to deskill people, a position espoused by the prominent craft theorist and socialist William Morris (Morris and Salmon, 1994). They frequently foster holistic making practices where one person or a community of similarly skilled makers has the autonomy over a production process, responding to materials with an intimate knowledge of the tools they employ and guiding the aesthetic considerations that are often inherent in the making, a kind of literacy that theorist Glenn Adamson (2018) calls "material understanding."

In this paper, we will present some of the emergent themes of the study: Thinking in and Resisting Binaries; Impact of Time; Nostalgia for the Hand; Generational Difference/Bias; New Models of Learning; and Communication and Agency. For the purposes of this text, we have focused on a jewelry perspective.

2. Thinking in and Resisting Binaries

Throughout the interviews we noticed varied responses to identifying the analog and digital, or hand and machine, as binaries. While some interviewees stressed a continuum, others emphasized difference. As faculty member Kathleen Morris indicated:

Those two areas of digital and [the] hand, really, there's a lot of interplay between the two . . . I don't feel that one is particularly privileged over the other and in fact I don't feel that there is a concrete separation between the two. I feel that they represent different stages in a process.

In some cases, however, students reacted to the challenges of integrating or moving between hands-on studio and digital learning methods. One student stated, "I did not enjoy that we were learning complex digital technologies and softwares [sic], like Rhino, while working by hand as well. [The course] should be more concentrated on one thing at a time" (Anonymous, Final Survey, Study ID 180058). Conversely, another stated, "I like using both hand and digital techniques simultaneously" (Anonymous, Final Survey, Study ID 180066).

Overall, students did indicate preferences—82 percent of participants in the final survey strongly agreed or agreed that they "prefer to work in hands-on processes of designing and making," while 96 percent strongly agreed or agreed that "using digital technologies for design expands or opens up new approaches and possibilities."

3. Impact of Time

Another prevalent theme was the implications of time when working digitally. As technician Laurie Wassink described, "The immense amount of time needed to operate and maintain this equipment is vastly undervalued and overlooked."

From the student perspective, initially 78 percent strongly agreed or agreed that "using digital machinery in production saves me time." This percentage increased in the final survey to 88 percent strongly agreeing or agreeing. This result could indicate a discrepancy between the experience of students and technicians. Whose time is saved? Is learning to outsource effectively and ethically an important aspect of the learning experience?

In addition, students reported that there is often a long wait for a machine and/or technician to become available. One student complained that when using digital technologies in design process and production that it was "Very time consuming and not always necessary" (Anonymous, Final Survey, Study ID 180009). On the other hand, technicians pointed out the need for scheduling production for multiple class projects in order to manage both their own and the students' time more effectively.

4. Nostalgia for the Hand

Nostalgia or preference for the hand and direct use of materials and tools was evident in many of the comments made. For example, in the following quote, a student refers to the immediacy and authorship of working by hand when they stated that:

As an artist who wants to make handmade things I don't like the impracticality of having to make digital models of something you can just sketch by hand and make, if you don't want to. I don't like using technology as much as making things myself. (Anonymous, Final Survey, Study ID 180058)

Other students connected the handmade to embodiment and questioned the way the institution may place importance on the digital:

I perceive material work as linked directly with the body, and the erasure of the hand manipulated techniques offensive. I know the MAAD program is not pursuing this erasure, but I do worry about OCAD's digital prioritization. (Anonymous, Initial Survey, Study ID 180042)

Some students indicated strong opinions on the connection needed between the making of craft and the body or, as one student stated, "I am not a fan of using digital technology in my work, I feel as if it removes the object from the body, and I believe that the body is an important component to craft overall" (Anonymous, Final Survey, Study ID 180035).

In contrast many students did recognize the benefits of digital methods, tools, and technology. For example, one student conceded, "I had [a] negative view of digital technology/programs prior to this course. However the course helped me have more of an open mind to it. I enjoyed the course" (Anonymous, Final Survey, Study ID 180063). Another said, "I felt difficult at the beginning and after I got the result of the 3D printing, I felt more confident and I think it could be really helpful in the future" (Anonymous, Final Survey, Study ID 180034).

In the final survey, 98 percent of participants strongly agreed or agreed that "learning to use digital technologies is worth the effort." This sense of acceptance was noted in some comments, "It doesn't come easy to me to use computer programs but I know it's the way of the future" (Anonymous, Initial Survey, Study ID 180038) and:

Learning digital technology so you can avoid labour intensive work with potential health hazards long term is really important for me. Avoiding things link tendinitis or wax or metal allergies that can develop overtime for jewelers is important to me. (Anonymous, Final Survey, Study ID 180036)

5. Generational Difference/Bias

Concurrent with nostalgia for the hand were references to generational differences or biases, perhaps even ageist assumptions. Several faculty members spoke of the assumptions they make about the facility students have with certain digital applications, which means that they spend less time on instructing those methods. Faculty member Chung-Im Kim commented that "the young generation; they grew up with this new technology, for them it's not a big gap between analog and digital." Faculty member Marie O'Mahony considers the skills new students may bring to their post-secondary studies. "We're getting students . . . with . . . digital language. So the language that is new as they're coming in to study . . . is often the making."

Students are not all of the same generation, however, and some acknowledged a connection between age and an awareness of analog and digital difference. As this mature student stated, "I believe that being relatively old, that I understand the importance of analogue process, as well as the impact of the digital revolution. . ." (Anonymous, Initial Survey, Study ID 180042). Others stated more subtle differences in their experience, "I am 22 and feel as though people who attended school just after me learned more in terms of programs such as photoshop etc. where as [sic] I just missed being a capable [sic] with such programs" (Anonymous, Initial Survey, Study ID 180026).

6. New Models of Learning

References to new models of teaching and learning were foremost in the responses. Unlike traditional craft learning methods, which typically involve a student learning from a teacher's demonstrations, all the faculty participants identified as being predominantly self-taught when using digital technology. As Chung-Im Kim explained, "I learned [textile design] through [a] very traditional educational background . . . digital technology I learned from books, online and also from my niece and that became a seed [for] how to approach the students."

Faculty member Greg Sims was exposed to 3D design using digital software while pursuing his masters degree in the UK. The role of teaching yourself or ways in which instructors continue to learn was further explored, as Sims stated:

I was introduced to it there—I don't think I was ever taught . . . From there it became about just learning it on my own and eventually teaching it with the little knowledge that I had and that's really when you learn something is when you have to teach it. With every little problem that students came up with, just finding those solutions gave me a very good understanding of the software.

Faculty also suggested they have observed other models of learning, such as student to student, technician to technician, and online sources such as YouTube videos. Most of the interviewees discussed "learning the hard way" and conversely through play. They also, however, stated that they strive to keep the digital manageable for their students through short demonstrations, guided processes, and step-by-step technical learning, hoping to make it slightly easier for them.

Jewelry students' interest in and adoption of digital technology has varied over time. As Sims said:

Initially asking students to have software running on a laptop became a struggle over time I think students have adapted and understood that this is an important part of their learning we're also figuring out what kind of access to the machines that students can have, whether it's through technicians, with technician assistants, or if there's circumstances where students can start to access it directly and start to learn how to operate that machinery.

As Sims went on to suggest, the physical location of a class could also affect adoption and relevance of digital technology for the students. Three-dimensional design techniques have typically been taught at OCAD U in a computer lab rather than a jewelry studio, which may further emphasize a sense of difference. He described this separation: "When you're teaching and working in a studio [that] doesn't have any of that equipment or doesn't allow you to pull out a laptop then that can be problematic." Does separating digital learning from the craft studio make it harder for students to learn digital skills as a tool for their jewelry design and making?

The final student survey yielded interesting insights about the ways that students perceive they learn digital technology. When asked to rank resources, it was evident that "being shown or discussing digital technologies with the course instructor" was considered the most helpful. The students ranked "licensed resources available through the school (e.g., Lynda.com)" and "watching my peers" as least helpful.

In our institution there has been an administrative push towards online learning, such as comprehensive courses that companies like Lynda.com provide, as an accessible and inexpensive resource. The student survey suggests that they prefer to be shown digital design processes in person.

Autodidacticism or self-teaching and the role of technicians were recurring themes. An interesting observation from technician Darrell Currington was that it takes a year to train a student monitor to be comfortable operating the Rapid Prototyping equipment in a service centre. As he stated, "I'll give them the base safety training [and] then say, 'play around with it, make something that you've always wanted to laser cut' I find that they seem to learn better when they have their own projects in mind."

7. Communication and Agency

One of the most important themes we noted is the issue of agency, control over process. Participants in part one of the study questioned whether students had full control in the making process. As Director of Studios Nick Hooper observed, "We may just not be familiar with how we can mess with some software and processes digitally and how we can tweak things and/or make those . . . mistakes which are so critical to creative processes." Consequently, we ask where can the students make the mistakes Hooper refers to, which are so necessary to deepen learning and engagement, when they are a step removed from the machine? How are they translating their ideas to or through technicians?

Concurrent with agency is the necessary communication to translate ideas and design intentions to others. Technician Darrell Currington noted the need to manage student expectations given the digital equipment available and the limitations of the technology. He further posited that "There has always been a lack of communication between faculty and shops and studios. . . . Faculty just assume that, 'it'll get done,' but there are limitations to the facilities we have in the school."

Following on from managing student expectations around machine capabilities there is also the issue of translating a 2D screen representation into a 3D printed object. As Sims explained:

Initially there is always that big surprise in a discrepancy between what [students] see and what they understand through this two-dimensional sort of flat screen and what actually comes out of it there's always mix ups and scale issues and even just something that looks great on the screen can come out feeling very heavy and awkward.

Technicians report that some faculty members rely heavily on them to help the students translate their ideas while others directly assist students to navigate dimensionality, materiality, and scope when using digital processes.

Limited access to the machines is a barrier to students' ability to manage their own learning; as one student stated categorically, "I would 100% pay extra for the ability to use these machines without first having to chase a tech down between the hours of 10–4 on a Tuesday or whatever—the loss of independence is stressful" (Anonymous, Final Survey, Study ID 180045).

Greg Sims, speaking about the possibility and learning opportunities inherent in a deep understanding of digital affordances, reflected on an experience he had while advising a graduate student who built a 3D ceramic printer from scratch, as part of an exploration of technology in service to craft processes. The student, Samantha Sherer, had a background in jewelry and ceramics. Sims observed that she was initially skeptical about what digital technology could offer but:

Once she got in to actually sort of running the machine it was at that point that she really started to recognize what it meant and what she could do with it so she really saw the possibilities. She had an intimate understanding of the technology that was running it. She knew exactly how the machine was built and therefore if anything went wrong she could fix it. So, at that point then she really kind of jumped in to the possibilities of making and that's where she started to experiment with small little glitches in how something was made.

Another interesting aspect of agency is intentional or unintentional failure. Currington uses this awareness as he navigates his role as a technician who is expected to maintain and operate machines:

Remember that we're an art school and they're here to experiment and learn. That's why I like that we were able to purchase cheaper hobbyist 3D printers . . . [some students] want to see the machine fail, they don't want something successful . . . initially that was a bit of a struggle for me because I'm more technically focused and my job is that the machine never fails.

Marie O'Mahony reflected on aspirations of a manufacturer who was seeking to test the boundaries of their products:

I remember speaking to some manufacturers that were setting up innovation labs back in Frankfurt earlier in the year and they were saying that what they really want to do is work with students who break their machines because that means they've really taken their machines and pushed it to the limits and beyond.

Digital technology always involves a level of collaboration—at the very least with unseen programmers. However, our interviewees identified the need for close communication between students, technicians, and faculty. It is one thing to interact and play with a machine you have direct access to but it is a struggle to work with something you can't see or touch.

8. Conclusion

The project has generated many discoveries and the research team intends to broaden the range of focus to craft-based programs in institutions across Canada. The thoughtfulness and expertise of our participants was extraordinary, making it very

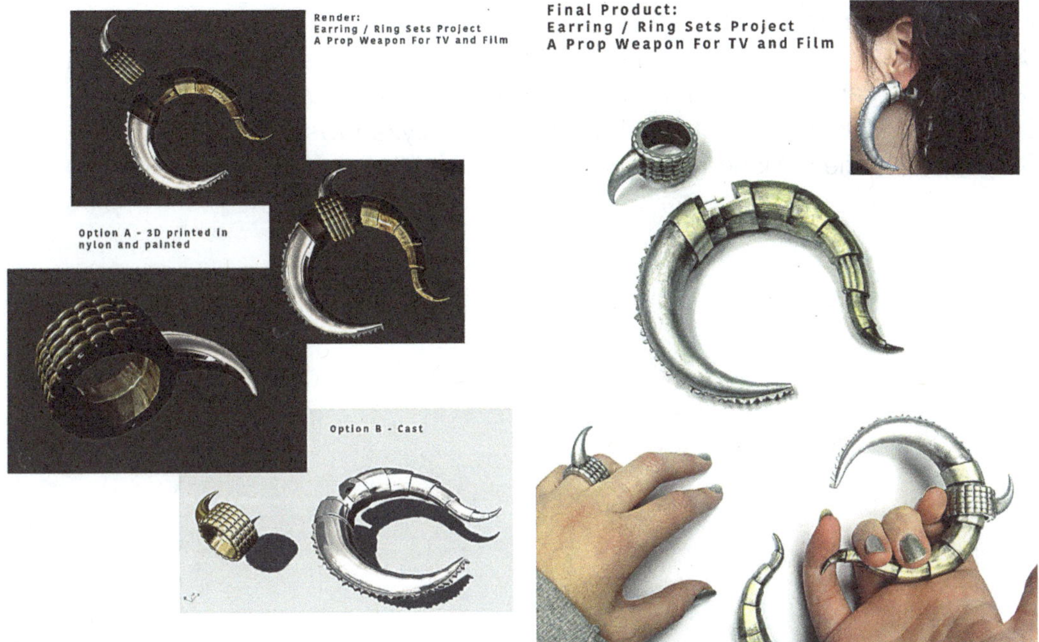

Figure 2. Anonymous, Study ID 180036, Earring/Ring Sets Project: A Prop Weapon for TV and Film, 2018, Instructor Greg Sims, OCAD University.

difficult to pare down our findings and raising more questions for future explorations, such as: how to provide access to self-serve digital equipment; how to understand waste within this context; how to weigh digital gain and analog loss; what impact the increased outsourcing of production will have; how to balance competing demands for space and resources within the institution; and ultimately, whether we are de- or re-skilling students. As Marie O'Mahoney queried, "How do we equip [students] for what they have come in to learn from us . . . how do we futureproof them?"

In our identified themes—Thinking in and Resisting Binaries, Impact of Time, Nostalgia for the Hand, Generational Difference/Bias, New Models of Learning, and Communication and Agency—we have endeavored to reflect the voices of our community. Their unique perspectives have helped us to deepen our understanding of our pedagogical goals and the experiences of our students, technicians, and faculty. We are grateful to all our participants for their candor and generosity.

Acknowledgements
Co-Investigators Cary DiPietro, Travis Freeman, Greg Sims; Research Assistants Claire Bartleman, Keiko Hart, Enna Kim, Ellie Manning; Participants Darrell Currington, Nick Hooper, Chung-Im Kim, Stan Krzyzanowski, Kathleen Morris, Greg Sims, Marie O'Mahony, Laurie Wassink, and the students of MAAD.

References

Adamson, G. 2018. *Fewer, Better Things: The Hidden Wisdom of Objects.* New York: Bloomsbury Publishing. https://www.bloomsbury.com/us/fewer-better-things-9781632869647/.

Alfoldy, S. (ed.) 2007. *Neocraft: Modernity and the Crafts.* Halifax: Press of the Nova Scotia College of Art & Design.

Braverman, H. 1974. *Labor and Monopoly Capital: The Degradation of Work in the Twentieth Century.* New York: Monthly Review Press.

Harrod, T. 2007. *Otherwise Unobtainable: The Applied Arts and the Politics and Poetics of Digital Technology.* In *Neocraft: Modernity and the Crafts*, edited by S. Alfoldy, 225–39. Halifax: Press of the Nova Scotia College of Art & Design.

Jönsson, L., 2007. Rethinking Dichotomies: Crafts and the Digital. In *Neocraft: Modernity and the Crafts*, edited by S. Alfoldy, 240–48. Halifax: Press of the Nova Scotia College of Art & Design.

Labb, A., and E. Neely. 2014. "Making Way for Maker Culture." *EDUCAUSE* 49, no. 2: 58.

Morris, W., and N. Salmon. 1994. *Political Writings: Contributions to Justice and Commonwealth 1883–90.* England: Thoemmes Press.

Press, M., 2007. Handmade Futures: The Emerging Role of Craft Knowledge in Our Digital Culture. In *Neocraft: Modernity and the Crafts*, edited by S. Alfoldy, 249–66. Halifax: Press of the Nova Scotia College of Art & Design.

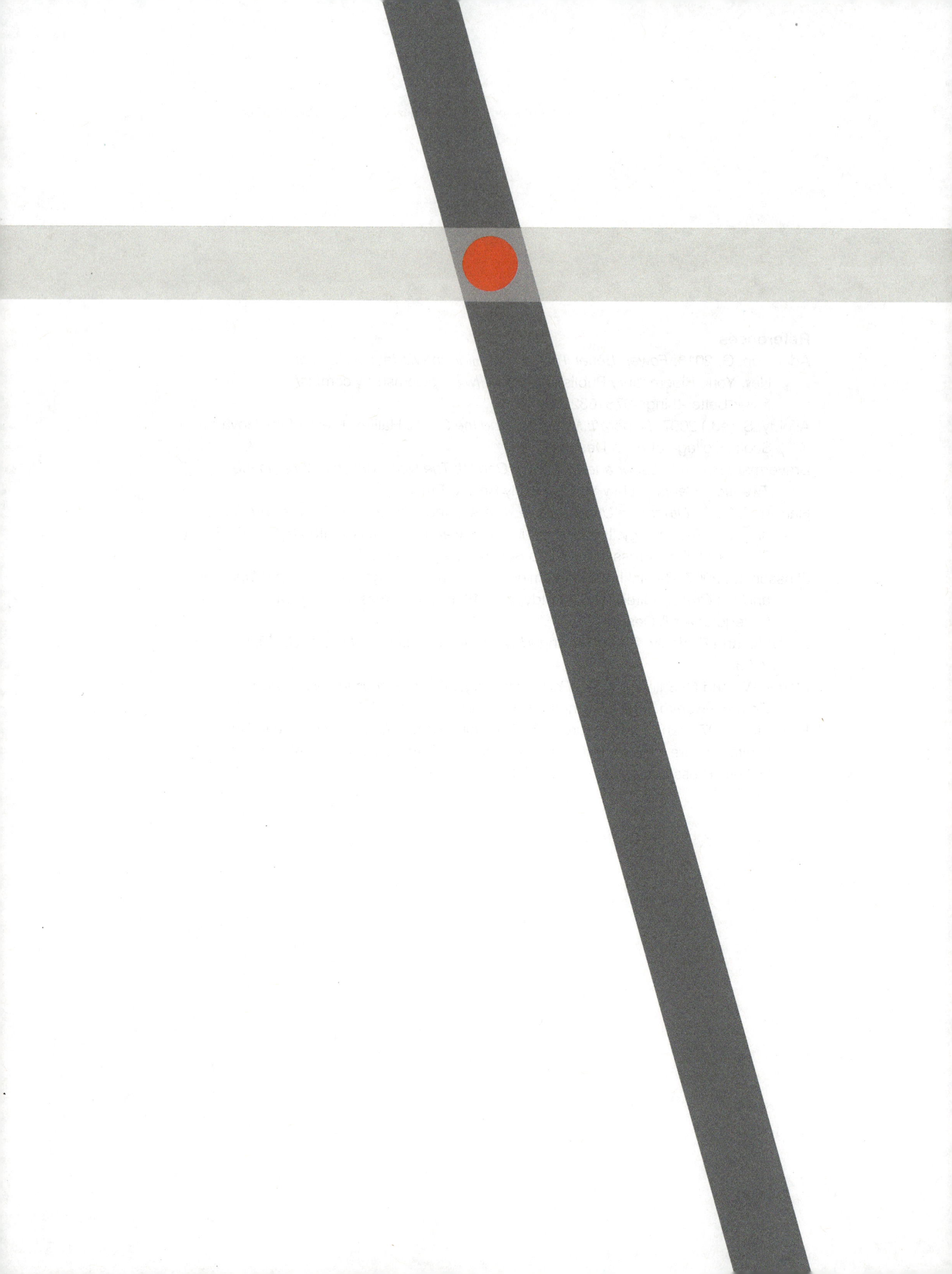

Materializing Humanbeingness in Jewelry through Digital Transformation

Christine Lüdeke, School of Design, Pforzheim University, Germany

Abstract

More efficiency and convenience is a common driver of progress, and similar to the industrial revolution before it, both have played a large part in the advance of the digital revolution. While a focus on improved efficiency in certain contexts brings real benefits and new opportunities, in others it can detract from or even reduce traditionally essential values. In general we are in such a quandary today. On one hand we increasingly recognize the dangers of committing to the seduction of the digital to the exclusion of human-driven and -touched values, resulting in an increased awareness and appreciation of handcraft in the design and fabrication process—whether as one-offs or small or large scale series. At the same time, as we advance through the stages of integrating new technologies (substitution, augmentation, modification, redefinition), this awareness is leading to hybrid approaches between analog and digital, resulting in genuinely interesting advances in design, fabrication, and distribution. Focusing solely on the design potential within the jewelry context, we are currently at the modification stage of integration, using digital technologies in best case scenarios to advance aesthetic languages, ironically still within a classic "tools" context. A close examination of the fundamental definition of "digital" however, reveals a common denominator to a fundamental attribute of jewelry—both in their essence deal with connectivity, creating bridges of understanding and communication that decode abstract behavior. On a basic level, the digital process excels in grasping complex information and through creating abstract patterns (with zeros and ones) enables their translation into more comprehendible mediums. It is this unique quality of creating bridges between the unseeable and the tangible that presents a holistic design potential. More specifically, digital technologies give us the opportunity to explore aspects of being human as points of departure for new hybrid approaches. While already certain digital technologies integrated in jewelry objects reflect aspects of the wearer or the relationship between wearer and environment, and as such influence the design and "behavior" of the jewelry, the hybrid here is more of a combination than a synergetic evolution. State-of-the-art digital technology and its potential make it possible to actually interpret human behavior patterns and attributes and interaction with our environment as a new transformative approach in imagining and designing jewelry. This paper will be looking at uniquely digital processes in exploring aspects of human being and behavior and, combined with currents in craft traditions and the maker movement, proposes a new potential for developing jewelry design languages.

Materializing Humanbeingness in Jewelry through Digital Transformation

The thing about digital is, at some point, everything in the human experience still comes down to be being some type of tactile.

The thing about technology is that we as a species invent it, take it to its extremes, and then incorporate it in a basic, society-shaping way.

Know it, use it, hack it.

Societies have always been shaped more by the nature of the media by which we communicate than by the content of the communication (McLuhan, 1964). In a digital society, the medium becomes the embodiment of the content (Negroponte, 1995, cited in McCullough, 1996).

Humans, being the efficiency-oriented animals we are, create technical developments often based on "improving" and thus replacing traditional technology. The improvement typically focuses on a specific issue such as producing more items in less time. The specific focus on solving a particular issue inevitably raises new conundrums, such as a nuanced question of value, the role of humankind, or the relationship between what is made, the maker, and the user. We continue to experiment with and push the boundaries of the available technology, letting our curiosity squeeze every drop from the possibilities. To paraphrase Descartes (or continue his train of thought): I exist, therefore I make. This specific pattern—substitution, augmentation, modification, and then redefinition[1]—is how we as a species, and Western society specifically, deal with new and persuasive technologies.

The first stage—substitution—is, as it's name suggests, a one-to-one application of new technology within a specific context. An early example of this is the

1 SAMR, a framework developed by Dr. Ruben Puentedura showing the impact of teaching and learning new technologies, also works as a description of how societies as a whole deal with and integrate new technology.

development of the handcraft tools and processes we look at as traditional today. At one time, a hammer was state-of-the-art new technology, enabling humans to exert more power on manipulating material, than hitherto with just our hands. This is technology applied at its most fundamental—as an extension and amplification of what humans (can) make, enabling us to realize our (not yet recognized) potential. So first we substitute, replacing traditional methods and processes with ones defined by the new technology. Our reference is what we know; initially the goal is not to change the forms we make but rather how we make them—quicker, more precise, more efficient. The function of the applied new technology is the same as the one it replaces.

Unsurprisingly, as all tools and technology each have a distinct character, these leave traces—be it the anonymity of perfection, the possibility of new forms, or the ability to work with new materials, until now not possible. Thus in the augmentation stage we begin to add on to the direct tool substitute, discovering and adding new functions and abilities inherent in the new technology's DNA. These include new formal languages and using inherent qualities such as ease of repetition for specific, design-defining actions, all the while remaining within the specific context of the application, such as forming material.

As we learn what the new technologies can do beyond the initial role they were developed for, we enter the third stage, where we begin to modify not only how we use them but also the contexts within which we position our understanding of the technology as well as of design. For example, 3D printing has superseded it's role as efficient intermediate step to being end-use manufacturing, and as a result introduces not just new materialities but also has the potential to change the relationship between making and the end user. This coupled with the democratization of this technology and the advent of maker labs has contributed to a new understanding of what a final material can—and can't—be, as well as placing digital technologies squarely into the handcraft purview.

Craftsmen have always had the tendency to personalize their tools, to appropriate them by honing, modifying, or expanding them. In the early phases of digital technology, a digital design program was imposed upon designers, quite soon confronting them with limitations within the program, and thus exerting a disproportionate control on how and what was designed. Until relatively recently the programs were also mainly closed source, so difficult to adjust and modify to one's personal needs. With the advent of open source, it is becoming more possible to hack the digital possibilities and create, similar to traditional craftsmen, one's personalized digital tools. This has led to the designer being able to intervene directly into the production process—and therefore also in the eventual design, harkening back to the general principles of craft. Thus computer-aided design (CAD) and 3D manufacturing processes are no longer solely part of a process; they are increasingly becoming a partner in the evolution of design languages and the maker user relationship. This also includes combination and hybrid processes with an unencumbered interaction between digital and analog techniques. The jewelry field is currently in this phase and will continue plumbing its depths, with these approaches and capabilities most likely becoming part of our collective designer and craftsman's toolbox.

And yet, as the integration process is not a consecutively linear but rather an overlapping phenomenon, we as a society are currently entering the final, redefinition stage in parallel. While on the one hand this entails the expected pendulum swing to a more discriminating analysis of the digital and it's effect on our lives, it also embraces a creative understanding and exploring of what this technology can do, inherent to its own capabilities, and not just as an extension or development of existing technologies and our historical relationship to them. Part of understanding this is to look at what digital fundamentally means.

Digital basically means describing phenomena within a system of numerical values attributed to them. Simplifying the binary number system to zero and one allows for an easier and more efficient implementation (Lister et al., 2003)—a classic example of pattern recognition and application.

The binary code traces back to 2000 BC and the abacus, in essence predating human industrial civilization. The jacquard weaving card (developed in early nineteenth century) is recognized as an important physical step leading to the highly complex development of binary code application. Thus on a basic level, this means the digital process excels in grasping complex information and through creating abstract patterns (with zeros and ones) enables their translation into more accessible mediums. Taken at face value, this does not mean that to be digital designs, for example, have to created in a CAD environment, 3D printed or use digital capabilities as a source of quantitative measuring and feedback. The latter reduces "digital" to the lowest common denominator and limited understanding of what it is—its reduction to the most easy and direct association is co-opted as a design signifier that in turn reinforces and propagates that simplistic definition. "Smart" bracelets and their ilk and are common representatives of this prevalent thinking.

However, regarding "digital" more abstractly as the unique ability for creating bridges between the unseeable and the tangible, transforming complex phenomena into comprehensible entities, is where it really gets interesting.

Then this sounds familiar.

What is jewelry if not a tangible, haptic interpersonal bridge conveying the intangible emotions and points of view that make us human? It is no coincidence, that to adorn oneself predated the development of clothing, not only in the context of physical but also psychological and metaphorical protection, communication, and definition of standing within a specific social group. As is often noted, jewelry in its essence works on a communicative iconic level, quoting but in the best sense also transcending cultural and social codes. While the game rules change according to context, this essence is the same whether as part of the democratic principle of multiples and series jewelry or revered as a one-off unique statement by a specific artisan. It communicates and creates access—both visually and haptically—in a dialog with the body. Not only in that it is worn on the body, but also in how it interacts with it.

Recognizing that the body is not wholly independent of a specific environment, jewelry often takes on the role of specific, under-the-skin cultural and social commentary. In that jewelry is worn, the body acts as an amplifier of that which it seeks to express, from an interplay between material and form in relation to the wearer's point of view, to simply expressing the joy of being alive.

The success of this expression is closely tied to a sensitive and commanding understanding of handcraft principles. Traditional craftsmanship is still considered by many a keystone in the culture of making. *Tékhnē* (Greek for "art, handicraft" and at the root of the word "technique") refers to the rational method involved in making an object, implying the principle of knowledge over matter and the application of a skill that is fundamental to its development (Pye, 1968). Craft involves an ongoing manipulation of material with a specific skill set and the intimate knowledge of particular materials, practical arts, and techniques, the application of which intrinsically manifest the character of the resulting artifacts.

This becomes—in addition to the underlying concept—a defining factor in the nature of the pieces. The aesthetics and feel of the jewelry object are important for the wearer because of how they connect to their own subjective experiences. So one could say, craft is defined as much by the user as the maker or process involved does. There is a holistic, symbiotic relationship in defining craft between the subjectivity of the processes that determined it and the outcome and how it is experienced by the non-maker as well as the maker. Craft is a humanistic endeavor—the maker's attention to detail and caring about the result leads directly to the maker also caring about the user. It is a direct individual-to-individual transfer, affirming our human existence with each other.

It is at this intersection of reasserting humanism that the next-level potential of what we call digital technology presents itself. If we consider digital at its most fundamental to be a technical way of capturing and communicating complex (including unseen) information, then early photography, as has been well documented, is a godfather of digital perception, on the cusp between virtual and analog, analog referring here to the process in which one set of physical properties can be stored or conveyed in another "analogous" form (Lister et al., 2003). The new "form" is subjected to cultural coding that allows the original properties to be, as it were, recreated for the viewer, who may be physically separated from the original. The recreation thereof in itself adds a layer of abstraction, thus augmenting the viewer's experience beyond the original, through the maker's personal experiences as well as those of the viewer.

A mitigating factor in confirming our existence is through experiencing our environment, involving active and reactive interaction with each other and our surroundings. How I make a mark—and with which part of my body—defines in the moment who I am in relation to myself and this interspatial context. We are in a perpetual sensorial exchange with ourselves and that which surrounds us. We constantly displace the invisible material of our environment solely through our movement—defining not just us but impacting as well consciously or subconsciously our environment. All our perceptions and resulting cognitions are mediatized through our bodily experience.

We experience this space—this mutual feedback of existence—through our senses. What is of interest within the context of this paper are the senses that go beyond the classic exteroceptive senses (visual, auditory, olfactory, gustatory, and tactile/haptic) with which we interpret the world around us. These are the interoceptive (which help us understand what is going on inside our bodes and include senses for blood pressure, temperature, and pain perception) and proprioceptive, related to the sense of movement and balance that informs our awareness of body position in space, also known as kinesthesia. As Salter (2016) notes, the immersive nature for example of contemporary art operates not just in sense categories, but on the body itself. Artists who work with interoceptive senses create new ways of expressing their intentions and for the recipient of their work to experience them. A much larger palette, encompassing complex layers of the human experience, is investigated and played with. This goes far beyond the classic dualities of vision and audio, vision and touch, smell and taste.

Digital media translate the notion of three-dimensional space into the virtual realm and thus open up new dimensions for relations between form and space . . . the trans-physical aspect of the virtual environment changes traditional modes of experience that are initially defined by gravity, scale, material, etc" (Paul, 2013, p. 8).

The cross- and multimedia basis of digital art endows it with a strong spatio temporal structure. Its aesthetic makeup has traditionally integrated fundamental features of motion in that it alters space and time. The aesthetic media transformations that define these spatio-temporal shifts often take place from one sensory modality to another (Gsöllpointner et al., 2016). The binary nature of the digital propagates such sensorial dualism, not just accelerating the complex interdependent processes of stimuli, sensation, and perception but allows artists another level of capturing stimuli and transferring them into digital but also analog form. A type of digital synesthesia—Gsöllpointner and colleagues (2016) also call it a sense of empathy —is created. The ability to change perspectives—literally and metaphorically. The post-digital approach of bringing the digital to a physical world is included: "neo-materiality often highlights this condition by turning code and abstraction into the material framework of an object" (Paul, 2015, p. 553). As with traditional craft, in which the attuned craftsman asks, "What can this medium do?" as much as "What do I wish to do with this medium?" (McCullough, 1996, p. 199), embracing the fundamental attributes of the digital as a medium like any other in one's palette allows the contemporary artist and designer to use its intrinsic advantages sensitively and appropriately—and to continuously experiment with and form it.

Thus we begin to see that we can use digital technologies to read and capture essences of being human that are not graspable through traditional craft technology. The hybrid manifestation of these digital qualities in the physical world, for example the convergence of the digital and the analog into tactile objects in connection with the body, is the potential for new aesthetic languages and interactions between jewelry and the maker, jewelry and the wearer, and between the wearer, the jewelry, and the observer. Hybridization takes on additional new meanings in digital and post-digital contexts, embracing according to Alexenberg (2011) "art forms that address the humanization of digital technologies through interplay between digital, biological, cultural, and spiritual systems . . . between high tech and high touch experiences, between visual, haptic, auditory, and kinesthetic media experiences."

As a designer it's not (only) about designing the final object, but about (also) designing the system, the philosophy that allows the object to be made. The gamut is wide between transforming (digitally) visualized phenomena into material (e.g.,

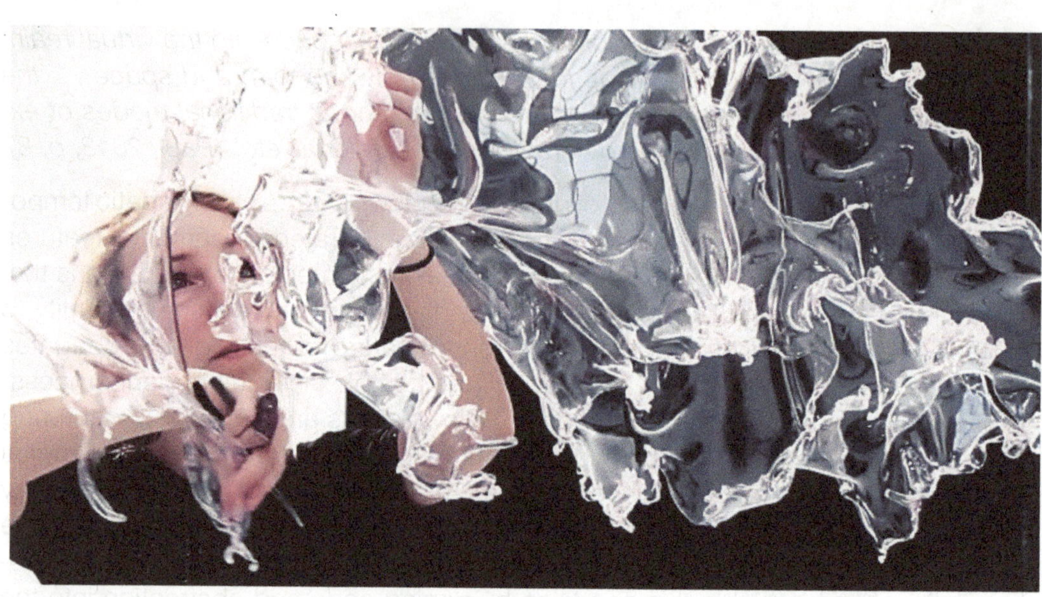

Figure 1. Iris Van Herpen, 2013, SPLASH Project SHOWstudio. Vidoe still: SHOWstudio.

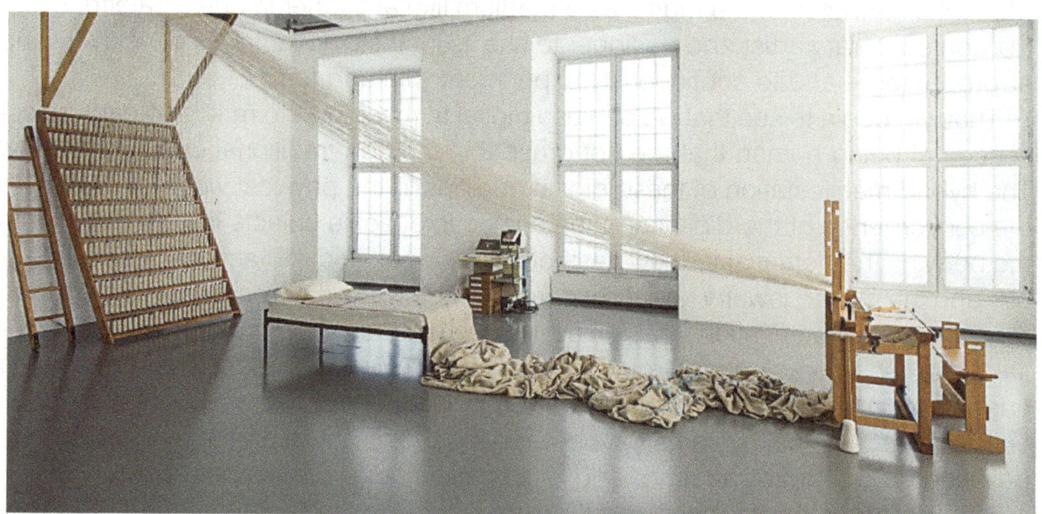

Figure 2. Janine Antoni, 1993, Slumber, Dokumenta 14, Collection National Museum of Contemporary Art, Athens, Installation view, ANTIDORON, The EMST Collection, Fridericianum, Kassel. Photo: Nils Klinger.

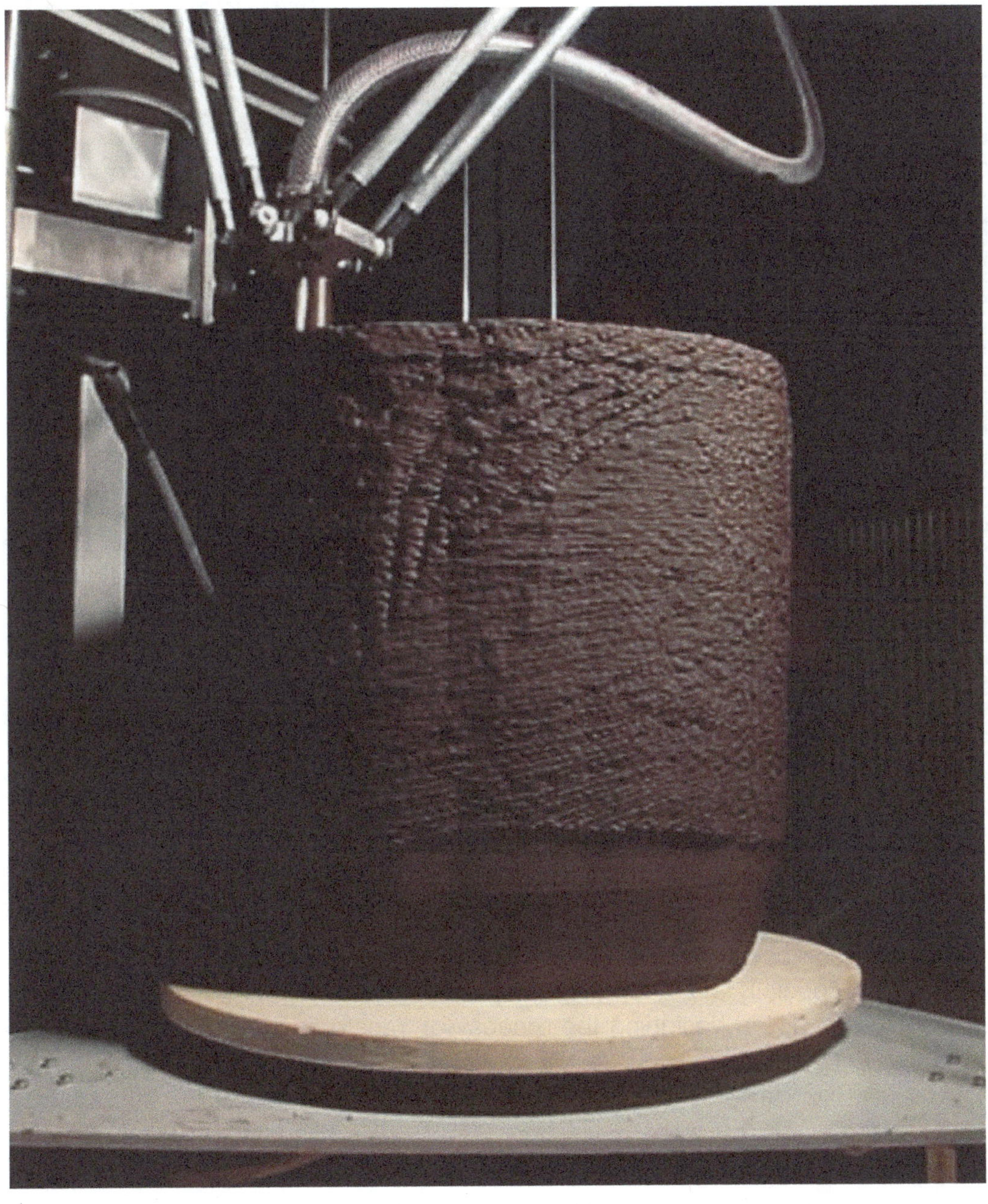

Figure 3. Oliver Van Herpt and Sander Wassink, 2015, Adaptive Manufacturing, Vibration Printer. Video still: Van Herpt/Wassink.

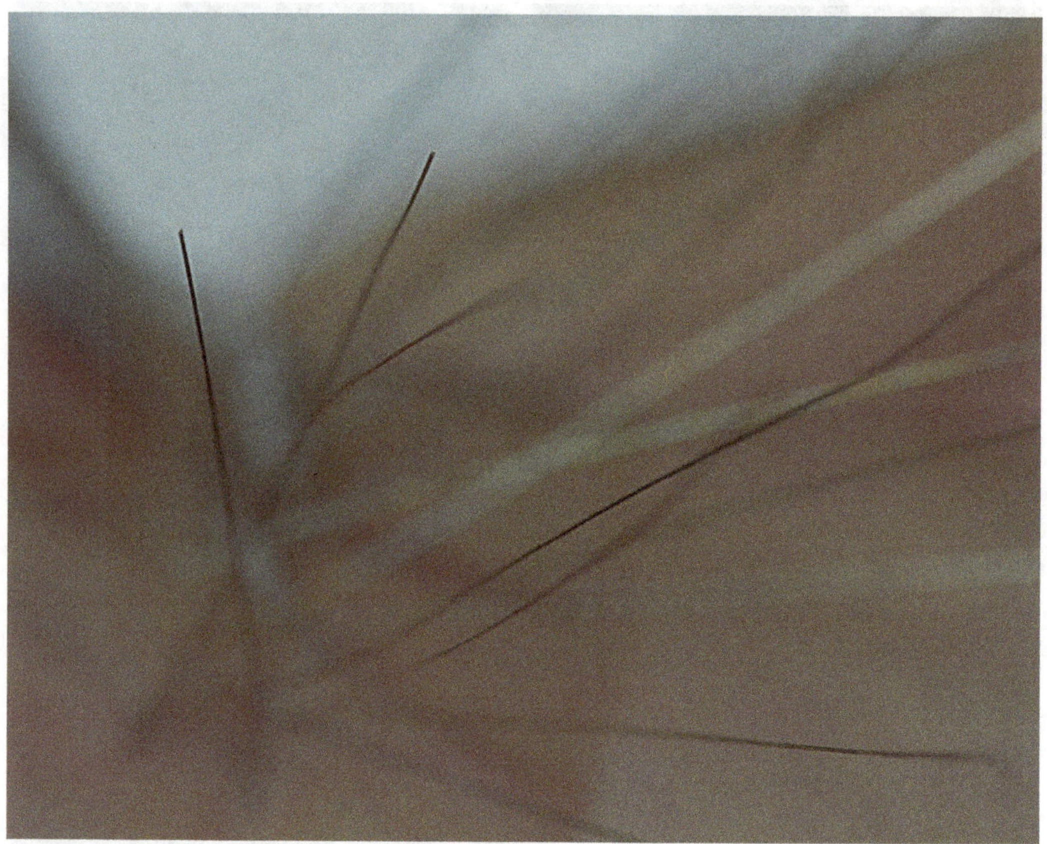

Figure 4. Eva Knoch, 2018. Atmungsaktiv.
Photo: E. Knoch.

Van Herpen[2]) or using them as part of the crafting tools (e.g., Antoni,[3] Van Herpt/Wassink[4]). Especially the latter is gaining interest and experimentation in the art and objects world. In designing the process of transformation, creating the rules

2 Iris Van Herpen, 2013, SPLASH Project SHOWstudio. Using stereoscopic photography of water splashing on a body, Van Herpen manipulates material to achieve that visual effect an repositions it back onto the body. See figure 1.

3 Janine Antoni, 1993, Slumber. Harnessing the REM brain waves while sleeping to manipulate a jacquard weaving machine, Antoni creates a blanket "woven of dreams" for the dreamer as she sleeps. See figure 2.

4 Olivier Van Herpt and Sander Wassink, 2015, Adaptive Manufacturing, Vibration Printer. Taking up vibrations of the Earth to guide the ceramic extrusion 3D printer, Van Herpt and Wassink create topographical structures in a vessel made of clay (earth)—Earth to earth. See figure 3.

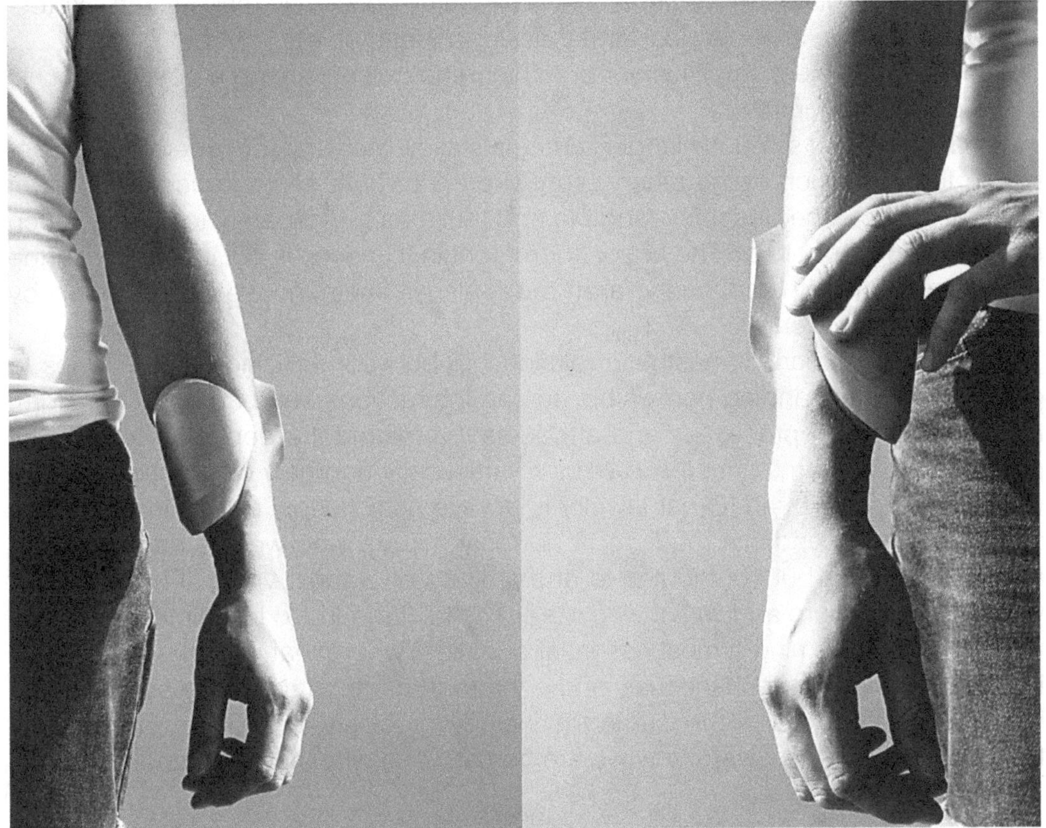

Figure 5. Johanna Seibert, 2019, Touch Hunger.
Photo: J. Seibert.

of play, the designer imparts a craft sensibility that converges the abstract binary data with the potential of not just experimenting with new visual languages but also formal relationships to the body.

Preliminary jewelry research projects at Pforzheim University are exploring amplifying states of the human experience through a symbiotic relationship between digital technology and craft sensibilities. For example, Eva Knoch aestheticizes the small but indisputable movements that our bodies constantly make as an expression of being alive in her project Atmungsaktiv (Breathable).[5]

The material object amplifies our breathing and pulse, lending a poetic dynamic to the physical adornment.

Johanna Seibert's Touch Hunger[6] bracelets allow the wearer of one of the bracelets to feel the touch of the other, even when not in the same space—the act of thinking of someone becomes tangible and thus has the capacity to literally touch the one being thought of. The act of adornment in this case is not just external (the visual shape of the object on the arm) but is also intimate, not seen—felt solely by the recipient, the wearer.

It is this holistic and synesthetic relationship between utilizing digital means to grasp and understanding non-visible human interactions and haptically transform them through craft processes and attributes that plumb the depths of true digital potential. At the same time it allows us to artistically find new connections to that which makes us human. Great jewelry is always both deeply rooted in and at the same time transcends its medium. It not only mirrors who we are as individuals and as a society, but contributes to and shapes on a most visceral level the development of culture and with it who we are, what it means to be human. At a time where this is becoming a most essential question, where that what we as humans invent and develop simultaneously and perversely contributes to a lessening of our humanity, we can utilize this same technology precisely to explore and express through jewelry in new ways why we are human. And why that is a good thing.

5 Eva Knoch, 2018, Atmungsaktiv. The fine wires of the jewelry pieces take up and amplify the body's quiet moments of breathing and pulse. See figure 4.

6 Johanna Seibert, 2019, Touch Hunger. Incorporating bluetooth and Arduino, when one wearer touches their bracelet, the other feels a vibration on their skin on the inside of their bracelet. See figure 5.

References

Alexenberg, M. 2011. *The Future of Art in a Postdigital Age: From Hellenistic to Hebraic Consciousness*. 2nd ed. Bristol: Intellect Ltd.

Gsöllpointner, K., R. Schnell, and R. Schuler. (eds.) 2016. *Digital Synesthesia: a Model for the Aesthetics of Digital Art*. Berlin: De Gruyter.

Labaco, R.T. (ed.) 2013. *Out of Hand: Materializing The Postdigital*. Museum of Arts and Design, London, UK: Black Dog Publishing.

Lister, M., J. Dovey, S. Giddings, I. Grant, and K. Kelly. 2003. *New Media: A Critical Introduction*. 2nd ed. New York: Routledge.

McCullough, M. 1996. *Abstracting Craft: The Practiced Digital Hand*. Cambridge, MA: MIT Press.

McLuhan, M. 1994. *Understanding Media: The Extensions of Man*. Cambridge, MA: MIT Press.

Paul, C. 2013. "Objecthoods from the Desktop." In *Out of Hand: Materializing The Postdigital. Museum of Arts and Design*, edited by R.T. Labaco, 8–13. London, UK: Black Dog Publishing.

Paul, C., 2015. *Immateriality to Neo Materiality: Art and the Conditions of Digital Materiality*. In *ISEA 2010 Vancouver (proceedings of the 21st International Symposium on Electronic Art)*, 255-555. Vancouver, Canada.

Pye, D. 1968. *The Nature and Art of Workmanship*. Cambridge, UK: Cambridge University Press.

Salter, C. 2016. "Sensing Digital Art: Aesthetic Acts Beyond (the Two) Synthesia(s)." in *Digital Synesthesia: a Model for the Aesthetics of Digital Art*, edited by K. Gsöllpointner, R. Schnell, and R. Schuler, 59–64. Berlin: De Gruyter.

Further Reading

Adamson, G. (ed.) 2010. *The Craft Reader*. Oxford, UK: Berg.

Hatch, M. 2013. *The Maker Movement Manifesto: Rules for Innovation in the New World of Crafters, Hackers, and Tinkerers*. Columbus, OH: McGraw-Hill Books.

Hope, C., and J.C. Ryan. 2014. *Digital Arts: An Introduction to New Media*. UK: Bloomsbury Publishing PLC.

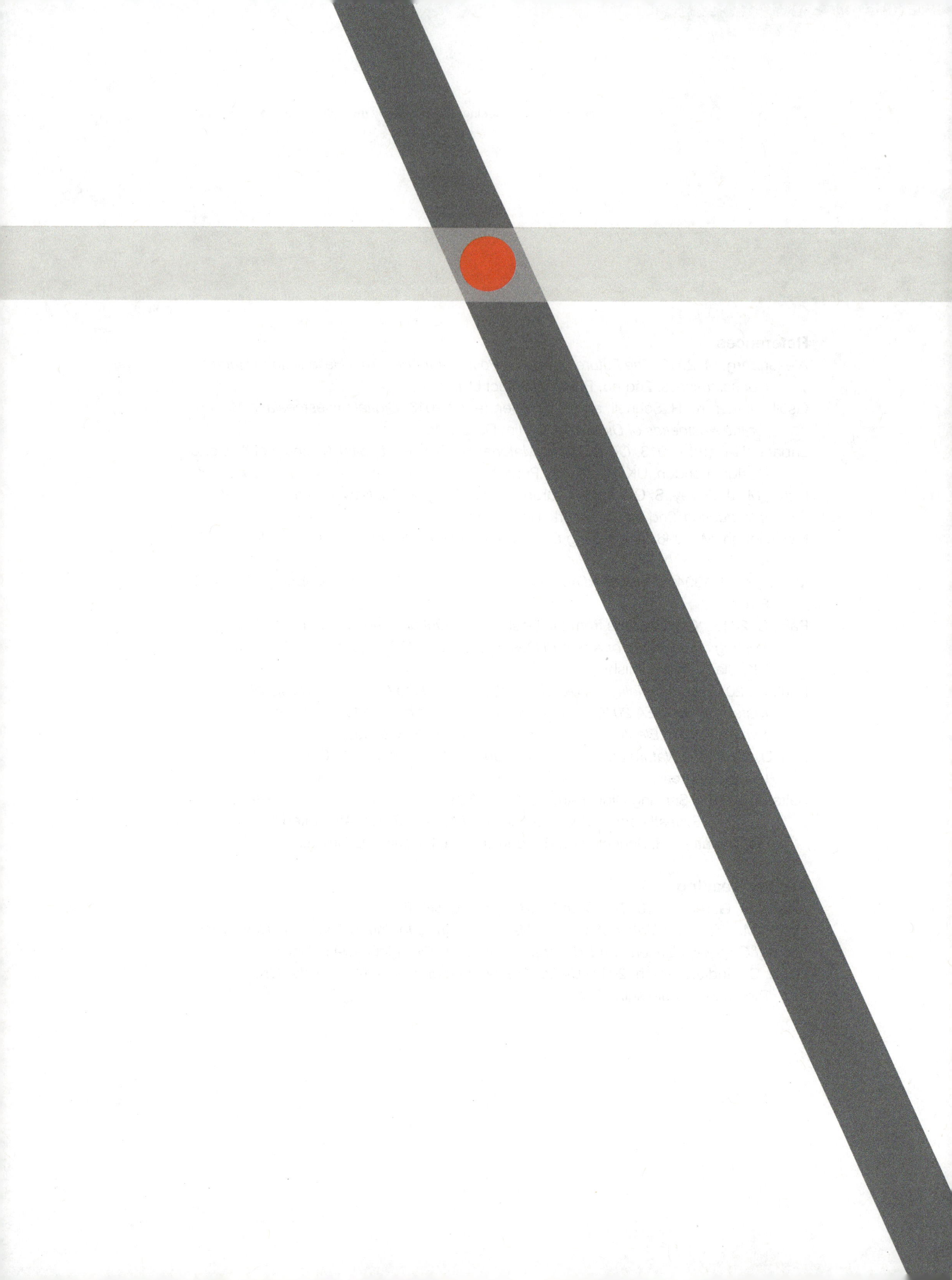

Hand vs. Machine: Three Methods of Jewellery Making

Kadri Mälk, Estonian Academy of Arts, Tallinn, Estonia
Sofia Hallik, Estonian Academy of Arts, Tallinn, Estonia

Abstract
In the contemporary context there is a mutation of some sort happening to jewellery as one of the most physical and material of all the art forms by means of its absorption into cyberspace and its interrelation with the Machine. That is exactly why the concepts of digital craft and handwork lie at the heart of this paper.

It is very beneficial to have new technologies coming in because it opens up the scope of what we can do, but it is fundamentally important before that to learn making things without a machine. On the one hand, machine and technology are "spiritualized" by some researchers and makers as if it was a living being, on the other hand, some have handwork on the foreground. This conflict carries a highly intriguing nature and is similar to the conflict that occurred during the emergence of photography. Benjamin states that "earlier much futile thought had been devoted to the question of whether photography is an art. The primary question—whether the very invention of photography had not transformed the entire nature of art—was not raised" (Benjamin, W., 1969, p. 8).

What if both hand and machine could have really blended in a ready object? Digital craft represents the idea of a work that comes from the digital environment but is still highly crafted, work that comes from the skilful combination of a hand with the machine, in which both digital and craft are 100 percent complementary to each other. Using these concepts, it is possible to define the influence of digital technology on the essence of jewellery and also answer the question of what happens in between when digital and physical, immaterial and material meet.

1. Kadri Mälk: the Trace of Fingers

We invest a kind of psychic energy in a piece of jewellery we make, while inputting our efforts, time, attention—and love!—in making of the piece. Such energy might be seen as part of the self, since their origin, where the work is grown out of, is the

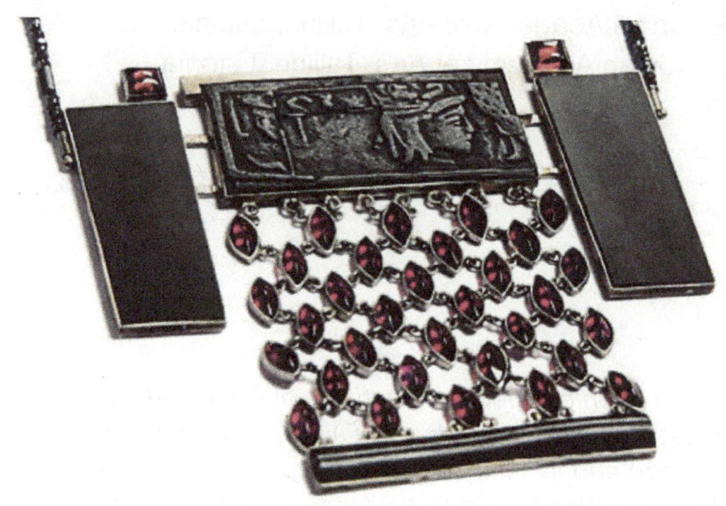

Figure 1. Kadri Mälk, Invisible Hands, neckpiece, 2006. Photo credit: Tiit Rammul.

self. The human self is mostly imperfect. So, an almost invisible imperfection can make the piece!

Handmade objects are unique as they are charged with their maker's spirit and energy, the fingertips' touch, and when passed on to another person, some of the energy is transformed, the extension of the maker's self is transmitted in an unmediated way. The belief in affinity, in shared sensibility, as we respond to handmade objects in an unconditional way, and feel cheated by the manufactured objects, is vaguely lost.

The significance of the hand-made object is often kind of highlighted. The handmade object bears the witness of the human hand that shaped it, and brought it into life. In contrast to factory-made objects that bear no trace or witness to the machine that made them, and in a sense represent the impersonal, the objects that were made by hand carry within them the memory of their maker, a piece of themselves. There is a great intimacy between the maker of the object and the object they make, and this intimacy is felt once again when another person's hand touches the object. Contact magic, sympathetic magic. Simply put, the law of personal contact, personal touch.

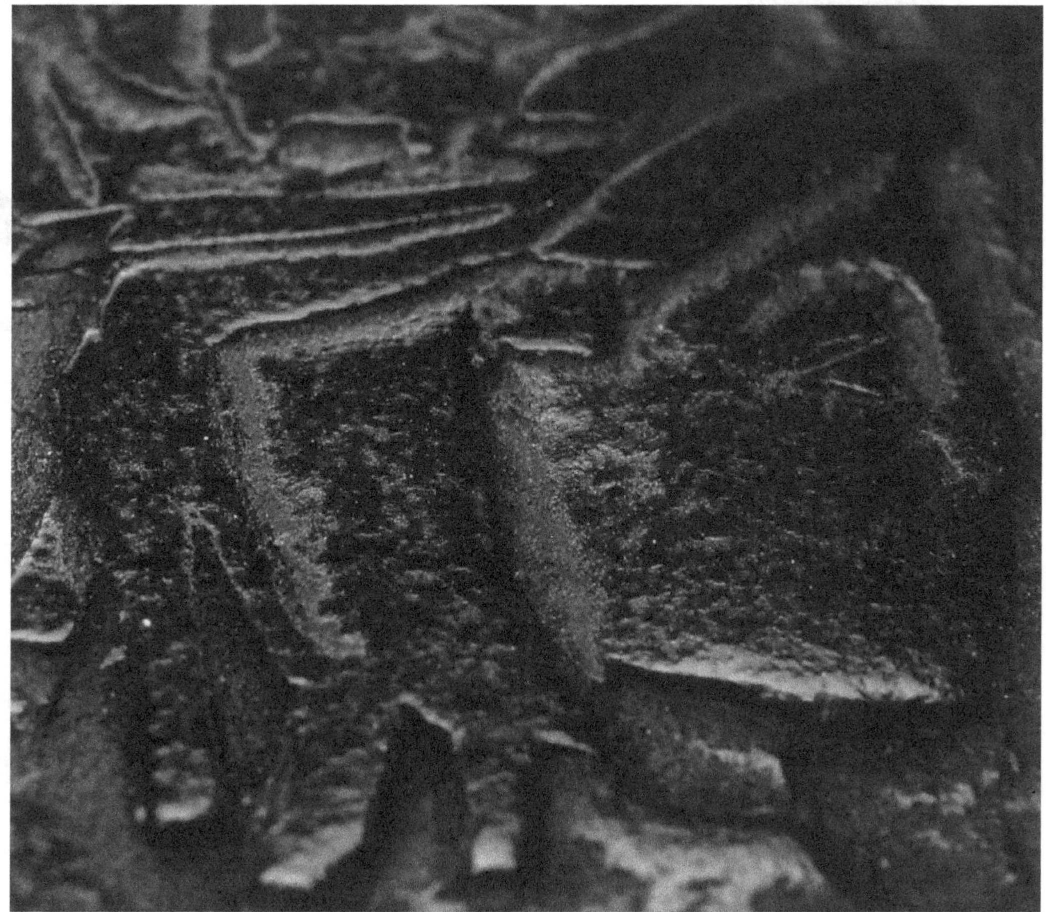

Figure 2. Kadri Mälk, Invisible Hands, neckpiece fragment, 2006. Photo credit: Tiit Rammul.

The quiet slow acts of the hand have created the world we live in. All handmovements can be sensed as archaic. Their speed and precision may have grown, but the purpose is the same. The glory of the human hand—is it a consistent magnitude? The real greatness of the hands lies in their patience. But how did the hands acquire their patience? How did the fingers get their fine sensations?

Monkeys turn fingers into the fine instruments as we feel them today. The finger-exercises of monkeys are the oldest we know. We thought that rummaging in a friend's hair has the practical purpose to find something, but as a matter of fact

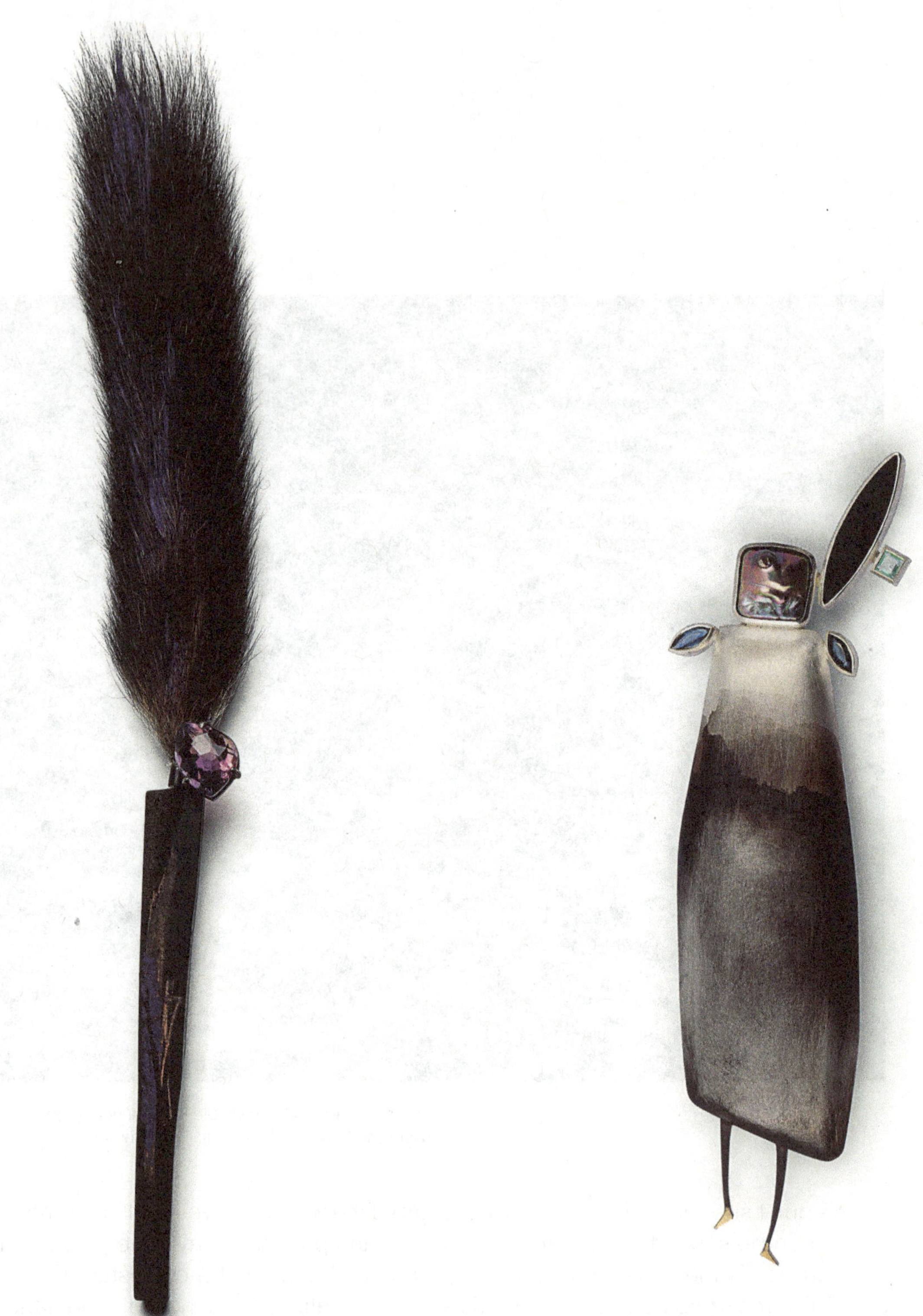

Figure 3. Kadri Mälk, Unfaithful Julia, brooch, 2019, 300 mm, ebony, silver, ametrine, paint, tail of a black fox, courtesy of Maria Mägi, Estonia. Photo credit: Tiit Rammul.

Figure 4. Kadri Mälk, Manfred, brooch, 2014–15, 115 mm, silver, gold, paint, pearl, onyx, emerald, sapphires, tears. Photo credit: Tiit Rammul.

and the monkeys are driven by the nice feeling created by the fingers in their hair. This requires well-coordinated fingers, a precision and convergence of the eyes.

The sensitivity of fingers developed at the same time as their strength. Tool making developed in tandem. Human beings invented tools to extend what hands could make—but in the final instance, every tool must respond to the hand.

2. Sofia Hallik: Digital Craft

WOA (work of art) is an acronym (Foreman, 2014) used in cyberspace correspondence, allowing its participants to expedite and therefore make the process of communication more effective. Along with 2G2BT (too good to be true), 2EZ (too easy), and IVL (in virtual life), WOA is basically, but not solely popular among the Internet Generation which "refers to a generation that has had access to the Internet from an early age . . . known as the Millennial Generation, born between the early 1980s to 2000" (Foreman, 2014, p. 58). Such technophiles (although it would be unwise to bind relation to technologies by generational framework—lots of people, including artists and researchers, born before the 80s can be considered as technophiles) work with technologies rapidly both in the workspace and social areas, while their adaptation to binary codes seems an absolutely natural course of events.

In my PhD research (supervisors Prof. Kadri Mälk and Dr. Jaak Tomberg) I study the influence of digital technologies, such as computer-aidd design (CAD), 3D scanning, 3D printing, and glitch, on jewellery, which is one of the most ancient arts and crafts. All the way through the twentieth century, jewellery is still one of the tools that allow us to emphasize the beauty of the material and the refinement of its treatment. Jewellery is composed of many techniques, just to mention a few of them: forging, casting, repoussé, chasing, stamping, engraving, filigree, granulation, niello, enamelling, and metal inlay. Through the millennia, humankind has studied these crafts and passed knowledge from one generation to another. According to Jean-Jacques Rousseau (1979), the process of creating a piece of art is what influences the author. Therein lies the difference between handwork and the usage of the machine. For example, handwork often implies more "intimate" relations between author and WOA, given that in this kind of link only the material, the author, and the WOA are engaged.

material—artist—WOA

However, in the contemporary context there is a mutation of some sort happening to jewellery, as one of the most physical and material of all the art forms, by means of its absorption into the digital world and its interrelation with the machine. The machine here means digital technologies, for example CAD, 3D printing, and CNC milling, that refer to the presence of computation—the use of computers, especially as a subject of research or study. Technological development gave birth to the machine that was able to assist, complement, or replace hand; the reliance on the machine is often described negatively, associating it with mechanization and capitalism (and by hand I infer any handwork that includes different material processing techniques; I would also like to point out that the use of a hammer or an electric drill, for example, also pertains to handwork). This machine embodies mass production that is opposite to craft. The topic here is the application of the machine to handcraft, specifically, the application of modern digital technologies by designers and artists. I aim to analyse the changes in jewellery making and perception that are the result of technological development; I aim to explore skills, working methods and approaches emerging from digital craft and intertwining relations between handwork and the machine.

What interests me the most is not the answer to the question *how* the object was made, but *what happens* in the process of its creation by using:

- the hand exclusively
- the hand and the machine in equal proportions
- the machine exclusively

In the following I will refer to these methods as follows: handwork, hybrid work, and machine production.

The aforementioned "what happens" is related first and foremost to the author's vision/attitude. I would like to focus on mundane things in the life of an artist, things we don't pay attention to, dismissing them usually as casual or banal. I would also like to differentiate those things by *modus operandi*.

These include skills that are necessary for different kinds of work, the author's vision appropriated in the process of WOA creation, and also the positioning of the artist's inner self to the outside world.

What also interests me is how exactly does one specific method influence the selection of materials and techniques used in the process of making jewellery, and how does the context frame the usage of materials and techniques. In other words, what can be made using only digital technologies, what we cannot achieve using only the hand, and vice versa? And also, what are the difficulties and advantages associated with hybrid work?

At the heart of this practice-based research lies the body of work (jewellery or/and series of objects) that is the result of the aforementioned processes: handwork, hybrid work and machine production. Therefore, I will try not only to answer the question, "Does the outer appearance of jewellery change (and if it does, then in what way)?" but also, does the jewellery's function and objective change after the implementation of digital technologies?

One of the aims of my research is to clarify the impact of the digital on the essence of jewellery in general, as well as the impact on jewellery making, representation,

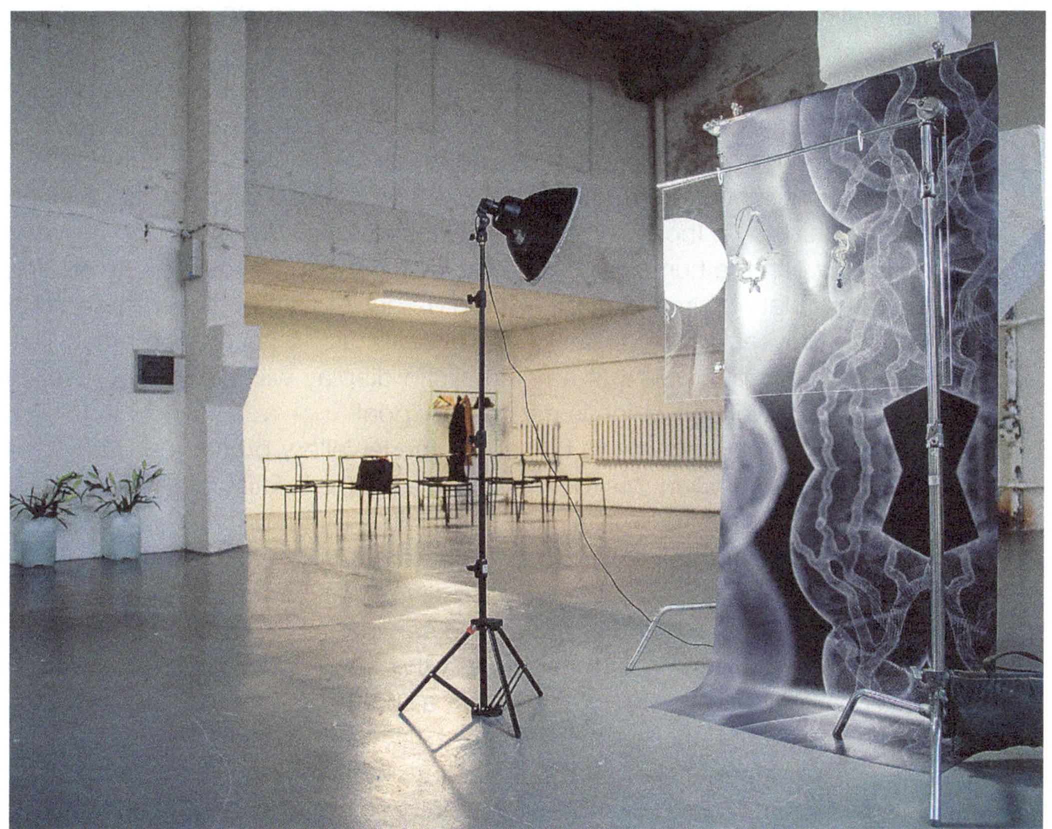

Figure 5. Sofia Hallik, Tangibility Matters display, 2018, ARS project room. Photo credit: Sofia Hallik.

and perception. This research is directly connected with my creative work, to be more exact, the jewellery that I create using digital technologies and/or hands. The primary focus of the given research is on the creation of a body of work that consists of three types of jewellery, reflecting the essence of handwork, hybrid work and machine production (of the WOA). In this way it will be possible to research in practice the influence of digital technologies on the process of jewellery creation. It will also be possible to analyse the influence of this process on the author.

3. Sofia Hallik: Peer-Reviewed Exhibition, "Tangibility Matters"

The second solo peer-reviewed exhibition that was part of my PhD project took place in the Tallinn ARS project room on November 15 and 16, 2018. It is important to point out that the series of jewellery is the central element of the given exhibition. At first, this may seem obvious, but we can't leave out the fact that we usually experience an exhibition as a whole. Besides the objects themselves, the way of displaying, the location, and the printouts also affect the experience of the exhibition. During my work I encountered an unexpected problem: a predominance of the mode of presentation over the jewellery itself. I looked for a way to support the idea of closeness between the human and the machine through the display by adding digital screens, digital pictures, and by using a drone. At some point I realised that I want to position myself as a jewellery artist and not as an installation artist. This way I arrived at the conclusion that a minimalistic display will allow the viewer to concentrate on the jewellery, which is my primary goal.

It is inexplicably difficult for me to talk about the jewellery presented during the "Tangibility Matters" exhibition. Maybe this is because the tactility of a given object is more important for me than words. Half of the time spent on making the jewellery passed in a digital space where 3D models were created and 3D printing took place. This in turn isolated me from the possibility of applying my handwork skills to jewellery making. Up to a point I required the services of a 3D printing company (3D Koda OÜ), but as it turned out, aside from the absence of tactility, I was deprived of the possibility of observing and above all controlling the printing process, and this confused me greatly.

During the "Digital Meets Handmade: Jewellery in the Twenty-First Century" international symposium that I participated in at the Fashion Institute of Technology in New York on May 15–17, 2018, the internationally renowned jewellery artist Annika Pettersson emphasized that when an artist gets a 3D printer in their workshop and no longer has to get that service from the intermediaries, a possibility for experimenting emerges. Businesses that deal in 3D printing often refuse to do something that doesn't follow the rules. More often than not, only "safe" and standard requests are accepted. An artist can achieve a very different result if they own a 3D printer. A possibility arises to take a risk, to find new ways of achieving a desirable outcome.

To allow myself a possibility to immerse deeper into the 3D printing world, I decided that I needed my own 3D printer. How do I feel myself while unpacking a new machine? I feel a pleasing anxiety and an energy surge, because I believe that this new helper will allow me to do something that I don't fully understand yet. This positive attitude ends abruptly, as I encounter the first lag—the screen stops working, which means that even a test print is impossible. Would it have been more convenient to order printing from a third person or printing company, receive the printed models in the mail, and not bother with the machine purchase? No. After the system update the lags are gone. I am confident that the printer will allow some experiments. I am interested, for example, in wax printing that can be used for precious metal casting and also porcelain printing. I am interested in the result of premeditated violation of rules of the maintenance of the printer. But what exactly is the nature of my collaboration with the machine?

Recently, I stumbled upon an essay by Dorinne Kondo titled "Polishing Your Heart: Artisans and Machines in Japan" (2005). As it is seen from the title, anthropology professor Kondo writes about the relationship between artisans and machines in Japanese culture. The author tells about the new year tradition of some Japanese craftsmen to make gifts for their machines, which are not seen only as instruments. "There was a special spiritual presence in all of their machines . . . But it wasn't a love of machinery as machinery, but of machinery as some kind of spiritual extension of themselves. For them, machines were extensions of themselves as spiritual beings, as creators of things, things of high quality" (2005, p. 410).

This tradition is determined by the presence of so-called Shinto spirits, or *kami*, in the Japanese culture, who inhabit the living and also inanimate objects. "Trees, rocks, waterfalls, and other natural formations can be imbued with *kami* and are sometimes worshipped as sacred" (Kondo, p. 410).

Drawing a parallel with the objects presented during my exhibition, I would like to point out that not only my hands participated in the process of jewellery creation. I consciously integrated the machine into the making process, which means that there is a new intermediary in the chain *artist—WOA*. Now the aforementioned chain becomes:

artist—machine—WOA

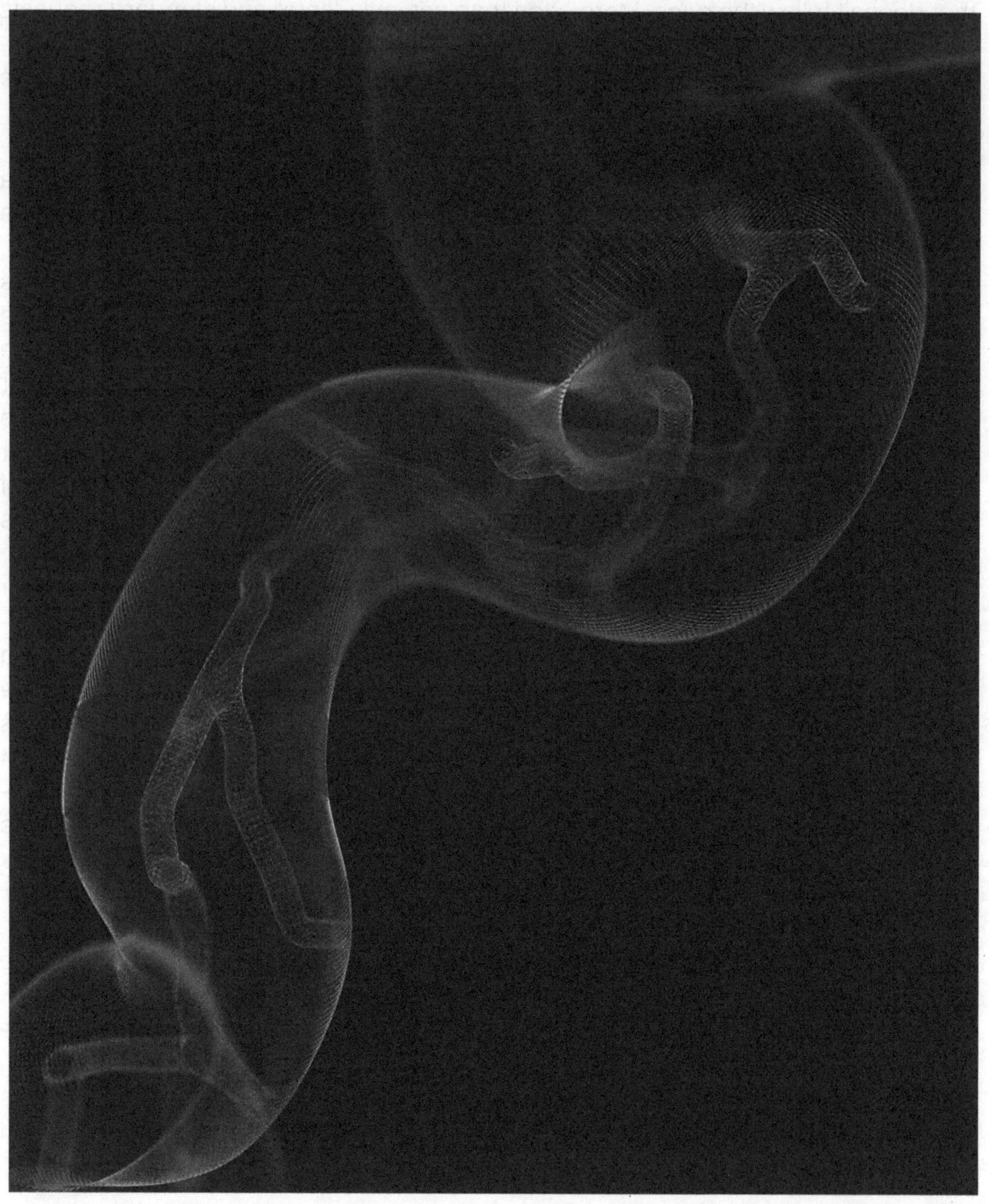

Figure 6. Sofia Hallik, Tangibility Matters, 3D render of a brooch. Photo credit: Oskar Narusberk.

Is it fair to stipulate that I use the machine not only as an instrument? Did it really become my partner? Instead of being a banal instrument, can the machine be a medium? The machine participates in the process, which in turn influences the result. This participation is not limited to the manufacturing of jewellery; it dictates the possible alterations in the material, texture, shape, etc. That is why we can conclude that there is some closeness between the human maker and the machine. I am not seeking spirituality in the digital, but I cannot reject the idea that as a result of the implementation of the machine in the process of work, there originates a bond between the author and the machine, and the link between them is a WOA.

I would also like to try to find an answer to the question of how exactly the implementation of digital technologies influences the jewellery's function and objective. It is important for me to raise the topic of the difference between jewellery as a general idea and jewellery as an object. The second one is intended for an exhibition space, a museum or a private collection, it is a piece of jewellery whose function does not correspond to the primary idea of jewellery—to ornament, protect, or symbolise something on the human body. I consider my latest works as a result of an experiment, and they cannot blend into the generally accepted framework of jewellery. This is due to the fact that the shape of the jewellery was formed in a 3D program, and my goal was to create an aesthetically satisfying shape. The human body was not taken into account. It is necessary to point out that one of the ways to make jewellery implies the initial understanding of what part of the body will be 'ornamented' and how it will be 'ornamented'. This allows for the creation of a shape that not only looks laconic on the body but is also (relatively) practical. This approach seems to me the most accurate one, but while working on the objects presented during the exhibition, I neglected that rule. The stage of fitting the object to a body was moved closer to the end of the process, when the shape was already being printed. Therefore, the machine influenced the function and the objective of the jewellery.

I am critical of the "just add a pin to an object and it will transform into a brooch" method employed by some artists. But in the case of "Tangibility Matters" I intentionally ignore the rule that governs my work in other situations. In this case, I wanted to find a balance between handwork and digital production.

That is why the body is not my goal or final destination.

I described the digital part, but we should not forget that half the time allotted for the creation of these series of works was given to handwork. Works on display are wearable objects that are a hybrid of handwork and digital production. While working on jewellery, I feel a need of touch and tactility, while an object that is made using 3D printing appears as an empty form that demands substance. In the world

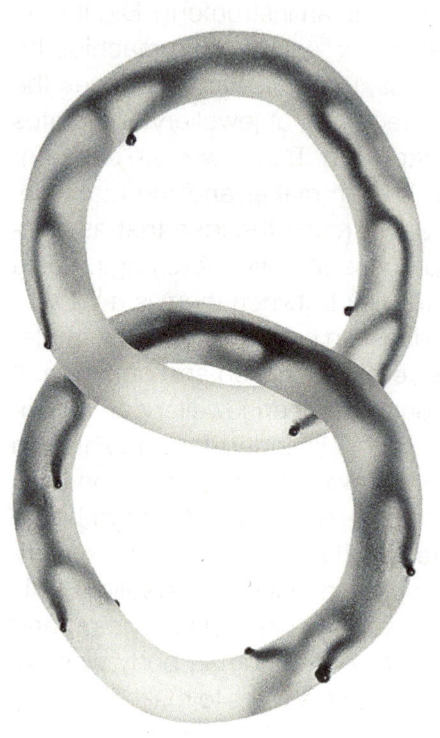
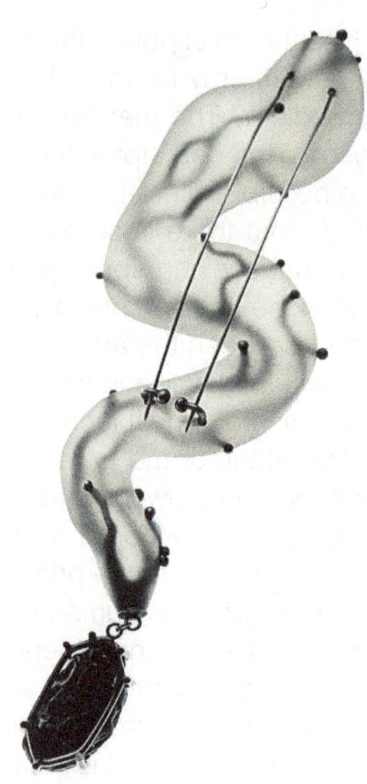

Figure 7. Sofia Hallik, Tangibility Matters, brooch on left 2017, object on right 2018. Photo credit: Sofia Hallik.

of tech, because the process of work using CAD or 3D printing excludes tangibility, I am lacking physical contact with the WOA.

In his book "Hammer and Silence: A Short Introduction to the Philosophy of Tools" (2015), Jyrki Siukonen focuses especially on hands, handwork, and tools, and their interaction with technological development. His research is especially important in the context of my work, since the author takes notice to the mundane 'things' that are usually left unnoticed in the process of making of WOA. Siukonen defines the process of creation first and foremost as a process you can experience with your hands or your whole body. For example, you can feel nailing with your hand and your forearm. Even with the advent of new technologies that expand our capabilities, we need to understand why handwork is so important. In this regard, McCullogh writes, "hands are the best source of tacit personal knowledge because of all the extensions of the body, they are the most subtle, the most sensitive, the most probing, the most differentiated, and the most closely connected to the mind . . . Hands also discover. They have a life of their own that leads them into explorations. For example, a sculptor's feel for a material will suggest actions to try, and places to cut. Learning through the hands shapes creativity itself" (1998, p. 7–8).

That is why I am peaceful while spending the quiet evenings in my studio alone with jewellery. Handwork is one of the most important and pleasant moments in my life, akin to prayer or meditation. As exemplified by this exhibition, handwork accompanied by machine production enables me to achieve a result impossible with strictly handwork, and vice versa. The works presented during the exhibition originate from two contradictory principles, digital production and handwork, and embody the mutual closeness of human and the machine. One of the features of such closeness is the fact that we demand more and more from the machines and from ourselves. While demanding more, and striving for better results, the line between real and digital is blurring. In other words, while people approach the digital world, technology becomes more and more humane.

References

Benjamin, W. n.d. *The Work of Art in the Age of Mechanical Reproduction.* Accessed November 15, 2016. http://web.mit.edu/allanme/www/benjamin.pdf.

Foreman, K. 2014. *Social Media Dictionary: A Modern Guide to Social Media, Texting, and Digital Communication.* USA: Social School 101 Press.

Kondo, D. 2005. "Polishing Your Heart: Artisans and Machines in Japan." In *The Book of Touch,* edited by C. Classen, 409–411. Oxford: Berg Publishers.

McCullogh, M. 1998. *Abstracting Craft: Practiced Digital Hand.* Cambridge: The MIT Press.

Rousseau, J. 1979. *Emile, or, On Education.* New York: Basic Books.

Siukonen, J. 2015. *Hammer and Silence: A Short Introduction to the Philosophy of Tools.* Finland: The Academy of Fine Arts at the University of the Arts Helsinki.

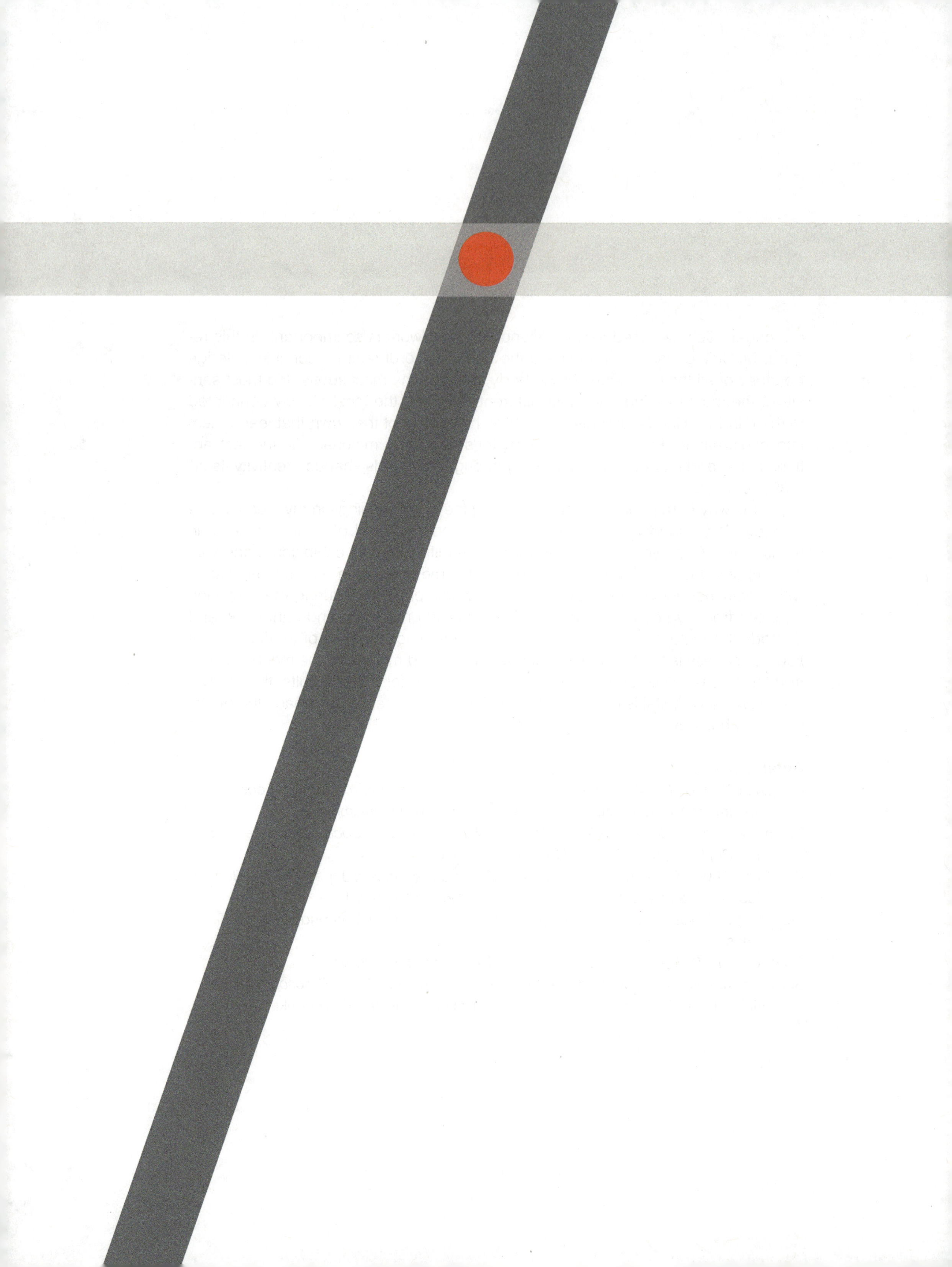

A Virtual Tradition

Kim Nelson, Fashion Institute of Technology, NY, USA

Abstract

The traditional techniques and methodology of jewelry design have inspired and informed centuries worth of delightful objects. These are the skills I apprenticed with more than twenty-five years ago—lead holders and graphite, gouache and brush, vellum and T-square. When I approached digital technology some five years later, I did so from a traditional perspective. Software was chosen based on its ability to accommodate a traditional approach. Above all, aesthetic fidelity was paramount. Aesthetics were my job.

When I discuss digital manufacturing with handcraftsmen, I often compare traditional and digital jewelry making with reality and virtual reality. Manufacturing decisions can easily go awry in the virtual space of digital media; concrete, real-life demands and decisions can become obscured by the hermetic digital environment. Tools and a bench are reality. A monitor and keyboard become virtual reality. This is not the case with design. The design process has always been abstract, always virtual: the object doesn't exist outside of the mind, until it is prodded to life with the point of a pencil or brush. Traditionally, the third dimension is more conceptual than real. Exploration through traditional maquettes and studies yields useful but approximate results. Digital technology endows the designer with the power to explore their inspirations and ideas fully. Myriad variants can be developed and assessed with a fraction of the energy previously required. No stone need be left unturned. The digital design process can be fully integrated. 2D and 3D cross-pollinate. Digital maquettes and studies are no longer guesses; they are as accurate as the designer wishes them to be. The result is a more deeply evolved design supported by real data. Traditional design processes are virtual reality by comparison.

Clients may still voice a preference for hand-drawings and gouache renderings. The perception is that these design artifacts are intrinsically more valuable, more precious than a digital print. But I am an applied artist in the most concrete sense of the phrase; my work is always a means to an end—the end being a realized, three-dimensional article. The value of design lies in its content, and I have found digital content to be superior. If it wasn't I wouldn't use it.

When I was an apprentice, my mentor often stated that his ideal asset would be a designer capable of carving their own waxes. That way, nothing would get lost in translation. As soon as I stepped into the virtual environment, I recognized I could readily become as fluent in digital modeling as I was with design. I now work as a digital model maker as often as I do a designer. There is no pause or translation between my design intent, my design process, and the finished model. The potential for this immediacy and fluidity might be digital design's greatest asset.

In my current role as an educator, I strive to extend this powerful virtual platform to my students. In their hands, these digital tools will open doors, expand horizons, and reshape our industry.

A Virtual Tradition

The traditional techniques and methodology of jewelry design have inspired and informed centuries of delightful objects. These are the skills I apprenticed in more than twenty-five years ago—lead holders and graphite, gouache and brush, vellum and T-square. My interest and experience with digital technology were not academic in origin. My introduction was through the factory floor of the commercial jewelry industry. This was 1997, and large-scale jewelry manufacturing had recently begun using solids-based parametric modeling software to feed their CNC milling machines. The motivation was not higher aesthetics. The goal was consistent and precise cutting of metal molds for plastic injection. The software used was for industrial designers and engineers, not artists. In fact, design integrity was regularly a point of contention; parametric solids modeling could be an awkward tool for exploring fluid organic form, and an errant undercut could result in sophisticated and expensive hand-cut lead inserts. My jewelry experience up to this point had been with the premier New York jewelry firm Carvin French. There, design intent had been a paramount concern, and I had often been discouraged from designing around production concerns. (The level of craftsmanship and the nature of the product at Carvin French all but removed such concerns anyway.)

But I had come to Louisiana in pursuit of large scale jewelry production experience, so I focused on learning to design the other way around—to ask first how the product would be made and then to design with a constant eye on the production process. This was fine—interesting even. Then I heard murmurs in the trade about

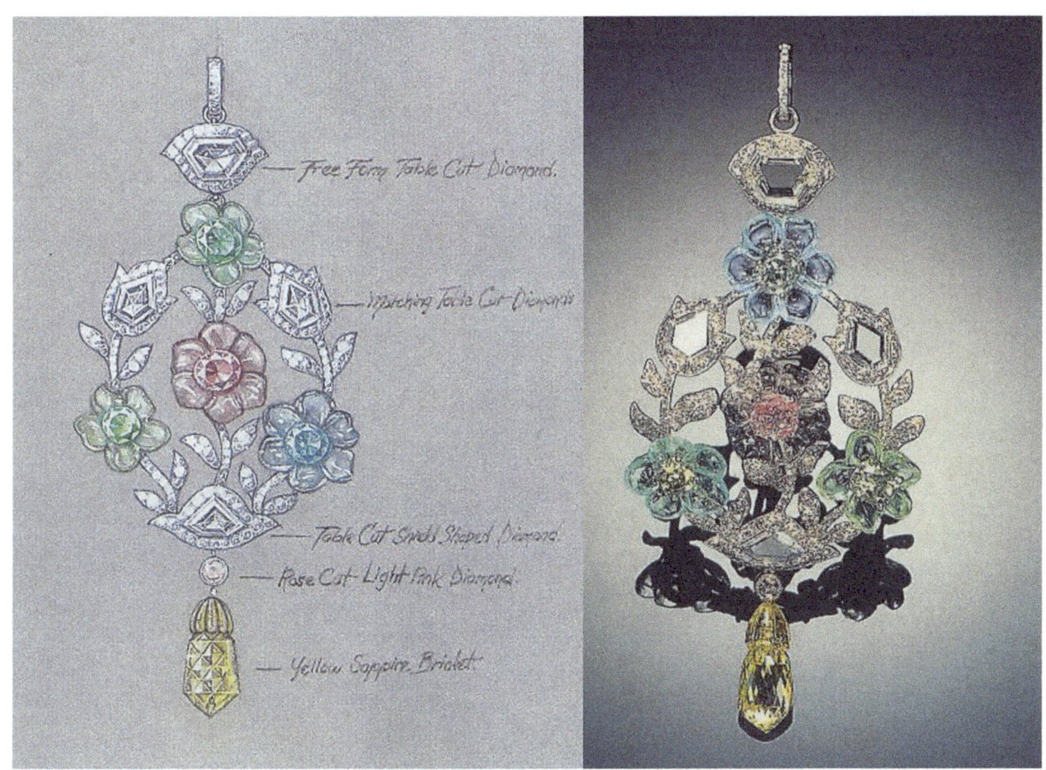

Figure 1. Traditional gouache design presentation.

digital design being on the horizon. These rumors were always dismissed in the telling: it would be impossible to design jewelry on a computer; jewelry was too sophisticated. The problem was, I'd heard this all before.

Prior to my work as a jewelry designer, I had worked as an illustrator. For a decade, illustrators denied the significance of digital technology using the same logic: the computer was fine for page layout, typesetting, or even simple graphics, but illustration was too sophisticated to be threatened—and that's how most of us saw it . . . as a threat, not an opportunity. By 1990, digital media had inundated the publishing industry. I was an oil painter, a purist, and I wouldn't lay hands on a computer. (I wouldn't know how.) Demand for traditional media illustration dwindled,

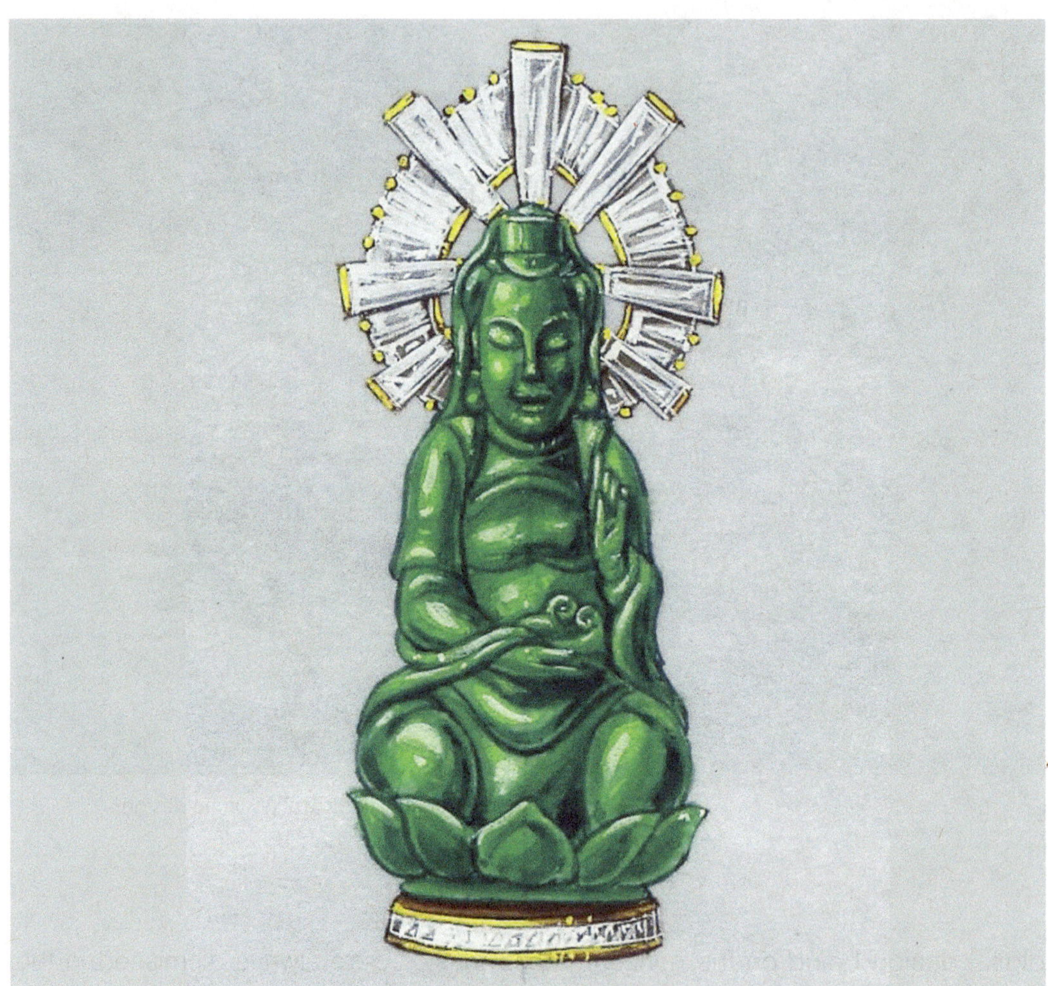

Figure 2. Traditional gouache design presentation.

and this—combined with my stubbornness—had been a key motivator to my leaving the illustration field for the jewelry industry. Eight years later, I was sitting at my elegant drawing table with its floating drafting arm, and if I was certain of anything, it was that jewelry was not too sophisticated to design with a computer. In fact, with its diminutive scale, generally geometric and symmetrical foundations, and its demand for precision, jewelry was an ideal candidate for computer-aided design (CAD) design. I decided this time I would get out in front of the digital wave rather

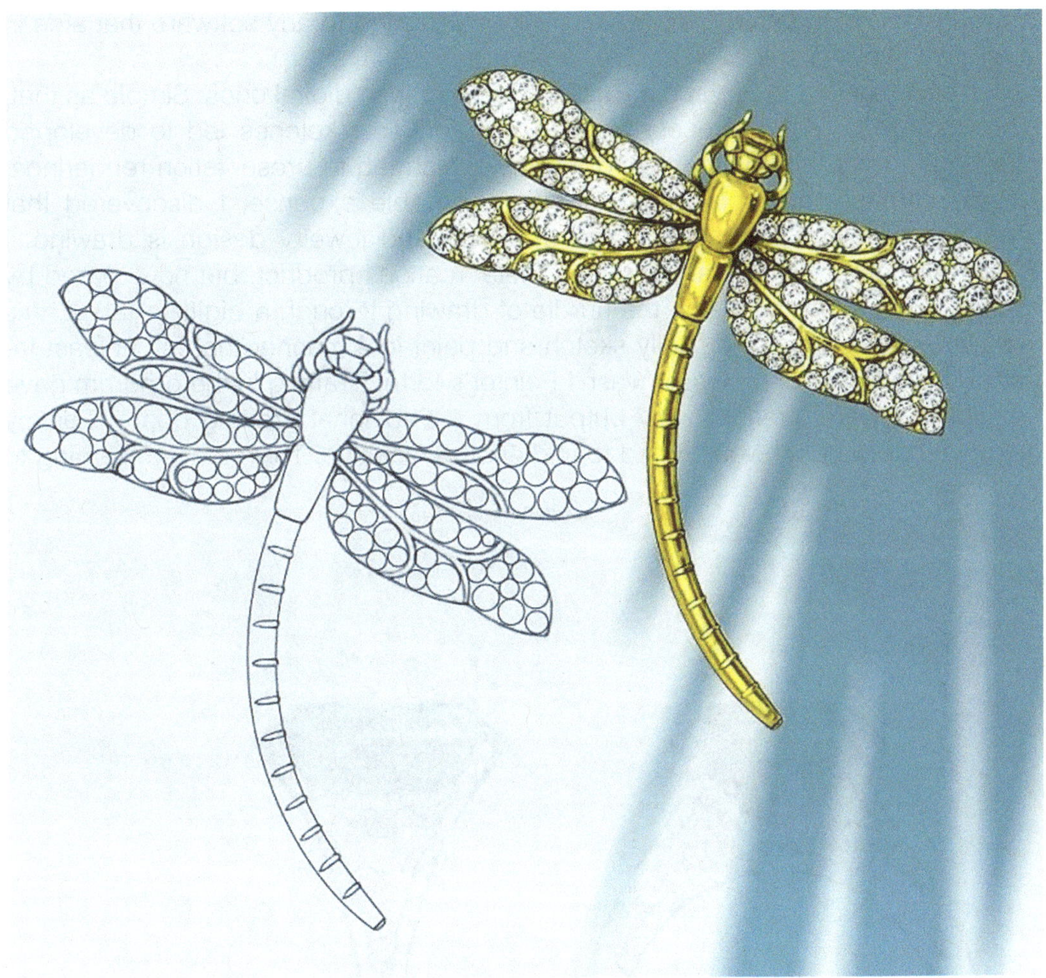

Figure 3. Digital design presentation.

than be drowned by it. As I charted my path into digital design, I did so from a traditional perspective with my guiding principle being a refusal to compromise. While I accepted catering my designs to meet the needs of the CAD operators in the factory, in order to utilize CAD in my own work it had to be adaptable to my needs. Above all, aesthetic fidelity was paramount. Aesthetics were my job. Since I will be using the term CAD repeatedly in this paper, it is important to define its meaning: CAD stands for computer-aided design. CAD refers equally to 2D graphics software and 3D modeling software. I will be referring to any software that aids in the product design process as CAD software.

Initially, I sought to replace my traditional tools with digital ones. Simple as that. The traditional design process worked well for me: sketches led to developed drawings, which led to technical drawings, which led to presentation renderings. To my surprise, disappointment, and considerable expense, I discovered that graphics software didn't encourage drawing—and jewelry design is drawing. I eventually found Painter (at the time a Metacreations product, but now owned by Corel), and once I overcame the hurdle of drawing through a digitizer tablet, this software allowed me to digitally sketch and paint in a manner that felt at least familiar. Unfortunately, precision wasn't Painter's forte. Drafting in the program gave results that were inferior to my output from a traditional drafting board. For my technical drawings, I would need to find another solution. This entailed learning to

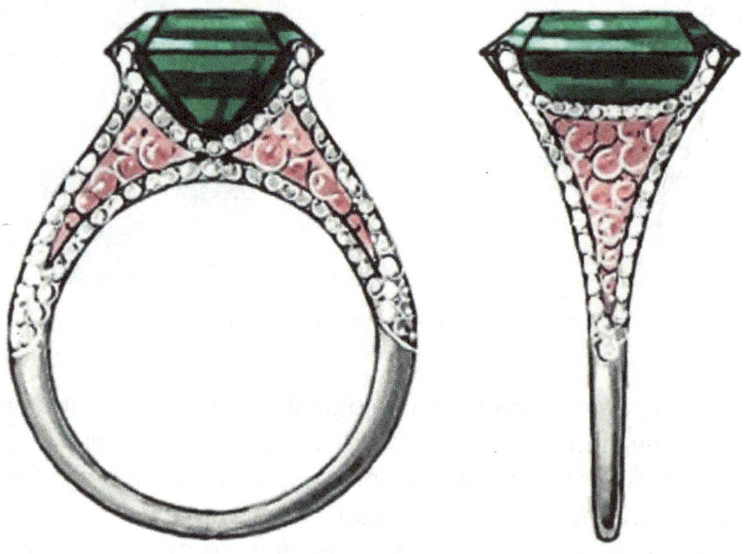

Figure 4. Digital design sketch.

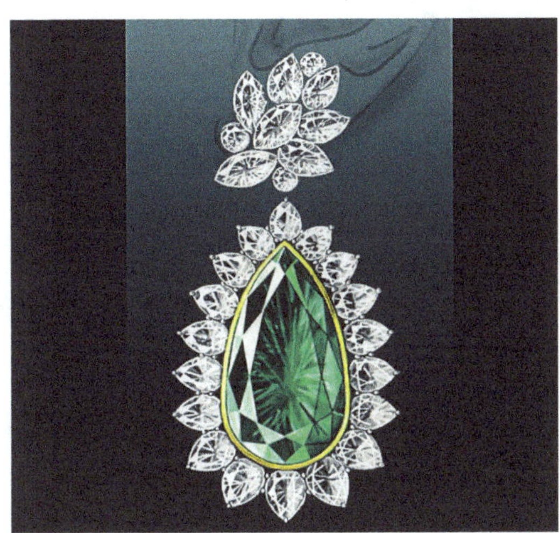
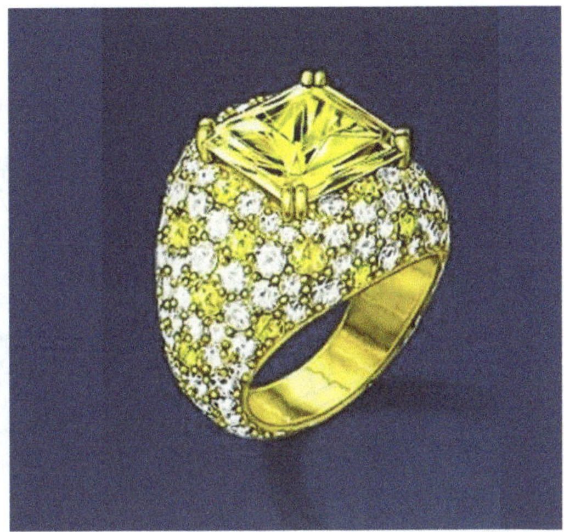

Figures 5 and 6. Digital design presentations.

use vector-based drawing programs like Freehand, Illustrator, and CorelDRAW. I pushed control-points and dragged handles to bend mathematical curves to my will. The results were cleaner and more precise than anything I could do by hand, but the process was cumbersome. Two fundamental truths of CAD had become clear to me: I couldn't achieve everything I wanted with a single software solution, and CAD wasn't always, or even usually, faster.

I returned to Carvin French a year later. . .and my laptop, drawing tablet, scanner, and printer came with me. Eyebrows were raised. A couple of days in, I printed my first design and delivered it to André Chervin, my employer and mentor. He was pleased. He spoke with some relief to how my time working in commercial jewelry hadn't stained me, about how I "hadn't lost a thing." He then made the point that work of this caliber would never come from a computer. I then confessed he was holding a printout. He refused to believe me until I told him to loupe it. He did. "Formidable," he said. So I'd done it. I had reached the point where my digital work had met or even surpassed my traditional efforts, even to the eye of the most demanding expert. I finally had arrows in my quiver for the digital invasion when it came. But so what? Output-wise, the work was the same: a carefully considered and presented jewelry design on a letter-sized sheet of paper. At first glance, it would appear I'd devoted two years and countless hours of effort only to arrive where I'd started.

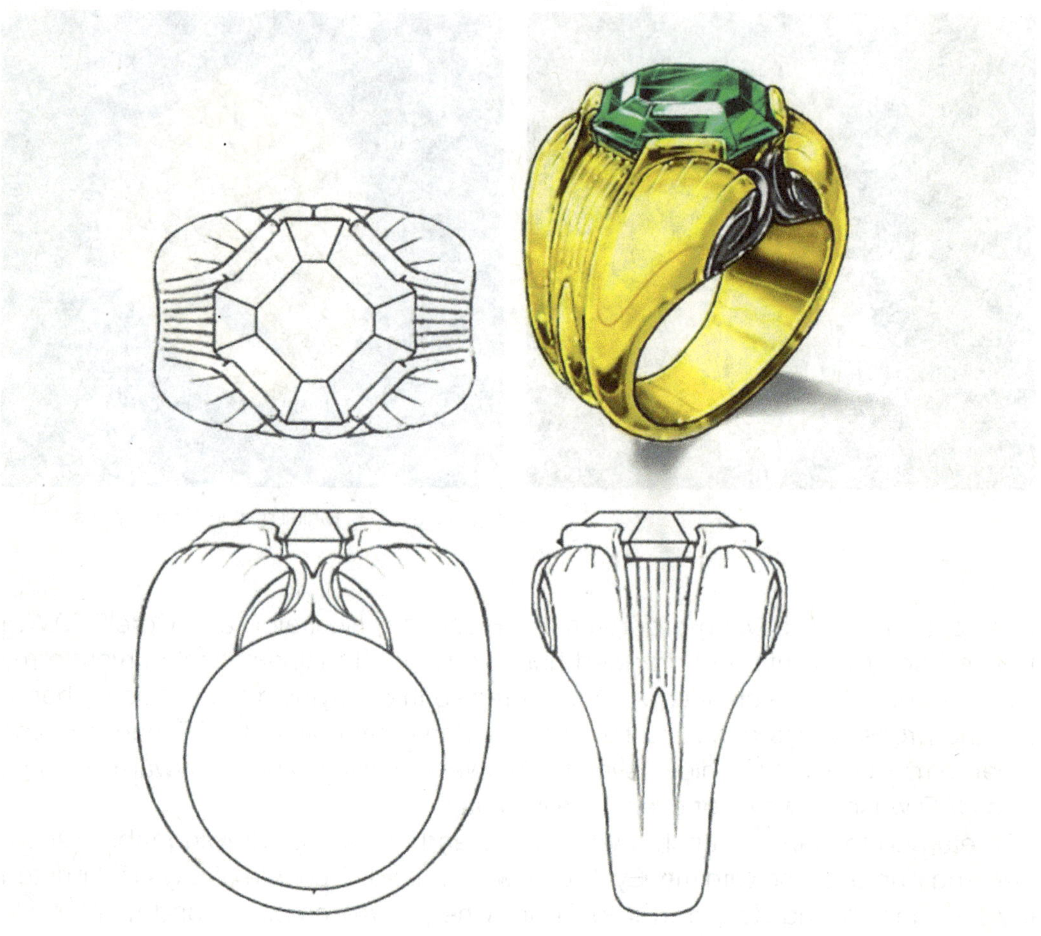

Figures 7: Digital design presentation.

There's much more to a jewelry design than lines and color on paper. We're talking about intent, content, and process. In my experience, CAD has proved superior across the board. Undo alone is worth the price of admission—as is access to perfect geometry and symmetry. Without sounding like a technical manual, graphics software allows for layered content, which makes exploring and finessing design options much more efficient and fluid. My design process is lossless.

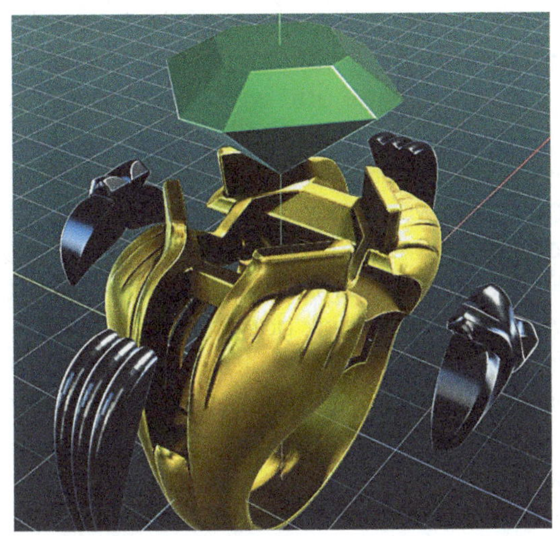

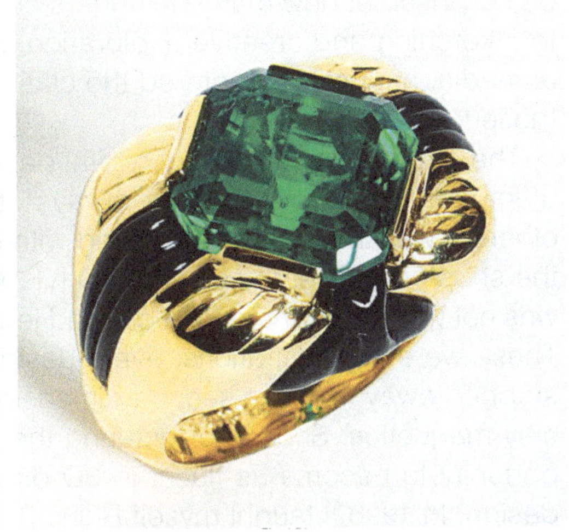

Figures 8 and 9. CAD production model and final piece.

I have immediate access to every iteration or path I've explored. In a professional environment, most design time is devoted to client or designer driven revision. A proper design can witness a dozen variations. With traditional media, any one of these changes can demand starting over. With digital media, this is almost never necessary. The entire development process is immediately accessible and readily adaptable. No 6H pencil can match the precision or accuracy of a vector-based CAD drawing, and presentation renderings are unbeatable for their consistency and durability; I can't count the number of gouache renderings I've seen sacrificed to the bottom of a coffee mug. I can print countless copies of any presentation I like, as well as email it around the globe in its native format. The reference gathering and communication advantages of 2D CAD should be obvious, and there are numerous other benefits I could list, but suffice it to say, it took CAD just ten years to overtake the jewelry design field and rightfully so. Some developments have been unexpected. Much of jewelry design has become cut-and-paste, and drawing, never an overabundant skill[set] in the jewelry industry, has been downplayed even further. I find both of these trends lamentable, as I do the ease with which intellectual property is being plagiarized. And I continue to be surprised at how many designers continue to resist the power of digital media for sketching and creative exploration. For my part, I never returned to traditional media, not until I re-entered the classroom years later and was asked to teach those tools.

The greatest advantage of digital design is its intelligence. In a traditional manufacturing environment, I was always one voice working in concert with several others. I was the front line, working with clients to create problems that the rest of the shop would get to solve, and while I possessed rudimentary bench skill, that was not what I was there for. I created jewelry with my pencil, gouache, and vellum. These were not illustrations; every design was a plan for a sculpture, and I often stepped away from the second dimension to prove my designs by crafting wax or clay maquettes. Soon after entering the virtual environment, I recognized the opportunity to become as fluent in 3D digital modeling as I was with 2D computer design. In 1998, I taught myself Rhino 3D, a NURBS-based surface modeler, and I discovered creating maquettes was an ideal way to master the program. Traditional wax or clay maquettes had been necessary and useful, but they provided very limited and approximate results. Digital maquettes and studies weren't guesses; they were as accurate and detailed as I wished to make them. CAD technology endowed me with the power to explore my inspirations and ideas fully. Myriad variants could be developed with a fraction of the energy previously required, and I could review these variants in 3D, in real time. Now no stone needed to be left unturned. My digital design process had become fully integrated. 2D and 3D cross-pollinated. Design jpegs were dropped into Rhino, and Rhino's vector lines were readily converted and pulled back into Painter. I was drawing and sculpting simultaneously. André often stated his ideal asset would be a designer capable of carving their own waxes; that way, nothing would be lost in translation. Eventually, I developed enough CAD vocabulary to model any piece I could imagine. Of course, those two basic laws of CAD still applied—I couldn't do it all in one program, and it wasn't necessarily faster than creating a master model in wax. But further translation was no longer required. I had become what André would have considered an ideal creative asset.

I regularly discuss digital manufacturing with handcraftsmen, and in these conversations, I often compare traditional and digital jewelry making with reality and virtual reality. Manufacturing decisions can go awry in the virtual space of digital media. Concrete, real-life demands and decisions easily become obscured in the hermetic digital environment. Tools and a bench are reality. A monitor and keyboard are not. This is not the case with design. The traditional design process has always been abstract, always virtual. The object doesn't exist outside of the mind, until it is prodded to life at the point of a pencil or brush. The third dimension is limited to a conceptual construct struggling to become real. Using a digital design process results in a more deeply developed design that is supported by real three-dimensional data. This gives the designer a clearer understanding of their work, and this understanding leads to design confidence. Some years ago, I had a shop foreman come to me with concerns over my design. He accused me of having inaccuracies in my technical drawings and boldly declared my piece to be impossible, a "rocket ship that couldn't fly." The ring was a complex and asymmetrical design, and to draw it comprehensively would have required a minimum of five orthographic views. My client wasn't interested in waiting for, or compensating me for, that much work. If the design had been done traditionally, I would have had doubts, and those doubts would have led me to release creative control to the shop foreman. But the ring had been developed digitally. I pulled the detailed maquette up on my screen and asked the foreman where he saw inconsistencies. He left my office in silence. Later, he returned to discuss a legitimate setting concern, and we discussed the piece while rotating the digital maquette on my screen for reference. The digital design process gave me the confidence I needed to support my design intent and a credible venue for me and the foreman to have an intelligent, productive conversation about his setting concern. In a professional product design environment, traditional design processes are virtual reality by comparison. My digital designs are more informed and intelligent than my traditional designs ever could have been which is why I choose to create digitally.

Much of the current conversation surrounding digital technology's impact on the jewelry world centers on innovation. I did not approach digital technology to find a new or innovative way to create jewelry. I am passionate about traditional craftsmanship and fine jewels, and traditional methods work just fine. Premier quality craftsmanship was the DNA, the brand of Carvin French. But there was some irony surrounding their craftsmanship: if you didn't know what you were looking at, the craftsmanship was so fine it was almost invisible. Their jewelry was primarily about the design and materials—most often important gemstones. Craftsmanship, or goldsmithing, brought the design and materials together, but it rarely took center stage on its own. A jeweler once told me that if you could tell his hands were behind a piece, he'd failed. His workmanship had to be mastered to the point where he became invisible. His only purpose was to craft a given design accurately. Mastery was the key concept. There were master-craftsmen, master-goldsmiths, master-lapidaries, master-wax carvers, and master-model makers. Materials weren't obeyed, they were mastered . . . subdued. As a designer and model maker, mastery is the concept I have always relied upon in my pursuit of beauty. CAD allows for maximum mastery over the product development process. For me, innovation has been a side effect. I continued to pursue CAD technology because it allowed me to create better jewelry.

Clients still occasionally voice a preference for handdrawings and gouache renderings. The perception is that these design artifacts are intrinsically more valuable, more precious, than a digital print. But a mere artifact of the design process is all any design presentation is. I am an applied artist in the most concrete sense of the phrase; my work is always a means to an end—that end being a realized, three-dimensional article. The value of a design lies in its content: the inspiration, insight, understanding, and experience that rest behind it. Digital design content is more complete, more deeply explored, and more informed. This renders it more valuable. It is also more durable; I have a library of design reaching back nearly twenty years, and all of it is still pristine and readily accessible. Digital design even makes communication easier, and at the end of the day, the chief obligation of a design is to communicate. Still, the customer is always right. When asked, I still take pleasure in pulling a point on my kolinsky sable brush and splashing new jewelry into existence.

In my current role as an educator, I strive to provide a rich and varied learning experience for my students based on a variety of methods and media. While my personal preference leans towards digital media, I believe it is critical for students to have full exposure to traditional processes and techniques. In my design courses, I teach and demonstrate a traditional approach in detail. But from the very start, CAD can play an important role. We do not allow our associates degree students to specialize, which places students who may have little native interest in design behind desks in an array of drawing and design courses. CAD can be a great equalizer for these students. While having drawing ability is helpful and important when designing jewelry, CAD programs offer an element that traditional media can't: consistency. Given time, every student can use this consistency to coax credible design work from CAD software. By the time students leave our program, it can be very difficult to discern the students without native ability from those who entered our program as accomplished graphic communicators. This success gives students confidence and promotes further interest in the design process. Competency with graphics software also enhances their employability. CAD drafting and modeling are also introduced in the first semester. One of our greatest limitations our program faces is time, and digital model making has provided important assistance in this area. An early project for my CAD modeling students is a filigree ring based on individual designs. This is not a simplistic project, and it challenges students' patience and concentration. When the project is complete, the students print their rings so they can have the finished dimensional object in front of them. Then I ask, "I understand this was a very difficult project, but how long would it take you to acquire enough skill to make these rings by hand?" Most of our students have scant metals experience before joining us, so I rarely get an informed answer, but my point is made: none of them could imagine making their ring by hand. Truthfully, to accurately hand fabricate a filigree ring with a repeat pattern—to specification—would require a level of skill and precision that few of our students could achieve in two years. This acceleration in their ability to realize complex jewelry items is most obvious in our graduating student show, where students display their final completed pieces alongside the original designs that inspired them. The finesse and sophistication their work displays is often the result of their fluency with digital technology. Returning to the design aspect of our curriculum, by their second year our students are connecting the dots. They understand and appreciate the importance of using digital maquettes to verify design intent, and are comfortable moving design information between 2D and 3D CAD applications, as well as incorporating scanned analog information as part of their creative process. This will allow them to go forward with their professional goals and development as individual artists with the confidence and power CAD tools provide.

In summary, CAD tools can be approached from a traditional perspective and incorporated into a traditional design development process. This is how I brought digital technology to my own work, and how I continue to apply digital technology to product development. My involvement with CAD software has led to innovation in my work, mostly in the form of vastly improved design exploration, verification and veracity, but innovation has never been my motivation. I still believe in and promote a traditional approach to jewelry—only using digital media. For example, CAD technology allows for much finer details than are available by hand, and some digital production methods such as metal sintering are even capable of expressing this detail in a finished piece. But at what point does detail become small enough to lose its significance and come across as a texture? And at what point does a texture lose meaning and read as poor finishing? How should a prong setting function? How should it look? Such questions cannot be properly assessed without exposure to traditional methods and materials. It is my grounding in the traditional processes behind design and manufacturing that have enabled me to benefit richly from the power and flexibility of digital media.

Further Reading

Bennett, D., and D. Mascetti. 2017. *Understanding Jewellery.* Woodbridge, UK: ACC Art Books.

Berenguer, M., and J. Pastor. 2012. *Drawing for Jewelers, Master Class in Professional Design.* Atglen, PA: Schiffer Publishing.

Clements, M. and P. Clements. 1998. *Avon: Collectible Fashion Jewelry and Awards.* Atglen, Pennsylvania, US: Schiffer Publishing, Limited.

Cole, R. 1976. *Perspective for Artists.* Mineola, NY: Dover Publications.

Galli, M., N. Giambelli, D. Riviere, and F. Li. 1997. *The Art of Jewelry Design: Principles of Design, Rings and Earrings.* Atglen, PA: Schiffer Pub Ltd.

Galli, M., D. Riviere, and F. Li. 1997. *Creative Variations in Jewelry Design.* Atglen, PA: Schiffer Publishing Ltd.

Giesecke, F., and J. Dygdon. 2014. *Modern Graphics Communication.* Upper Saddle River, NJ: Financial Times Prentice Hall.

Habsburg, G. 1996. *Faberge in America.* London: Thames & Hudson.

Hornung, C.P. 1946. *Handbook of Designs and Devices.* Dover pictorial archive. Mineola, NY: Dover Publications.

Meyer, F. 2010. *Handbook of Ornament.* Newcastle, UK: Cambridge Scholars Publishing.

Pinton, D. 1999. *Jewelry Technology.* Edizione Gold.

Rudoe, J. 1997. *Cartier 1900–1939.* New York: Harry N. Abrams Inc.

Snowman, A.K. 2002. *The Master Jewelers.* London, UK: Thames & Hudson.

Stuller. *The Mountings Book.*

Tait, H. 1986. *Seven Thousand Years of Jewellery.* London: British Museum Press.

Threinen-Pendarvis, C. 2007. *The Painter Wow! Book.* San Francisco, CA: Peachpit Press.

Untracht, O. 1982. *Jewelry Concepts and Technology.* New York: Doubleday.

Woolton, C. 2010. *Fashion for Jewelry: 100 Years of Styles and Icons.* Munich: Prestel.

Pixels Bejeweled: Modern Media, Contemporary Jewelry, and the Replication of Desire

Sasha Nixon, NY, USA

Abstract

This paper will consider how American jewelry artists Anya Kivarkis, Mary Hallam Pearse, and emiko oye examine how visual mediators create, alter, and perpetuate perceptions of adornment in a critical reconsideration of jewelry's traditional place within Western society. Contact with "high jewelry" designs are often filtered through visual mediators from magazines to social media, from the silver screen to images of cultural heritage. Kivarkis recreates jewelry exactly as it appears in movie stills, fashion spreads, and celebrity red-carpet photographs. She reinterprets it as interrupted, the jewelry cut off by the wearer's body and occasionally coated in industrial paint, subverting its value. Pearse's series Girls Play Games *references children's dexterity games, transforming the pursuit of adornment into a game. She digitally prints images from fashion magazines onto aluminum, deliberately placing the handmade and the mass produced in counterpoint with the visual culture of desire. Oye works from pixelated images of historical "high jewelry" to reconceive these iconic pieces out of LEGO©—a material with sentimental rather than monetary value. In so doing she questions societal assumptions about the nature of "heirloom."*

Introduction

This paper will consider how American jewelry artists Anya Kivarkis, Mary Hallam Pearse, and emiko oye—oye chooses not to capitalize her name, which has been respected in this paper—examine how visual mediators create, alter, and perpetuate perceptions of adornment in a critical reconsideration of jewelry's traditional place within Western society. As with any artistic pursuit artistic intent is of principle importance and it is this that will be discussed here. In line with this directive the majority of the sources used for this paper are the artists themselves—either through discussions with the author or from published interviews and artist statements.

Contact with "high jewelry" designs are often filtered through visual mediators from magazines to social media, from the silver screen to images of cultural heritage. Kivarkis recreates jewelry exactly as it appears in movie stills, fashion spreads, and celebrity red-carpet photographs. She reinterprets it as interrupted, the jewelry cut off by the wearer's body and occasionally coated in industrial paint, subverting its value. Pearse's series *Girls Play Games* references children's dexterity games, transforming the pursuit of adornment into a game. She digitally prints images from fashion magazines onto aluminum, deliberately placing the handmade and the mass produced in counterpoint with the visual culture of desire. Oye works from pixelated images of historical "high jewelry" to reconceive these iconic pieces out of LEGO©—a material with sentimental rather than monetary value. In so doing she questions societal assumptions about the nature of "heirloom."

The jewelry discussed in this publication is seen through digital photographs, an assemblage of pixels formed together to approximate a 3D object in 2D space. Contact with "high jewelry" designs, like those from well-known jewelry houses or other independent icons of the goldsmith's art, is often filtered through such visual mediators. A visual mediator generates an image or video of an object—in this case jewelry—in a way that allows visual exposure to something without ever having physically occupied the same space. Today these mediators—movies, fashion spreads, celebrity red-carpet coverage, and images of cultural heritage—are often distributed on digital platforms. The work of all three jewelry artists focuses on desire for opulent jewelry created by the presence of jewelry in digital and print media. How they critique the digital presence of jewelry in modern life and its relationship to adornment, however, is unique.

Anya Kivarkis

Anya Kivarkis recreates jewels worn in paparazzi snapshots, movies, fashion spreads, or historical paintings. Rather than creating replicas, she incorporates distortions of perspective and glare created by the intervention of the image between viewer and jewelry into each piece and represents parts obscured by the image or the wearer's body as blank spots. The natural interaction between the wearer's body and the jewelry from the perspective of the image is re-fabricated as a interruption and distortion of the jewelry (Nixon and Kivarkis, 2018). Through this process her work becomes about the image as interpretation.

Kivarkis often manipulates perspective by overlapping jewels drawn from one or multiple images. *Winona Ryder, Lost Jewels, 3 Views,* for example, is a single piece created by superimposing three different perspectives shown in separate

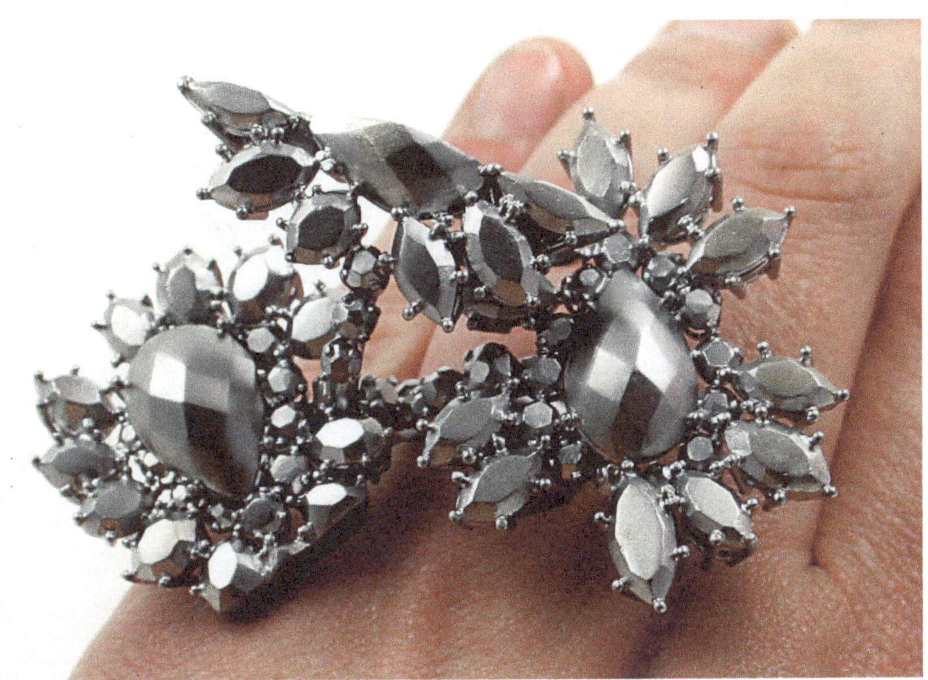

Figure 1. Anya Kivarkis, Winona Ryder, Lost Jewels, 3 Views, Ring, 2010, silver. Courtesy the artist.

photographs (Figure 1). When worn, the perspective of Kivarkis's pieces seems disjointed. It is only when the ring is viewed from a particular angle that the wearer and the jewelry seem to come into sync and occupy the same optical space for a second before disassociating again. In that single moment in which the perspectives align, the wearer and observer are part of an interactive encounter where the jewelry and the wearer achieve the same perspective as the original image from which the jewelry was recreated—at least in part (Nixon and Kivarkis, 2018). In a few select works, Kivarkis's pieces are recreated and filmed. Returning them to their cinematic context with the bodies removed adds yet another layer of digital mediation between the viewer and the artwork.

Images or videos of jewelry are sometimes poor in quality or obscured by glare. These distortions are particularly characteristic of quickly captured photographs like those of celebrities moving through space. Kivarkis represents these

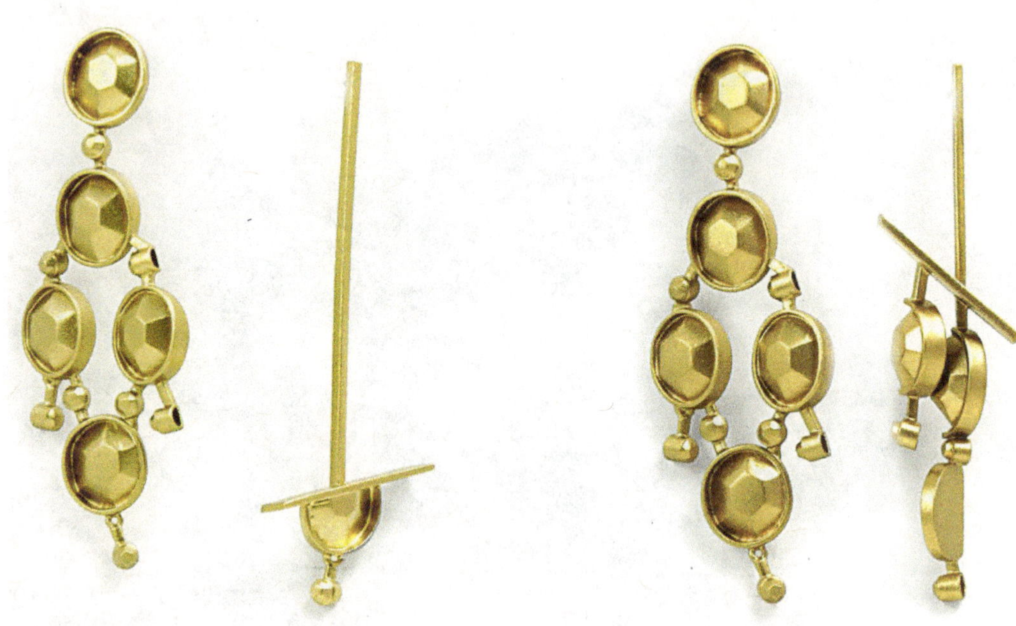

Figure 2. Anya Kivarkis, two pairs of earrings from the *Miley Ray Cyrus, Red Carpet 2008* series, 2009, silver, gold paint. Courtesy the artist.

peculiarities by piling jewels on top of one another to create a mass in which each object is obscured or by placing silver bars on top of the delicate jewels underneath to create a visual barrier which resembles a ray of light (Nixon and Kivarkis, 2018). The visual obstructions have become adhered to the 3D object and are inseparable from it as it exists in the photograph, as Kivarkis makes clear through her work.

Kivarkis creates all her work by hand, laboriously carving stones from rods of silver (Nixon and Kivarkis, 2018). The dichotomy between the highly tactile process of making such complex pieces and the purely visual digital medias from which she pulls her inspiration adds potency to her concept. By critiquing modern media obsession with extravagant displays of preciousness, Kivarkis establishes her own paradigm for value. For example, she sandblasts the surfaces of her pieces to take some of the vitality out of the precious material. In diminishing the sparkle,

Kivarkis transforms the original jewels into something incisive. Jewelry is often valued for its reflectiveness and shimmer. Dulling the surface draws attention to the expected flashiness of the form through its absence. For her series *Vanishing Point*, Kivarkis used paparazzi snapshots of celebrities at red carpet events. Her piece *Miley Ray Cyrus, Red Carpet 2008*, has been coated in gold spray paint as a mockery of the lustrous precious gold of Cyrus's actual jewels (Figure 2) (Cummins and Kivarkis, 2014). Her reinterpretations of digital images—as in the *Miley Ray Cyrus, Red Carpet 2008* series—represent jewelry in a single moment preserved by visual media. This series mapped Cyrus's movements through the movements of her earrings as preserved in paparazzi images (Nixon and Kivarkis, 2018). The earrings show the afterglow of strobing camera flashes at the Golden Globes award ceremony. Each pair of earrings in this series extends and suspends time by replicating the way moments are preserved for the public in social media.

Mary Hallam Pearse

Contemporary jewelry artist Mary Hallam Pearse contemplates desire and value in relation to fashion. Pearse's *Girls Play Games* series transforms the pursuit for adornment into a game. She took the images used in this series from current and vintage fashion spreads. Through the addition of interactive stones, encased in a form evocative of children's dexterity games, the fashion images are taken out of their original context and become playful and ironic (Figure 3). Pearls and diamonds in her work roll freely inside small frames instead of being set permanently like most fine jewelry. The rounded gems scurry atop images of traditional precious jewelry digitally printed on aluminum and under glass lids. These small frames are meant to invoke children's dexterity games, but by substituting precious materials for the usual steel ball bearings, Pearse commits her pieces to the adult sphere (Hallam Pearse, 2017). The free-rolling gems ricochet off the sides of the frame as the shadowbox is manipulated, just as in the youthful toys from which she draws inspiration. Marked with impressions on the aluminum base, the diamonds and pearls can be temporarily set in place through delicate tilting movements. Enlisting the wearer in a game where inattention leads to the loss of any progress towards setting the stones in their proper places causes contemplation of how society lures consumers towards the pursuit for the perfect jewel. Eventually the game must be given up, causing the pearls or diamonds to cascade out of their places, emphasizing the unattainability of desire (Figure 3).

The use of industrial components and processes such as aluminum for the bases of her games, the digital transfer printing process through which she incorporates

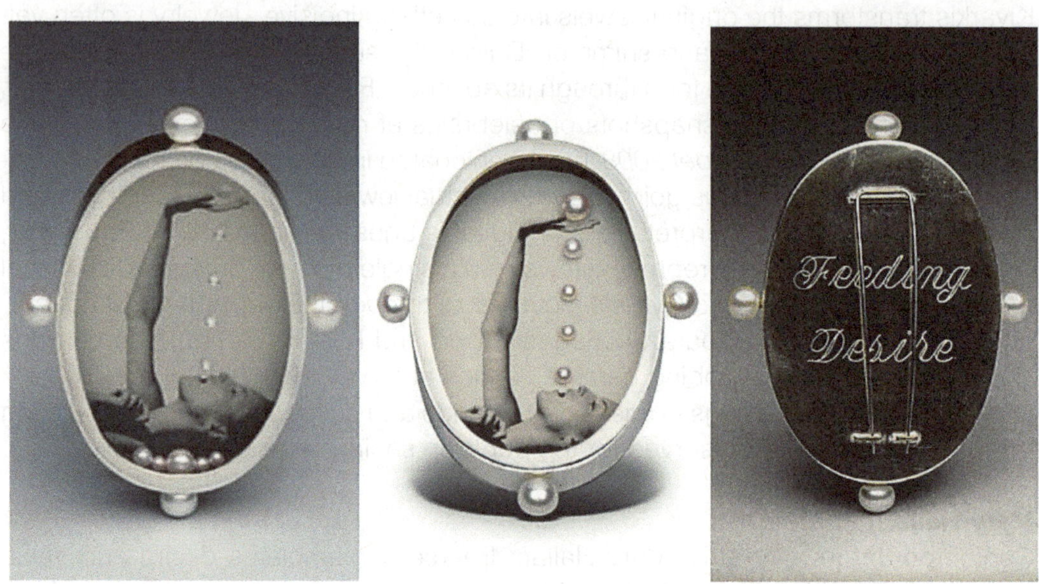

Figure 3. Mary Hallam Pearse, Feeding Desire, 2008, digital photograph, aluminum, silver, pearls, glass. Courtesy the artist.

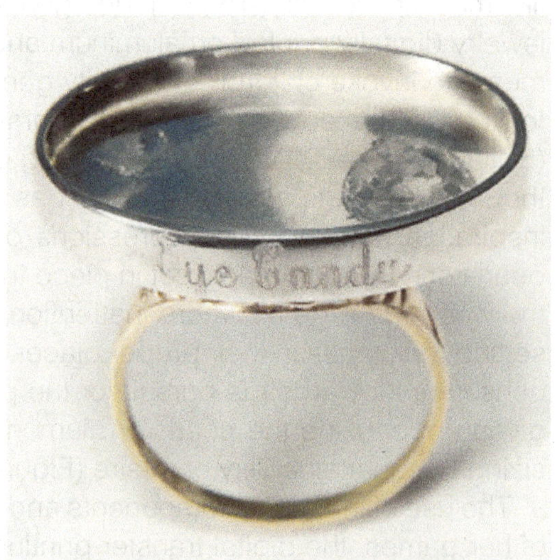

Figure 4. Mary Hallam Pearse, Eye Candy ring, ca. 2013, silver, gold, digital photograph. Courtesy the artist.

images from fashion spreads, and laser-engraving allow her to comment on the large-scale industry that manufactures consumer desire (Hallam Pearse, 2017).

Pearse's obviously playful figural pieces use imagery evocative of consumption digitally transferred from fashion magazines, arguably a vehicle for perpetuating the desire for a fictional look that was fabricated through the collaboration of many people including a photographer, model, and the magazine. Some of the images selected by Pierce evoke that consumption literally. She pours pearls and diamonds into mouths and across lush lips. Others are more subtle and emphasize illusion. Pearse's *Eye Candy* ring has those words laser engraved along the rim and the illusion of a large diamond digitally printed on the inside of an even larger shining silver disk (Figure 4). These techniques sharpen the focus of visual culture's emphasis on extravagant jewelry (Habermas, 2011). By isolating images of people and making them interact with gems she creates small decadent worlds that are almost a caricature of the contemporary chase for the precious. By printing images of stones, she adds yet another layer between the viewer and the original stone which was already unattainable as a photograph of a stone rather than the stone itself. Through the digital printing process, the stone becomes a ghost—requiring the shine of the metal beneath to provide the semblance of life. The laser engraved phrases spell out what gems do while the engraved and polished surfaces of the silver stand in for the facets of a stone, providing the sparkle. By replacing the large diamond with the digitally printed illusion of that stone on a shining and engraved silver disk Pearse asks whether it is the materiality of a jewel that matters or the appearance of it (Callahan, 2010).

emiko oye

Breaking almost entirely with traditional jewelry materials, emiko oye reinterprets famous examples of virtuosic jewelry. A well-known necklace created by Cartier in 1972 for Elizabeth Taylor is one such piece (Figure 5). Oye works directly from digital images of these historical pieces, images that have been widely and famously reproduced but few have ever seen the actual jewelry in person. Oye deliberately pixelates these images and uses them as sources to build replicas using LEGO© pieces (oye, 2017). She believes that using LEGO© as physical pixels to replicate historical pieces addresses the fact that much of the jewelry we are aware of is seen through the filter of computer screens (oye, 2017).

The title of oye's piece *La Reine de Pèlerin* references the famous drop-pearl in the necklace, La Peregrina. La Peregrina (Spanish for "the wanderer") is one of the most renowned pearls in history. It was discovered in the sixteenth century and

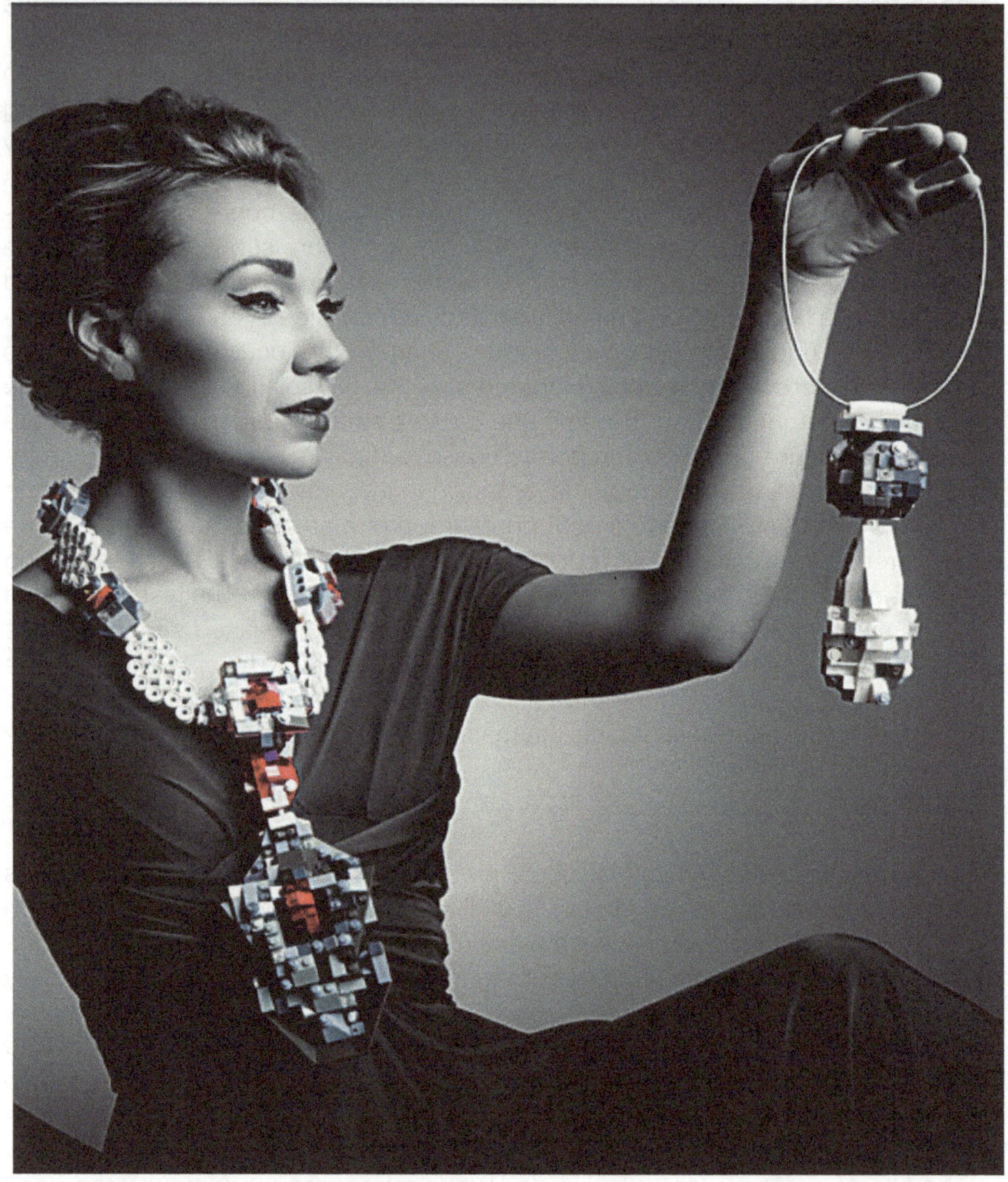

Figure 5. emiko oye, La Reine de Pèlerin, convertible neckpiece, 2013, LEGO®, argentium silver, coated copper wire, coated steel cable. Photo: Marc Olivier Le Blanc 2016, styling: Joui Turandot, hair and makeup: Shana Astrachan of Fox & Doll, courtesy the artist.

owned by several European royal families. Its movements can be traced through royal portraiture, including those of King Philip II of Spain, Elizabeth of France, and Margaret of Austria (Muller, 2012).

Oye's selection of significant pieces that have circulated for centuries emphasizes the meaning and importance of heirlooms beyond monetary value. In her artist's statement she asks:

What is an heirloom but a time traveler, embedded with a rich personal history, crossing the generations to invoke stories and nostalgic memories of loved ones, childhood, past lives. Held dear to our hearts as part of who we are, these objects and treasures may not appear to be precious for any other reason to the casual observer. Once we are gone, what value do our "heirloom" pieces have to future generations and cultures? What if we consider the power of a heirloom as coming from the materials it's made from? (oye, 2017)

Oye's necklaces replace the diamonds, rubies, emeralds, pearls, and platinum of the original designs with LEGO©, which in turn evoke memories of childhood and play. Deviating from materials traditionally associated with jewelry, oye reconsiders what is valuable, and how other factors such as memory and nostalgia influence value (oye, 2017). Another necklace oye chose to interpret is by Cartier and was once owned by the Duchess of Windsor. The necklace was first set with gems repurposed from the Maharani of Baroda's anklets. After the Duchess discovered that her gems had once adorned the ankles of the Maharani, she exchanged them for a 48.95 ct emerald pendant by Harry Winston. The large emerald had once belonged to King Alfonso XIII of Spain (Papi and Rhodes, 2005). The materiality and provenance of the gems themselves were as important to the Duchess as the beauty of their setting. Oye's oversized execution emphasizes her design's "thingness" and the material effects of the object's size on the wearer. Oye's necklaces take over the body, conforming the wearer to it instead of vice versa. In the wake of these monumental LEGO© jewels, the gemstones and precious metals that composed the originals appear inconsequential; what was previously seen as opulent and extraordinary now seems small and understated.

Conclusion

Anya Kivarkis, Mary Hallam Pearse, and emiko oye contemplate ideas of value and reality in a culture that is increasingly ephemeral and where contact with physical objects is often mediated through images on digital platforms. By critically considering the materials and methods used, these artists have created complete wearable artworks that critique adornment and its place in society. Inspiring new ways of thinking about adornment and value through the influence of modern media, these artists' practices are indicative of the current direction of contemporary art jewelry. All three take on the subject of historical and traditional "fine" jewelry through the lens of value hierarchies and material culture (Malpass, 2015). Today, that includes the ever-present digital image, which often substitutes for reality.

Recognizing the photograph as a mediator between the viewer and the object is not immediately intuitive. As viewers, the tendency is to take photographs as impartial. Behind that impartial facade though, the photographer had a perspective from which they took the image, and anyone looking at the image is seeing the jewelry through that lens, which was further altered or focused by the person who made it available on a public platform. At minimum there are two layers of interpretation, and the limitations of a 2D digital medium describing a 3D physical object, between the viewer and the jewelry. Information is lost in translation and other aspects are overemphasized or digitally augmented. In the case of jewelry photography, often the intent is to engender desire or reinforce our perception of jewelry's role in society.

These three jewelry artists help illuminate how our digital world is changing our relationship with adornment. Is jewelry on a screen as real as the jewelry that you wear? Does it matter? Does exposure to digital jewelry affect our preferences, our desires? Do incomplete images result in imaginary pieces of jewelry? How does the timelessness of the digital image affect our understanding of the world and the jewelry in it? Answers to these questions are nuanced and lead to a questioning of the fundamental nature of jewelry and its value systems within our culture—essential to these jeweler's practices (Lindemann, 2011). Their work encourages awareness of the digital image and its influence over our perspectives and desires. This critical eye is ever more important as digital images become increasingly prevalent lest we mistake red carpet snapshots for careful records of jewels, carefully composed fashion photographs for what our desires should be, or luxurious jewels for our heirlooms.

References

Callahan, A. 2010. "Mary Hallam Pearse: That Little Something." *Ornament* 34: 38–43.

Cummins, S., and A. Kivarkis. 2014. "Anya Kivarkis: September Issue." *Art Jewelry Forum*. https://artjewelryforum.org/anya-kivarkis-september-issue.

Habermas, T. 2011. "'Diamonds are a Girl's Best Friend' The Psychology of Jewellery as Beloved Objects." In *Thinking Jewellery: On the Way Towards a Theory of Jewellery*, edited by W. Lindemann, 96–107. Stuttgart, Arnoldsche.

Hallam Pearse, M. 2017. "Artist's Statement." Sent to author, December 10, 2017.

Lindemann, W. (ed.) 2011. *Thinking Jewellery: On the Way Towards a Theory of Jewellery*. Stuttgart: Arnoldsche.

Malpass, M., 2015. "Between Wit and Reason: Defining Associative, Speculative and Critical Design in Practice." *Design and Culture* 5: 333–56.

Muller, P. 2012. *Jewels in Spain, 1500–1800.* Madrid: El Viso.

Nixon, S. and A. Kivarkis. 2018. Oral History Project Interview.

oye, e., 2017. "Artist's Statement." Sent to author, November 3, 2017.

Papi, S., and A. Rhodes. 2005. *Famous Jewelry Collectors*. London: Thames & Hudson.

Glitch in the Copy: Research into Noise Artifact in Digital Reproduction

Annika Pettersson, Konstfack University, Stockholm, Sweden

Abstract

This research project brings together jewelry as a craft with an open manufacturing technology practice governed by an experimental approach towards a craft practice. The purpose is to investigate "noise" artifacts that are created by digital reproduction techniques and to examine how the findings relate today's craft practice.

My starting point for this research project was to investigate the effects of copy in relation to jewelry and digital (re)production. The project was a year-long exploration into the process of copying and (re)producing a specific jewelry piece with digital technology.

With any form or media, copying is only possible to a limited degree of accuracy, often depending on the quality of technique and equipment used within the process. A mold can only be cast a certain amount of times before it begins to degrade and affect the integrity of the copy. This degradation, or generational loss, could be understood as "noise" or as "noise artifacts." The research project entitled "Glitch in the Copy" takes its inspiration from a fascination with this "noise" distortion.

The artistic practical research is framed in craft practice within the contemporary jewelry field. The digital reproduction methods that have been used within the process are 3D printing and 3D scanning. The research project has developed a method for these digital reproduction techniques to create an iteration-based production line that examines a continuous development of noise artifacts.

The result of the practical research has been analyzed on the basis of visual expression and the findings have been related to glitch art theory and the concept of material markers. In this research project, digitally crafted jewelry is created in a multi-stage process and the result is a series of wearable jewelry pieces.

1. Introduction

This project is situated in the context of contemporary jewelry, which is a term that describes the broad range of activities that exist in the field of jewelry, including studio jewelry, art jewelry, and author jewelry, or research jewelry. Contemporary jewelry history dates back to roughly 70 years ago, signifying a shift of focus to the author, with value assigned in accordance with uniqueness and experimentation rather than raw material value (Skinner, 2013).

Contemporary jewelry began to move away from the world of public use or adornment roughly 70 years ago. It moved away from the public domain, instead orienting itself to the gallery, on the plinth, and in the museum. Adopting notions of autonomy resonating with the visual art field, the contemporary jewelry pieces were no longer ordered by a patron. Rather, the pieces were created for an artistic expression based on the maker's vision (Besten, 2011).

In the craft field, a digital revolution has taken place creating crossroads for the innovative craftsman. The digital revolution can be defined as a massive change within digital technologies altering the way knowledge is generated and objects are materialized in all fields from product manufacturing to arts and crafts. During the 1980's and 1990's, new digital possibilities of production became accessible to makers due to the digital revolution of CAD (computer-aided design) (Johnston, 2015).

In recent years, a significant change has taken place as makers, artists, and craftsmen began to embrace digital technologies in their work. As machines of manufacture can produce copies, the quality of handmade and the norm of uniqueness is blurred.

This research project embraces contemporary methods of making that originate from the digital revolution. In this research project, digital fabrication has been used as a method and as a tool.

1.1. Methodology

Data has been collected through a practical research where a craft studio practice has been the focus. The methodology is set within the scope of artistic experimental research, investigating the aesthetic changes that are created by a digital (re)production process based on iteration.

This project investigates the preferred aesthetic of 3D scanners and 3D printers. The physical findings have been aesthetically and formally analyzed and the result has been compared and related to the material marks left by the creator, the handmade, and the machine-made. The main content areas of thinking that have been examined are of glitch art and craft theory.

1.2. Methods

Methods of reproduction that have been used are 3D scanning and 3D printing. The decision to focus on these two digital reproduction methods was determined due to the fact that 3D scanning and 3D printing are techniques which are commonly used by today's craft practitioners. The 3D scanner used in this research project is called David SLS-3. The 3D printing has been outsourced to one of the leading 3D printing companies to ensure that the prints maintain a constant high quality throughout the research. The research pieces have been printed in a high definition plastic, since it serves as the material that is the most accurate in terms of surface, shape, and detail.

2. Glitch

Glitch art is the practice of using digital or analog errors for aesthetic purposes by either corrupting digital data or physically manipulating electronic devices. A glitch is defined by Dutch artist Rosa in the paper "Glitch Art Momentum":

I describe the glitch as an (actual and/or simulated) break from an expected or conventional flow of information or meaning within (digital) communication systems that result in a perceived accident or error. A glitch occurs on the occasion where there is an absence of (expected) functionality, whether understood in a technical or social sense. (Menkman, 2011, p. 9)

In 1984, mathematician Claude Shannon was investigating the concept of absence of functionality within digital technology. In Shannon's book *Mathematical Theory of Communication*, he explains how messages and information are transferred, and how during this transfer, external noise is introduced to the signal while it is in transmission, obscuring the purity of the signal (Shannon, 1964).

This kind of external noise has a particular materiality and enters into the equation as unplanned variations and random error. When information is moved from one place to another it requires transformation. During this transformation point external noise is added.

This point of transfer is essential because it reveals something about the relationship between raw information, the machine, and the spaces connected together for the purpose of transmission (Menkman, 2011).

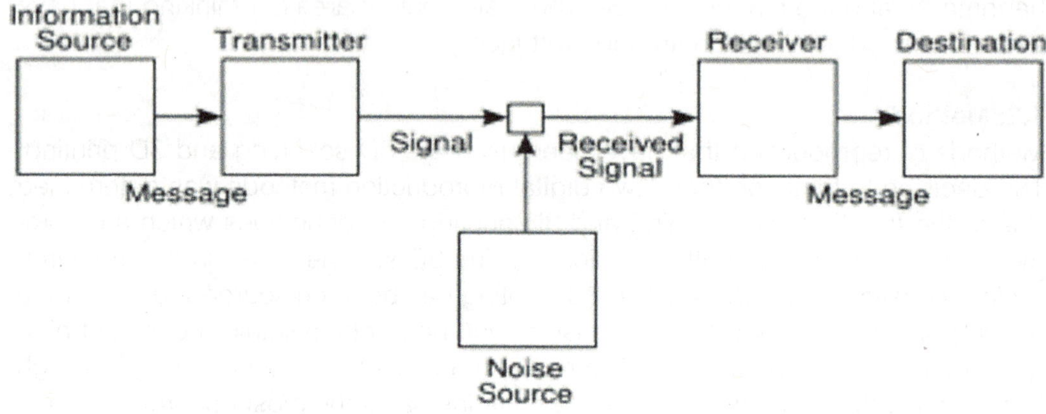

Figure 1. Showing Claude Shannon's communication theory in symbols.

Menkman states that there are three occasions where a glitch can appear, aligning with Claude Shannon's thoughts of the transformation of information. These are the three stages that have been analyzed through practical research:

- *Encoding.* The process of 3D scanning physical jewelry; a recording and storing process.
- *Decoding.* The process of 3D printing, binary data, 0s and 1s stored in a computer translated to a tool path code. This code is then sent to a 3d printer that physically renders the information and creates a physical 3D print.
- *Feedback.* A loop or repetition of a procedure applied to the result of a previous application.

By using these specific methods and techniques, the practical research is structured to encourage glitches to occur. The glitches that have appeared can be seen as an intimate experience with a machine and a program when a system is showing its hidden information and its inner workings: its strengths and its weaknesses (Menkman, 2011).

3. Material Markers

Designer and woodworker David Pry wrote the book *The Nature and Art of Workmanship*, in which he discusses the workmanship of certainty and the workmanship of risk. Pry defines the workmanship of risk as "using any kind of technique or apparatus, in which the quality of the result is not predetermined, but depends on the judgment, dexterity, and care which the maker exercises as he works" (Pry, 1968, p. 20)

Production in this case involves the risk of failure. The workmanship of certainty, on the other hand, relies on industrial production, where the process should guarantee the result, without any risk involved.

When using digital techniques, one is using a more complex system for reproduction, since a computer (a complex instrument based on a logic often unknown by its user) can behave in unpredictable ways. Malfunctions or failures are hidden behind the slick surfaces and complex code languages of computers. Each of these new and improved techniques will always have their own fingerprints of imperfection (Menkman, 2011). To use Pye's terminology, 3D scanners and 3D printers are not performing the workmanship of certainty, but rather they are showcasing the workmanship of risk.

Most people experience these fingerprints as negative (and sometimes even as accidents). This project emphasizes the positive consequences of these imperfections by showing the new opportunities they facilitate (Verbruggen, 2013).

Material Markers

Material markers of the artist's "hand" were common when the arts and craft movements were active; one could find the appearance of visible brush strokes, imperfections, and natural variations in manufacture, such as hammer marks or other abnormalities. These marks, which at one point signified unskilled craft, are now seen as a signifier for the handmade and crafted in contrast to the mass produced or machine made. The material markers show a physical production—both glitches and other historical errors show the faults within the perfected machine as the material markers once did in craft production (Betancourt, 2017).

Using digital techniques to extract information from the physical world will always leave an imprint on binary information. The machine used will always leave its mark in the code and in the structure of the extracted information. Tools and equipment are extensions of the body that carry the thought of the maker, wholly different from the autonomous production of machines (Charny, 2011). Computers, on the other hand, are different from machines; they interpret and translate information.

In this translation, changes occur and noise is added as described by Shannon in *Mathematical Theory of Communication*.

4. Practical Research

The role of practical research can be seen as a sequence of actions that set in motion a curiosity to go beyond what is already known—a nonverbal language used to find and generate new knowledge, creating new ways of thinking through engagement with material, techniques, and ideas.

This project's practical research consists of a series of repetitive actions based on iteration. The process is based on a repetition of a procedure that is applied to the result of a previous application. The practical research can be divided into four steps:

- 3D scanning
- Storing binary information
- 3D printing of the stored binary data
- A physical representation of binary data

The practical research starts with an original piece of jewelry that is 3D scanned. The binary information is then stored in a computer. The stored binary information is transferred to a 3D printer that creates a physical rendered copy of the binary information. The physical result of this series of actions is titled Scan_1. This copy is now the starting point for the second series of actions, which creates a production based on iteration and feedback.

5.1. Original

The practical research starts with an original piece of jewelry that was selected based on a set of requirements relating to the digital reproduction techniques and function.

- The original should be a brooch. A brooch is a piece of jewelry that is least dependent on the body, which gives it a freedom within its physical presence. A brooch allows the jewelry piece to drastically change without any loss of wearability.
- The original should be a classical piece of jewelry. Aesthetically, the original should represent an iconic piece of jewelry. A unified reconcilable original with a defined aesthetic will show possible transformations more clearly.
- The original should have fine details. The details will give the project a valuation parameter, a scale to measure the changes.

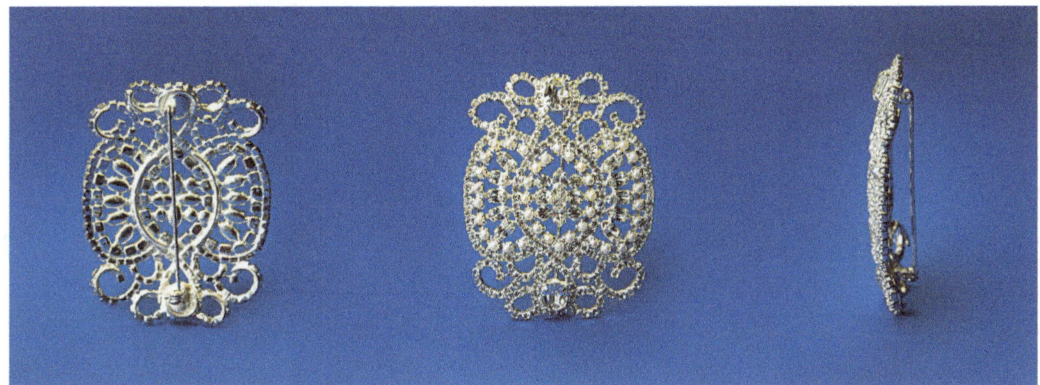

Figure 2. Picture of the original Victorian brooch that has been used in this research. From left to right: back, front, and side views of the brooch.

- The original should have a complex shape in relation to the reproduction methods used within the practical research. This means that the original piece of jewelry's form should be challenging to 3D scan and 3D print. This forces the machines to work on a high capacity and show their inherent abilities and aesthetic.
- The original piece for this research project is a classical Victorian brooch. This piece of jewelry meets all the qualifications as it is a brooch, it is a classical piece of jewelry with many fine details, and it has a complex shape.

5.2. Process—Finished Pieces

It is important to separate the process from the finished jewelry wearable pieces. In the practical research, the pieces have been printed in a high definition plastic. The high definition plastic is the most accurate material to 3D print in, but the material does not function well in a finished piece of wearable jewelry.

The finished jewelry pieces have been 3D printed in aluminum. The physical qualities of the aluminum do not limit the finished jewelry's size; instead, it gives the finished jewelry a solid feeling with a substantial weight.

Within this research project, the act of 3D scanning and 3D printing have been performed twenty times. After the process had been repeated fifteen times the aesthetic changes began to decrease. From Scan_15 to Scan_20 very little new data was found, and therefore it became a natural ending point for the practical research.

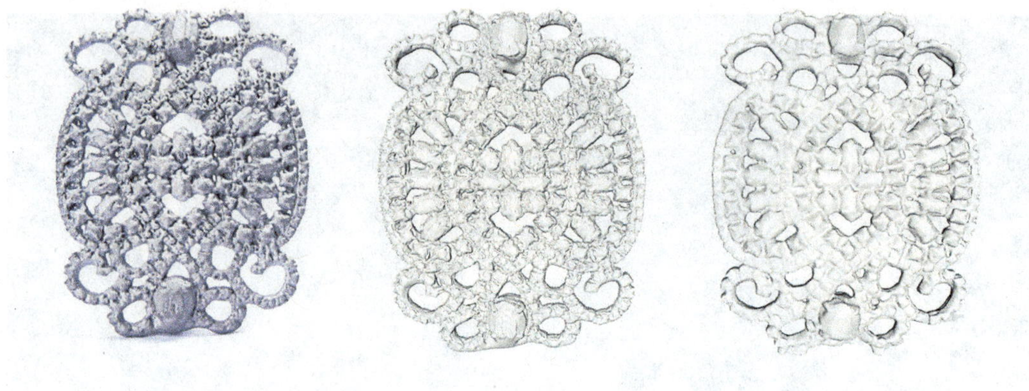

Figure 3. From left to right: Scan_1 in aluminum, Scan_1, and Scan_10.

In this paper, the Scan_1 and the Print_1 will be analyzed and after that every fourth scan. This will give a total of six different snapshots of the processes: Scan_1, Print_1, Scan_5, Scan_10, Scan_15, Scan_20, each scan that is analyzed will be so in relation to four criteria: details, holes, shape, and expression.

Scan_1

A comparison between the first 3D scan and the 3D print of the first scan shows that there are some minor formal differences in translation.

- Details: The edges are of a slightly wider diameter in comparison to the original jewelry piece.
- Holes: No changes have occurred.
- Shape: The bottom large corner tilted slightly, giving the piece a less symmetrical appearance.
- Expression: No changes have occurred.

Scan_5

- *Details:* The smaller details have been blurred, all individual shapes are still distinguishable but their distinct shapes are now blunt. The individual shapes no longer have a clearly defined shape; instead, their shape has merged together with the base construction.

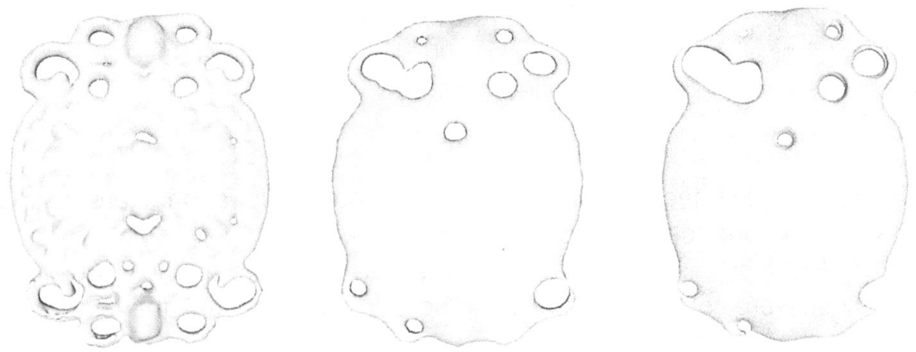

Figure 4. From left to right: Scan_10, Scan_15, and Scan_20.

- Holes: The holes are becoming slightly smaller, but they still obtain their distinct original shape.
- Shape: The overall shape resembles the original; it still has all the recognizable elements. Scan_5 appears to be thicker and heavier. This is caused by the negative spaces between the individual shapes decreasing in mass.
- Expression: The piece is softer in its expression and is no longer sharp and distinct.

Scan_10

- Details: The smaller refined details are gone, but one can still trace the bigger details such as the bigger stones in the upper and lower part, and one can still see traces of the medium-sized individual stones. All stones now appear as protuberances in the surface.
- Holes: The smaller holes located on in the center on the sides have either totally disappeared, or they have decreased significantly in size. The bigger holes have been slightly deformed in various ways, and all remaining holes are rounder.
- Shape: Scan_10 has kept its silhouette form. The upper part is denser, and the two arch shapes next to the big top corner are now thicker and bulkier. In the middle part, the negative space that used to define the individual parts are filled and the surface is smoother.

- Expression: Scan_10 general expression is much heftier and smoother due to the fact that all its parts have been rounded. Many details have been removed and the shape appears simplified.

Scan_15

- Details: All the surface details are now gone; no individual parts are distinguishable and the surface is comparatively smooth.
- Holes: All the smaller holes have disappeared and there are no traces left of the holes that were once present. The big holes are still present; they have lost their original shape and are now circular.
- Shape: The overall general shape is simplified and has big smooth surfaces without any details. The piece is no longer symmetrical; there are differences between the upper and lower parts, as well as between the right and left parts. The silhouette is now more streamlined.
- Expression: Thicker both physically and aesthetically. The big smooth surface gives the piece a solid, sleek feeling, and the rounded edges create a simple spherical impression. The lack of details gives Scan_15 an appearance to be more simple and uninformed in its expression.

Scan_20

- Details: There has been little change in details in the comparison between Scan_15 and Scan_20. All of the fine details were gone by Scan_15, and the transformation is now less present.
- Holes: Three of the holes that were located in the bottom part of Scan_20 are enlarged and losing their outer wall; there is now a dent in the outer shapes.
- Shape: The shape of Scan_20 has minor changes in comparison to Scan_15. The overall shape is now slightly more simple; the shape feels more oval.
- Expression: Scan_20 has a minimalistic and fluid expression. It feels more light and airy due to the delicate, thin material that occurs along the outer contours.

6. Conclusion

This research project investigated the type of glitches or noise artifacts that have been created by a digital reproduction of 3D scanners and 3D printers. Glitches have become a prominent aesthetic of the arts in the late twentieth century, reminding us that our control of technology can be illusory, revealing digital tools to be only as perfect as those that build them. Glitches are a part of digital technology; one can say that it is inherent in the medium.

During this research project, a piece of classical jewelry has been translated between a physical state and a digital state, and the research shows that the shapes simplify, details disappear, and holes get filled. The overall shape gets rounded, and the length and the width decrease while the thickness increases.

Halfway through the practical research, a shift took place; the process of 3D scanning and 3D printing became easier, fewer errors occurred, and the results became more accurate. Just like the expression, the practical research became smoother and simpler the further the practical research progressed.

The overall shape changed, becoming digital friendly, adapting to the production methods. After twenty scans, the aesthetic had changed to the point where it had become digitalized to fit the digital reproduction process. The production process based on iteration opened up for glitches and noise artifacts to occur resulting in a change in the aesthetic of the outcomes.

A classical Victorian brooch changed every time it was translated from binary code to tangible object. In this research project, a classical piece of jewelry was transformed into a contemporary brooch, not shaped by a human hand, but by a digital reproduction process.

References

Betancourt, M. 2017. *Glitch Art in Theory and Practice: Critical Failures and Post-Digital Aesthetics.* New York: Routledge.

Charny, D. (ed.) 2011. *Power of Making: The Importance of Being Skilled.* London: Victoria & Albert Museum.

Menkman, R. 2011. *Glitch Art Momentum* [e-book]. Amsterdam: Institute of Network Cultures. https://networkcultures.org/_uploads/NN%234_RosaMenkman.pdf.

Pry, D. 1964. *The Nature and Art of Workmanship.* Reprint 1995. London: Herbert.

Shannon, C. 1964. *Mathematical Theory of Communication.* 10th ed. Urbana: University of Illinois Press.

Skinner, D. 2013. *Contemporary Jewelry in Perspective.* Asheville, NC: Lark Crafts in association with Art Jewelry Forum.

Verbruggen, D. 2013. "The Digital Craftsman and His Tools." Conference. Falmouth, UK. http://unfold.be/pages/the-digital-craftsman-and-his-tools-essay.

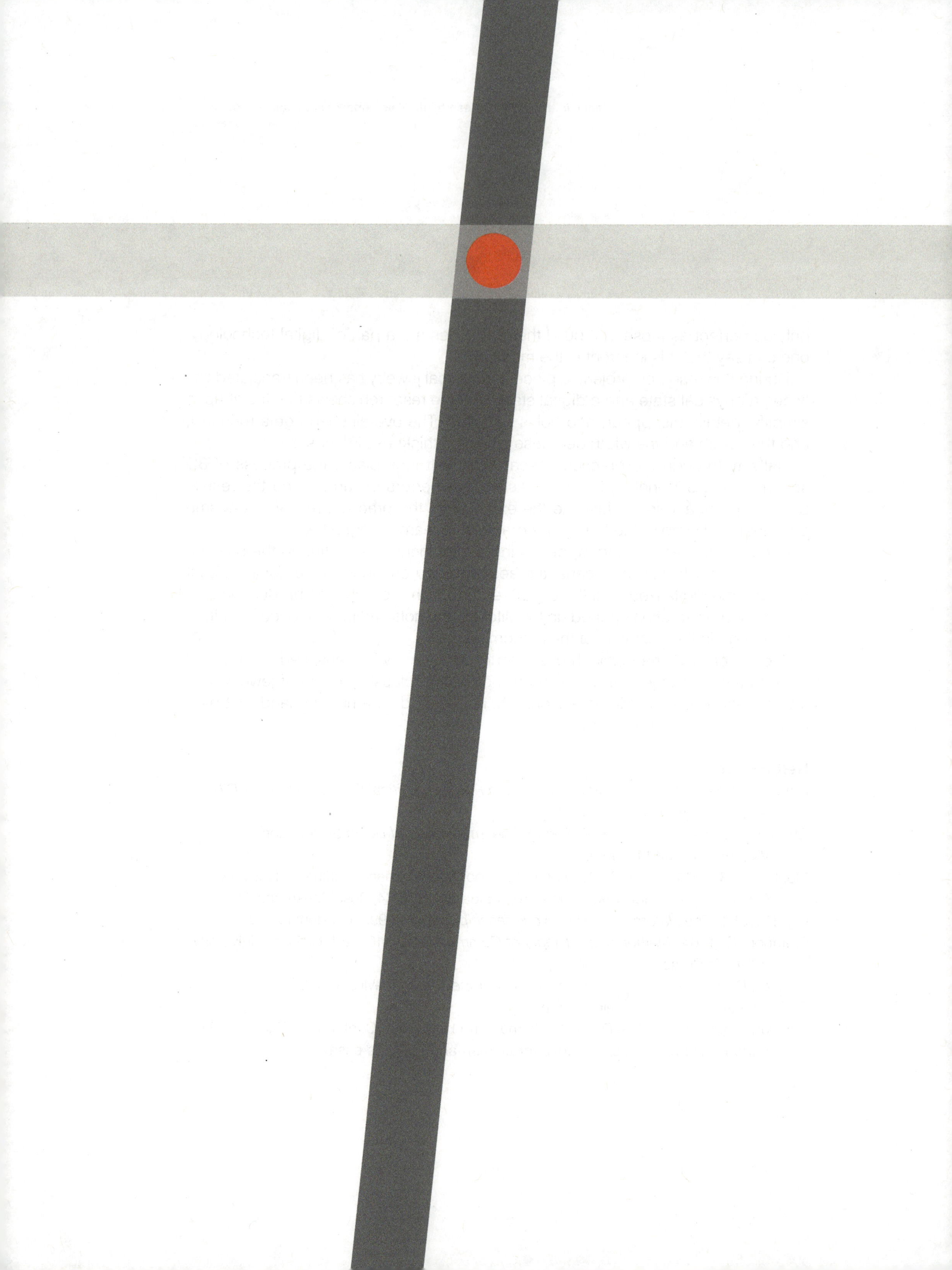

Future Carriers of Our Past

Paulina Sierra, Universidad Iberoamericana, Mexico City, Mexico

Abstract

On May 2017, my path crossed with the Xico Valley Community Museum in the Chalco Valley in the State of Mexico and instantly fell in love with the community work they were exerting.

While spending some time there, I stumbled upon small fragments of broken pots and vessels on the premises. Not at all an unusual event, figurines, obsidian knives, and even fossils are usually found not only in the museum but in the grandeur of the Xico Valley. These are remains of Aztec, Teotihuacan, Coyotlatec, Chalco Polychrome and Toltec cultures that date back to pre-Classic and even Pre-historic periods.

More often than not, budgets for educational or restoration purposes in countries are diminished and, in some instances, completely severed. With these incoming tides of abandonment crashing against preservation, Future Carriers of Our Past is an art project that pretends to reappropriate some of these fragments, by creating a silver base to transform them as pendants.

By transfixing the decaying object unto a wearable piece, it converts the carrier into a living entity that can safeguard these pieces of jewelry. Not only, these actions provide a one of a kind adornment that denotes the craft from the pre-Hispanic artist, but the "emphatic responsibility" of being akin to another civilization through the bearing of a significant object from the Mexican culture.

Future Carriers of our Past

"Who owns History? Everyone and no one . . ."
—Eric Foner, Who Owns History?: Rethinking the Past in a Changing World

On May 6, 2017, my journey crossed with the Chalco Valley in the State of Mexico, a rough municipality that resides adjacent to the eastern side of Mexico City. Settled just north of that green-patterned basin, between two extinct volcanoes, lies the

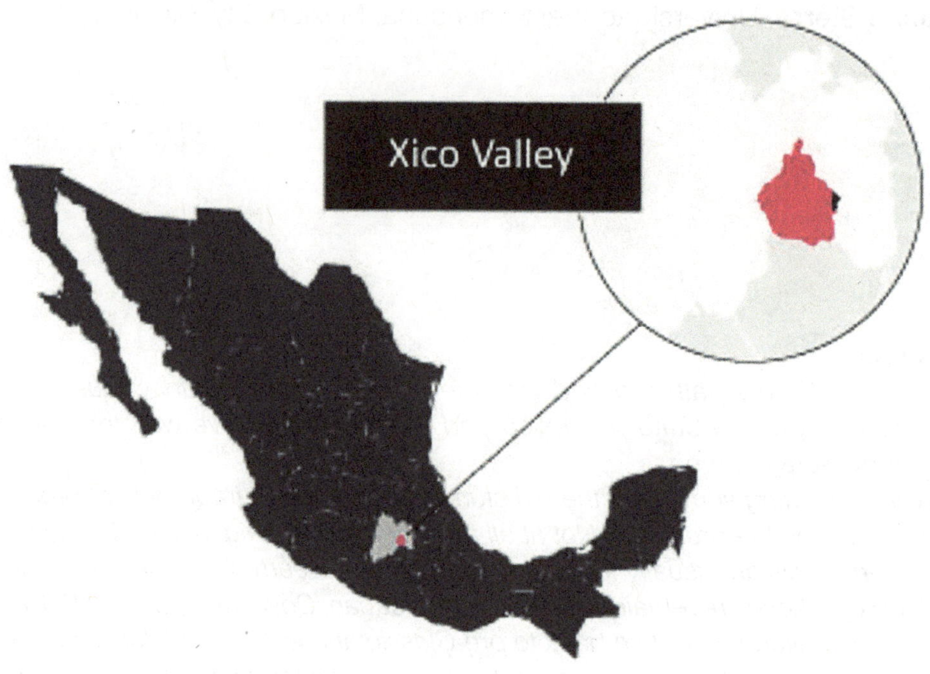

Figure 1. Xico Valley Location. Source: Author, 2017.

Xico Valley Community Museum, also known as the Ex-Hacienda of Xico, one that according to Rivero, in his book published at the beginning of the twentieth century, rested Hernán Cortés, the famous Spanish conquerors' country house awarded to him by the king of Spain in 1529.

Of all the fortunes that excite my imagination to think, I'm at the exact same place where the conqueror came to rest and whose grandeur was perceived by Napoleon as the most notable in history, and that the valley there, was once a lake and the eternal snowy peaks of those mountains were contemplated by that extraordinary being in many dawns similar to this one, not only in the quality of light but on the amount of joy, poured upon these pages. (Rivero 1911, p. 104)

Four hundred years after the Spanish conquest, a wealthier Spaniard, Iñigo Noriega, "built a superb palace in the shape of a castle, with four lean towers, artistic gardens and lush trees" (Rivero, 1911, p.103) upon the frail vestiges of the conqueror's country house.

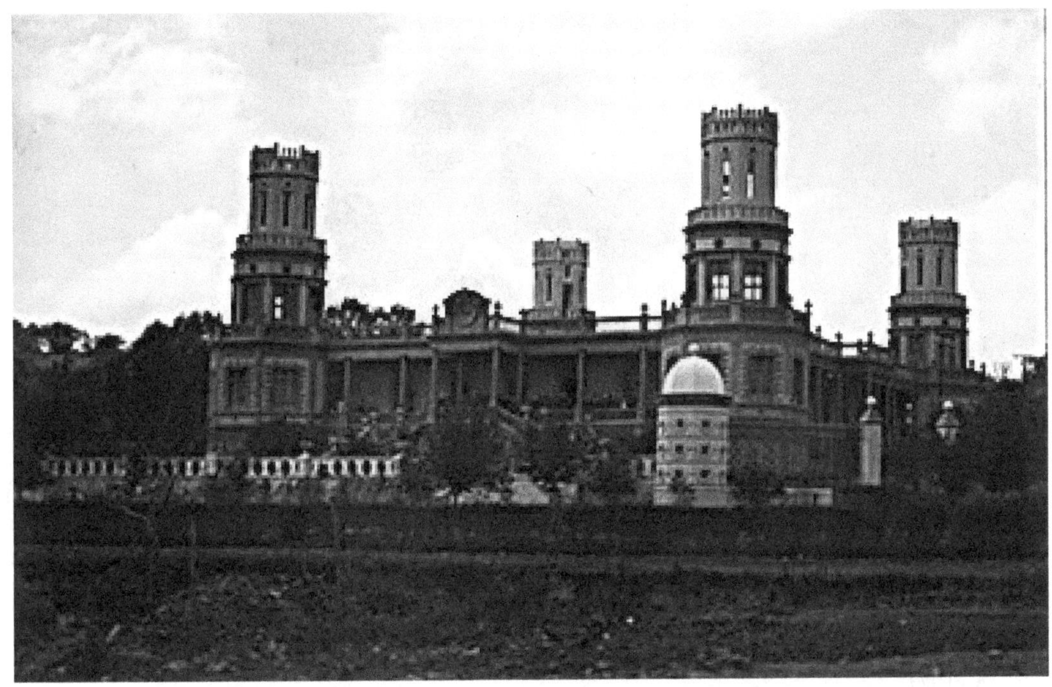

Figure 2. Former Hacienda of Xico built by Noriega. (CronistadeNuestroAntiguoIxtapalucaChalco, 2014)

Today, this resilient complex has a slow yet ongoing restoration that barely survived the Mexican Revolution in 1910, a later land expropriation, and the final desiccation of the lake in the 60s. Since June 1996, it is home to the Xico Valley Community Museum fueled by a humble yet powerful vision: to keep the story of the Chalco Valley and its inhabitants in one place. While the space itself is probably what anyone would expect from an underbudgeted community museum, visual art classes, walking tours to the crater, and a small library keeps local and foreign visitors successfully pouring in. Foreign visitors pour in even though the site is adjacent to "the largest favela (shanty town) in the world." (Waldrep, 2015). The residents live a precarious existence, under constant threat of violent crime. This reality plagues the people who live not only in the Chaka Valley, but also in the neighboring boroughs of Neza City and Iztapalapa.

While I was there, I stumbled upon small fragments of pots and vessels that seemed antique but was not expecting them to be original. By original, I mean

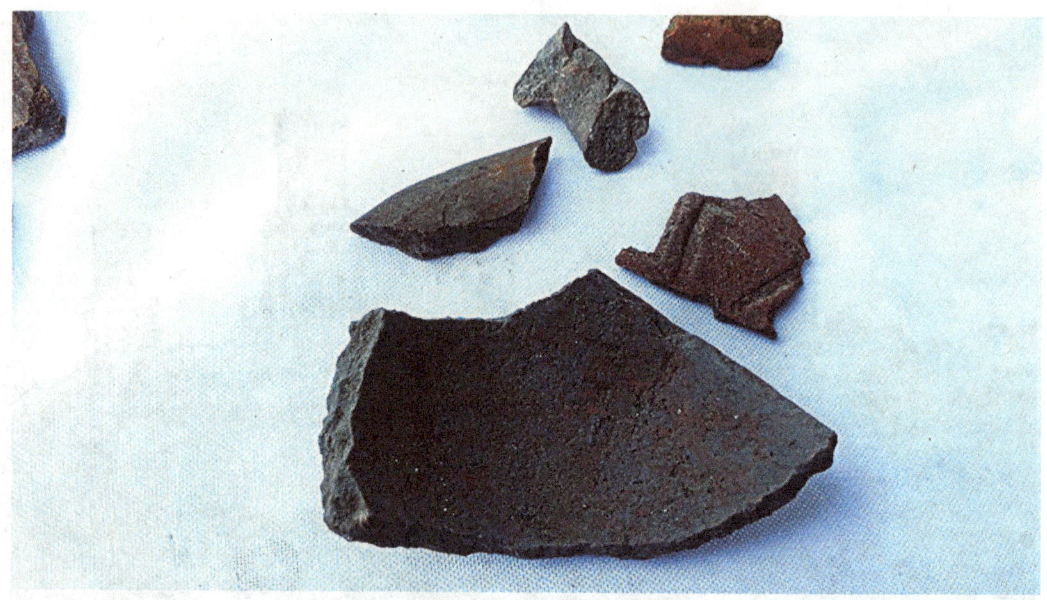

Figure 3. Fragments of pots and vessels found at the Xico Valley Community Museum May 2017. (Sierra, 2017)

authentically dating from the first century after the birth of Christ. Yet through a conversation with the museum's director, Genaro Altamirano, on May 29, 2017, in search for their authenticity, he replied briskly: "Oh, yes, these are scattered all over the valley. Long time ago, this place was a busy commercial spot and a convergence of trade and different cultures through the lake. Some of these we keep as people bring them over to us but there are so many we end up putting them in boxes or people sometimes end up creating their own collections or using them as ashtrays upon dusty bookshelves."

To the irreversible loss of our past, my heart sank in despair.

But then, I decided to do some research.

According to María Villarreal, National Coordinator of the Instituto Nacional de Anthropologia e Historia (INAH)'s legal division in 2007, "More than a million of archeological pieces are in private hands and . . . the National Institute of History and Anthropology in Mexico can grant their use as long as these are registered" (Aguilar, 2007). From those registered pieces it is clear the people never become the real owners, as these will always remain national heritage.

Additionally, according to the Federal Law of Monuments and Archeological, Artistic and Historical Sites (2018), "any individual can keep the pieces as long as they are registered to avoid their illegal sell." While this holds true for pieces found in demarcated archeological zones, what regulation was offered to Pe-hispanic fragments? I couldn't find any. In addition, the ambiguity in regards to the relevance of any artistic, historical, or archeological monument (not fragment) resides in terms of "the following characteristics: representativity, determined stylistic current, innovation degree, used materials and techniques" (Ley Federal sobre Monumentos y Zonas Arqueológicos, Artísticos e Históricos, 2018).

So, on October 7, 2017, I went back to the museum to ask Don Genaro if he could show me the pieces he kept orphaned, unacknowledged in plastic blue bins. Some of these samples were spectacular, they seemed as if, after a long period of darkness, they slowly yawned and awakened to their full glory.

After a long conversation, he agreed to donate the tiniest ones, which he then helped me, catalogue one by one. The final selection of twelve pieces are by no means large, nor fragments that by themselves represent key parts of a larger one; they were also, definitely not made from human bones, carved out of precious stones, fossils, or have codices inscribed within them.

Ten items are identified as belonging to five unique cultures: Teotihuacan (100–650 AD), Coyotlatelco (650–900 AD), Toltec (900–1200 AD), Aztec II (1200 AD) and Polychrome Chalco (1200–1520 AD). One of them is generic, meaning it could belong to any culture, due to the lack of formal information about it, and is catalogued from an unknown period.

Some of these cultures rose to their full domination as they met with others for trade and power while others declined as they clashed in sanguinary battles against each other. Whatever fragment is found any place, no matter how insignificant, it is what remains of our culture as a whole.

As soon as I closed the lid of a small aluminum box where I kept them momentarily, I directed myself to a prominent jeweler, Tanya Moss in Mexico City, whose valuable skills with her atelier forged, bent, and lovingly encased these fragments of our culture into something that intended to salvage the loss of our past.

The results were simple yet beautiful. By transfixing the object into a wearable piece, that immediately transforms the carrier into a living entity that can safeguard these pieces. And while these actions also provide a one-of-a-kind adornment that denotes the craft from a pre-Hispanic artist, they enhance what Jonas in his book *The Imperative of Responsibility: The Search of Ethics for the Technological Age* explains as "the emphatic responsibility," or a duty to use techne ethically towards

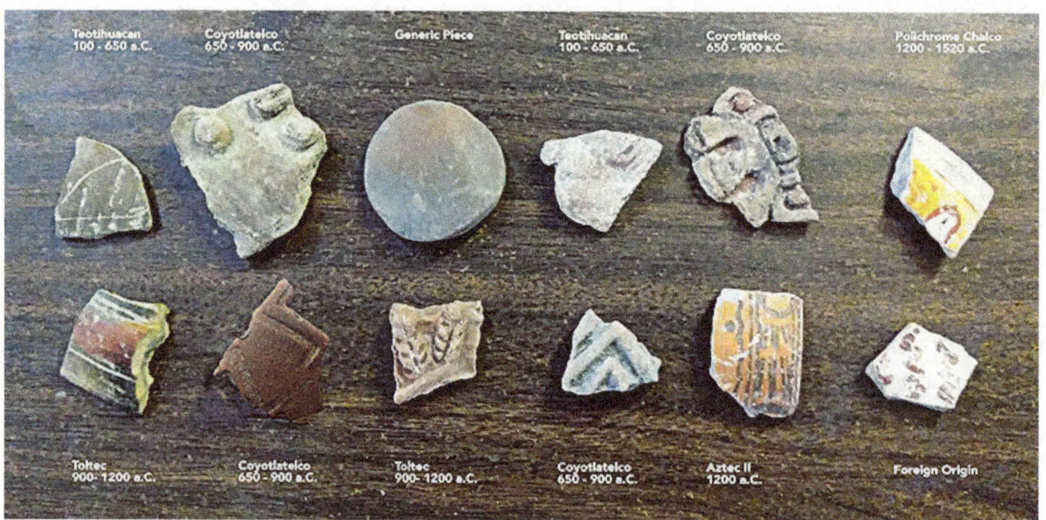

Figure 4. Final selection of twelve fragments.
(Sierra, 2017)

the future in standards "of solidarity, of sympathy, of equitableness, indeed even of compassion" (Jonas, 2000, p. 42) and, in this particular case, of being akin to another civilization through the bearing of a significant object from the Mexican culture through the jewelry craft.

That there be future bearers of it, so as to ensure its very perpetuity in the world, comes first in the hierarchy of duties. But of course, to impose it on future subjects presupposes that we have not prejudiced their capacity to bear it. (Jonas, 2000, p. 42)

Call it electricity or a jewelry collection, we have come to understand how a craft, a technique, or any technology can become a legacy in itself and how it may entitle a responsibility on the one who uses, owns, or wears it. Quality and the value of this "handcraftsmanship" (L'Ecuyer et al., 2010, p. 22) has become a way to recognize humanity's fleeting and defining moments, social dynamics and ideals.

Another way to interpret this issue of influence and appropriation is to recognize that studio jewelers, since the 1940's have had their own agenda rooted in the history of jewelry. They (and the wearers of their work) express criticism of what they perceive as the bland conventionality of mass-produced objects and the ostentatious display of wealth in precious gemstone jewelry. They seek to make a new kind

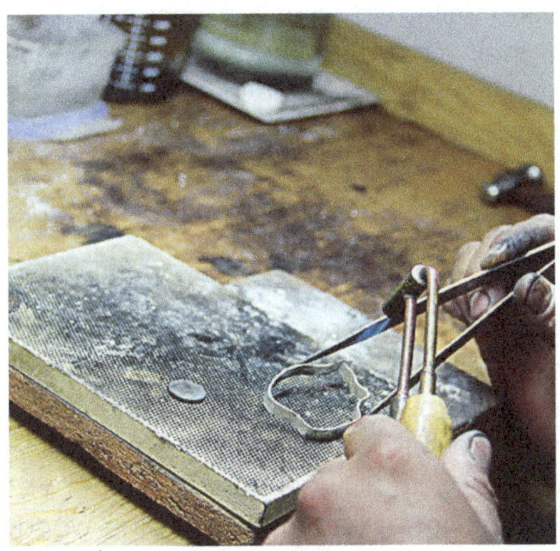
Figure 5. Tanya Moss Atelier. (Tanya Moss, 2017)

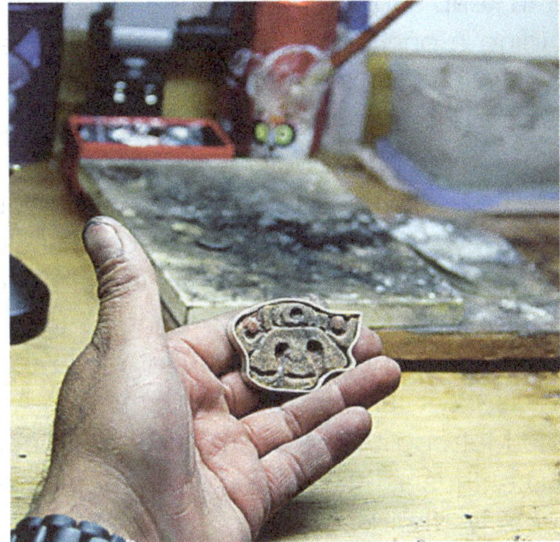
Figure 6. Tanya Moss Atelier. (Tanya Moss, 2017)

of adornment that privileges individual expression, nonconformity, and aesthetic and intellectual values. (L'Ecuyer et al., 2010, p. 27)

In regards to the jewelry pieces from the Xico Valley, I believed there was a possibility to explore a self-funded artistic process that could become a path towards the ownership of our heritage and subvert the traditional notion of preservation through any institution exceeded in their capacities.

In order to pose this question, all pieces were signed in the back, installed and displayed in a collective art show called *Timeless Fragments* (Sacquegna, 2017) at the Palazzo Nervegna in Brindisi, Italy where I decided to showcase them within a timeline, under their original creation date and the wonderful culture it belonged to. At the show's opening, someone who had been aiding the installation process came over and gave me a present. It was a seashell fossil. "We found this while we were building our house in Lecce," a historic in the Apulia region. "Maybe you can do something wonderful with this too," she said. It suddenly dawned on me how every culture had it's wonderful, anonymous relics, silently looking at the living, maybe feeling unappreciated, bored even. Had I touched a common human preoccupation somehow?

To be completely honest, the whole purpose of the project was also to make a little revolution of my own, a humble one, that is. To recuperate the initial investment and keep supporting the great effort of the Xico Valley Community Museum by providing a one year jewelry course to one of their most dedicated volunteers. This was not a self-determined decision; she was the one, when interviewed on May 29, 2017, stated that if she could have the possibility to learn one skill to teach courses at the museum, jewelry would be it.

The beginning of a cycle has been set, so she can hopefully enjoy the acquiring of a new set of skills, but also give back to a community whose frailty and lack of opportunities can become an important catalyst of change.

On a conceptual level, I hoped to raise some questions that may or may not be pondered upon. First, what is the relation between a museum and the objects it displays through their collections? A great example of this, the "MediaLab at the Metropolitan Museum of Art has been working with Creative technologists and 3D enthusiasts, using photogrammetry and hand-held 3D scanners, to render objects in [their] collection into 3D models that [anyone] can share with the world. [The MediaLab] encourages everyone to use [their] content, which represents the world's cultural heritage, to create their own creative works" (Metropolitan Museum of Art). This digital gesture that originally sparked from preservation efforts now allows users to edit and 3D print some of the museum's heritage in unforeseen ways, but most importantly, keeping history alive.

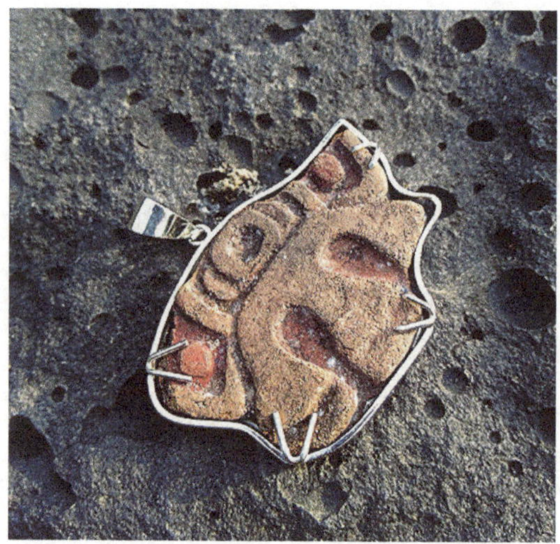

Figure 7. Future Carriers of Our Past: Coyotlatelco Period. Source: Author, 2017.

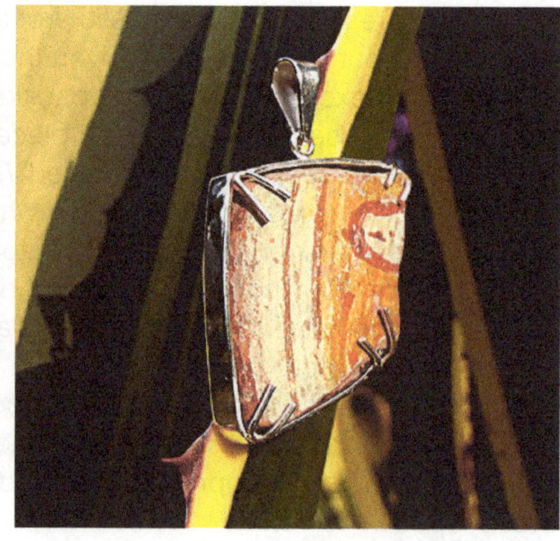

Figure 8. Future Carriers of Our Past: Polychrome Chalco Period. Source: Author, 2017.

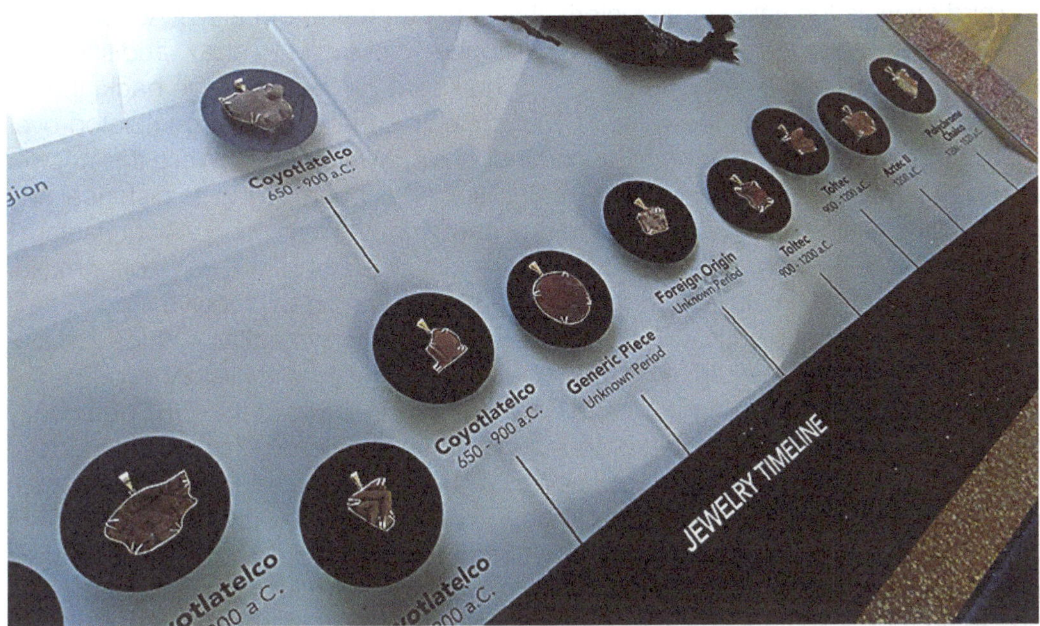

Figure 9. Future Carriers of Our Past at the *Timeless Fragments* show at Palazzo Nervegna, Brindisi, Italy in December 2017. (Sierra, 2017)

Second, if history can no longer be preserved by institutions due to several socio-economical circumstances of a country, whose duty, if not a private one, is it to help salvage our past? On March 21, 2019, museums, historical sites, and zoos in the US, received an update from the Financial Accounting Standards Board (FASB) to account for artwork and dinosaur bones. In its amendments to Subtopic 958–360 a disclosure was added in regard to works of art, historical treasures, and similar assets. It establishes: "A collection-holding NFP shall disclose its organizational policy for the use of proceeds from deaccessioned collection items, including whether those proceeds could be used for acquisitions of new collection items, the direct care of existing collections, or both. If the collection-holding entity allows proceeds from deaccessioned collection items to be used for direct care, the entity shall disclose its definition of direct care" (FASB, 2019). What this means is museums can now have the opportunity to sell, for example, a copy of a not-so-pristine valuable photograph hanging from a donor's home to aid the photograph collection on its premises.

Third, what is the value of an historical asset once reappropriated? According to Cathy Clarke, chief assurance officer at CliftonLarsonAllen LLP, a tax, auditing, outsourcing, and wealth advisory in the US: "Who knows? How do you go back and do the math and say what is the value of your collection that you've accumulated over 100 years? What's the value of . . . dinosaur bones?" (White, 2019). While this answer may be vague, the Gettysburg Museum of History has been selling its historical artifacts online, assigning the objects as direct care from the institution: "All artifacts . . . are from the Gettysburg Museum of History's collection/archives. . . . We offer museum documentation on all artifacts and relics sold by us. You will receive a document verifying the items authenticity. All money raised by the sale of artifacts helps to maintain the Gettysburg Museum of History" (Gettysburg Museum of History, n.d.).

The range of objects and prices is wide, from King Edward the VII's personally owned cigar for $495 USD to a copious lock of Senator Henry Clay's hair in a case for $1,699 USD. Hypothetically speaking, whatever craft added to any of these pieces could possibly be added to the original purchased price. But then again, when it comes to the Mexican territory, where uncatalogued, unaccounted, broken pots and vessels of any archeological period can not be officially assesed, the value, again, becomes murky.

Finally, I believe that, as an individual right to become an originator of all sorts, maybe artists can become part of a country's history, by acquiring a sense of duty towards the country's heritage to conserve and shelter through happy carriers the evidence of an already invaluable previous craft.

References

Aguilar, J.C. 2007. "Más de un millón de piezas arqueológicas, en manos de particulares; el INAH las registra y autoriza "concesión de uso." *La Crónica*, August 19, 2007. http://www.cronica.com.mx/notas/2007/318188.html.

Financial Accounting Standards Board. 2019. *Accounting Standards Update, Not-for-Profit Entities (Topic 958), Updating the Definition of Collections, (2019). No. 482.* https://fasb.org/jsp/FASB/Document_C/DocumentPage?cid=1176172375318&acceptedDisclaimer=true.

Foner, E. 2003. *Who Owns History? Rethinking the Past in a Changing World.* New York: Hill and Wang.

Gettysburg Museum Of History. n.d. *Other Historical Artifacts.* https://www.gettysburgmuseumofhistory.com/product-category/other-historical-artifacts.

Jonas, H. 2000. *The Imperative of Responsibility: In Search of an Ethics for the Technological Age.* Chicago: University of Chicago Press.

L'Ecuyer, K., M. Finamore, and Y. Markowitz. 2010. *Jewelry by Artists: In the Studio, 1940–2000.* Boston, MA: Museum of Fine Arts Publications.

Ley Federal Sobre Monumentos y Zonas Arqueológicos, Artísticos e Históricos, 1972 (Revised text 16–02–2018). Diario Oficial de la Federación. http://www.diputados.gob.mx/LeyesBiblio/pdf/131_160218.pdf.

Metropolitan Museum of Art. 2019. *Thingiverse.* https://www.thingiverse.com/met/about.

Rivero, N. 1911. *Recuerdos de Méjico: 1910.* Havana, Cuba: Rambla y Bouza.

Sacquegna, D. 2017. *Frammenti senza tempo, festival di arti visive e performative a Brindisi.* https://www.primopianogallery.com/en/15203–frammenti-senza-tempo.

Waldrep, M. 2015. "Scenes from Neza: Mexico's Self-Made City." *National Geographic Society Newsroom*, March 26, 2015. https://blog.nationalgeographic.org/2015/03/26/scenes-from-neza-mexicos-self-made-city.

White, N.M. 2019. "Museums Selling 'Priceless' Treasures Get Accounting Break." *Bloomgberg Tax,* March 21, 2019. https://news.bloombergtax.com/financial-accounting/museums-selling-priceless-treasures-get-accounting-break.

Image References

Sierra, P. 2017. Xico Valley location. Former Hacienda of Xico. Mexico City. Courtesy of the artist.

Cronistadenuestroantiguoixtapalucachalco. 2014. State of Mexico. https://www.facebook.com/NuestroAntiguoIxtapalucaChalco/photos/pcb.691768080916590/691766194250112/?type=3&theater.

Sierra, P. 2017. Fragments of pots and vessels at Xico Valley. State of Mexico. Courtesy of the artist.

Sierra, P. 2017. Final selection of 12 fragments. State of Mexico. Courtesy of the artist.

Moss, T. 2017. Jewelry process documentation. Mexico City. Courtesy of Tanya Moss's staff.

Moss, T. 2017. Jewelry process documentation. Mexico City. Courtesy of Tanya Moss's staff.

Sierra, P. 2017. ***Future Carriers of Our Past: Coyotlatelco Period.*** Mexico City. Courtesy of the artist.

Sierra, P. 2017. ***Future Carriers of Our Past: Polychrome Chalco Period.*** Mexico City. Courtesy of the artist.

Sierra, P. 2017. ***Future Carriers of Our Past: Coyotlatelco Period.*** Mexico City. Courtesy of the artist.

Sierra, P. 2017. ***Future Carriers of Our Past at the Timeless Fragments Show.*** Brindisi IT. Courtesy of the artist.

Discursive Jewellery, Marine Plastic Waste, and Mediational Aesthetic Recontextualization

Synne Skjulstad, Westerdals Department of Communication and Design, Kristiania University College, Oslo, Norway

Abstract

This paper discusses the concept of discursive jewellery, defamiliarization, and digital mediational presentation and aesthetic recontextualization as part of a practice-led discursive design inquiry, which takes ocean plastic waste as the main design material. In the ongoing project to which this paper refers, pieces of ocean plastic waste are explored as a material for discursive jewellery—in tandem with digital presentation and mediation as part of an aesthetic recontextualization of this material. It sketches out how the digital and the handcrafted may be understood as intertwined factors in processes that seek to make us look at this material anew and as expanding the discursive space for such a deeply problematic material. The jewellery addresses the problem of marine plastic pollution. Each piece of jewellery is designed as a gentle material nudge towards setting reflective processes about a pressing environmental issue in motion.

1. Sadly, Every Shore Is a Treasury

Sadly, every shore is a treasury. This paper takes as its point of departure a Norwegian, Oslo-based practice-based research project labelled *Seabling.* In this project, ocean plastic collected from the shores of the often perceived "pristine" fiords of Norway take centre stage. The project explores how context and visual presentation may interfere with the ways this material may be perceived as part of a discursive approach to design. In this practice-based design research project, jewellery serves as an open platform for material exploration and embodied communication. As there is a growing awareness of the threat marine plastic pollution poses to our marine eco systems, as multiple tons of plastic waste pile up by the minute, this project investigates the ways through which contemporary jewellery may aid us in addressing this global problem on a micro level, and as design-led acts of care for the ocean (Skjulstad 2019). As plastic waste is an increasingly familiar sight along our coast line, this is but a symptom of a larger problem; a tiny fraction of a growing plastic leviathan lies at the bottom of the sea.

An interdisciplinary body of work on the role of visual articulations in design research (e.g., Arnall, 2013; Dunne and Raby 2013; Auger 2013) informs the project. In combining perspectives on discursive design, as taken from Morrison et al. (2011), Arnall (2013), Mollon and Gentes (2014), as well as from Tharp and Tharp (2015, 2013, 2019), and practice-based design research methodologies (e.g., Sevaldson, 2010; Schön, 1983), we investigate ocean plastic debris as a material for jewellery. It does so by prompting the idea of mediation and visual articulations as vital in shaping ideas. For instance, Auger (2013) discusses various techniques for presenting a design speculation in ways that enable audience engagement and reflection. However, more than in speculative design, the project is positioned within a discursive approach to design (Morrison et al., 2011; Tharp and Tharp, 2019), where design for discourse, reflection, and debate is key. In addition, the project is informed by research and practice with a focus on fashion as practices and as discourse (Rocamora, 2013; Skjulstad, 2020). All these perspectives come together in how we approach jewellery as part of an explorative discursive material practice in design research. Drawing on Barret (2013, p. 64), artistic practice as a mode of enquiry and knowledge production entails an aesthetic awareness and knowledge as material processes. *Seabling* is thus a practice-based open-ended collaborative design research project into the material and discursive potential of ocean plastic waste, and the ways in which we may repurpose and refine it, ultimately aiming at making us look at this material as a resource astray.

In combing these approaches, and the bodies of work on which they build, we experience jewellery as an open and interesting discursive and mediational platform. This is part of the overarching goal of enabling us to rethink the value of this material, a material that is rapidly undermining the conditions for life on this planet. Jewellery is interesting as a case for exploring the potential of aesthetic recontextualization of objects made from such a material, as it is located at the complete opposite end of the spectrum to waste. Presented in the form of fully functional jewellery in contexts of design and fashion, the projects asks us to look at each piece of plastic aesthetically. Such a mode of address, drawing on Auger (2013), aims at involving the audience in taking part in a design scenario where tiny pieces of marine plastic are treated with great care as a precious material—thus offering an invitation to reflect on the possible idea of marine plastic as a pressing problem and potential resource.

In discussing the epistemology of practice, Schön (1983, p. 78) describes processes of designerly inquiry as represented as "a reflective conversation with the materials of the situation." Typically, a piece of our jewellery consists of one, or several pieces of ocean plastic, as they are found. We select the pieces we want to include in our materials repository without altering its shape. After a process of tinkering, we assemble them with sterling silver or gold parts, several of them custom made. The shape or texture of the plastic pieces are not altered, except for tiny holes. This exposes the material qualities of the plastic pieces, whilst also pointing back to the industrially designed objects they were part of before they ended up in the ocean. The various ways these objects have been broken, their shapes, angles, texture, and colour nuances are at the core of each piece of jewellery. In the case of earrings, pieces that relate to each other aesthetically, or that we find engage in a "dialogue" with each other, are combined. Some of the plastic pieces we select are melted, resulting in darker colours and more organic-looking shapes. Several plastic pieces are recognisable as fragments of specific objects, such as screw caps, whilst the origin and history of the original object is in most cases unknown to us. They carry the marks of time and the wear and tear of the ocean, shown as cracked and textured surfaces. Others have been bleached in the sun or polished by sand. The pieces we select are tiny fragments that usually are overlooked. However, by repurposing a few selected plastic pieces, the jewellery forms an invitation to look closely at each piece. Tharp and Tharp (2019, p. 8) refer to "discursive designs" as "good(s) for thinking," positioning designed objects outside of the commercial, utilitarian approach to design, but rather in the symbolic and philosophic realm of ideas, where they make visible the socio-cultural aspects of material culture. The jewellery is thus designed so as to trigger conversation and reflection on ocean plastic pollution. However, the visual presentation of the jewellery is incremental in processes of aesthetic recontextualization, ones that seek to make us look at this material anew. Examples of such discursive recontextualization are discussed more fully below. Central to the project is to explore what such aesthetic recontextualizations might interrupt our perception of the plastic pieces—and to promote the pressing need for immediate global political action on marine plastic pollution.

Speculative design approaches inform the project (Dunne and Raby, 2013; Dunne, 2008; Rynning and Skjulstad, 2017) by suggesting we ask questions such as, "What if?" *In this case, what if plastic pieces are treated as a valuable material in the context of jewellery?* As the research project has developed, the jewellery has opened up discursive spaces in which to discuss marine plastic pollution. This is taken up below. Central to the above-mentioned design approaches is that they are concerned with visually and materially asking questions and stimulating debate, dialogue, reflection, and if possible—action. Such design approaches are

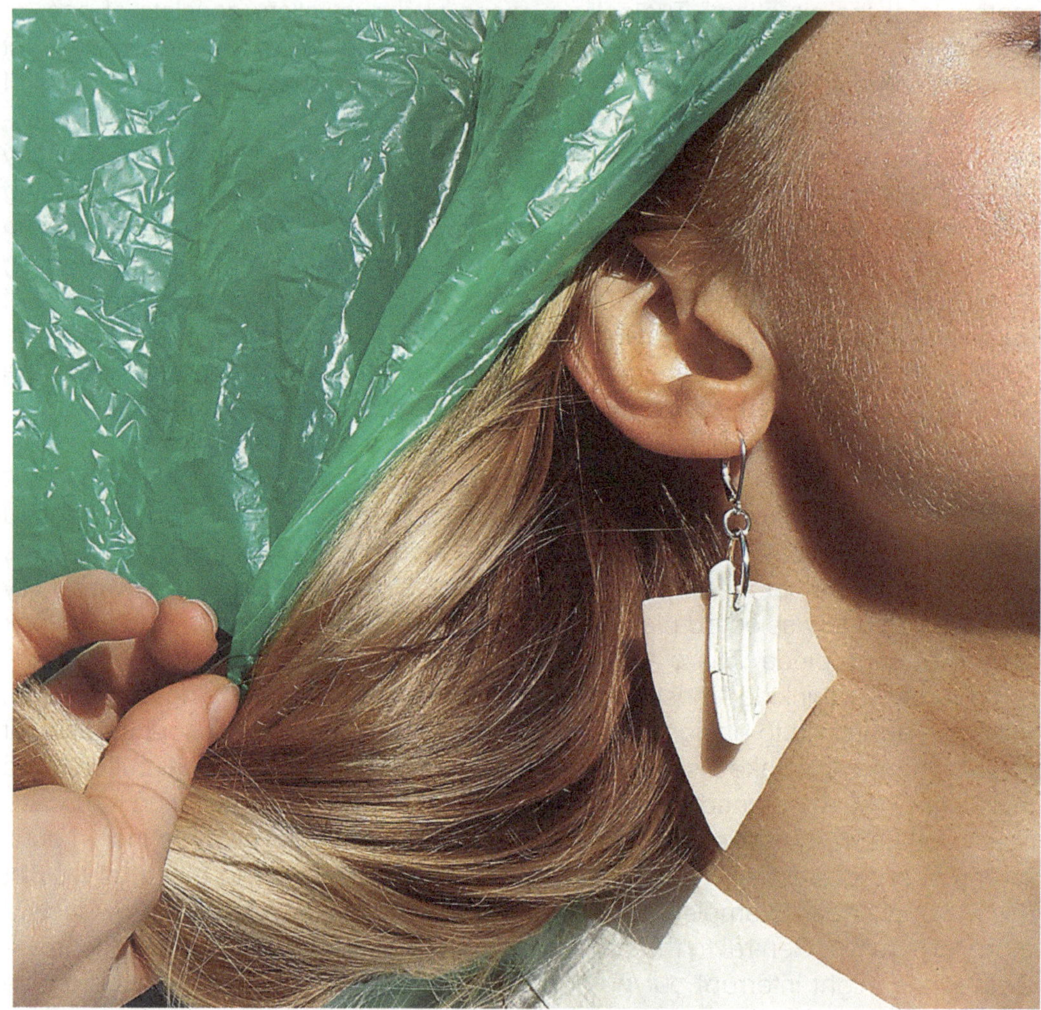

Figures 1 (above) and 2 (next page): Jewellery worn by a model and presented as a fashion accessory. All visual references to marine waste are removed.

concerned with the imaginative potential in design, and of making problems of a sociological, ethical, or psychological nature—often difficult ones—visible (Tharp and Tharp, 2013). According to Dunne and Raby (2013), speculative design may provide gentle nudges towards changing perception of a phenomenon. Exploration of a specific design material, as shown by Arnall (2013), may take place in tandem

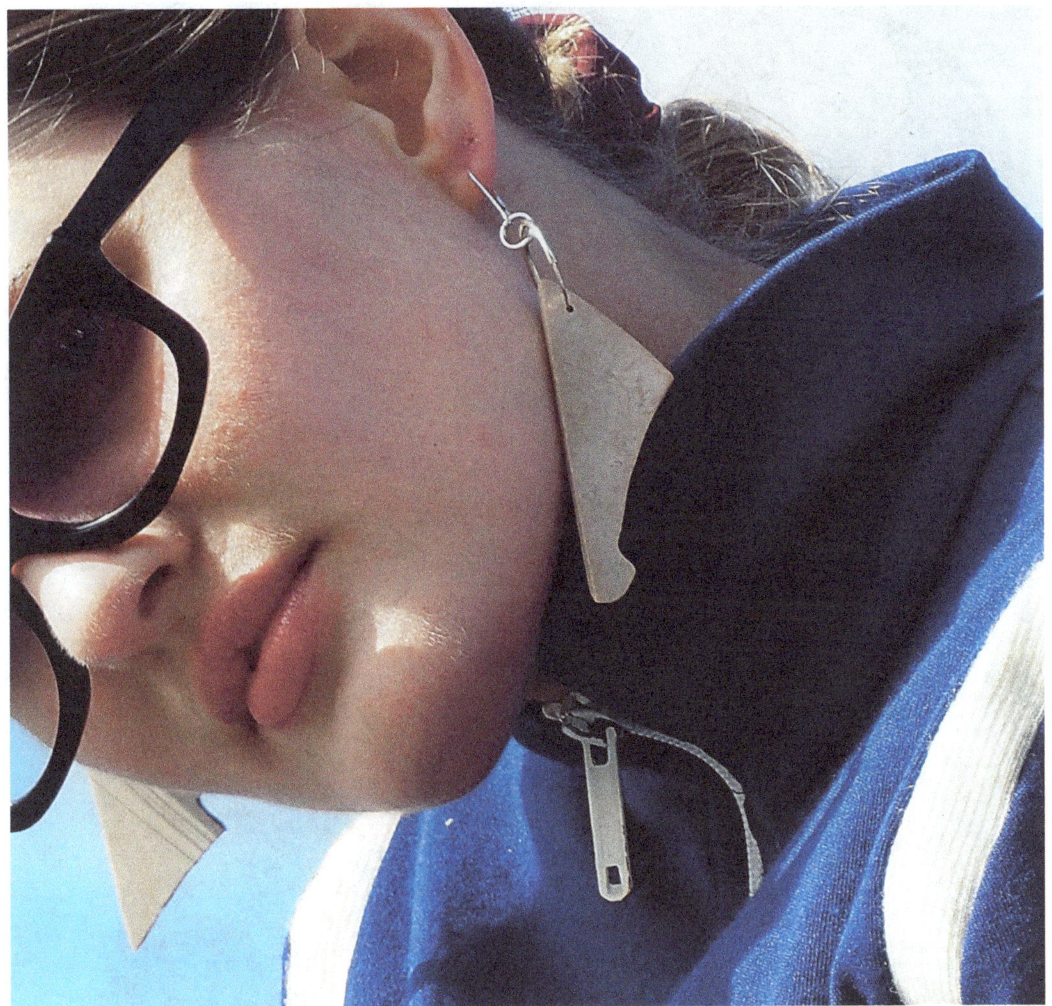

with visual mediation as an incremental part of the research process. Picking up on this, the role of visual presentation and the aesthetic properties of a given material is key. Drawing on Schön (1983) and Fallmann (2008), material knowledge is shaped via design practice as a close dialogue with and about a material, in our case marine plastic debris. As put forward by McCosh (2013), new insights may be

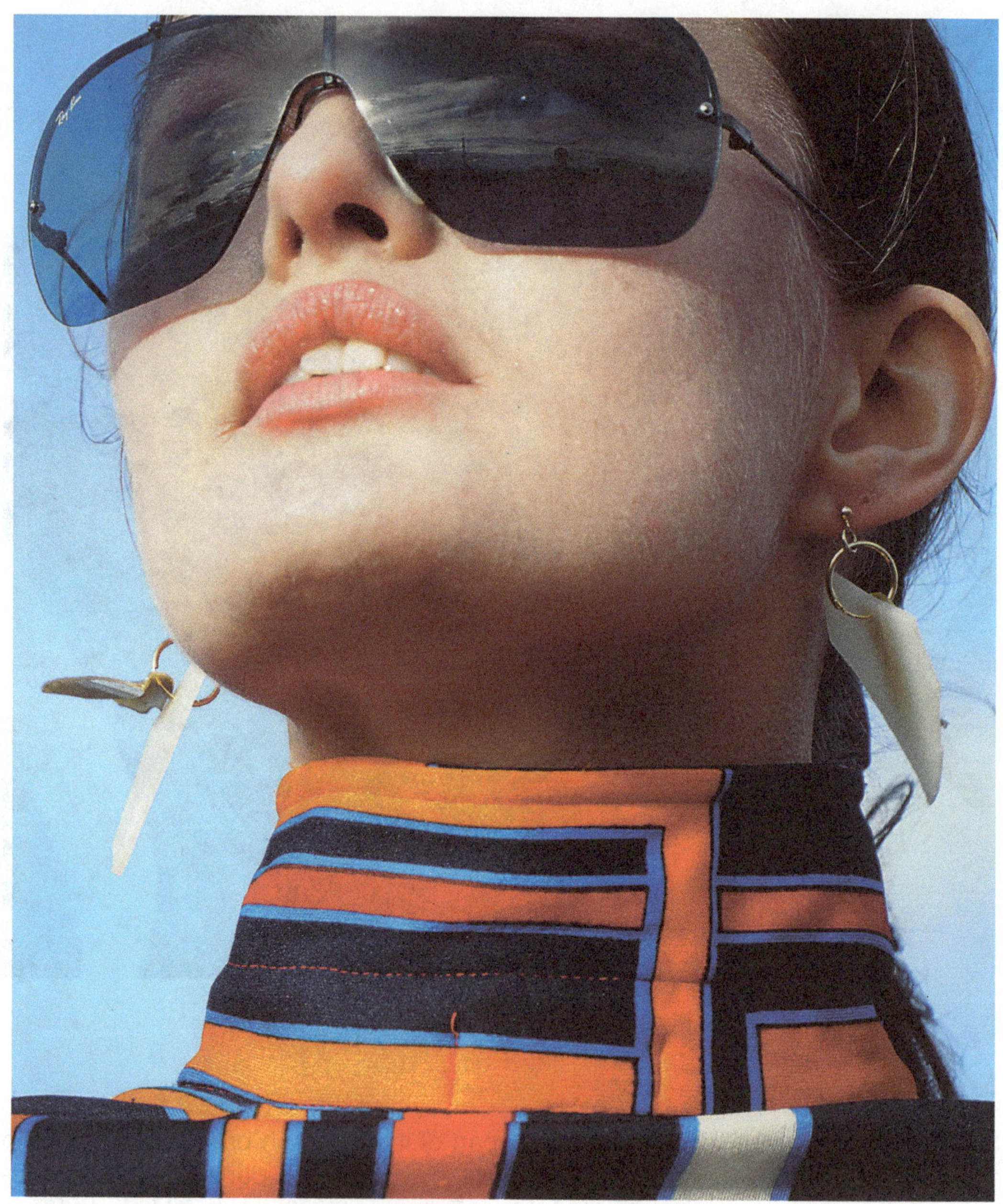

Figure 3. Jewellery worn by a model and presented as a fashion accessory. All visual references to marine waste are removed.

revealed through material practice. Our engagement with this material in the context of contemporary jewellery is aiming for what Dunne (2008, p. 147) refers to as an integration of critical design experiences into everyday life. As jewellery is worn on, or in close proximity of the body, the discursive potential is thus an embodied one (Negrin, 2013). In the context of jewellery, we find that the concept of defamiliarization, as developed by the literary scholar Victor Shklovsky (1917) informs this jewellery project as the material is removed from a visual ethos of pollution to that of jewellery. Such a visual recontextualization may generate friction, and thus also interest. In addition, the project is also informed by perspectives on digital mediation and presentation within fashion, where fashion is increasingly perceived as mediatized and as distinctive discursive practices (Rocamora, 2016; Skjulstad, 2020, 2017). Jewellery thus serves as an open-ended platform for discourse.

To briefly unpack the background of this project, it is necessary to backtrack to the summer of 2017, when my partner began to bring back selected pieces of marine plastic from his walks and kayak trips in the eastern part of the Norwegian archipelago. What began as an informal beach cleaning initiative and playful exploration of artistic repurposing of marine plastic waste gradually grew into a discursive design research project, as the project gradually bled into this author's work as a researcher and educator within an interdisciplinary design context in higher education.

2. From Waste to Jewellery

The transformation of worthless material into something precious is a recurring theme in the history of art, design, and also jewellery. Since the urinal titled *Fountain* signed R. Mutt, and attributed to Marcel Duchamp (see Mundy and Howarth, 2000), was placed into Stieglitz's gallery (Lynton, 1989, p.131), the role of the artistic object and its relations to institutional context has been questioned. In the history of art, found objects as well as relationships between culture and nature has been addressed by a wide range of artists. For example, the Italian 1960s (and its revival in the 1990s) movement *Arte Povera* as led by the curator and critic Germano Celant brought material considered as worthless into the gallery space (Lumly, 2010). In the context of sustainable jewellery, Manheim (2009, p.15) points to the ways in which the value of material in jewellery has been questioned in the history of art and jewellery, and specifically questions relating to transforming worthless materials into valuable ones. Pennie Jagiello (2017) has importantly studied what she refers to as anthropogenic debris as a material for contemporary jewellery. She defines this as "Human-made materials that has been discarded causing serious negative environmental impacts" (p. 4). Jagiello (2017, p.11) points to the rich practice of jewellers that have found materials at its core, such as Helen Britton, David Bielander, and Lisa Walker, among others. These have, according to Jagiello, been pivotal in raising debates about what jewellery can be, and what can be considered precious or non-precious. There are many similarities between Jagiello's approach to jewellery materials and ours. However, in contrast, we do not shape or alter the pieces of plastic we use in our jewellery.

3. Looking Anew

In popular jewellery that point to issues of sustainability, the jewellery itself plays a secondary role, as the "good cause" tends to become the main rationale for engaging with the jewellery. This is for instance the case in the 4ocean bracelet initiative, where the bracelet acts as a symbol for commitment to cleaning up the ocean. The bracelet is made from recycled glass and polyester, but the project is not presented as a *jewellery* project, but as an ocean cleaning initiative. The bracelets are thus created and mediated as discursive pieces that facilitate conversation about marine pollution. The bracelet is first and foremost a mediational device (Lash and Lury, 2009), a token for engagement with marine plastic pollution.

In order to nudge people into looking at found pieces of ocean plastic anew, to push perception in other aesthetic directions, we explore how the style associated with idealistic approaches to repurposing waste needs to be interrupted, even replaced, in order to afford the perception of ocean plastic as a possible design material outside of existing aesthetic regimes linked to sustainability. That is, by removing all visual elements that connotes plastic waste and polluted beaches, we aim at making one look at the plastic pieces closely. The main reason for this is for triggering reflection on the very existence of such plastic pieces as a symptom of a pressing problem. Incremental in this regard is Viktor Shklovsky's concept of "defamiliarization." In his 1917 essay, one that was translated and reprinted in 1965 titled "Art as Technique," Shklovsky discusses, how to make us perceive the familiar anew so as to experience the world without perception becoming dulled down by being perceptually worn. However, as Shklovsky discussed poetic language, his ideas on defamiliarization have informed other fields of cultural production. In terms of jewellery design, defamiliarization refers to luring the imagination to see beyond naturalised perception. According to Shklovsky, the object of our perception is there, but we do not really see it even as it is right in front of us. To escape this condition, and to make a phenomenon poetic, it is necessary to make the perception more difficult, to interrupt the habitual and to prolong the perception of it. This is taken up in practice in the ways through which the presentation and mediation of the

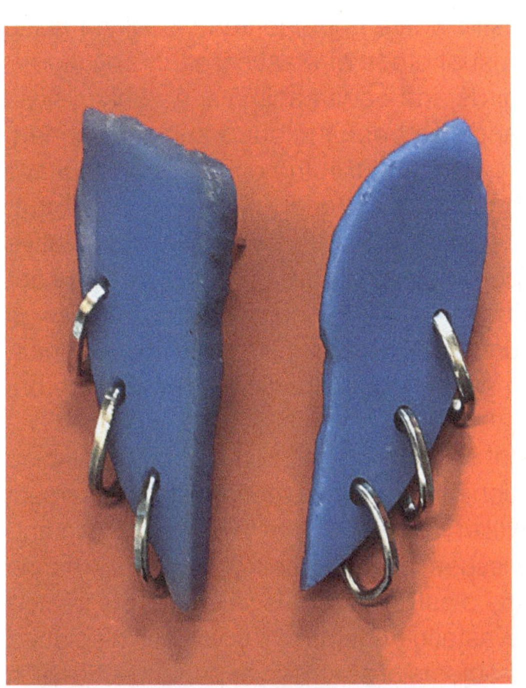

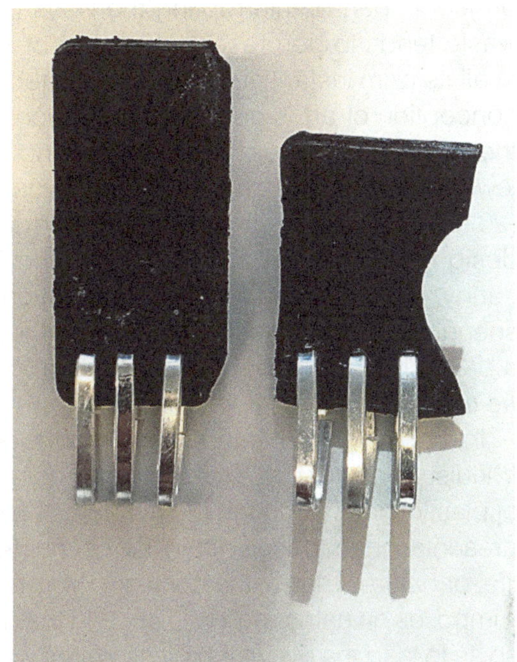

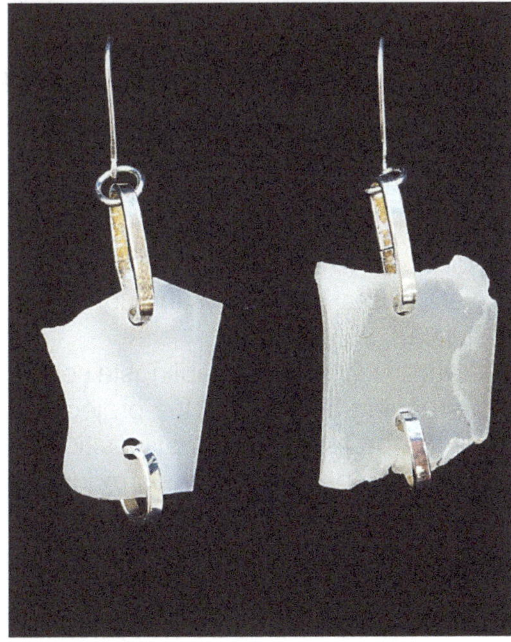

Figures 4, 5, and 6. Earrings made from found ocean plastic pieces. The plastic pieces are used as they are found. That is, they are not shaped by us, except for holes drilled for assembling them with sterling silver.

project is part of interrupting the ways plastic waste is presented visually. Plastic waste tends to be presented as part of a visual ethos of plastic beach pollution—in all its grim instantiations with molested birds and ocean animals. As Shklovsky's conception of art is open for discussion, and has been critiqued and questioned, the idea of making us look at something anew is fruitful in the context of discursive jewellery. However, the aestheticization of such a material may put what Auger (2013) points to as a perceptual bridge, a means through which a speculative design scenario may appear convincing, put into play by being represented as uncanny. As Auger argues, if a speculation becomes too uncomfortable, the design scenario may be rejected. However, the uncanny as a form of quiet disturbance, a balancing act between the familiar and the unfamiliar (drawing on Freud, the *unheimlich*), may trigger interest.

In applying and referencing mediational techniques of contemporary fashion (Skjulstad, 2020), we explore the combination of curation, selection, and refinement of plastic pieces through the medium of jewellery. This is combined with staging and presentation that does not initially connote issues of sustainability, beaches, marine life, or nature. That is, the context in which the plastic material is selected, the trauma it imposes on nature and wildlife, and the devastating effects of it is visually displaced so as to lead the eye to the plastic pieces as objects of aesthetic experience. Fashion photography has historically perfected the mediation of ambivalence as one of its defining features (Andersen, 2006). Such an ambivalence is part of the mediation, as the devastating effects of our material is visually removed from our mediation of the project. This may initially seem counterintuitive. However, the audience's own knowledge of ocean pollution and its consequences may provide a visually conflicting backdrop to the aestheticized mediations of ocean plastic jewellery. The digital in this sense thus refers to the ways the project is situated visually in digital media representations. According to Rocamora (2015), a media logic is engulfing more and more aspects of fashion, and mediational processes are pivotal in the ways through which fashion is not only mediated, but designed (Skjulstad, 2017, 2020).

As part of the mediation of the project the Instagram account @seablingsta serves as a platform for research mediation. Here, the running activities of the project are presented along with visual representations of the project. We aim at positioning the project as a site for exploring mediation, photography, and various modes of presentation. As the project is allowed to play itself out rather organically, a part of the project is also concerned with investigating how the jewellery may appear in other contexts than the ones we fully control. For example, an editorial context created by an independent journalist, a professional photographer and stylist, models, and a professional studio is anchoring, echoing Roland Barthes (1964), the jewellery in a visual ethos where the connotations that such context entails may guide the perception of the plastic pieces. For example, the project was featured in a series of articles in contemporary lifestyle magazines, such as *The Chromarty*, where the jewellery was presented as a means for reflection and critique, giving editorial space for a discussion of issues of marine plastic pollution. The jewellery thus serves as a Trojan horse for bringing up the issue of marine plastic pollution in contexts where this issue does not tend to be discussed.

4. Finding a Material

We are currently a collaborating with the organisation Nordic Ocean Watch, a project-based collective initiative dedicated to taking care of the ocean. The organisation is led by a group of surfers who took responsibility for cleaning the beach of Hoddevik, a bay surrounded by majestic mountains located in the Western part of Norway. Norway has for many years been providing oil to the industrial production of plastic and is still actively drilling for oil in the North Sea. We are currently working on a "Hoddevik" jewellery edition and are in dialogue with Nordic Ocean Watch on a project labelled Norwegian Trash, which will feature contemporary Norwegian design made from upcycled waste. Now, we are in the process of collaboration in sourcing materials, as this organisation is developing and installing infrastructures for marine clean-up activities along the coast of the country. As designers increasingly explore marine plastic as a design material, as the material is widely available, but still largely an undiscovered one, the various design explorations of this material seen as a whole presents marine plastic both as a problem that needs to be dealt with at a global scale, but also as a potential resource. It is, however, when large fashion brands such as Prada integrates marine nylon waste into their production of bags that such a material is fully seen as valuable. As sustainability initiatives now are becoming imperative within a variety of design contexts (McDonough and Braungart, 2009, 2013), including within the fashion industry, our explorative jewellery practice aims to provide a platform for discussions of such issues, including issues of green-washing, and serve as tangible examples of alternative material scenarios.

5. Implications: Contemporary Archaeology and as a Memento Mori

This project has a range of implications. In particular, we are interested in exploring how the kinds of ocean plastic pieces we use in our jewellery can be reconceptualised as precious, and as parts of products with aesthetic—and market value.

This is part of our interest in contributing to the conception of the value this material might have in circular economies. This opens for collaborations with organisations that are already involved in ocean plastic waste and waste management, as well for domains related to fashion, style, and design. Considering our approach to jewellery design in terms of contemporary plastic archaeology is one we are developping (Skjulstad, 2019). The plastic pieces in our jewellery tell us something about human life since the popularisation of plastic in the 1950s and 60s. Our material is made by humans and shaped by nature in processes beyond our control, marked by the passing of time and the forces of the ocean. These processes give the plastic pieces variation in nuances, patina, colour, texture, and shape. Each piece is a remnant of our near past and carries an untold story of our contemporary condition. Positioning ocean plastic within the context of contemporary archaeology, as an element of what Dibley (2018, p. 44) refers to as "technofossils" may open up for some of the more affective dimensions we explore. In the context of the onset of the Anthropocene, Dibley discusses contemporary debris, the layer of human activities and technologies as fossils to be. That is as a new sedimentary layer of the earth. Ocean plastic debris is an intrusive force among traces of human activity on the planet. This is a layer that according to Dibley (2018) may be conceived of as a memento mori and as a heuristic for envisioning a future planet without human inhabitants. Each piece of jewellery made from this material carries the story of our species. It points to the unpleasant thought of an unhabitable earth. In the context of the Earth's trajectory in geological time, ocean plastic is but one trace of human activity—along with everything from mobile phones to hydro dams, cities and shoes. The jewellery is made of the material of such prospective technofossils, and as jewellery these pieces will be folded into a readable future, one that paradoxically will be without readers. The jewellery may thus become, drawing on Dibley (2018, p. 48–49), affective objects.

6. Concluding Remarks

As ocean plastic pollution is one of the most pressing environmental issues of today, the discursive potential of jewellery made from such a material may serve as discursive embodied reminders of the gravity of the issue of plastic ocean pollution. In addition, they may facilitate dialogue and reflection on the need for immediate action on ocean plastic pollution, serving as aestheticized affective objects that carry our recent history—as well as our future prospects as a species. In this regard, looking closely at what is otherwise widely overlooked may interrupt the ways a tiny fragment of a screw cap is perceived.

References

Andersen, C. 2006. *Modefotografi: En Genres Anatomi.* Copenhagen: Museum Tusculanums Forlag.

Arnall, T. 2013. *Making Visible: Mediating the Material of Emerging Technology.* PhD diss., The Oslo School of Architecture and Design.

Auger, J., 2013. "Speculative Design: Crafting the Speculation." *Digital Creativity* 24 (11): 11–35.

Barrett, E. 2013. "Materiality, Affect, and the Aesthetic Image." In *Carnal Knowledge: Towards a "New Materialism" through the Arts*, edited by E. Barrett and B. Bolt, 63–72. New York: IB Tauris.

Barthes, R., 1964. "The Rhetoric of the Image (Rhétorique de l'image)." *Communications* 4.

Dibley, B., 2018. "The Technofossil: A Memento Mori." *Journal of Contemporary Archaeology* 5 (1): 44–52.

Dunne, A. 2008. *Hertzian Tales, Electronic Products, Aesthetic Experience, and Critical Design.* Cambridge, MA: MIT Press.

Dunne, A., and F. Raby. 2013. *Speculative Everything: Design, Fiction ad Social Dreaming.* Cambridge, MA: MIT Press.

Fallmann, D. 2008. "The Interaction Design Research Triangle of Design Practice, Design Studies, and Design Exploration." *Design Issues* 24 (3): 4–18.

Jagiello, P. 2017. *Remains To Be Seen, Worn and Heard: An Inquiry into Anthropogenic Debris Investigated through Contemporary Jewellery Objects.* Master of Fine Arts thesis, College of Design and Social Context, RMIT University. https://research bank.rmit.edu.au/eserv/rmit:162193/Jagiello.pdf.

Lash, S. and C. Lury. 2007. *Global Culture Industry.* Cambridge: Polity Press.

Lynton, N. 1989. *The Story of Modern Art.* 2nd ed. London: Phaidon.

Lumly, R. 2010. *Germano Celant: The Arte Povera Period.* https://www.domusweb.it/en/art/2010/10/31/germano-celant-the-arte-povera-period.html.

Manheim, J. 2009. *Sustainable Jewellery.* London: A & C Black Publishers Limited.

McCosh, L. 2013. "The Sublime: Process and Mediation." *In Carnal Knowledge: Towards a "New Materialism" through the Arts*, edited by Estelle Barrett and Barbara Bolt, 127–139. New York: IB Tauris.

McDonough, W., and M. Braungart. 2009. *Cradle to Cradle: Remaking the Way Make Things.* London: Vintage Books.

McDonough, W., and M. Braungart. 2013. *The Upcycle.* New York: The North Point Press.

Mollon, M., and A. Gentes. 2014. "The Rhetoric of Design for Debate: Triggering Conversation with an 'Uncanny Enough' Artefact" *Proceedings of Ume: Design Research Society Conference*, June 16–19, pp. 1–13.

Morrison, A., T. Arnall, J. Knutsen, E. Martinussen, K. Nordby. 2011. Towards Discursive Design. *Proceedings of IASDR2011, 4th World Conference on Design Research*, October 31–November 4, 2011, Delft.

Mundy, J., and S. Howarth. 2000 (revised 2015). *Marcel Duchamp: Fountain 1917, replica 1964.* https://www.tate.org.uk/art/artworks/duchamp-fountain-t07573.

Negrin, L. 2013. "Fashion as an Embodied Art Form." In *Carnal Knowledge: Towards a "New Materialism" through the Arts*, edited by E. Barrett and B. Bolt, 141–55. New York: IB Tauris.

Rocamora, A. 2016. "Mediatization and Digital Media in the Field of Fashion." *Fashion Theory* 21 (5): 205–522.

Schön, D. 1983. *The Reflective Practitioner: How Professionals Think in Action.* New York: Basic Books.

Sevaldson, B. 2010. "Discussions & Movements in Design Research.". *FormAkademisk*, 3 (1): 8-35.

Shklovsky, V. 1965 (1917). "Art as Technique." In *Russian Formalist Criticism: Four Essays,* 3–24. Translated by L. Lemon and M. Reis. Lincoln: University of Nebraska Press.

Skjulstad, S. 2017. "Who Wore it Best? Understanding Mediated Fashion as Design. NORDES, Oslo, Norway." Oslo ACT, June 15–17, The Oslo School of Architecture and Design/Westerdals.

Skjulstad, S. 2019. "Taking Care of Plastic: Discursive Jewellery and Anthropogenic Debris." Nordes, Aalto University, June 2–4, Helsinki, Finland. http://www.nordes.org/opj/index.php/n13/article/view/478.

Skjulstad, S. 2020. "Vetements, Memes, and Connectivity: Fashion Media in the Era of Instagram." *Fashion Theory,* 24(2), 181–209, DOI: 10.1080/1362704X.2018.1491191.

Skjulstad, S. and M. Rynning. 2017. "Transgressive Graphic Design: Defamiliarisation, Human and Non-Human Fusions." Presented at Cumulus Srishti, November 20–23, Bengaluru, India.

Tharp, B., and S. Tharp. 2013. "Discursive Design Basics: Mode and Audience." Nordic Design Research Conference 2013, Copenhagen-Malm. http://www.nordes.org/opj/index.php/n13/article/view/326/306.

Tharp, B., and S. Tharp. 2015. "What is Discursive Design?" *Core77*. http://www.core77.com/posts/41991/What-is-Discursive-Design.

Tharp, B., and S. Tharp. 2019. *Discursive Design: Critical, Speculative, and Alternative Things*. Cambridge, MA: MIT Press.

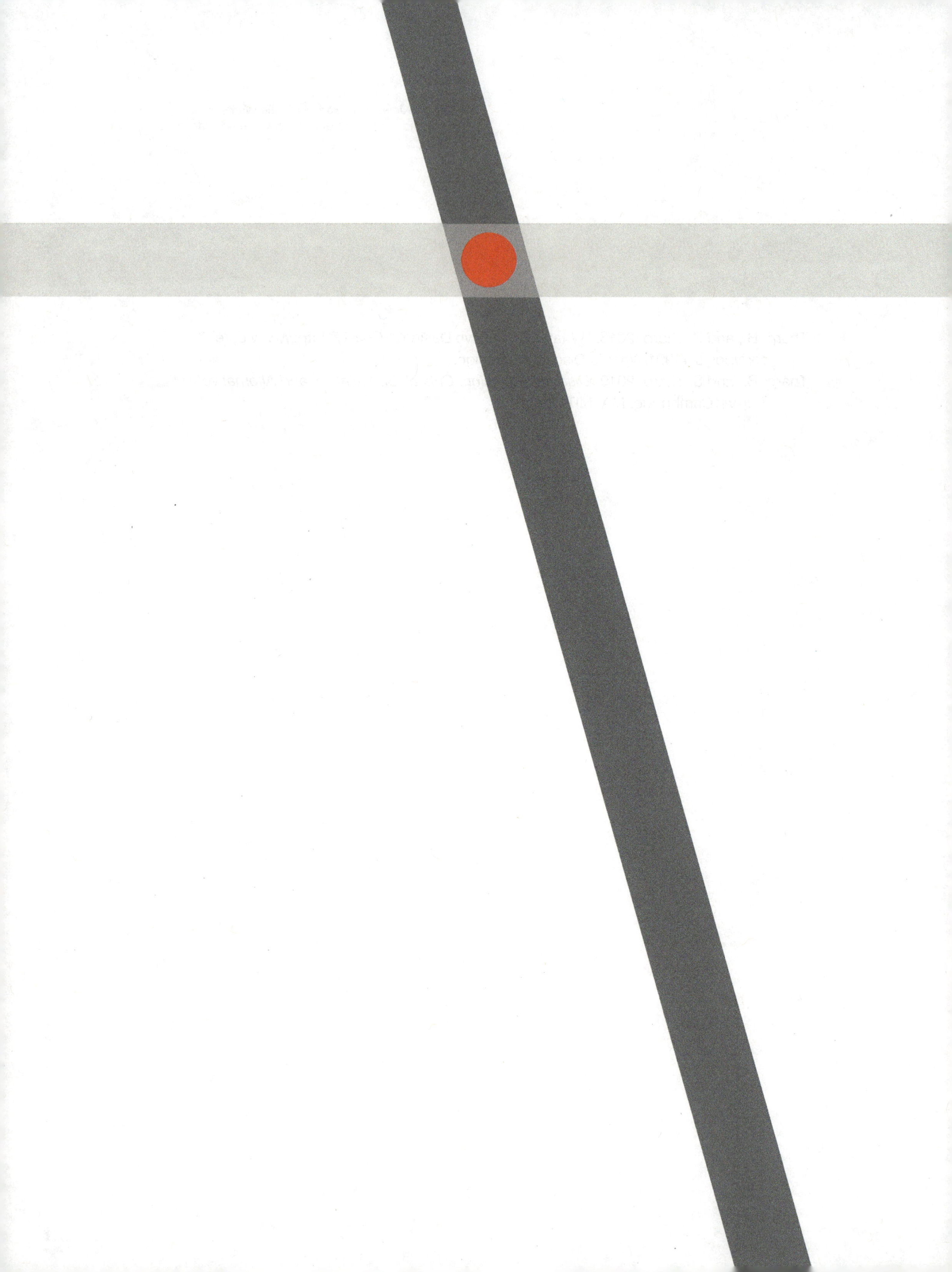

A Reexamination of Jewelers' Titles and Nomenclature

Donna Mason Sweigart, Rowan University, NJ, USA
Patricia Madeja, Pratt Institute, NY, USA
Ashley Marcovitz, Pratt Institute, NY, USA
Ho'o Hee, Pratt Institute, NY, USA

Abstract

Jeweler, Designer, Goldsmith, Artist, Maker: The titles by which we define ourselves are often the world's first introduction to our craft. But what do these labels say about us? Where do they originate? Are the ideas they express any longer relevant? Oppi Untracht's mandala A Polarized Convocation of Jewelers in 1982 mapped classifications within the jewelry community. Much has changed in the last thirty-six years. We seek to revitalize this schema so that it may reflect the trends of our modern discipline.

Most of the Western traditional nomenclature associated with jewelry production is rooted in Medieval or Renaissance terminology. Monikers often refer to: a specific action (engraver), a material (silversmith), a space (studio jeweler), or measure of work (journeyman). As innovations occur, processes are retooled and roles are relabeled. Hand-carved wax is matched by 3D-printed wax and the model maker parallels the CAD modeler.

Beyond announcing our skills, our titles also express the ideals of the time. During the industrial revolution we saw a resurgence of the title Craftsman, as the arts and crafts movement sought to mediate the cold uniformity of mass production. Their desire was to return to the romantic individuality of the hand. Similarly, our contemporary use of the title "Maker" is a rejection of traditional labels that confine us to a specific medium, process or product. Through use of the title Maker, we seek to proclaim that we are creators whose skills span an array of media and modes of production. We are nimble creatures, adept at navigating both the digital and physical realms. We are able to integrate new technologies as they evolve. Through the universality of the term Maker, we are able to resolve the conflicting adjectives that often describe the plurality of our skills: "Digital Handmade," "Post-digital Artisan."

By breaking down the constructs of traditional titles have we also opened ourselves up to being cast in the same category as the unskilled? With the democratization of knowledge, software, and means of production, is everyone a Maker? Will this title become tarnished like the word "handicraft"? It is time for contemplation of the titles we carry and their impact on the jewelry field at large.

A Re-examination of Jewelers' Titles and Nomenclature

Nomenclature

It is with the idea of looking at present-day practice we take on describing the common titles and naming practices of the jewelry field. In order to fully understand the present titles, we are utilizing Oppi Untracht's A Polarized Convocation of Jewelers as historical reference and updating present reflected practice.

This is an exploration of how our field represents its members through titles. It is important to look closely at how language relates people to work and how that practice has evolved and been adapted through the history of Western craft. Language defines skilled peoples in a variety of formats. "Skill" refers in this reference "to a combination of knowledge and manual dexterity" (Collins Dictionary of Business, 2006). These skills are identified by titles in several formats in our field. Formats of naming are often linked in language to specific skill, level of skill, material, space, or measure of work. Sometimes the title itself assumes a level of proficiency; for example, the title artisan is defined by skill. "Skilled workers—also known as artisans—usually commanded the highest wages for their craft." (Caron, 2004) Names that are related to level of skill would be Master and Apprentice. Our modern carry over from this naming is the Master Model Maker. A name that is related to both skill and measure of work is Journeyman. It shows skill as related to level of skill and as related to measure of work in time.

"By the fourteenth century, the word journeyman denoted "a daily worker," that is, one who worked for another for daily wages. He was distinguished from an apprentice, who was learning the trade, and a master artisan, who was in business for himself. Journey is derived from the Old French jornee, "a day, the length of the day" and "a day's work." (Journeyman, 2004)

Quite often labels that experts are assigned relate to their distinct skill set or action of their skill set, such as Engraver. Some titles are defined by the artisan's space, such as Studio Jeweler. A significant amount of titles in the jewelery field are predicated by their relationship to specific materials, such as Enamellist or

Goldsmith. Specifically, the term Goldsmith is both material and technique derived. "(Ger. Goldschmeid, or Nl. edelsmid, literally meaning one who forges in precious metals)" (Den Besten, 2011, p. 9) An appellation within language that encompasses all facets of these areas related to space, material, and process would be Lapidaries.

Convocation

All of these titles were distilled 36 years ago in Oppi Untracht's *Jewelry Concepts and Technology* a legendary manual on jewelery making, a book that is widely recognized, owned, and referenced by many. As Doubleday (Penguin Random House) will not grant permission to share the original figure in this paper we ask you to reference **A Polarized Convocation of Jewelers** on page 12. Figure 1–36 represents Untracht's view of the history and prevalent state of jewelery for the time. Untracht's specific view of the field was based on his status as an art jeweler, enamelist, craft writer, four-time Fulbright Scholar with trips to India (1957–59) and Nepal (1963–65) to study metal work, and his marriage to Saara Hopea, a Finnish designer. His words about the centric placing of the studio jeweler could be argued but this is his reflection.

We cannot speak of the world of jewelry today without giving due reconition to the artist-jeweler upon whom all developments center. He/she is both procreator/genetrix, begetter/conceiver of all the concepts endlessly poured into the jewelry object. The term artist-jeweler can be interpreted narrowly to include only influencial jewelers, but it can also have an all-inclusive meaning to incorporate both greater and lesser members of this ideaology and physically far flung family as long as their work contains an element of orginality. (Untracht, 1982, p. 11)

This diagram is titled "polarized" not to speak of opposition but to describe how the peoples relate to each other. "It must be made clear from the start that the arrangement of this seating plan is not to create hierarchy, nor to give undue prominence to any particular member, nor divide the family into opposing camps" (Untracht, 1982, p. 11). Untracht does say that these areas have instances of opposition in concept. Through this chart he acknowledges the diverse nature of the field. From the spirit of his justifications the chart was conceived with tolerance and introspection, a sort of assembly and uniting of the field. This notion is supported by the presentation at the Society of North American Goldsmith's conference in 2013 by academic Damian Skinner:

Scrupulously fair, Untracht is at pains to ensure we don't read the diagram as a hierarchy, or think that he favors one branch of the family over another, or that we read it as a division into opposing camps—even though, as he notes, some of the family isn't speaking to each other. All he wants to do is identify members and suggest how they might relate to one another. (Skinner, 2013a, p. 1)

Untracht briefly laments the lack of communication between the areas within the convocation. However, the entire language of this figure is related to the jeweler with some exceptions. Generally, Untracht never gives a reason for his lack of inclusion of the respectable/common/specific term "smith" as it relates to material or the field. There is evidence in the field from this time to suggest there had begun a schism with artist jewelers wanting to differentiate themselves from a variety of other titles as noted by Liesbeth Den Besten. Den Besten is an art historian, based in the Amsterdam region, who works as an independent writer, teacher, lecturer, and curator. Presently, she teaches jewelry history at Sint Lucas Antwerpen. She is the chairwoman of the Françoise van den Bosch Foundation for contemporary jewelry.

The New Jewelry had problems with its identity from the outset. The difficulty was not only in the positioning of the maker away from old-fashioned crafts notions such as goldsmith . . . but also in the identification of the field or practice, in order to distinguish from fine, precious, fashion, costume or commercial jewellery. (Den Besten, 2011, p. 9)

As Untracht was in his own right an artist jeweler, although outside of the main cohort of the New Jewelery as referenced by Den Besten, perhaps this omission of the smith is merely a reflection of his time. Although born and educated in the United States, his perspective was significantly external as his specialization and Fulbright studies were on historic and contemporary crafts of India and Nepal and he later spent most of his time writing from Finland.

Perhaps this separation of the smith from the list of metal specialists in the convocation is revealed in his comments noted from an interview with him in 2003 where he speaks of the ten–year history of the research for this book. He mentions how open American jewelers were to sharing information and agreeing to share their knowledge and participate in the book. He specifically states that he realized that this sharing of knowledge and technique was something he saw as inherently American in nature (Untracht, 2003). In whatever way Untracht's decision was made, it is this historical standard that we reflect.

Either way, we acknowledge the inherent trouble in his creating his diagram for the book. He desperately tries not to create hierarchy but it is clearly difficult when he is limited to a vertical format. He declares that there is no hierarchy but identifies and locates related members and perhaps inadvertently illustrates diversity in the field and creates unintended oppositions both within the vertical and horizontal format (Untracht, 1982, p. 11). As we studied the format to begin formulating questions we considered necessary, in order to gain deeper insight into current titles and nomenclature, we started to notice trends, omissions, and linguistic changes in the thirty-six years since the volume was first published. We also noted how it presents a simple diagram but is actually incredibly complex and afforded us a newfound respect for the amount of time and consideration that went into this undertaking.

Some of the power of Untracht's diagram comes from its visual qualities. A diagram brings into play spatial relationships and enables the viewer to trace a number of connections at the same time. It is both complex—a great deal of information—and simple—a single diagram. (Skinner, 2013a, p. 2)

In studying this figure we realized that it was essential that we reach out to the field in two ways to gather enough information to study this nomenclature and at the same time reinvigorate the mandala. For part of this we looked to job descriptions in the field during our months of research and we sent a survey out to professionals to gain insight into how they self-name, their reflections on the convocation, and what changes should be considered. The final version of the survey included these questions, which directly reference the image of A Polarized Convocation of Jewelers.

It is with these combined titles of employment advertisements and the responses to the shared questions that we reflect on the data to begin the process of contemporizing the convocation.

Terminology

Much of our research focused on how jewelers refer to themselves, but what about the titles we use to describe each other? What value do we place on each other's skills and how much has changed as far as what skills a single person is expected to have mastered? In order to answer these questions it was necessary to analyze terminology in the modern job market for jewelers.

Oppi Untracht—A Polarized Convocation of Jewelers, 1982:
Please reference the mandala when answering the following questions.

— *What is your title or how do you title yourself? If you were to self-title what would you call yourself?*

— *Does this title relate to Practice (e.g. enamellist, stones setter), Location (e.g. studio jeweler), Material (e.g. silversmith), Rank or Time period (e.g. journeyman), or Other?*

— *Oppi Untracht, in the early 1980's, describes the jewelry field through the Convocation of Jewelers. How do you see that Mandala significantly changing?*

— *What Jewelry professions have been lost? Which have been adapted?*

— *Where do you see yourself fitting in to a revised Mandala?*

— *How many co-workers do you have? What jobs do they hold?*

— *What is the objective of your making?*

— *Who do you consider your customer base?*

— *If you were to utilize a generic symbol for your position in the jewelry field, like what is used in Untracht's mandala, what would that symbol look like?*

Figure 1. Survey Questions.

We assessed about twenty-five job listings found online, from sources such as Indeed.com, Monster.com, LinkedIn.com, and directly on the websites of major jewelry companies such as Tiffany & Co and Stuller. The job listings' titles mostly fell into three categories: designers who illustrate by hand, CAD model makers, and goldsmiths, silversmiths, machinists, polishers, and setters, all of whom are titled traditionally according to the task they perform. Most listings for this last type of jeweler were looking for candidates with experience in multiple areas such as casting, fabrication, and setting (cite Sturgeon Bay WI job listing). The only company reviewed who did not require a multi-skilled jeweler in any of its listings was Tiffany & Co, in which the polisher, CNC machinist, watch repair jeweler, and assembler were only required do to the tasks associated with the title of the position.

The intersection between the job titles we found in the listings and Untracht's mandala is mostly focused on the bottom section of the original mandala, which

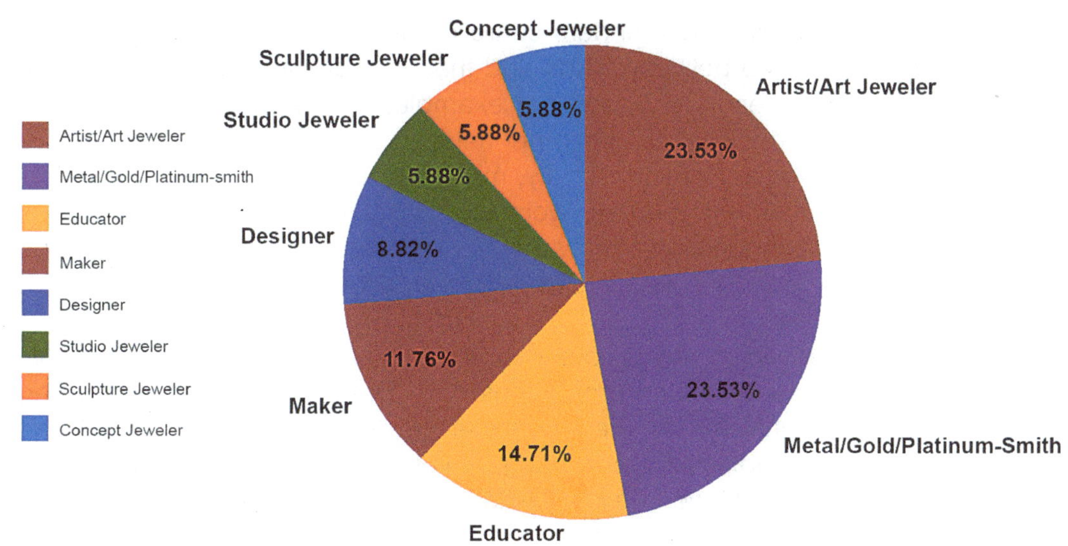

Figure 2. Self-Described Identification.

deals with production jewelry. The top portion of the mandala is geared towards independent artist jewelers, for which we did not find any job listings. We agreed that the industry area of the mandala was no longer accurate—the production titles listed do not encompass all skills and tasks a production jeweler might specialize in today's job market, and that the production section of the mandala was small in comparison to the many jewelers who work in that sector of the industry.

Another aspect of our research hinged on the field survey. There were approximately thirty responders to the survey of questions about self-identification, the changing of titles for the modern era, and the original A Polarized Convocation of Jewelers, which was attached to the survey. The goal of the survey was to have jewelers look critically at the role of titles in the modern age and at the mandala and to offer their suggestions for its revisions. The survey responders came from a variety of backgrounds—they identified as educators, makers, goldsmiths, artist jewelers, conceptual jewelers, and studio jewelers. About half responded that they work alone as a single practitioner, with the rest mixed between working in small studios and companies of ten to fifteen people. They identified their customer base as mostly wealthy art jewelry collectors or "design-oriented people."

When asked what their title refers to (practice, material, location, rank/time period, or other) over half responded "practice," and seven replied "other," with responses such as concept, technique and intent. When asked to analyze Untracht's mandala, many responders shared that they felt there is currently a good amount of overlap between fields and that one failing of the original mandala is that it "describes by division." For example, several responders felt that jewelry-trained individuals working in other fields such as sculpture should have a place on the mandala. Not surprisingly, many responders felt that some titles, such as Anonymous Ethnic Jeweler, were no longer politically correct. Another popular answer to the question of how the mandala should be changed was the addition of computer-aided design/computer-aided manufacturing (CAD/CAM) and digital processes.

Our survey asked which professions from the original mandala have been lost or adapted. While many said no professions have been totally lost, they agreed that some, such as chainmaker, are "endangered," and that the rise of CAD has caused a decline in traditional wax carving. Several responders also agreed that a production jeweler must know several skillsets in order to survive—a finding that was echoed in our job description research.

Lastly, we asked our survey responders to offer a symbol for their title, as is shown in Untracht's original mandala. Popular choices included a brain,

- ***GIA Certifications:***
  - *Graduate Gemologist*
  - *Graduate Diamonds*
  - *Graduate Colored Stones*
  - *Graduate Jeweler*
  - *Jewelry Design & Technology*
  - *Jewelry Design*
  - *Comprehensive CAD/CAM for Jewelry*
- ***Other Certifications:***
  - *Jewelry Design & Marketing Certificate—Pratt*
- ***Jewelry Design Degrees:***
  - *BFA, Jewelry Design, Pratt*
  - *Associate's, Jewelry Design, FIT*
  - *Cranbrook—Metalsmithing*
  - *Tyler—BFA or MFA, Metals/Jewelry/CAD-CAM*
  - *CCA—Jewelry & Metal Arts*
  - *U Kansas—BFA Metalsmithing & Jewelry*
  - *RIT—BFA Metals and Jewelry Design*
  - *RISD—Jewelry & Metalsmithing*
- ***Possible Career Paths, listed by GIA:***
  - *Appraiser*
  - *Auction House Jewelry Specialist*
  - *Colored Stone Buyer*
  - *Diamond Buyer*
  - *Diamond Sorter/Grader*
  - *Estate Jewelry Dealer*
  - *Gemologist*
  - *Inventory Control Specialist*
  - *Jewelry Business Owner*
  - *Jewelry Buyer*
  - *Lab and Research Professional*
  - *Merchandiser*
  - *Pawnbroker*
  - *Retailer*
  - *Sales Associate*
  - *Wholesaler*
  - *CAD Service Bureau Owner*
  - *CAD Technician*
  - *Jewelry CAD Technician*

Figure 3. Jewelry Education and Certifications.

suggesting the need for a broader, conceptual symbol, or something that represented digital work or the crossing between disciplines. It was clear from the results of the survey that today's jewelers found the mandala to be restricting for themselves personally but still accurate in many ways in describing different types of skilled jewelers.

In addition to collecting survey results and looking at job titles in the field currently, we reviewed the opportunities in jewelry education and certifications. In many cases these reference positions with multiple skill sets both within the field and related fields such as business and education. We know there may be countless more but we gleaned a general understanding through the many certificates and a variety of BFA degrees.

It is with all of this information that we undertook the examination and reinterpretation of the Untracht's convocation.

Reorganization of the Convocation

It was with hours of pouring over this diagram and our collected data that we realized we had to deconstruct the convocation to understand it more fully. With much discussion and adaptation, we decided that we would mainly honor Untracht's formation and some tenants of his original. We can all agree that this is a tool which is used to describe a complex and overlapping system and is imperfect in nature. We acknowledge that this outcome is considered organic and must continue to be adapted and changed. All of the decisions we made have been within the spirit of Untracht's original statement and recognize that "the remarkable diversity of interests exists within the family. In the light of such diversity, the only means of creating harmony within the family is through mutual tolerance." (Untracht, 1982, p. 11) It is with this tolerance that we began the process of editing the mandala to reflect the data and contemporary practice.

This resulted in several types of edits and label headings. There was recognition and agreement that some of the original document would be left. There was the identification of **Minute Areas**. There were additions of **New Areas** due to emerging technologies. There were also areas that were Added as it was agreed that they were left off in the original document. There was the need to make both **Label Edits** and **Position Edits**. Each of these labels are colored differently from the original black as to understand and identify the edits. They are color-coded as follows: Original = black, Minute Area = green, New Areas = red, Added = purple, Label Edit = blue, and Position Edit = pink.

During this process we recognized that there are several areas that are still practiced, but few people work in these areas. It was decided that we would include them as they were highly specialized. For the sake of the diagram we chose to label them **Minute Area** separately to visually illustrate that they are not common practice. The second section **New Area** represents the positions that are recent due to the technological shift in the field. Some of these areas have spread significantly to substitute other practices but not wholly replace, as in the case of hand and digital renderer. We also know that these areas in several cases may overlap or one person may hold multiple positions.

Added areas are sections that were omitted. The inclusion of these positions was essential, especially in the case of master model maker, which is a critical job in manufacturing. We were shocked to see that a bench jeweler was also not included in any format outside of the commercial/manufacturing section. Untracht deliberately says that this section "supplies a mass market by employing mass production methods, but art production jewelers ... create ..., often by hand technology" (Untracht 1982, p.11). We added bench jeweler as we see most jewelry repair shops to be outside of the direct manufacturing process, but they must be acknowledged as most consumers/patrons with fine jewelry are interacting with either mall or private jewelers that could fit into this sector outside of manufacturing. The addition of this area for the bench jeweler presented the opportunity to add the bench mechanic as well as the custom jeweler. As the technology changes so does the engagement of what technology is accessible to a singular jeweler.

The **Label Edit** was a striking area where the noticeable use of language led to the change of Anonymous Ethnic Jeweler to be more sensitive to the effects of colonialism, championing inclusivity, and changing the language to Indigenous/Ethnic Jeweler. The most significant change in these labels would be the central figure from Artist Jeweler to Contemporary Art Jeweler. This was completed due to a trend in the self-referencing language. For example, in Damian Skinner's moderation of a rapid-fire presentation during the 2013 Society of North American Goldsmith's conference each of the invitees or presenters in the field relate themselves to Contemporary Jewelry (Skinner, 2013a, p1–2).

Also edited was the title of Bench Worker to Bench Jeweler. There is a bit of an inference that bench workers are not qualified to be considered jewelers in the convocation or perhaps this is just lost terminology. This was a suggestion mentioned by Nanz Aalund in a conversation where she offered her thoughts on the mandala. We concluded that this sounded dismissive and needed critical updating. This

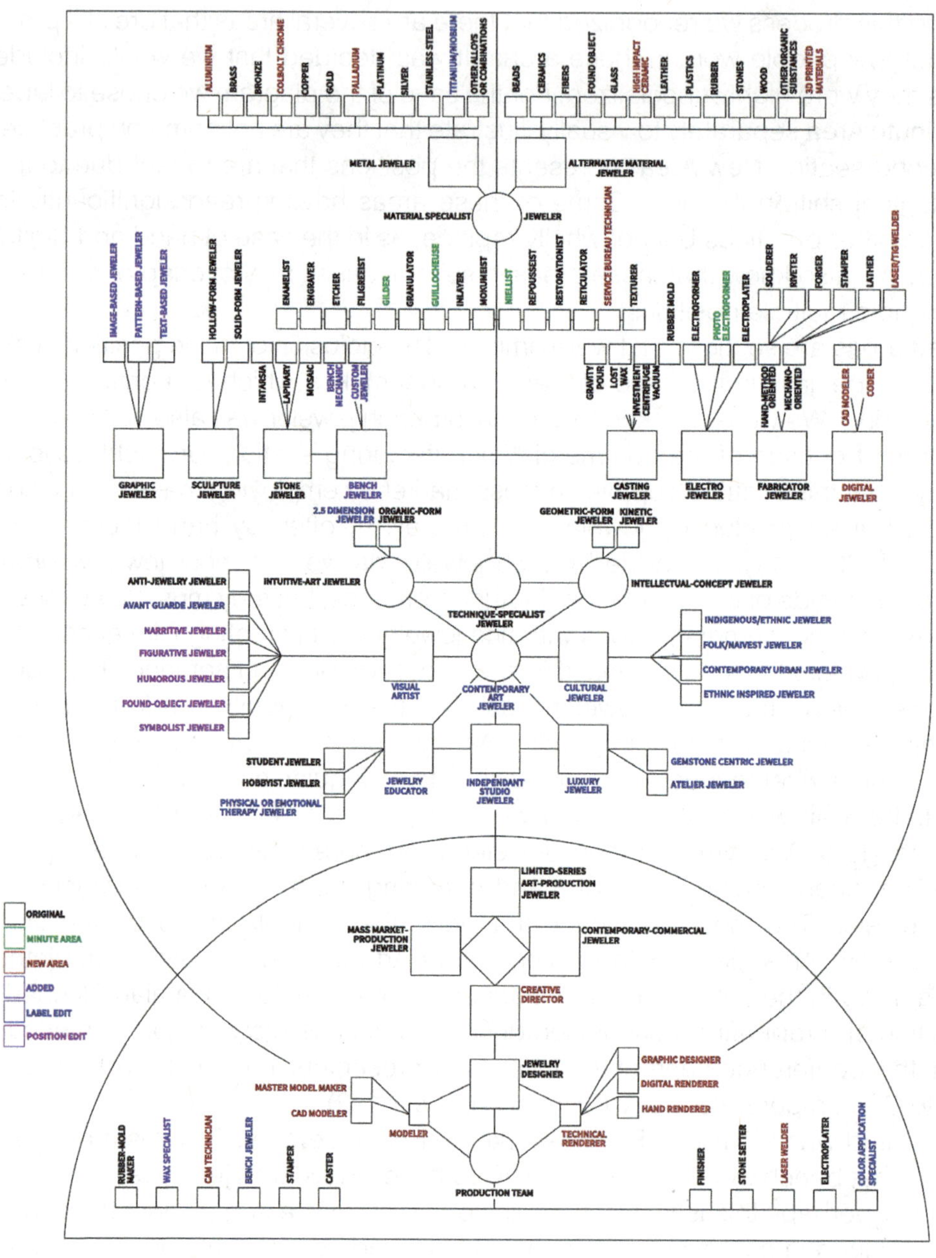

Figure 4. Color-Coded Edits to the Convocation.

was partially rectified with the expanded area outside of manufacturing as well as discussed in previous paragraphs. However, the Bench Jeweler then is positioned within two places in the diagram. This shows that this designation functions in multiple places within the field.

The most difficult part of this re-imagining was the **Position Edit** section. When looking at the Student, Hobbyist, and Therapy Jeweler, they had less in common with Expensive Stone Jeweler and the Prestigious Workshop Jeweler. So we flipped sides, to more closely position Folk/Nativest Jeweler, Indigenous/Ethic, Contemporary Urban Jeweler, and Ethnic Inspired Jeweler with the Expensive Stone Jeweler. This new match relates better to the material-driven nature of the central-right side of the diagram.

An additional necessary edit was to move the related jewelers attached to Graphic Jeweler to Visual Artist, which previously held the place of Rebel Jeweler. They did not conceptually branch off of Graphic Jeweler where they easily branched off of Visual Artist, a more generalized term. This entire movement created the widening of the figure/diagram, effectively changing the original diagram's proportions. The title Rebel Jeweler no longer made sense and was removed.

With these changes and many more not mentioned here, we agonized over positioning so that each jeweler was reflected in their space. Expanding arcs and umbrellas under which we as professionals fall. Even as we reflect on the re-invigorated diagram we see adaptations that could still be made.

Convocation

Part of the challenge for this convocation are the logos, which inhabit or represent each section. As part of the survey several mentioned the brain, as they see that conceptualization, thinking, or problem solving is a large part of their identity. With some suggestions from the three of us, Ho'o Hee has primarily taken on the formation of the logos. This is completed in such a way as to be as logical and representative of each designation as possible.

Reflections

In inspecting the revised figure we notice that there are many overlaps and areas that have become microscopic. We are left with some solutions and some questions. The research of job descriptions and survey responses reinforced what was already understood—jewelers must maintain multiple skills. It is through this understanding that most people in our field will fall under multiple descriptors and labels

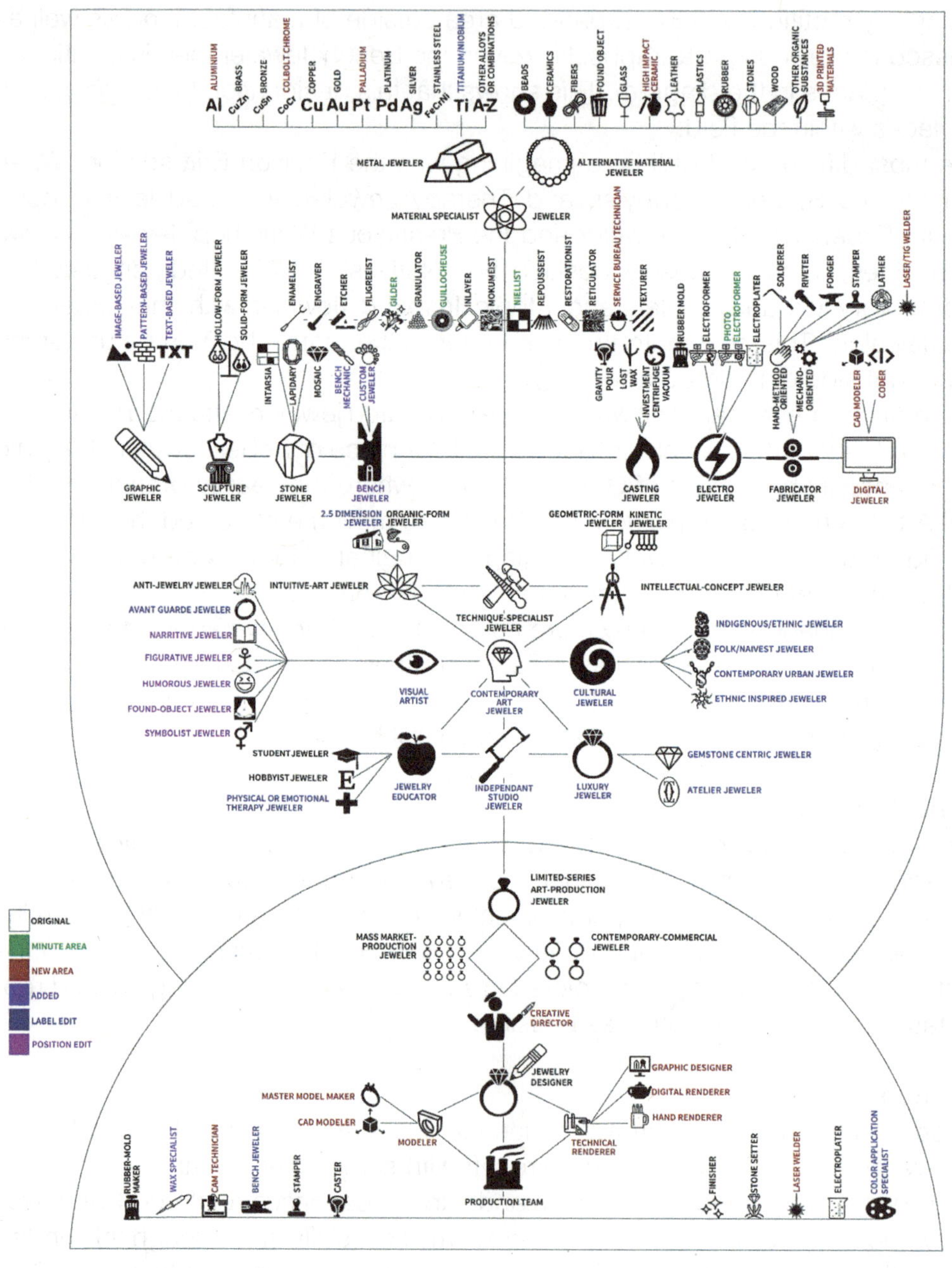

Figure 5. Revised Logos for the Convocation.

within the diagram. Are they so diverse they flow to disparate sides of the diagram? This appears to be common.

One of the questions that is still debatable is perhaps the term "smith"; should it be added to the top left row? With the highly regarded use of the name Goldsmith or Silversmith or one of North America's most important organizations based on Metalsmith should we include smith or is it just understood? Is it applicable to all of those metals? In researching Titanium-smith the term only seems searchable by a jewelry piece worn by a fictional figure on Star Trek Enterprise in 2269 as part of the episode "The Andorian Incident," which aired in October of 2001. (Memory Alpha, 2016) So we know that all of these terms are widely skirted and sometimes only theoretically categorize us properly. That being said the tradition and the terminology of the smith does not seem to be going away but seems deeply rooted in our history as well as our future. Is there a sense of elevation of the jeweler's status as it refers to the higher skill level? Does smith lend a credibility or specialization, establishment and knowledge of skill? We are reminded of the survey, where the two largest categories of self-naming are Artist/Art Jeweler and Metal/Gold/Platinum-Smith. However, we also recognize the titling of Jeweler is inline with the survey as 41 percent, the largest related title respondents, refer to themselves using nomenclature that contains "jeweler."

We have identified a few issues with our figure. Perhaps the upper labeled Bench Jeweler and related titles could be positioned where Luxury Jeweler is located, currently relating better to the other commercial jewelry areas. Possibly the Minute fields should disappear from the survey, but we found ourselves grasping at our history, wanting to preserve and respect the people who still work in these areas. These are thoughts that can certainly be addressed in the future.

One of the new titles that overarches this whole diagram is Maker. Just over 11 percent of professionals of our survey self-identify with the title of Maker. Is this title problematic? Unlike the term Master Model Maker, which encompasses a specific set of highly developed skills, the term Maker seems vague for its description of an unspecific set of skills. Are people making contemporary jewelry with skills so specific at this point they feel like they cannot describe themselves so generally? Is a maker the opposite to an artisan devoid of a specific craft, which is given up to be able to move between crafts? The root term is also popularized by the maker or DIY movement where people who do not have specific skill can create objects. Perhaps this term is allowing for a freedom that a more specific nomenclature would pigeonhole? When we consider terms like craftsman in the Art Nouveau Movement, it signified a return to the hand in response to the industrial revolution. Currently it is a sign of this post-digital age where generalist unspecific terminology is new and we have yet to see what the impact or space this distinction will inhabit. Conceivably there may be a response to this in a return to highly skilled areas of specificity. Or perhaps this trend of the title Maker will continue with our skills having to be diversified for success.

This has been a large undertaking but there is certainly room to develop an adaption of this diagram. It is a living project that invites discussion of categories to change, move, and add. This was completed by a group of jewelers from differing backgrounds, ages, and positions who self-identify and are frequently identified as: Artist (Anti-Jewelry Jeweler, Digital Jeweler and Educator), Studio Jeweler (Goldsmith, Educator), Maker (Digital Jeweler, CAD Technician, and Educator), and Jewelry Educator (Designer).

References

Collins Dictionary of Business. 2006. "Skill." *Collins Dictionary of Business*, 3rd ed. London: Collins. http://ezhost.utrgv.edu:2048/login?url=https://search.credoreference.com/content/entry/collinsbus/skill/0?institutionId=9822.

Den Besten, L. 2011. *On Jewellery: A Compendium of International and Contemporary Art Jewellery*. Stuttgart: Arnoldsche Art Publishers.

Journeyman. 2004. In *Word Histories and Mysteries*. Boston: Houghton Mifflin. http://ezhost.utrgv.edu:2048/login?url=https://search.credoreference.com/content/entry/hmwhm/journeyman/0?institutionId=9822.

Memory Alpha. 2016. *Titanium Smith*. http://memory-alpha.wikia.com/wiki/Titanium_smith.

Skinner, D. 2013a. "A Polarized Convocation of Jewellers Reconsidered." Presentation at the Society of North American Goldsmith's Conference, Fairmont Royal York Hotel, Toronto, Canada, May 16, 2013.

Skinner, D., 2013b. "The Jewel Mandala." Presentation at the Society of North American Goldsmith's Conference, Fairmont Royal York Hotel, Toronto, Canada May 18, 2013.

Untracht, O. 1982. Jewelry Concepts and Technology. Garden City, NY: Doubleday.

Untracht, O. 2003. Oppi Untracht Interviewed by Donna Mason Sweigart, Audio and PowerPoint Presentation. Part of MFA, Tyler School of Art, Temple University, August 2003.

Traditional Handcrafted Jewelry versus Contemporary Digital Jewelry Dictated by the Culture, Fashion, and Modern Trends of Hindu Families of Andhra Pradesh, India

Sarvani Vaddi, Department of Fashion Design,
National Institute of Fashion Technology, Hyderabad, India

Abstract

Jewelry formed the utmost important element of aadornment even before the invention of clothing in India. Tradition means the passing on of elements of a culture as guiding principle from generation to generation like gold and silver jewelry. Its possession indicated higher status in society as well. In Andhra Pradesh, a newborn baby boy is gifted with a gold chain, having a locket made out of two nails of a tiger embedded in gold. The local goldsmith handcrafts it with rubies and emeralds with utmost care. The maternal grandmother gifts this chain "Puligoru" (nails of a tiger) to her grandson, a symbol to bless him to grow as a brave man. Rice grains, cotton yarns, turmeric herbs, gold, silver, pearls, gems and fresh flowers are the materials used at various occasions as jewelry. This study focuses on the customs, rituals, designs, and materials used by Hindu families to celebrate various stages of life, like puberty of a girl, marriage, and seventh month of pregnancy, to express joy and to pass on the blessings and traditions. In the digital era, the beauty of traditional jewelry is at its plethora. Increased purchasing capacity of consumers and the advent of the modern designer has given rise to contemporary temple jewelry with elaborate and extensive use of precious and semi-precious materials. Digital manufacturing technologies made it possible to meet the increased demand for new categories of fashion jewelry trends to meet the changed lifestyles of modern consumers.

Introduction

In this robotic twenty-first century, we can find some people who do not wear a saree blouse but, adorn themselves with jewelry in certain parts of the state, like in Srikakulum district of Andhra Pradesh as shown in Figure 1. Tradition means the passing on of elements of a particular culture as guiding principle from generation to generation, like gold and silver jewelry. Its possession indicates higher status in

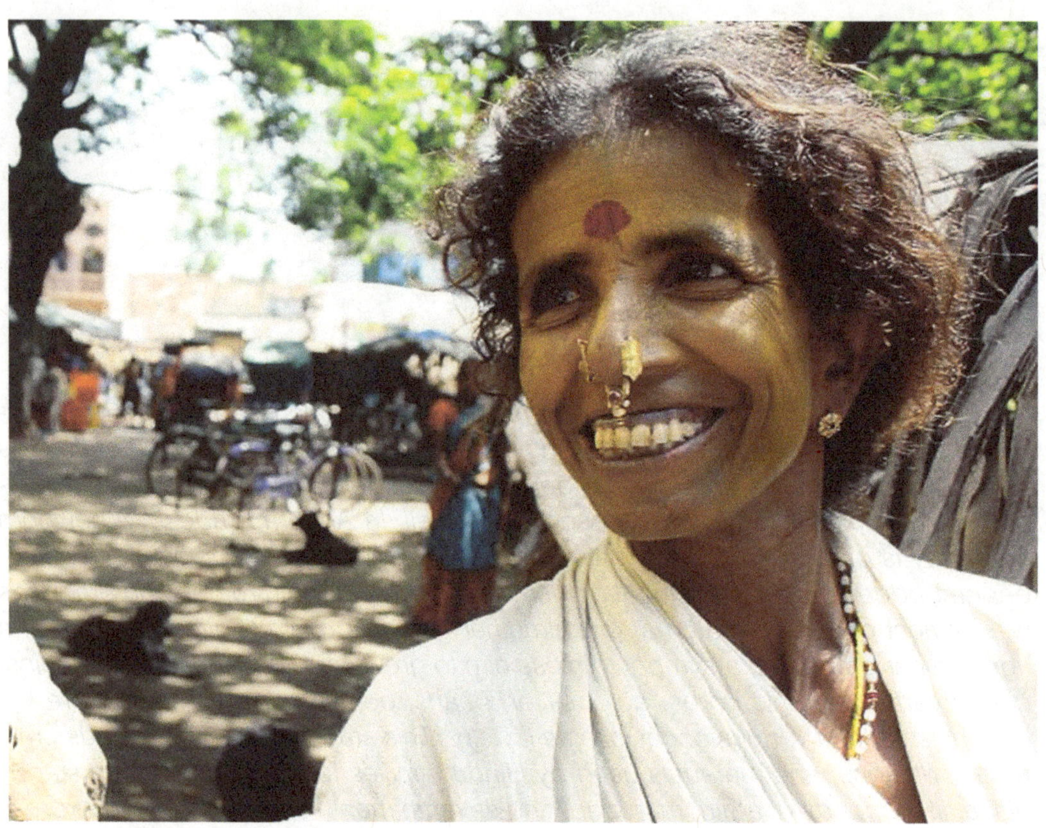

Figure 1. A woman wearing a nose ornament, ear studs, yellow cotton thread thaali and pearl string. She is not wearing a blouse but many jewelry ornaments.

the society as well. Rice grains, cotton yarns, turmeric herbs, gold, silver, pearls, gems, and fresh flowers are the materials used at various occasions as jewelry. In the digital era, the beauty of traditional jewelry is at its plethora. Increased purchasing capacity of consumers, and the advent of modern designers, has given rise to contemporary temple jewelry with elaborate and extensive use of precious and semi-precious materials. Digital manufacturing technologies made it possible to meet the increased demand for new categories of fashion jewelry trends to meet the changed lifestyles of modern consumers.

Methodology

The jewelry worn by various people differs among various age groups and castes in the Hindu society. The Padmashali community, who are the decedents of Markandeya, Son of Lord Shiva, is the weaver's community in the Andhra Pradesh state. Their customs, rituals, and practices are studied and documented. A sample of forty families with subjects from three generations were selected for the study in order to obtain detailed information about the customs and practices from the past seventy-five years. Photographic and videographic evidence was collected from their personal albums. Information was collected from the goldsmiths and jewelry stores to understand the current trends in jewelry designs.

Tools of research: observations were noted down. Questionnaires were designed suitably to collect information from three generations of subjects and personal interviews were taken with the support of structured interview schedules. Data was collected from the goldsmiths and jewelry store managers using structured interview schedules.

Results and Discussion

A married woman in her middle age wears a *Thaalibottu* chain, a black beads chain, and a necklace as her neck ornaments, along with a pair of earrings, one or two pairs of gold bangles, along with glass bangles matching to the colour of her sari. She wears golden finger rings, namely vanki, which is studded with czeds, jades, and pink. She also wears a gold finger ring engraved with goddess Lakshmi on it. A pair of earrings matching her necklace. Men wear gold chains as neck ornaments and golden finger rings with the face of Lord Venkateshwara engraved on it being the traditional one (Figure 2).

In Andhra Pradesh, a newborn baby boy is gifted with a gold chain with a pendent made out of two nails of a tiger embedded in gold. The local goldsmith handcrafts it with rubies and emeralds with utmost care. The maternal grandmother gifts this chain *Puligoru* (nails of a tiger) to her grandson on the occasion of his credle ceremony, which is celebrated on twenty-first day of his birth, as a symbolto bless him to grow as a brave man. The front and back view of the handmade *Puligoru* locket and chain shows that it is engraved with a lion's face, which is believed to be symbolic of bravery (Figures 3 and 4).

The contemporary digital designs in fig. 5 are Puligoru Pendants. They incorporate half-moon peacock motifs in mirror image with American diamonds, rubies studded in gold designs, imitation tiger nails and enamel material (Figure 5).

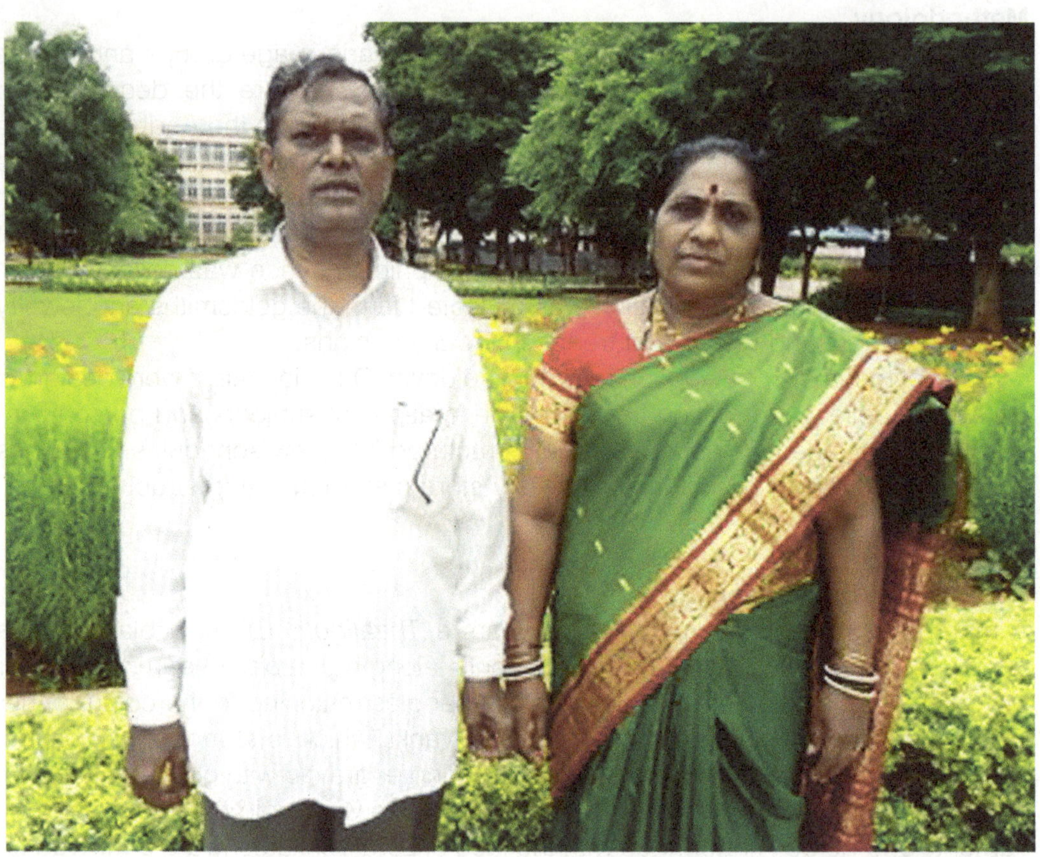

Figure 2. A middle-aged Hindu couple.

Baby girls, on the other hand, are gifted with golden chains at the time of the cradle ceremony celebrated on the twenty-first day after their birth. Once the baby girls are three months old, they are gifted with *Chevipogulu* golden earrings (Figure 6), which have sharp edges to prick into earlobes. It is customary that the maternal uncle gifts these earrings to his niece. If this is missed for any reason, the earlobes are pierced only in her third year. Earrings that can be directly pierced into the ear and twisted at the back are made out of 22 carat gold in 91.6 kdm purity. Later, when the girls are six years old, these earrings are replaced with *ringulu*, *buttalu* etc. so as to suit to the size of their face.

Ringulu are circular ear ornaments from a half inch to three inches in diameter with a latch opening and closure made in pure gold.

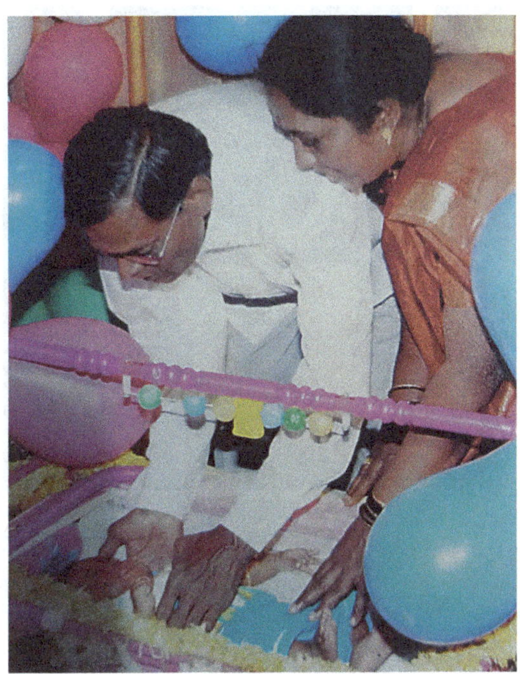
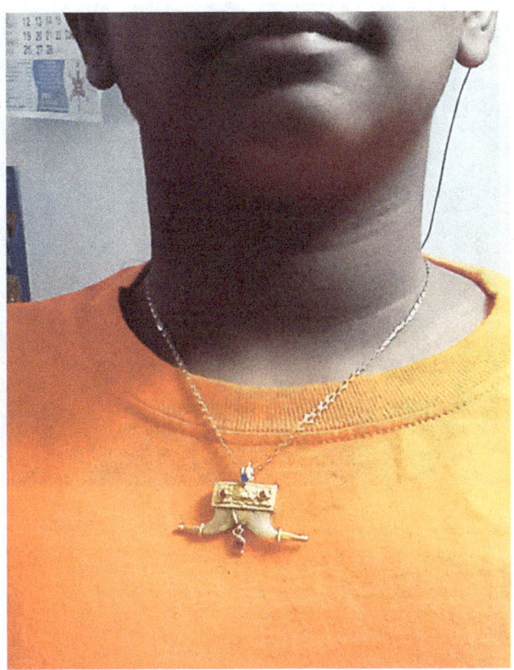

Figure 3. Cradle ceremony and a boy with *Puligoru* locket.

Poola jada, the hairstyle of young girls, is decorated with fresh flowers stitched to plaiting during festivals and marriages (Figure 7). With the advent of digital technology, handmade plaiting's are replaced by gold designs popularly called as *Bangaru jada* (Golden Plait). At the time of puberty, adolescent girls are decorated with all the pieces of jewelry to get the complete look of womanhood. A waist ornament, *Vaddanam* is a must have at the time of the celebration of puberty (Figure 8).

The *Chandra Haaram* moon necklace is made with a locket holding two to seven chains. The speciality of this chain is that the locket has the owner's names engraved for identity, as every woman would possess one such ornament (Figure 9).

Baasikalu are the ornaments on the forehead worn only during a marriage ceremony by both bride and bridegroom. Rice grains are woven in two to three rows and tightly placed on a piece of cardboard one inch in length and 1.5 inches in width (Figure 10). It is believed to be auspicious to wear such forehead ornaments while reciting the promises of marriage to each other. These days, the gold and artificial

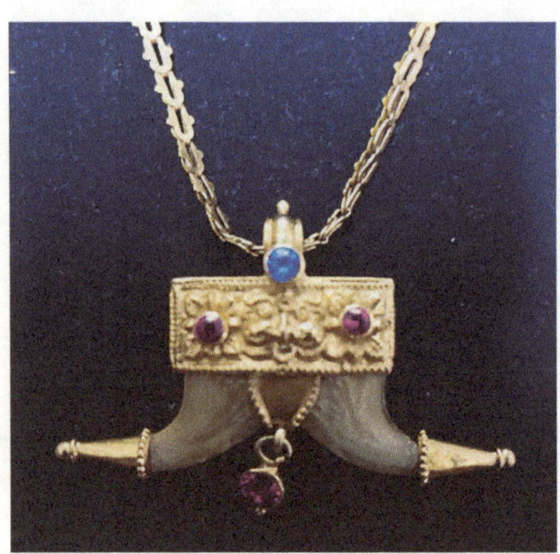

Figure 4. Front and back view of *Puligoru* locket design.

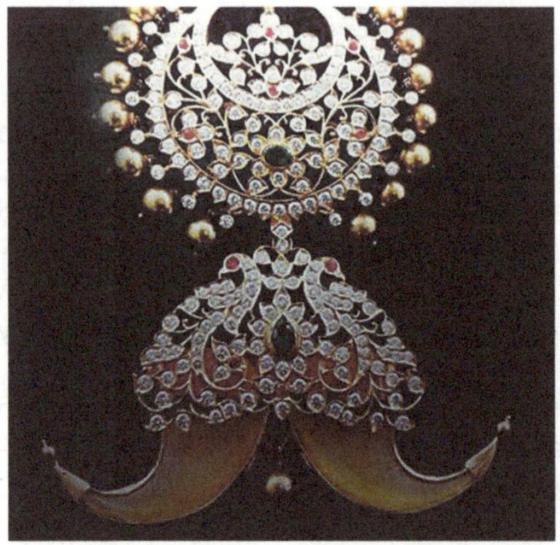

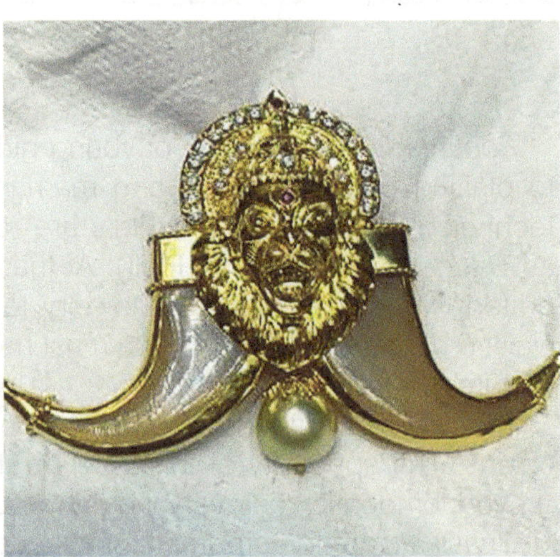

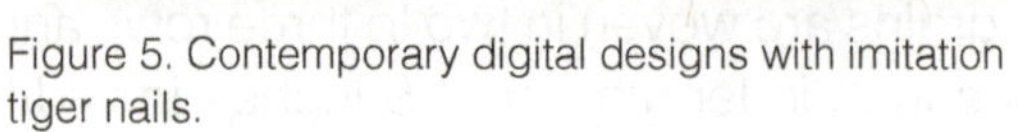

Figure 5. Contemporary digital designs with imitation tiger nails.

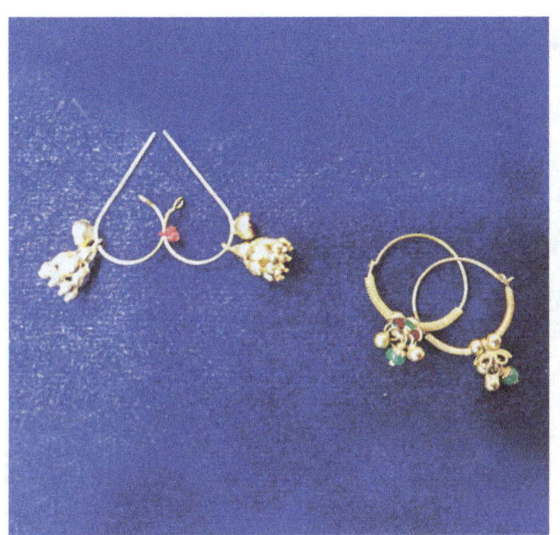

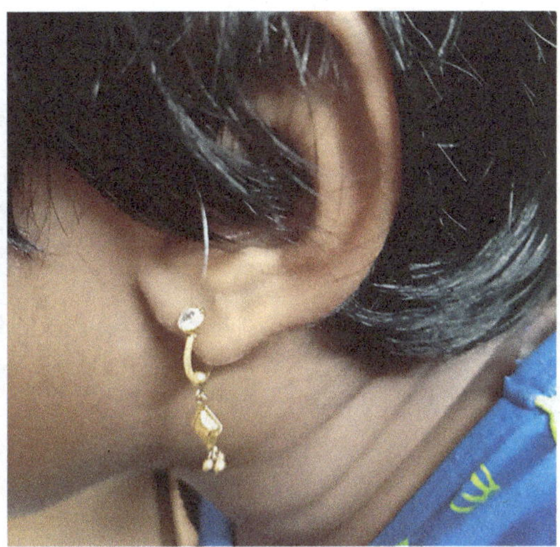

Figure 6. Chevipogulu earrings.

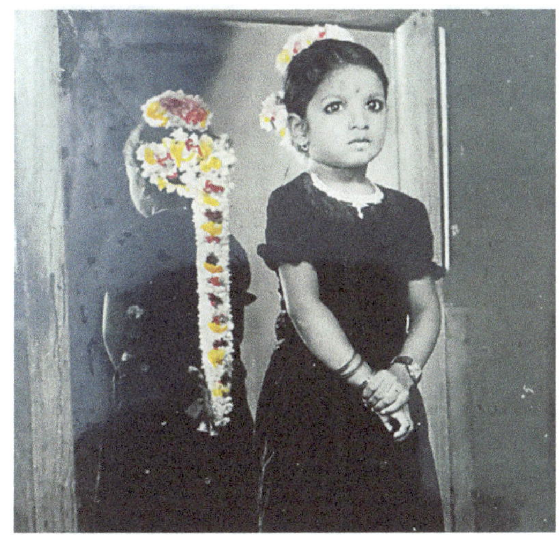

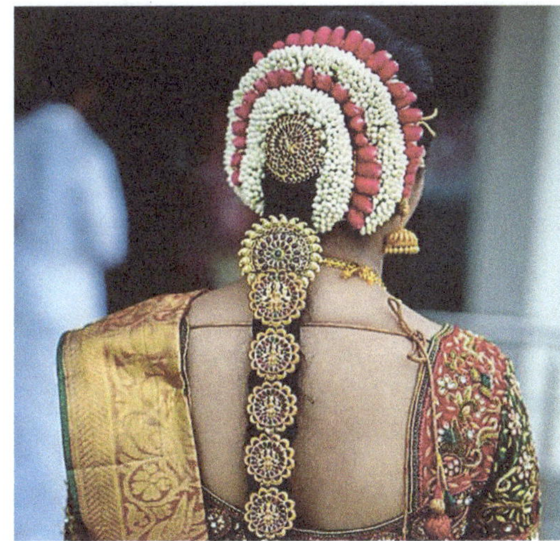

Figure 7. Poola jada.

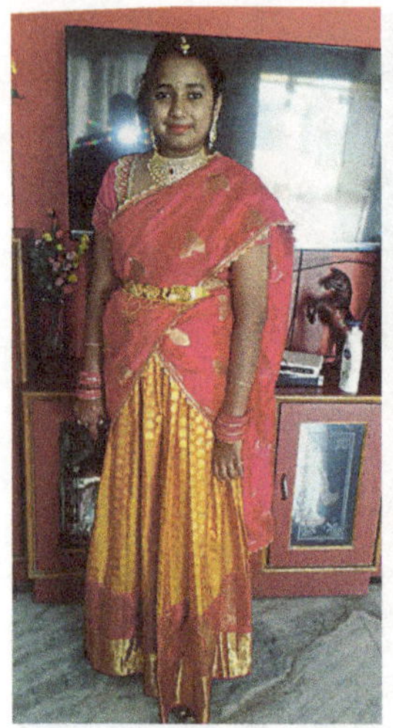

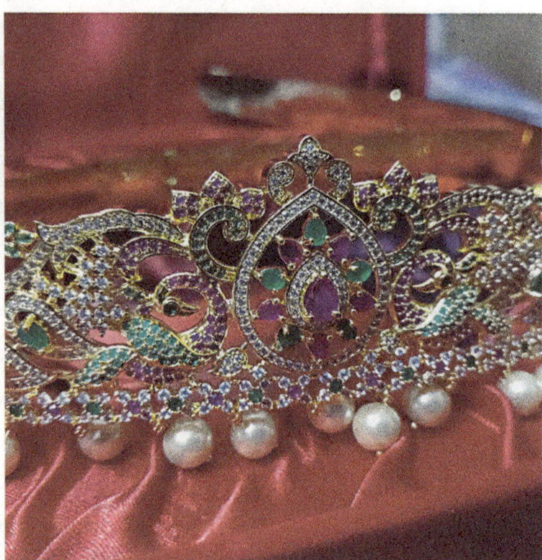

Figure 8. *Vaddanam*, a belt-like ornament.

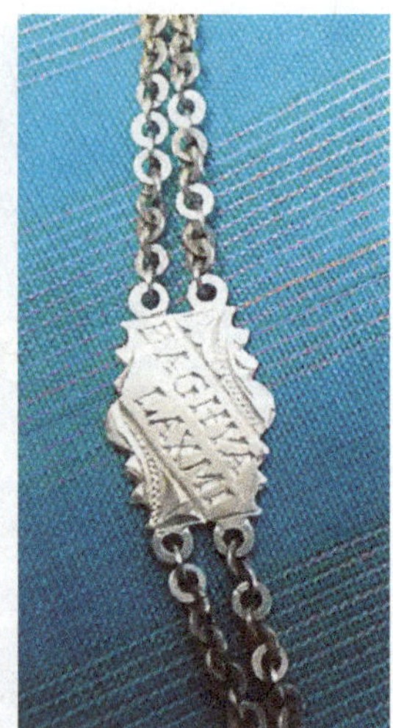

Figure 9. *Chandrahaaram* with name engraved.

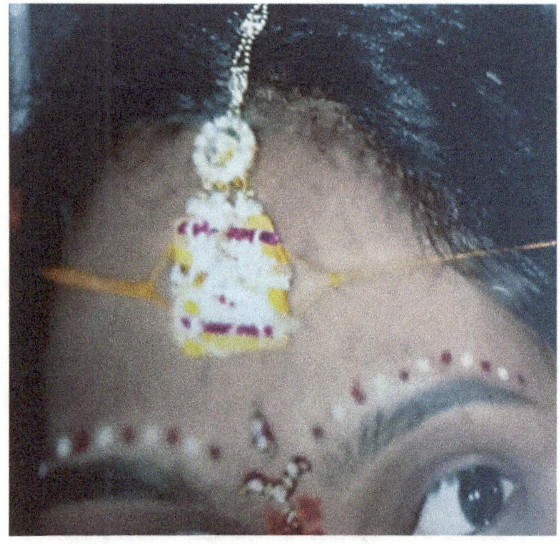

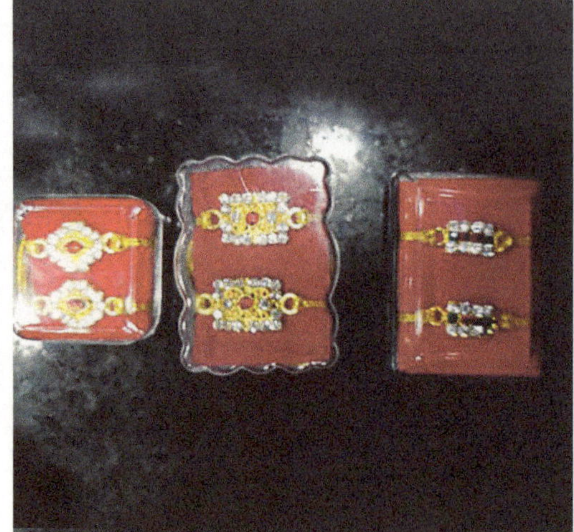

Figure 10. *Baasikaalu* ornaments on the forehead.

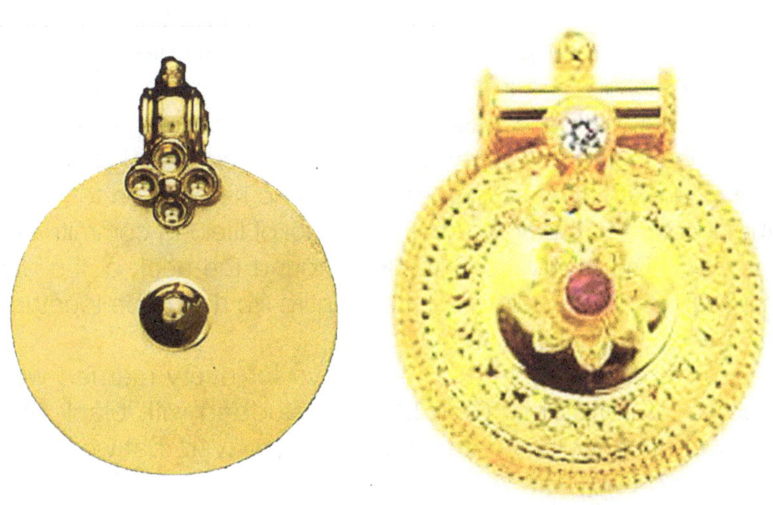

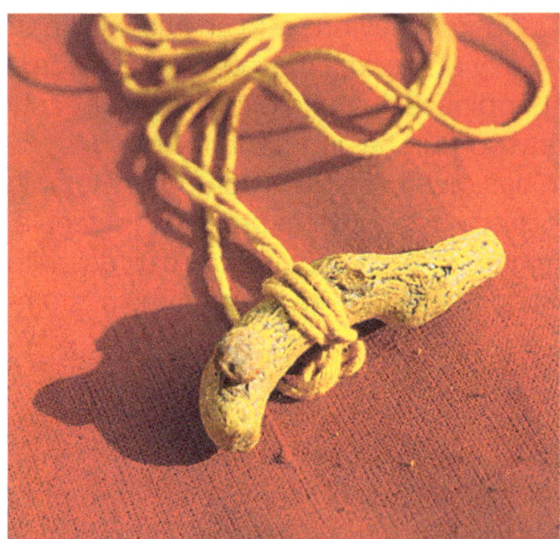

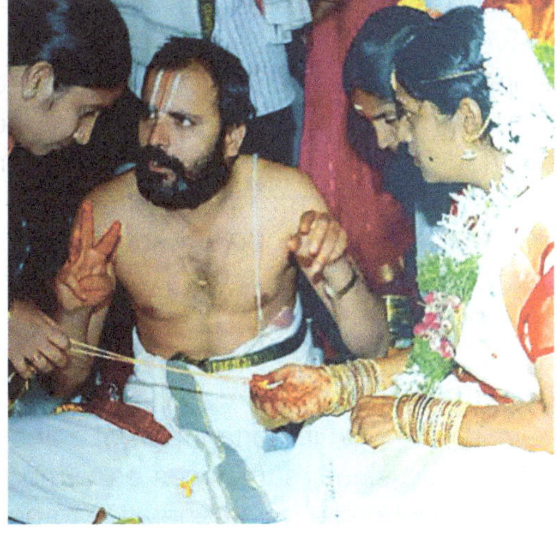

Figure 11. Stages of changes in Thaalibottu and the bride holding it during marriage ceremony.

gold designs replace the natural materials to suit to the choices of modern young consumers. Today, computer-aided digital designs are available for *Baasikaalu*.

Many changes have taken lace in the *Thaalibotlu*, from a turmeric herb to a flat handmade circular locket to an embossed locket with intricate digital designs. Fine cotton yarns are dipped in turmeric water and are twisted on the thigh by the elderly ladies in the family. Once the twist is inserted, a turmeric herb is tied to it at the center. This forms the auspicious *Thaali*, which is a symbol of lifelong commitment by the bridegroom (Figure11). The bridegroom ties this around the neck of the bride with three knots with a promise to stay with her for the entire life and to be together for the next seven births.

Digital black bead chains in gold is a must-have for every married woman as a symbolic indication of her status. Gold bangles studded with black beads are specially worn by woman after they are married. It is believed that wearing a black bead necklace will ward away evil forces.

Kaasula peru is a series of coins with goddess Lakshmi on them, forming a long necklace. Wearing such a necklace indicates prosperity and higher status among others. Digital designs have replaced the handmade *kaasula peru*. This can be worn by widows as well. This is the only necklace which remains and accompanies her till the end of her life.

Fresh flower garlands are sold by street vendors. They are also an essential part of every occasion. Handmade and digital jewelry along with the fresh flowers coexist in every celebration as an expression of happiness. In the digital era, the beauty of traditional jewelry is at its plethora. Increased purchasing capacity of consumers, and the advent of the modern designer, has given rise to contemporary temple jewelry with elaborate and extensive use of precious and semi-precious materials. Imitation jewellery, popularly known as 1 gm gold jewelry, is made out of brass with gold coating on it. Digital designs in imitation gold are also available for the customers who cannot afford to buy pure gold.

Conclusion

Jewelry forms an important part of celebrations in Hindu families: sometimes in the form of blessings, sometimes as symbols of commitments, sometimes as part of treasures inherited from generation to generation; many times, they accompany the wearer from childhood to the end of their life like a companion or friend. In this twenty-first century, as we are experiencing the drastic shift from computer-aided design and manufacturing of jewelry to computer incorporated digital jewelry; the customs, rituals, and culture of the people should be taken care of.

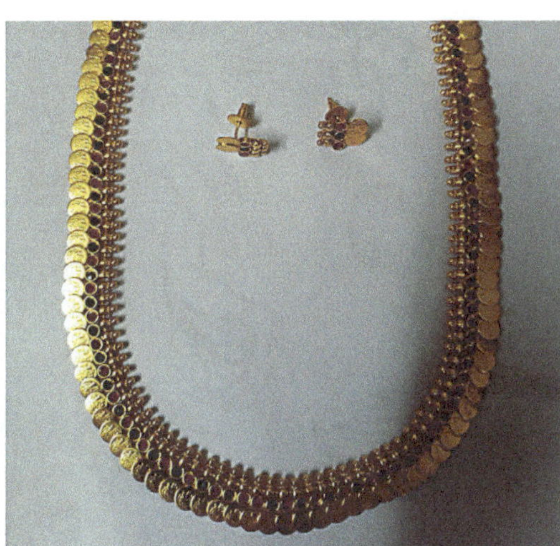

Figure 11. stages of changes in Thaalibottu and bride holding it during marriage ceremony.

Further Reading

Krzemnicki, S.M., and E.L. Cartier. 2017. "Fake Pearls Made from Tridacna Gigas Shells." *Journal of Gemmology* 35 (5): 424–429.

Handley, H.T. 2009. *Indian Jewellery.* Delhi: B.R.Publlishing Corporation.

Peacock, J. 2002. *20th Century Jewelry.* London: Thames and Hudson.

Balakrishnan, R.U. 2001. *Jewels of Nizams.* New Delhi: Department of Culture, Government of India.

Neubauer, J.J. 2001. *Chandrika-Silver Ornaments of India.* Manchester: Shish and Timeless Books.

BalaKrishnan, R.U., and S.M. Kumar. 1999. *Dance of the Peacock, Jewellery Traditions of India.* Mumbai: India Book House Limited.

Pandey, I.P. 1988. *Dress and Ornaments in Ancient India.* Delhi: Bharatiya Vidya Prakash.

Innovative Movable Structure Design for Jewelry Application Based on Integrated 3D Printing and Lost-Wax Casting Technology

Wei Xiong, Gemmological Institute, China University of Geosciences, Wuhan, China
Kaka Cheng, Gemmological Institute, China University of Geosciences, Wuhan, China
Liang Hao, Gemmological Institute, China University of Geosciences, Wuhan, China
Yan Li, Gemmological Institute, China University of Geosciences, Wuhan, China

Abstract

3D printing technology has brought unprecedented innovation in modern design and production. Governments, research institutions, and enterprises in many countries, including Europe, America, and China, have made great efforts with the development and application of 3D printing technology in various industries. In the jewelry industry, the 3D wax printing technology (wax-based slurry deposition for 3D printing) integrated with lost-wax casting method has been widely applied as an innovative production approach, becoming a relatively mature method for complex and novel jewelry fabrication. 3D printing technology is primarily used for substituting traditional manual molding methods, however, the advantages such as less molding geometry restriction and high molding accuracy have not been fully exploited for innovative jewelry design. In this paper, the design concept and principle proposed for jewelry movable structure are based on 3D printing technology and related lost-wax molding technique. The application of the "support column design and removal method" has realized the manufacture of various movable structures (e.g. ball sleeve movable structure, internal suspension movable structure, multi-spiral movable structure and axial movable structure). Through creative design, the movable structure and jewelry design are combined to make the jewelry more shiny, unique, and fitted. This not only takes the technical advantages of 3D printing but also realizes the creative design of jewelry.

1. Introduction

China's economy is transforming from intensive and heavy industry with large resource consumption to an innovative and creative hi-tech industry with high added value. 3D printing technology has made significant progress and is widely accepted in industries. The integration of 3D printing and digital technology provides unprecedented opportunities for the innovative development and manufacturing of jewelry in China. The 3D wax printing technology integrated with lost-wax casting method has been applied widely as an innovative production approach. The production approach is fabricated through a five-step process (Shapeways, 2018). First, the design model is printed in wax using a high-resolution 3D wax printer. The wax has a rich blue color, and its density and surface features are similar to traditional casting wax. This wax is printed using the multi-jet modeling (MJM) 3D printing process. Molten wax is deposited onto an aluminum build platform in layers using several nozzles that sweep across the build area. As the heated material jets onto the build plate, it solidifies. A different type of wax with a lower melting temperature is deposited under overhangs of the design model, acting as a supported structure. When printing is finished, the models are removed from the tray and placed into a heated bath that melts away the supported material. Then, the models are placed in the air to dry up. Next, the model is put in a container where liquid plaster is poured in. Once the plaster sets, the wax will be melted out in a furnace, and the remaining plaster will become a mold. Then, the molten metal is poured into the mold through a sprue gate and is set to be hard; the plaster will be kept for 12 hours prior to opening the mold by water injection, and the jewelry is briefly tumbled. Finally, jewelry is carefully cleaned and hand polished.

The integration of 3D wax printing and lost-wax molding technology quickly turns digital computer-aided design (CAD) data into precisely manufactured jewelry. The wax model used by the high-resolution 3D wax printer with high print resolution (up to 8,000 dpi) produces high-definition parts with crisp details and smooth surface. The support material is easy to remove in post-processing and preserves a jewelry's delicate features (3Dsystems, 2018). The wax materials can offer superior casting properties, fast melt out, no ash or residue, and no thermal expansion (Solidscape, 2018).

As a digital manufacturing tool, 3D printing bridges the gap between the virtual and physical world. Also, creative designers are given more space to express inspiration and ability, thus guiding future design innovation. This new digital manufacturing approach of the combination of 3D wax printing and lost-wax casting technology could offer the following five main advantages: 1) the small volume bespoke manufacturing using 3D printing and casting technology could meet the market demand for personal jewelry products with added value; 2) the rapid delivery speed of 3D printing and casting technology could comply with fashion jewelry, thus enabling the supply and sales of trendy jewelry in time; 3) high molding geometry with less geometry restriction of 3D printing and casting technology can achieve a highly complex and unique design, such as net-shape without welding spot, hollow, periodic, or movable structure; 4) the application of those two technologies is cost effective, using lightweight structure (such as hollow structure) that is

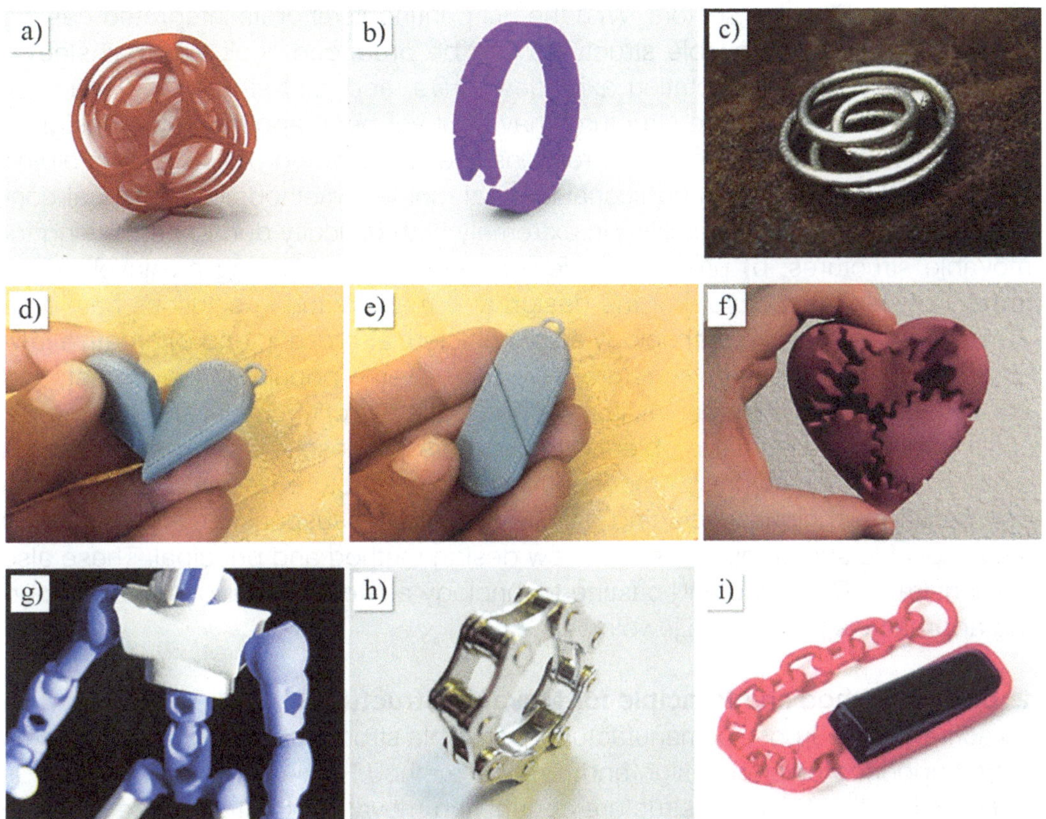

Figure 1. Design of 3D printing movable structure: a) Ball sleeve structure (Virtox, 2018), b) assembly structure (Badulaques, 2018), c) ball bearing structure (Terra Cotta, 2018), d) rotation axis structure (Gershoni, 2018), e) rotation axis structure (Gershoni, 2018), f) gear drive structure (Human Hive, 2018), g) joint structure (Kidmechano, 2016), h) chain structure1 (Friedrich, 2018), i) chain structure 2 (TomBot, 2018).

labor and material saving; and 5) the digital nature of 3D printing and casting technology can be combined with Internet-based cloud platforms to offer integrated design, manufacturing, e-commerce, and service, providing customers with precious and personalized jewelry products and experiences.

Although the advantages are many, as mentioned above, the advantages, such as high dimension accuracy and less geometry restriction, have not been made full use of in the jewelry industry. In contrast, the design innovation based on 3D printing and casting technology has been applied in other creative industries, such as culture innovation and fashion sectors. With the 3D printing itself or its integrated casting technology, various movable structures can be produced, including ball sleeve, assembly, ball bearing, rotation axis, gear drive, and joint structures (Figure 1).

However, these movable structures have not yet been applied to the design of metal jewelry products. The main reasons are as following: a) lost-wax molding geometry is restricted with traditional manual molding methods or numerical control cutting processions, resulting in extremely high difficulty during processing for movable structures; b) preliminary design and post-processing are involved for jewelry movable structure, but the design and manufacturing solutions based on 3D printing and casting technology are insufficient at present; and c) creative jewelry designs with movable structure have not become popular in the market, and consequently, many companies just want to make a profit from existing design.

To address the above problems, the authors propose a study on the design method and manufacturing process for movable structure based on 3D printing and casting techniques including ball sleeve, internal suspension, and spiral and axial movable structures by using a new design method and principal. These also demonstrate 3D printing and casting technology as advanced digital manufacturing approaches for creative jewelry.

2. Design Method and Principle for Movable Structure

To achieve the purpose of manufacturing movable structure, the authors propose a new "supported column design and removal method." "The supported column" is designed as the columnar structure connecting movable structures. The movable structures can separate two movable parts after the removal and be applied as "flow channel" among all movable parts of products during lost-wax casting. It can also act as a sprue gate, to avoid the effects on the bright surface of products with extra sprue gate setting on them, and it must be removed after lost-wax casting so that the structural parts can move easily.

The supported column should be designed according to the three important principles: 1) ***quantity***: the designed supported column should allow the casting of all product parts; 2) ***position***: the designed supported column should be easily removed during post-processing; and 3) ***cost***: minimum material waste should be considered for size and quantity of supported column. To achieve cost-effective design, computational simulation of the casting process has been applied to analyze/optimize the supported column. Moreover, after lost-wax casting, the removed supported column can be recycled.

3. Manufacturing Process of Movable Structure and Application

There are varieties of movable structures in jewelry fabrication, and the most common one is chain structure; hook structure for pedantry with innovative movable structure is less available in the market. As described previously, 3D printing and casting technique can be used to manufacture the movable structure. With this technique, the shape that is difficult to make by traditional technique can be produced now. This extended geometric freedom has greatly expanded designers' inspiration and imagination, enhancing artistic expressions as well as the functions of the jewelry. This 3D printing and casting technique has been widely adopted by the jewelry industry, due to its high quality and the reasonable cost of products. The following discusses the innovative design and implementation method for ball sleeve movable structure, internal suspension movable structure, multi-spiral movable structure, and axial movable structure based on the integration of 3D wax printing and lost-wax casting technology.

3.1. Ball Sleeve Movable Structure

Ball sleeve movable structure refers to the ball existing inside a hollow ball. The traditional handcraft skill for completing such a structure is associated with demanding skill and high expense. For instance, Figure 2 shows the craft master's high skill. Among sculpture arts with typical ivory or bone carving, an artist can engrave ball structure artware with more than 60 layers in maximum. Nevertheless, craft masters with such high demanding skill are very limited and thus the success rate of high-quality products is quite low, along with the need of long working hours and excellent fabrication skill. Such excellent works often become part of collections and are not available for consumers to purchase. With 3D printing and casting technology, the process complexity of movable structure manufacture could be reduced greatly, and would not be increased significantly with the increase of the layer number of balls. This allows designers to create such unique structures with original and innovative design out of craft restriction.

To make internal sleeve structure, the authors propose a novel "supported column design and removal method" (Figure 3a–b). All the parts are made of the same metal. However, in order to illustrate such complicated 3D design of internal sleeve structure, the authors use transparent glass, and red and green plastic to present external ball, internal ball, and supported column, respectively. With such a design, the supported column could be removed with tools after the casting process of all three parts. In this way, the external ball can be separated from the internal ball, and both parts become movable (Figure 3f).

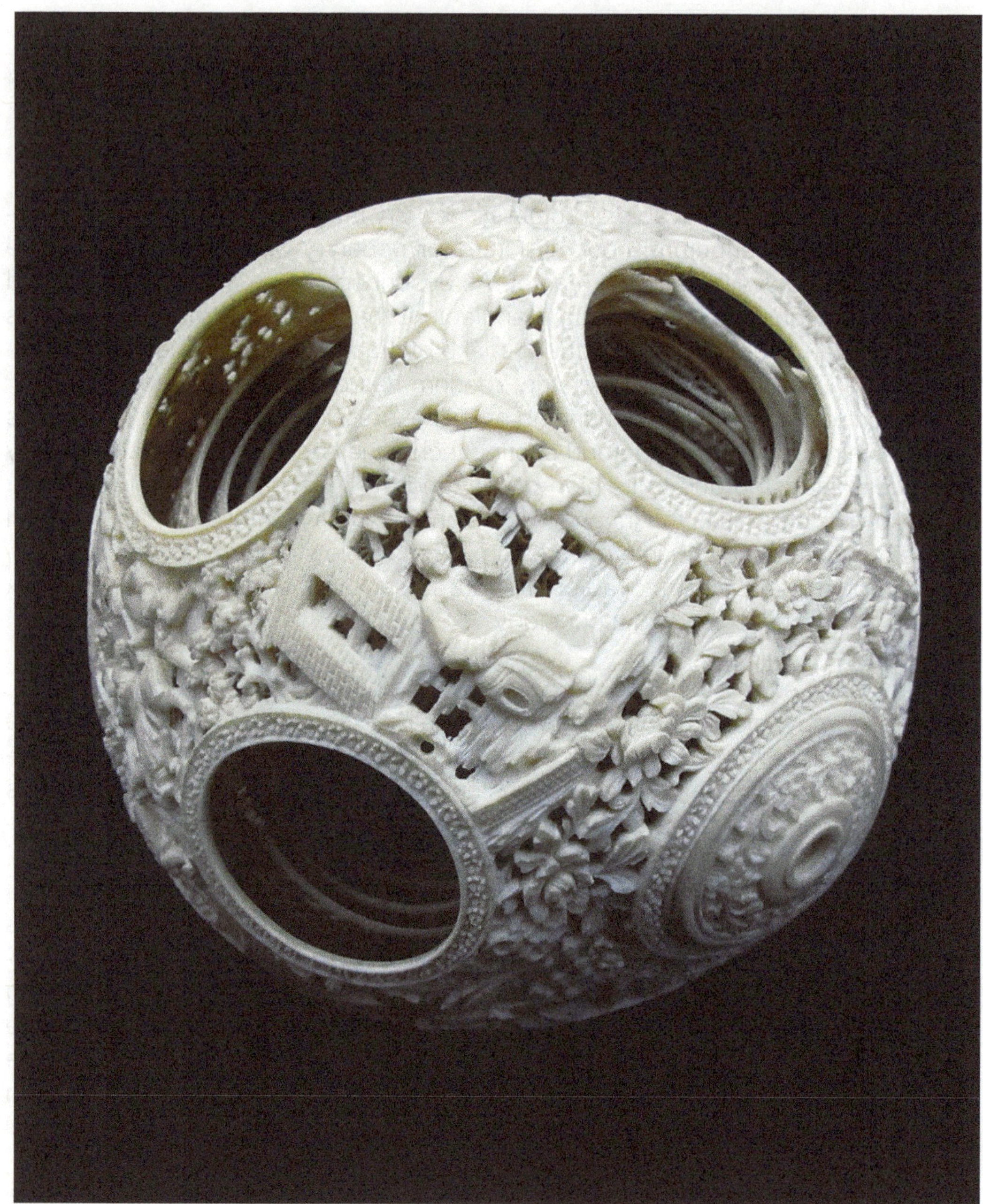

Figure 2 (above). Traditional ball sleeve ivory carving work (lwzholy, 2017).

Figure 3 (right). 3D rendering structural diagrams of ball sleeve: a) before removing the supported column; and b) after removing the supported column. Pictures of jewelry products with ball sleeve movable structure: c) 3D renderings; d) physical picture before removing the supported column; e) physical pictures after removing the supported column; and f) final product.

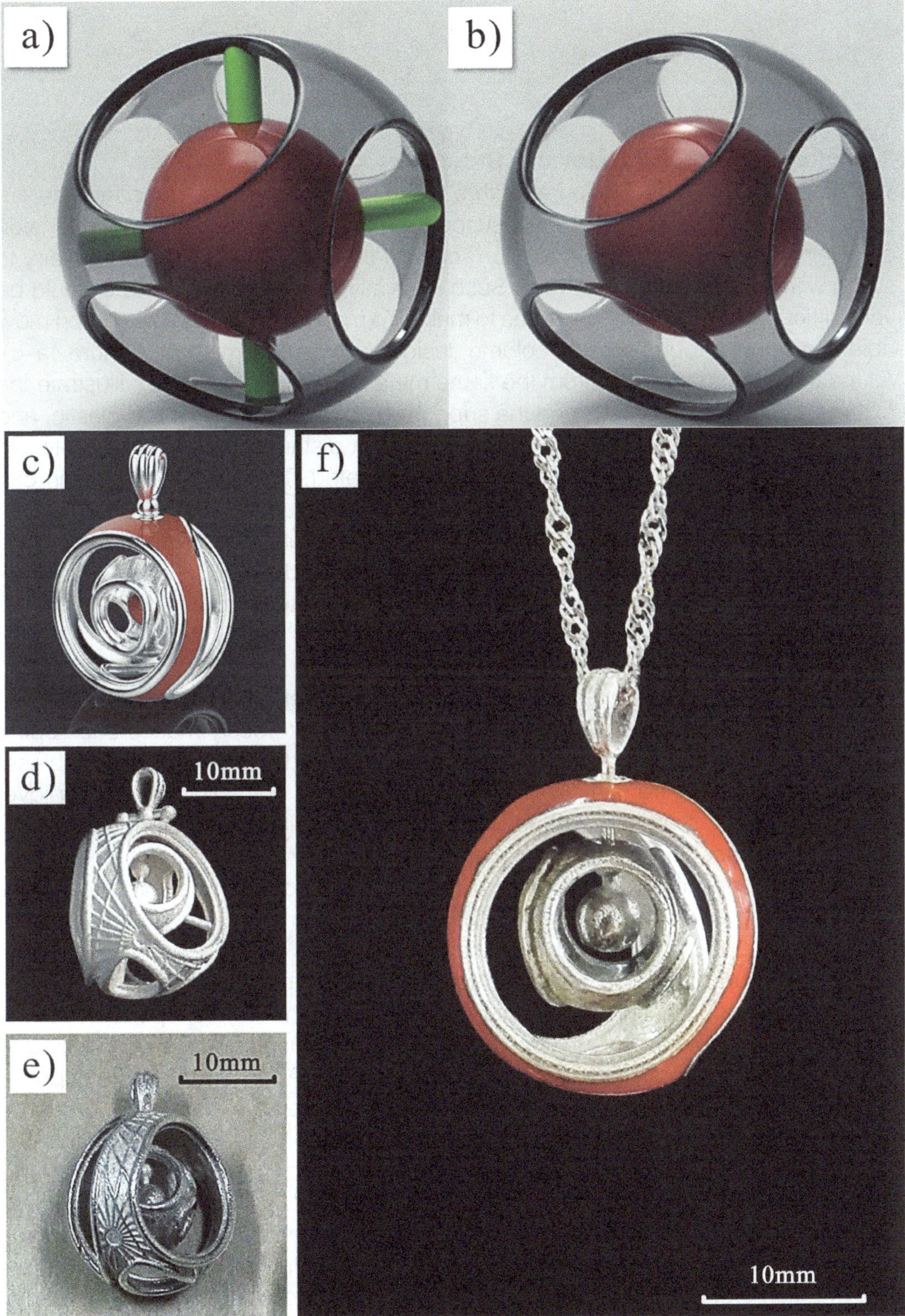
a)
b)
c)
d)
10mm
e)
10mm
f)
10mm

3.2. Internal Suspension Movable Structure

The most common suspension structure is the hooked part in a pendant. The authors propose the design of a novel suspension movable structure in the inner side of jewelry. The "concealed suspension" can be created and it allows the jewelry to swing with the motion of customers. Such innovative suspension structure would be very difficult for traditional techniques to make. To make the internal suspension movable, the authors apply "support column design and removal method" (Figure 4a–c). All the three parts are made from the same metal. Similarly, the authors illustrate the external ball, the internal ball, and the supported column with glass, red plastic, and green plastics, respectively. Two links with certain distance are designed between the internal and external ball to keep them separated. The supported column can be removed with tools once the casting is finished. Thus the external ball can be separated from the internal ball, and the small internal ball can be suspended as a movable structure. In term of suspension design, it should carefully consider and calculate the gravity effect in order to determine its final shape (Figure 4g).

3.3. Spiral Movable Structure

The spiral movable structure is similar to the double helix structure of DNA. It can be applied for innovative design for rings. Design dexterously makes each spiral band with a movable gap. It enhances the creativity and symbolizes a good blessing. As shown in Figure 5, it consists of three symbolic spiral bands: one for love, one for fidelity, and another for friendship. Trinity, a collective design, can be devoted to life's most memorable and eternal love.

The "supported column design and removal method" is the same for multiple spiral movable structures (Figure 6a–b). All parts are made from the same metal. Similarly, the authors illustrate the different spiral bands with red, orange, and blue plastics and supported column with green plastics. Keep certain distance between each spiral band. The supported column is designed in a ring shape to avoid deformation during the casting process. The sprue gate used for casting is linked to the supported column to easily remove in later stage. After removing the supported structures, three spiral band encircling strings become separated and can be movable (Figure 6f).

3.4. Axial Movable Structure

The well-known axial movable structure is the butt hinge. The structure of the traditional manufacturing process requires specialized equipment and complex steps. The creation of a butt hinge begins with two leaves. Each leaf is machined on one

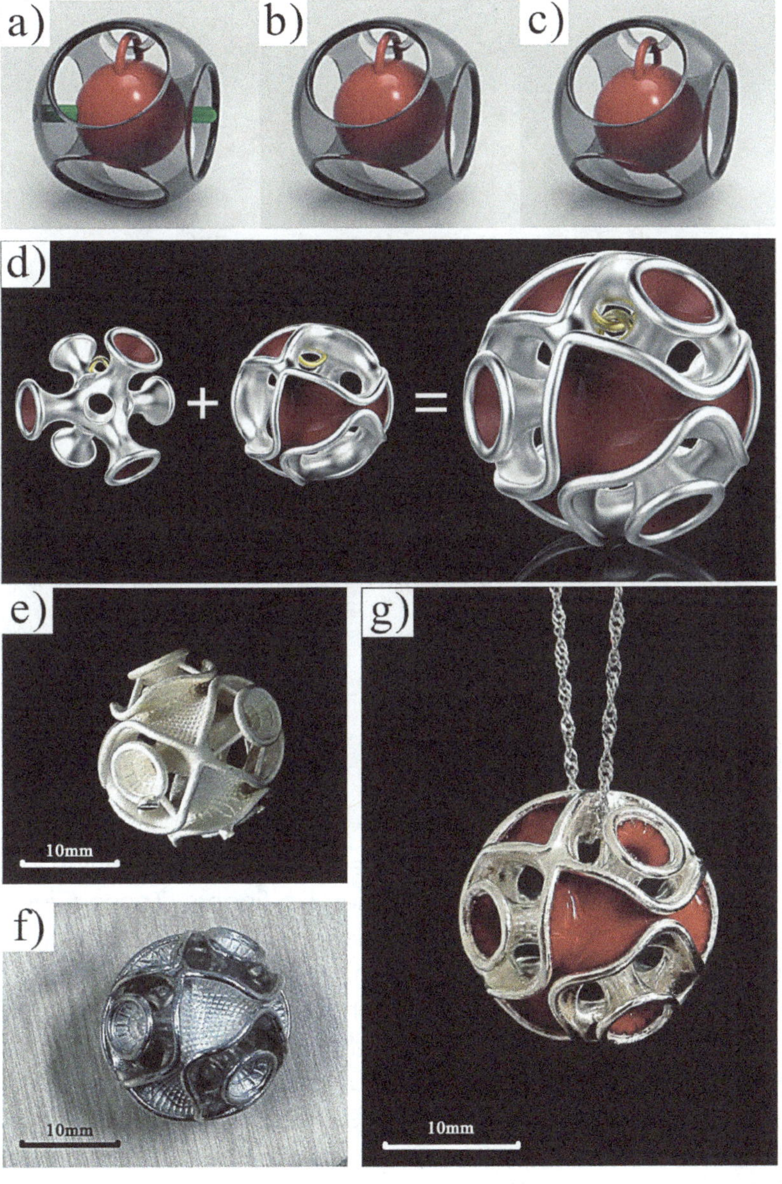

Figure 4. 3D rendering structural diagrams of internal suspension: a) before removing the supported column; b) after removing the supported column; and c) the shape under action of gravity. Pictures of jewelry products with internal suspension movable structure: d) 3D renderings; e) physical picture before removing the supported column; f) physical picture after removing the supported column; g) final product.

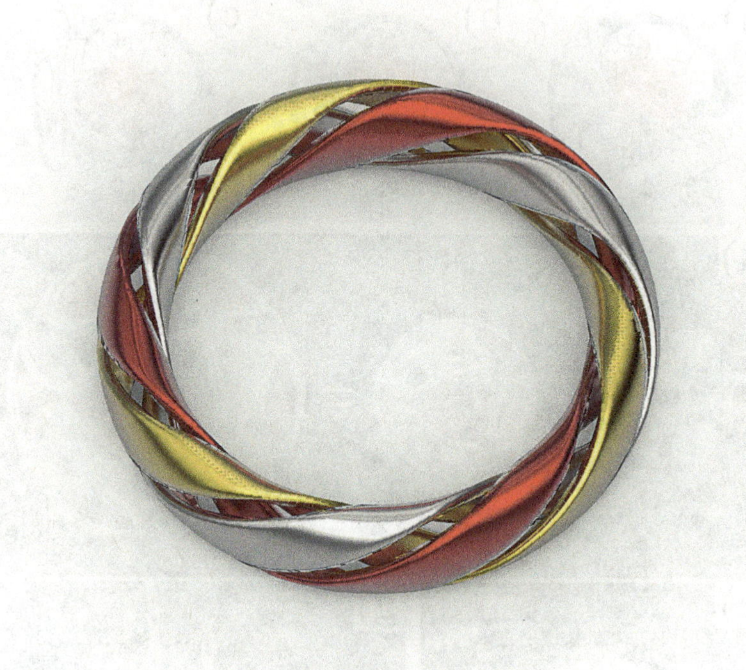

Figure 5. Structural diagram of trinity ring with spiral movable structure.

of its edges by the cutting machine; at the end of that machining process, the machined ends can interlock with each other like fingers. Those fingers are then curled by stamping machinery into a circular shape called knuckles. The leaves are then aligned so that their knuckles align, and then a removable or permanent pin is inserted, joining the two leaves and forming the hinge. The whole machining and assemblage is then complete (*Hinge Manufacturers*, 2015). The hinge structure of leaves and pin can be shaped with 3D printing and casting methods, so that the trouble brought by assembly is avoided successfully and designers have more room to design unique hinge structures for jewelry. The authors illustrate one of the leaves with semi-transparent plastics, the other with red plastics, and the supported column with green plastics. Similarly, all parts are made from the same metal. Keep certain distance between the two knuckles of leaves in order to keep them

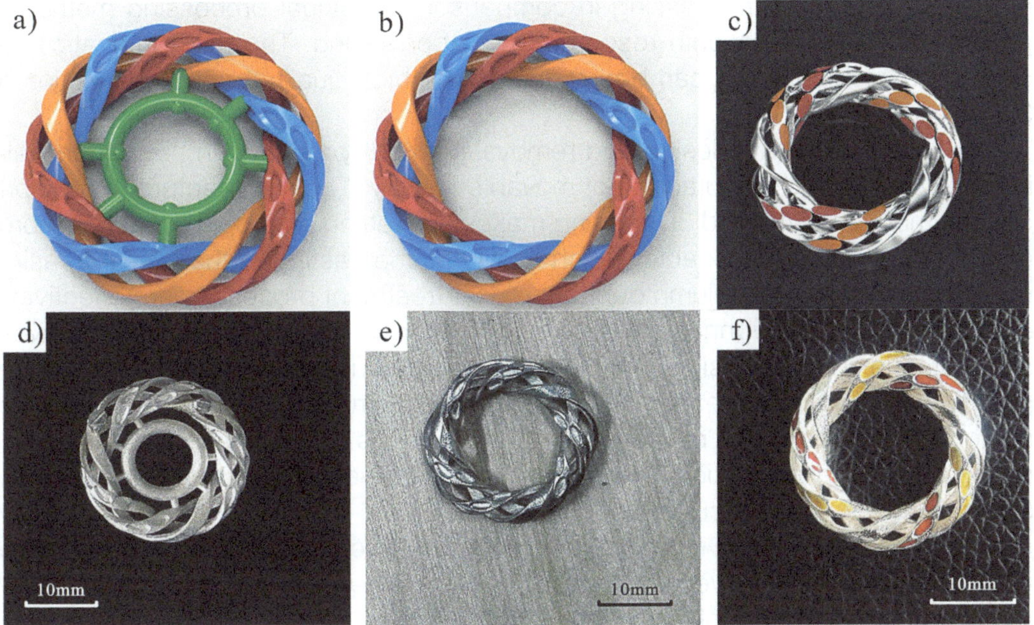

Figure 6. 3D rendering diagrams of spiral movable structure: a) before removing the support column; and b) after removing the supported column. Pictures of jewelry products with spiral movable structure: c) 3D renderings; d) physical picture before removing the supported column; e) physical picture after removing the supported column; and f) final product.

separated. After removing the supported structure, the two leaves become separated and can be movable.

4. Conclusion

3D printing technology has brought fundamental changes to jewelry design and manufacture. It spans the technology gap between the virtual and physical world, so that the creative designers can be given more freedom to express their inspiration. The integrated 3D wax printing and lost-wax casting technology, as a new type of digital manufacturing approach, could offer a few advantages including rapid delivery, low cost, and high quality. The rapid manufacturing benefits from 3D MJM and seamless integration between 3D wax printing and lost-wax casting methods, which simplifies fabrication procedures, improves efficiency and achieves automatic production processing in comparison to manual processing methods, and therefore achieves both resource and labor saving. The most intricate and unique geometric jewelry can be produced with high quality by high-resolution a 3D wax printer.

The "support column design and removal method" proposed in the paper realizes the design and manufacture of movable jewelry. The manufacture of support column made by CAD and 3D printing makes the setting of support columns more accurate and more reasonable, which facilitates the casting of the jewelry, easier removal of the support column during the post-treatment process, more effectively avoids the surface roughness caused by the support column removal, and saves material. The creative design with the movable structure is conducive to make the jewelry more shiny, unique, and fitted. The movable structure jewelry swing with the motion of customers and reflects the gleaming gems and metal in the sunlight—giving the jewelry exceptional vitality and attractiveness. Moreover, the movable structure jewelry can be customized for the individual according to personal body characteristics to improve user experience. We believe that in the near future, more and more jewelry with novel movable structures created by 3D printing technology will become a new trend of fashion.

References

3Dsystems. 2018. *ProJet SD/HD 3500 Series.* http://www.3dsystems.com/3d-printers/professional/projet-3500–hd.

Badulaques. 2018. *I Miss You! Ring.* https://www.shapeways.com/product/SLA6P4WBH/i-miss-you-ring?optionId=40746772.

Friedrich, S. 2018. *Violetta L - Bicycle Chain Ring.* https://www.shapeways.com/product/GTB4ZDLA3/violetta-l-bicycle-chain-ring-us-9–19–mm?optionId=9381394.

Gershoni, Y. 2018. *Illusionist Heart Pendant.* https://www.shapeways.com/product/QBRSDXV4X.

Hinge Manufacturers. 2015. http://www.hingemanufacturers.org.

Human Hive, The. 2018. *Gear Heart.* https://www.shapeways.com/product/FVU9GDEL6/gear-heart?optionId=0.

Kidmechano. 2016. *V3 Muscle Arm Set.* https://www.shapeways.com/product/BHER4RPAH/v3–muscle-arm-set?optionId=43537611&li=marketplace.

Shapeways, 2018. *How It's 3D Printed.* https://www.shapeways.com/materials/silver.

Solidscape. 2018. *Solidscape-STUDIO-data-sheet.* http://www.solid-scape.com/products/3d-printers/solidscape-studio.

Terra Cotta Personal Fabricators. 2018. *One Ring to Rule the Ball.* https://www.shapeways.com/product/456ACYNFJ/one-ring-to-rule-the-ball.

TomBot. 2018. *Chain Holder for Fitbit Flex.* https://www.shapeways.com/product/6323UXUGY/chain-holder-for-fitbit-flex?optionId=36079763.

Virtox. 2018. *Gyro the Cube.* https://www.shapeways.com/product/WPYSJMPYT/gyro-the-cube?optionId=40681150&li=marketplace.

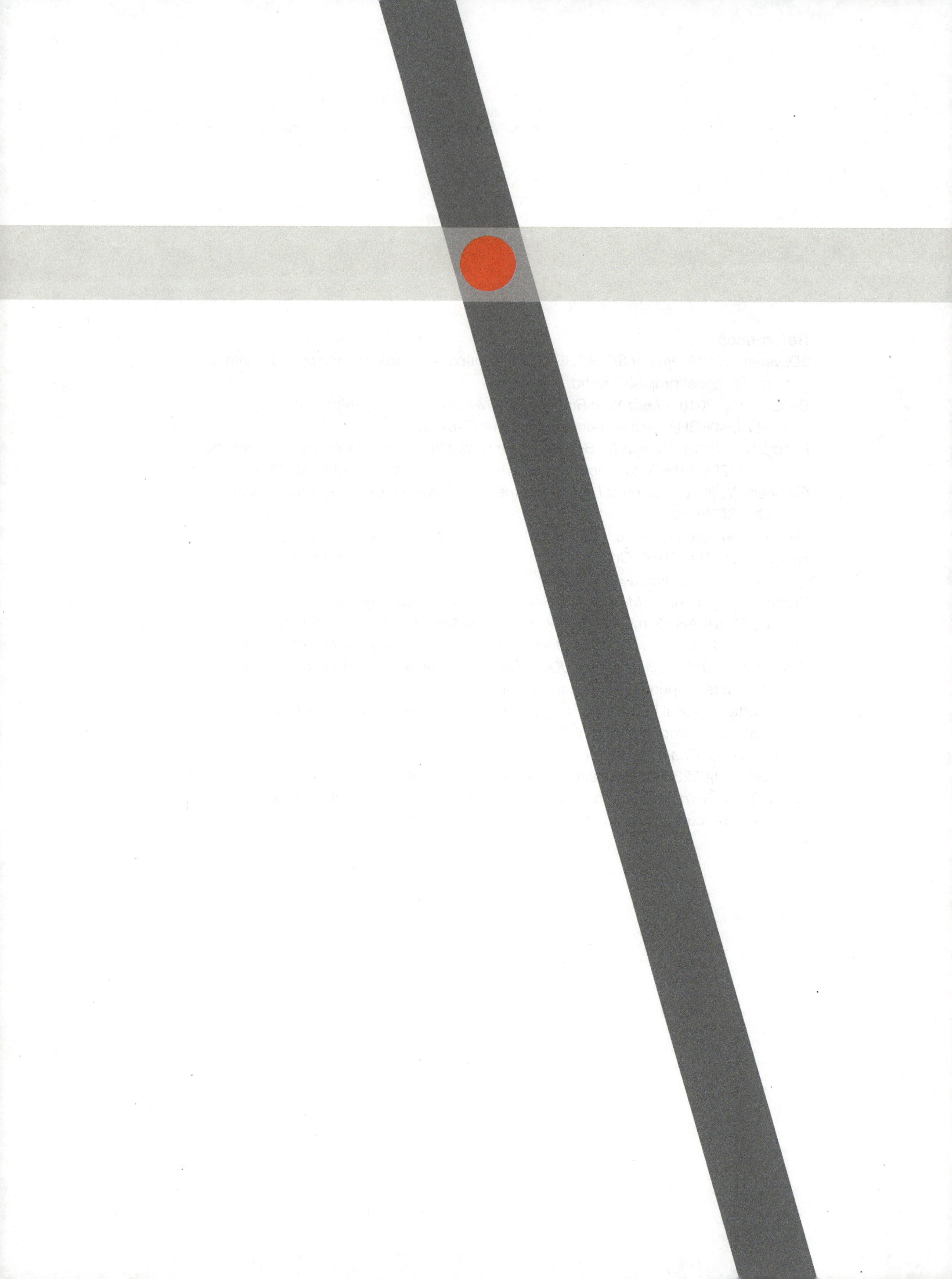

Digital Humanity and the Visualization of the Jewellery Archive and Kinematic Reinterpretation of Historic Jewellery

Yu Xinan, Shanghai International Institute of Design & Innovation, China
Zhao Qian, Shanghai International Institute of Design & Innovation, China
Ren Lisha, College of Design Innovation Tongji University, China

Abstract

Since its inception, the word "digital" has always been labelled as a "tool" of precise engineering, efficient production. Except for some rare and special cases, digital has never been treated as a fundamental part of jewellery creation, which is highly related to emotional or cultural context.

Today, digital is no longer merely technics, but a way of thinking and philosophy of creation that reveals the very nature of the universal connection of everything and provides us with a completely new perspective for recognizing the world in front of or behind us.

This paper mainly introduces two research projects hosted by Jewelry Accessory Lab (JALAB) in 2017, which were all related to "digital technology and jewellery in history."

The first project is mainly about using a series of natural language processing (NLP) and visualization scripts to make a linguistic study of jewellery archives. The second project is about finding morphological rules in the Giampaolo Babetto necklace made in 1994, and creates an easy-to-use design tool, so that people with no background of jewellery or design skill can also create things that are not only inspired from Babetto necklace structure but also incorporating their own creativity.

1. Introduction

Since 2015, a series of digital humanities organizations and related research has been developing fast in the cross-field of art and science. Digital is not only connected with technical means of creation, but also a sublime way of thinking and creating. Data not only reveals the essence that everything is extensively connected all over the world but also provides us with a new perspective and insight, for the reality in front of us and the knowledge behind us. There are easy-to-use online analysis tools for the public, such as Google Ngram or Voyant, as well as complicated natural languag processing (NLP) scripts developed for professionals.

Tongji Jewellery Accessory Lab (JALAB) actively explores how to apply modern digital technology to the collection, interpretation, and recreation of jewellery heritage from both linguistic and morphological points of view, and actively explores possibility of integrating digital language and cultural content.

This paper mainly introduces two research projects hosted by JALAB, which were all related to digital technology and jewellery from museums:

— digital humanity and visualization of the jewellery archive
— digital simulation and reinterpretation of historic jewellery

These two projects are relatively independent, the purposes of which are not to discover new truths in jewellery history or to create new technology, but to apply existing digital techniques to the jewellery field, read the jewellery history from different angles, and verify the effect of different combinations of method in the digital humanity study of jewellery documents; the purpose is also to find morphological rules in jewellery itself and to create easy-to-use design tools, so that people with no background of jewellery or design skills can also create things that are not only derived from jewellery history but also incorporate their own creativity.

2. Digital Humanity and the Visualization of the Jewellery Archive

The first project is mainly about using digital methods to make a linguistic study of jewelry archive.

As a preliminary attempt, we used Google Ngram first to do a simple keyword search and analysis of twentieth century achieves in Google's online library (Figure 1). The curve shows that "art jewelry" didn't start from the 1960s as it is usually thought, but from the end of the nineteenth century; its first peak appeared in the 1930s, which coincided with the active period of early "jewelry artists" such as Raymond Templier and Jean Després, the avant-guard jeweller from France. Then, the curve of "art jewelry" began to match "contemporary jewelry" from the 1980s. The second peak appeared in the 1990s, which shows that the origins of "art jewelry" and "contemporary jewelry" are completely different. Only in the later period of the 1980s, the two movements gradually show signs of integration.

These results are really encouraging because Google Ngram is not specifically designed for jewellery and its archives cover all topics of publications, but the curve it draws can be roughly consistent with human historian's conclusions, proving the great potential of this method.

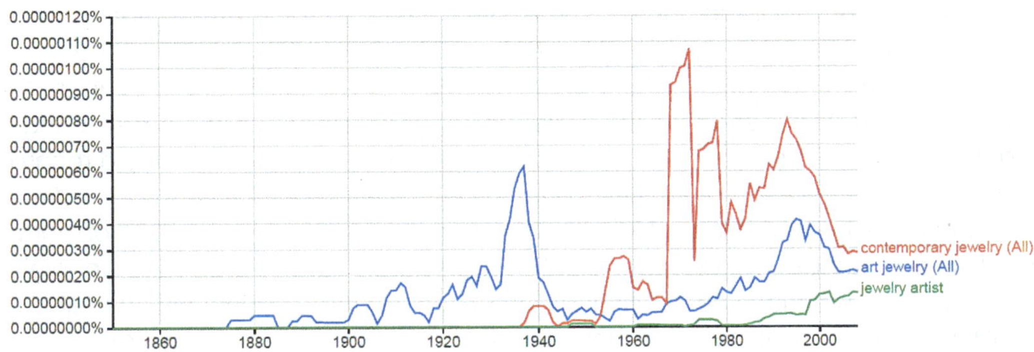

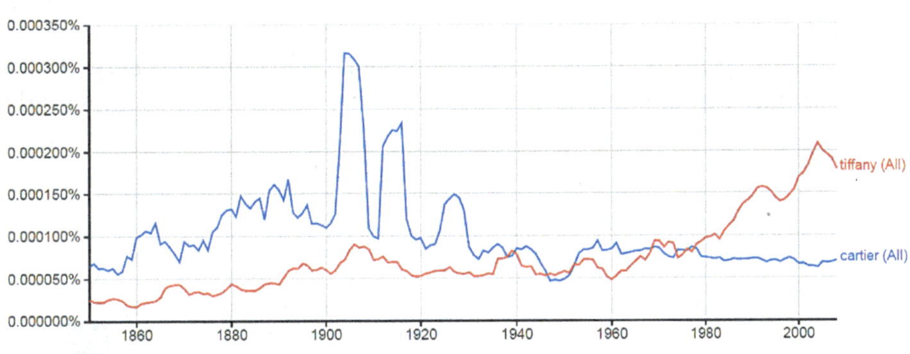

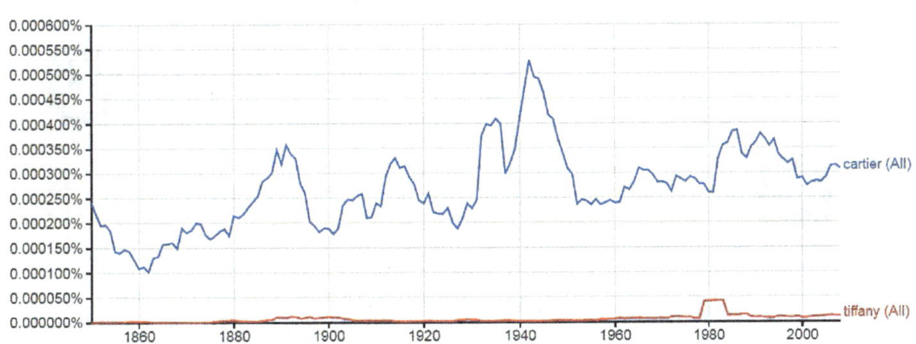

Figure 1. Curve of “contemporary jewelry,” "art jewelry,” and “jewelry artist” from 1860 to 2000 by Google Ngram.

Figure 2. Curve of “Cartier” and “Tiffany” in English publications from 1860 to 2000 by Google Ngram.
Figure 3. Curve of “Cartier” and “Tiffany“ in French publications from 1860 to 2000 by Google Ngram.

Besides, the search results for the same topic based on different languages are also very different. For example, the peak of "Cartier" in English (Figure 2) appeared from the 1910s to the 1920s while the peak of "Cartier" in French (Figure 3) appeared in the 1940s and the 1990s. People from different linguistic backgrounds might have very different perceptions and concerns when they interpret and record trends.

However, although Google Ngram can chart frequencies of any set of comma-delimited strings using sources published between 1500 and 2008 in Google's text corpora in American and British English, French, and German, which is about 5 million books, it is still not all of them. So, its inferences are not always reliable.

The second tool we use is NLP from Stanford University, with the help of which we made a comparative study of two important jewellery books. One is *Twentieth-Century Jewellery: From Art Nouveau to Contemporary Design in Europe and the United States* (2010) by Alba Cappellieri, and the other is *Jewels & Jewellery* (2008) by Clare Phillips for the Victoria and Albert Museum. We scanned the archive first

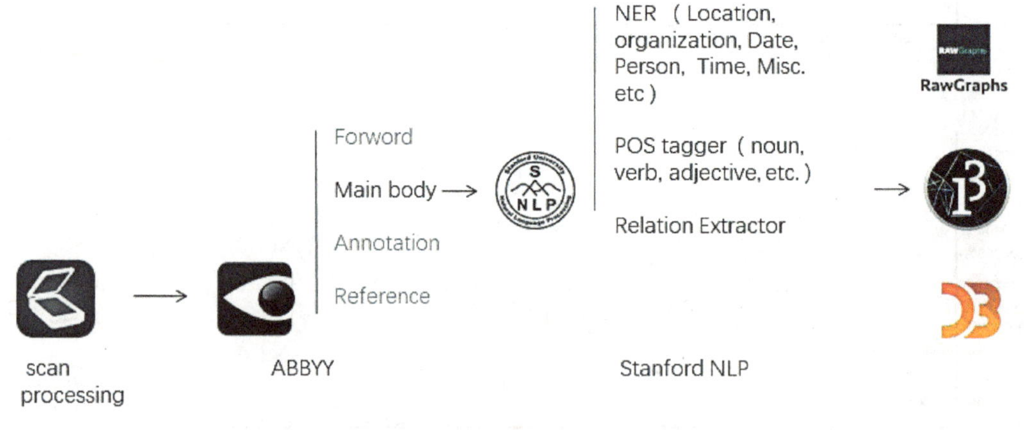

Figure 4. The process of data mining, evaluation, and visualization.

and converted it into plain text format, used Named Entity Recognizer (NER) and POS Tagger (Part-Of-Speech Tagger) to extract keywords, which included all verbs, adjectives, nouns, organizations, names, locations, and times from the text. And then, all the keywords were sorted, compared, classified, and finally visualized by scripting with Processing, RAW Graph, and D3.js (Figure 4).

If we take verbs (Table 1) as an example, after removing the auxiliary verbs such as "was, were, is, has, etc.," we sorted the rest and found that "made" had been used ahead of "designed," "produced," and "exhibited," which showed the importance of "make" behaviour in the context of this book.

Based on the frequency of the vocabulary, we see the similarities and differences between these two books written by British and Italian scholars. Firstly, both books pay special attention to the time of the early twentieth century. In the table of people's names (Table 2, Table 3), British scholar Clare Phillips writes

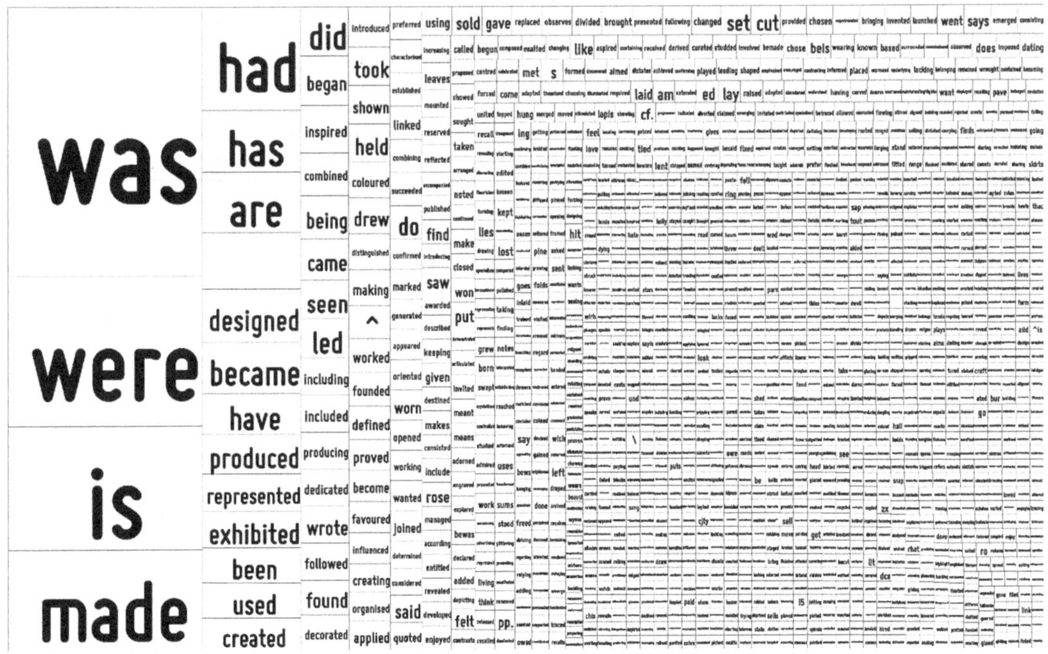

Table 1: Frequency of all verbs in *Twentieth-Century Jewellery: From Art Nouveau to Contemporary Design in Europe and the United States* (2010) visualized with code from *Generative Design* (2012).

more about individual jewellery artists or jewellers with goldsmithing backgrounds like Charles Ashbee, Gerda Flockinger, and Georgie Gaskin, while Italian scholar Alba Cappellieri quotes more about fine jewellery enterprise and big families like Fouquet or Cartier (Table 2).

In addition to the preferences differing by countries, we also compare the frequency of these keywords in specific historical periods. According to the contents of the books, we divided them into several major historical stages: 1919–1929, 1929–1946, 1947–1967, 1968–1978, and 1978–2008 (Table 4). We found some interesting changes: from 1919 to 1978, "new" is always on the top of the adjectives list, one of the most important attributes when we talk about jewellery history. From 1978 to 2008, however, the last two decades of twentieth century, "new" drops to the fifth place, and "such" replaces it, moving into first place. This shows that beginning from the 1980s, in the contemporary context, "new" was no longer the

Table 2: Frequency of all people's names from *Twentieth-Century Jewellery: From Art Nouveau to Contemporary Design in Europe and the United States.*(2010) visualized with code from. *Generative Design* (2012).

primary consideration to describe design or jewellery. People paid more attention to the story behind "new." Meanwhile, another adjective "precious" gradually decreases in frequency over time, revealing the transition of jewellery values over the twentieth century.

The breakthrough of natural language processing and cognitive computing enables us to access massive amounts of data in a highly efficient way. Currently, our attempts in this field are still early, and there are a lot of problems still to be solved. Due to the recognition problem when the English library reading text mixes with English, French, and Italian, the recognition error rate of people's names is still high. On the other hand, since we used the standard NER and POS tagger library, with no optimization for jewellery vocabulary and phrases, the outcome was full of recognition errors, such as tagging Art Deco or New Look into two words rather than a phrase. These are all expected to be solved in the following studies.

Table 3: Frequency of all people's name of *Jewels & Jewellery* (2008) visualized with code from *Generative Design* (2012).

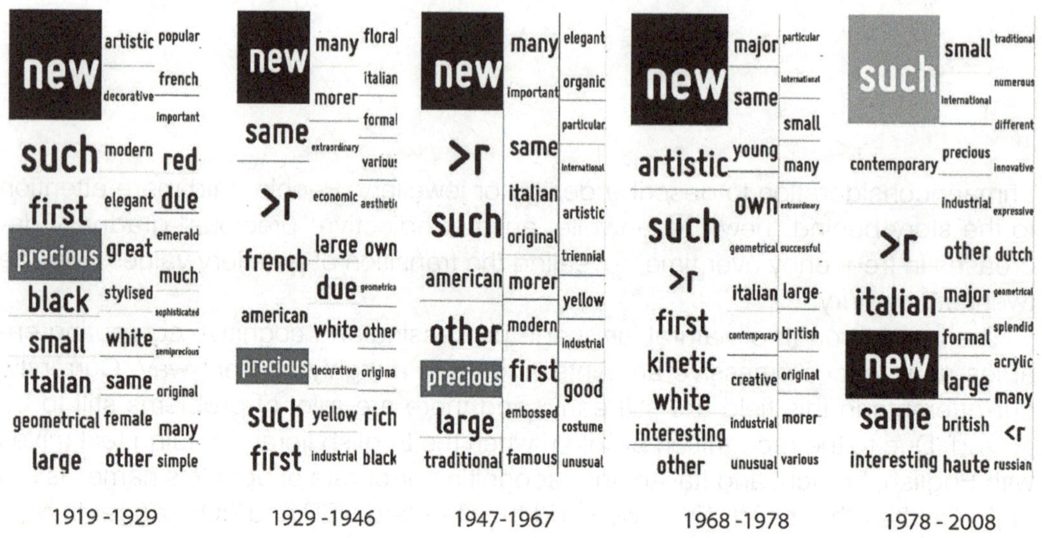

Table 4: The variation of adjective rank in *Twentieth-Century Jewellery: From Art Nouveau to Contemporary Design in Europe and the United States* (2010) visualized with code from *Generative Design* (2012).

3. Digital Simulation Kinematic Reinterpretation for Historic Jewellery

The second project is about digital simulation and the reinterpretation of a specific design of a Giampaolo Babetto necklace made in 1994, a very important piece of contemporary jewellery from Padua, Italy.

The purpose of this study is to find morphological rules in the Babetto necklace, and create an easy-to-use design tool so that people who have no background of jewellery or design skills can also create things that are not only inspired by the Babetto necklace structure but also incorporate their own creativity.

We analysed the connection logic of Babetto necklace and found there are only two types of hinge modules (Figure 5). If we take a look at its singular module and mark the surface with the open window as the criterion plane, then the hinge 1 is located on the edge of the window, while the hinge 2 will be located either on the left up or right down positions of the opposite window. According to these rules, these two types of cubes are marked as LU (left up) and RD (right down), and a different combination of LU and RD can form a different shape of necklace.

Then we used Maya (MEL)script to generate the entire necklace with a different combination of the cubes. The entire necklace is generated from a single cube as the initial piece and duplicated, every new cube one by one with angles following a simple sequence. It turns out that the whole piece always grow straight ahead and would never be able to become a closed loop if it just follows one fixed sequence (Figure 5). Then we reanalyzed the original design of the Giampaolo Babetto necklace and found there is actually a hidden repeated pattern inside (Figure 6).

```
polyCube -name "MyCube0";
        $v0 = eval("pointPosition MyCube0.vtx[0]");
        $v1 = eval("pointPosition MyCube0.vtx[1]");
        $v2 = eval("pointPosition MyCube0.vtx[2]");
        $v3 = eval("pointPosition MyCube0.vtx[3]");
        $v4 = eval("pointPosition MyCube0.vtx[4]");
        $v5 = eval("pointPosition MyCube0.vtx[5]");
        $v6 = eval("pointPosition MyCube0.vtx[6]");
        $v7 = eval("pointPosition MyCube0.vtx[7]");
        int $n=10;
        for($i=1;$i<$n;$i+=2){
        //51 13 5
          duplicate -name("$MyCube"+$i);
          $a = `angleBetween -euler
           -v1 ($v5[0]-$v1[0]) ($v5[1]-$v1[1]) ($v5[2]-$v1[2])
           -v2 ($v1[0]-$v3[0]) ($v1[1]-$v3[1]) ($v1[2]-$v3[2])`;
        rotate -r -p $v5[0] $v5[1] $v5[2] $a[0] $a[1] $a[2];

        $v0 = eval("pointPosition MyCube"+$i+".vtx[0]");
        $v1 = eval("pointPosition MyCube"+$i+".vtx[1]");
        $v2 = eval("pointPosition MyCube"+$i+".vtx[2]");
        $v3 = eval("pointPosition MyCube"+$i+".vtx[3]");
        $v4 = eval("pointPosition MyCube"+$i+".vtx[4]");
        $v5 = eval("pointPosition MyCube"+$i+".vtx[5]");
        $v6 = eval("pointPosition MyCube"+$i+".vtx[6]");
        $v7 = eval("pointPosition MyCube"+$i+".vtx[7]");

        print ("pointPosition MyCube"+$i+".vtx[0]");
        //10 03 0
        int $o=$i+1;
        duplicate -name ("MyCube"+$o);
        $b = `angleBetween -euler
           -v1 ($v1[0]-$v0[0]) ($v1[1]-$v0[1]) ($v1[2]-$v0[2])
           -v2 ($v0[0]-$v3[0]) ($v0[1]-$v3[1]) ($v0[2]-$v3[2])`;
        rotate -r -p $v0[0] $v0[1] $v0[2] $b[0] $b[1] $b[2];

        $v0 = eval("pointPosition MyCube"+$o+".vtx[0]");
        $v1 = eval("pointPosition MyCube"+$o+".vtx[1]");
        $v2 = eval("pointPosition MyCube"+$o+".vtx[2]");
        $v3 = eval("pointPosition MyCube"+$o+".vtx[3]");
        $v4 = eval("pointPosition MyCube"+$o+".vtx[4]");
        $v5 = eval("pointPosition MyCube"+$o+".vtx[5]");
        $v6 = eval("pointPosition MyCube"+$o+".vtx[6]");
        $v7 = eval("pointPosition MyCube"+$o+".vtx[7]");
                    print ("pointPosition MyCube"+$o+".vtx[0]");

        }
```

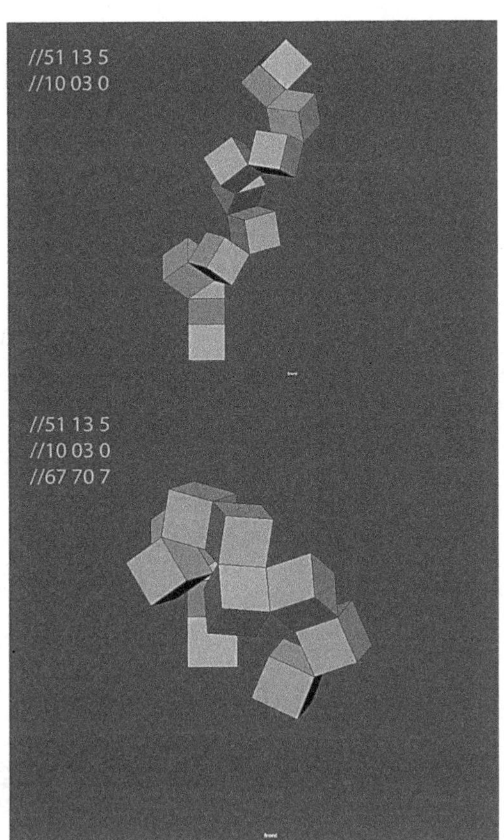

Figure 5 : MEL-script for generating the necklace (left); the cube grows straight ahead and will never be able to become a closed loop (right).

So, we decided to switch the path, from simulating the final form of the necklace into simulating the initial form, by setting the hinges position between each cube when they are all folded, thus ensuring that all cubes can be seamlessly connected and finally become a closed loop. There are eight relative states between each module: vertical-up; vertical-left; vertical-down; vertical-right; horizontal-up, horizontal-left; horizontal-down; and horizontal-right. Using these eight combinations, not only can we reconstruct the original Babetto necklace, but also successfully develop 4x4, 6x6, 8x8 squares, and even more complicated freeform shapes, for example an animal-like shape (Figure 7), into a Babetto necklace.

For further study of this project, we coded an interactive interface for customizing the space of each cube and the size of the hinges, with eight sets of buttons and two sets of input boxes. When pressing the button, the system will create a hinge with dynamic properties. Every two modules connected by hinges will repel each other and automatically unfold the entire necklace (Figure 7) by Newtonian

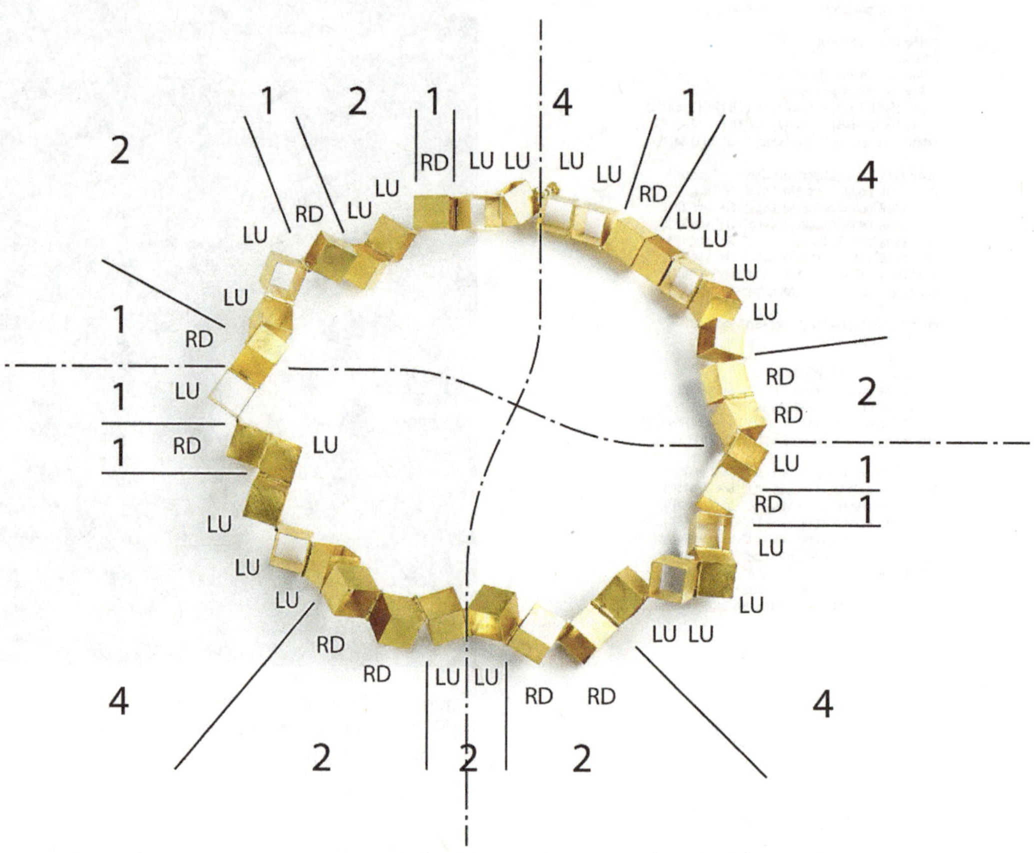

Figure 6. Hinge types and structure pattern of the Giampaolo Babetto necklace.

force from the negative gravitational environment. This function provides not only a highly dynamic and aesthetic process, but also a great deal of freedom, allowing users to intuitively adjust the position of the hinges based on their dynamic effects.

In the following tests, we found that these eight states are not enough to cover all the possibilities, so we added two additional relative positions, tilt-up and tilt-down. By flexibly using combinations of these ten states, these tools can theoretically unfold any shape of cube patterns.

We put all the buttons in one panel and named it the HINGE 2.0 (Figure 8), so that people with no professional background of jewellery or design skills will be able to unfold any pixel image, geometrical shape, alphabet, or even figurative

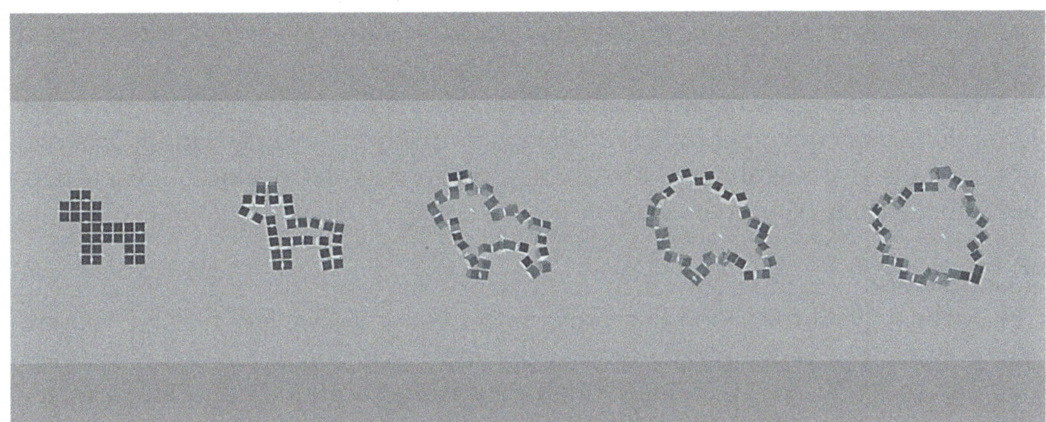

Figure 7. The expansion process of a dog-shaped necklace.

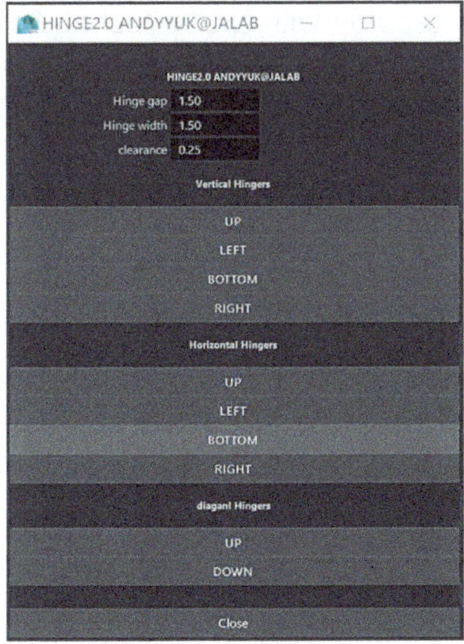

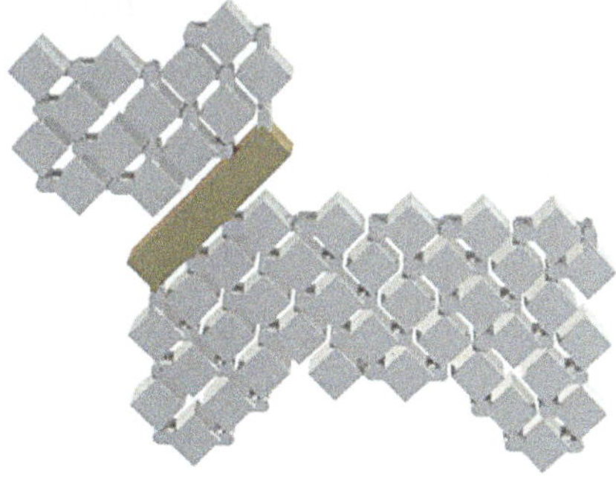

Figure 8. The interface of HINGE 2.0 and the animal-shaped necklace with Babetto necklace structure.

theme such as an animal into a "Babetto necklace." After obtaining the digital model, people can also 3D print their design into tangible products.

When unfolded, this necklace completely inherits Babetto's abstract geometric form, but it can carry specific information after being completely folded. This project attempts to break the barriers of art and integrate the design of avant-garde with the creativity of ordinary people.

4.Conclusion

The technological revolution has profoundly changed jewellery history. The jewellery industry was seemingly among the most "conservative;" many jewellery companies today are no different than they were two hundred years ago, and many use medieval jewellery materials. Skills, design, and values have continued but, fundamentally, new methods, new cultures, and new possibilities following technological revolution have always been the driving force. Two major jewellery discoveries of the nineteenth century, platinum and diamonds, relied on the breakthrough of steam-powered vessels and navigation technology. The birth of fashion jewellery in the twentieth century also relied on mass produced plastic. The ready availability of this versatile, colorful material inspired designers to use it as they created new fashion. The profound changes that have come with digital technology have brought infinite vitality to jewellery. Even if digital technology will probably not be the last word in the jewellery design of our time, it will inevitably become a strong bridge connecting the past while creating the future.

References

Phillips, C. 2008. *Jewels & Jewellery*. London: V&A Publications.

Cappellieri, A. 2010. *Twentieth-Century Jewellery From Art Nouveau to Contemporary Design in Europe and the United States.* Milano: Skira Editore.

Bohnacker, H., B. Gross, and J. Laub. 2012. *Generative Design: Visualize, Program, and Create with Processing.* Mainz: Princeton Architectural Press.

Google Books Ngram Viewer. 2012. https://books.google.com/ngrams.

The Stanford NLP Group. 2017. *The Natural Language Processing Group*. https://nlp.stanford.edu/software.